LAWYERS' ETHICS AND PROFESSIONAL RESPONSIBILITY

The University of Law
incorporating The College of Law

This book
fessio
autho
in En
stude
parts
legal
and p
tice
and i
from
are c
posin
they

pro-
the
yers
luate
four
ering
lities
prac-
thics
racts
ssues
s and
al as

Lawyers' Ethics and Professional Responsibility

Andrew Boon

The University of Law

Braboeuf Manor
Portsmouth Road
Guildford
Surrey GU3 1HA

·H A R T·
PUBLISHING

OXFORD AND PORTLAND, OREGON
2015

Published in the United Kingdom by Hart Publishing Ltd
16C Worcester Place, Oxford, OX1 2JW
Telephone: +44 (0)1865 517530
Fax: +44 (0)1865 510710
E-mail: mail@hartpub.co.uk
Website: http://www.hartpub.co.uk

Published in North America (US and Canada) by
Hart Publishing
c/o International Specialized Book Services
920 NE 58th Avenue, Suite 300
Portland, OR 97213-3786
USA
Tel: +1 503 287 3093 or toll-free: (1) 800 944 6190
Fax: +1 503 280 8832
E-mail: orders@isbs.com
Website: http://www.isbs.com

Hart Publishing is an imprint of Bloomsbury Publishing plc.

British Library Cataloguing in Publication Data
Data Available
ISBN: 978-1-84946-784-1

Typeset by Forewords, Oxford
Printed and bound in Great Britain by
CPI Group (UK) Ltd, Croydon CR0 4YY

In memory of David and Dorothy Boon

Preface

A lot has changed in the regulation of the legal profession in recent years. It is not too dramatic to say that there may not be legal professions as we have known them for centuries for too much longer. There will inevitably be pressure for regulation driven by perceived consumer concerns rather than professional concerns. It is important that aspiring lawyers understand what is involved in such a shift.

My aim in this book was to provide a concise and accessible text covering the main principles of lawyers' ethics but also the principles of legal professionalism which underpin them. Students who require more detail can consult my other book on legal ethics, *The Ethics and Conduct of Lawyers in England and Wales*. In *Lawyers' Ethics and Professional Responsibility* I have drawn on more material on lawyers' ethics from across different jurisdictions. This breadth of material is intended to promote discussion about lawyers' ethics generally. The main examples are from England and Wales, which is the system I know best.

Another purpose of this book is to present students with small examples of original material. The backgrounds to the case extracts are based on Westlaw digests. These samples are generally followed by questions about the material. This approach is intended to maintain interest and engagement, encourage application of principles and promote thinking about the issues. I hope it will encourage readers to recognise that the answer is not always obvious and usually not of a right/wrong type.

I believe that it is worth students learning about lawyers' ethics and professional responsibility for its own sake. Understanding the subject may have the long-term benefit of making them more thoughtful about ethics while in practice. As more attention has been paid to the legal ethics, this subject has become increasingly controversial. It has been argued that the legal role is immoral, and alternatives have been proposed. I think it is important that these arguments are understood and debated. From my point of view the most useful outcome of students learning the subject will be that they will understand better the fundamental importance of the legal role.

Grasping what lawyers do, and why, will hopefully increase appreciation of how society depends on the legal role being performed well. This should lead students to gain sufficient awareness and motivation to follow debates in the profession with interest. They may then engage with debates surrounding rule revisions and the like. In time, I hope, a former student of lawyers' ethics will articulate a new vision of the subject that will serve a future generation of lawyers, and society, well.

My thanks are due to all at Hart Publishing for their usual efficiency in dealing with the text. I am particularly grateful to Bill Asquith for encouraging me to produce it and for comments on a sample chapter. I am also grateful to my students in legal ethics and professional responsibility. Their engagement with the subject has given me a good idea of what background is needed by students. I hope their experience has helped me to pitch the book at the right level.

Andy Boon
Gray's Inn
London

Contents

Table of Cases

United Kingdom

Court of Justice of the European Union

United States of America

Table of Legislation

United Kingdom

Table of International Instruments

Table of Secondary Legislation and Quasi-Statutory Codes

Statutory Instruments

Part I

Systems

Roles and Values

Introduction

Are lawyers necessary? They exist in all developed societies and handle very similar kinds of work, typically dispute resolution and transactions. Some academics have, however, suggested that most of what lawyers do could eventually be done by machines. If this were to happen, would society lose anything by the disappearance of lawyers? If lawyers offer anything that machines do not, it is the sensitive handling of important issues in human affairs. This involves the application of practical wisdom informed by ethics.

What Are Lawyers' Ethics?

Ethics is a branch of philosophy concerned with how people make good and right decisions on problems with a moral dimension. In most people's everyday lives this is not problematic; they follow their own conscience. They may have to live with some criticism if people disagree with their choices, but they probably are not troubled by the fact that others have a different moral perspective. Members of various occupations are sometimes required to make decisions that go against others' idea of what is right in ordinary situations. These people are professionals. Lawyers, together with doctors and the clergy, form a triumvirate of learned occupations that most people regard as professions.

Professionals often perform a vital role in society. They undergo extensive training for their work. They are often inducted into a moral system that seems to stand at odds with the standards of everyday life. These systems are often written down in codes of professional ethics. Among professionals, lawyers have one of the most controversial moral systems. It requires them to defend murderers, abusers and terrorists with the same vigour as they would defend an innocent child. The explanation for this situation lies in the nature of the society in which we live and of the legal system it has produced.

Systems and Roles

The ethics of lawyers arise in the context of the tasks they perform. They also derive from the nature of the lawyer's social role. This, in turn, depends on the legal system within which they work. This is determined by the nature of the state, by which we mean an organised political community.

The Liberal State

In the Western world, liberal states predominate. Rather than being ruled by the will of a single person, power is distributed. This system helps to ensure that individual rights and collective freedoms are respected. Liberalism is often associated with the Age of Enlightenment. During the seventeenth century, philosophers argued that people had rights to life, freedom and property. John Locke proposed that a 'social contract' existed between a government and its people to protect liberty.[1] It was legitimate to remove governments which broke this social contract.

Revolutions in France and the US established states based on the values of liberty and equality. In England, the English Civil War was an important step in establishing the supremacy of parliament. The 'Glorious Revolution' of 1688 is a less dramatic but equally significant moment in England's progress towards a liberal democracy. It was a decisive step towards a liberal and democratic state. This marked a significant shift in social organisation from feudalism to liberalism. This marked a number of changes; in the system of rule, the position of the individual in society and the role of religion.

Anthony Giddens, the British sociologist, notes the growing commitment in Western liberal democracies to human emancipation from exploitation, inequality and oppression, and to institutions promoting justice, equality and participation.[2] In the evolution of liberal society, autonomy, the individual's

---

[1] J Locke, *Second Treatise of Government* (Indianapolis, Hackett, 1980).
[2] A Giddens, *Modernity and Self-Identity: Self and Society in the Late Modern Age* (Cambridge, Polity Press, 1991) 212.

right to choose, has become a dominant theme. This applies not only to issues of politics and religion, but to the individual's rights as a consumer.

Constitutional regimes protect the right to hold property,[3] support contractual relations between people, defend people's right to privacy, and support and promote their autonomy.

The last of these is important. Liberalism is based on the idea that every individual can pursue their notion of good in their own way, provided it does not impinge on the rights of others to do likewise. Liberalism supports capitalists and businesses by protecting them from the democratic will of the majority while providing protection to other minorities.

Principle	Feudalism	Liberalism
System of rule	Autocracy	Democracy
Individual position	Inherited position	Liberty and equality
Belief system	State religion	Secularism

The liberal theory of the state is based on the idea that the state is one social institution amongst many, each of which has its proper sphere. The state grants authority to other institutions in the fields of special competence of those other institutions. On grounds of efficiency and expediency, and as a moral principle, the state should not interfere in the spheres of other institutions. The power and authority of the state is therefore limited. It is regarded as improper for the state to go beyond these notional boundaries.

The second principle of the liberal theory of the state is that the powers of the state should be distributed amongst many centres. A common division at the level of government is between the legislature, the executive and the judiciary. This is usually referred to as the separation of powers. However, centres of power outside of government should also be encouraged. Therefore, for example, a free press is an important element in open and transparent government. The system of 'checks and balances' established in this way guards against the abuse of power by any one part. It also enables different centres of power to scrutinise the conduct of other parts. This helps to guard against corruption.

The third principle of the liberal theory of the state is that penalties should be proportionate and in accordance with the fault principle. Strict liability should be imposed only exceptionally.

---

[3] GC Hazard Jr and A Dondi, *Legal Ethics: A Comparative Study* (Stanford, CA, Stanford University Press, 2004) 92–93.

The Rule of Law

If the liberal state is to succeed in its objectives the legal framework must support individual rights and collective freedom. This framework is built around the idea of the rule of law. This is the fourth and final principle of the liberal theory of the state. In the liberal state, legal systems are controlled by autonomous rules. Max Weber, one of the founding fathers of sociology, called this system 'legalism'.

The idea that people should be ruled by law, rather than by any individual, was advocated by the Greek philosopher Aristotle. An important milestone in the conceptualisation of the rule of law was the document known as Magna Carta signed by the English King John in 1215. History has cast John as a bad king, given to capricious and arbitrary rule. Magna Carta was signed at the insistence of his barons.

While Magna Carta was not totally successful in controlling royal power, it took on great symbolic significance for future generations. It was used to legitimise the French and American revolutions on the grounds that the government had lost the moral right to rule. Magna Carta is, in effect, an early statement of the importance of the rule of law and civil and human rights. It defines the role of the state in relation to its citizens.

Consider this example of a paragraph from Magna Carta:

20. For a trivial offence, a free man shall be fined only in proportion to the degree of his offence, and for a serious offence correspondingly, but not so heavily as to deprive him of his livelihood. In the same way, a merchant shall be spared his merchandise, and a villein the implements of his husbandry, if they fall upon the mercy of a royal court. None of these fines shall be imposed except by the assessment on oath of reputable men of the neighbourhood.

The Constitutional Reform Act 2005

Section 1 This Act does not adversely affect—

(a)   the existing constitutional principle of the rule of law, or
(b)   the Lord Chancellor's existing constitutional role in relation to that principle.

Under section 17 the Lord Chancellor is required to swear the following oath:

'I, [name], do swear that in the office of Lord High Chancellor of Great Britain I will respect the rule of law, defend the independence of the judiciary and discharge my duty to ensure the provision of resources for the efficient and effective support of the courts for which I am responsible. So help me God.'

Q1.1 What was the purpose of Magna Carta?

Q1.2 Which principle of the liberal theory of the state could paragraph 20 of Magna Carta be said to reflect and why?

Q1.3 Is the rule of law important today? If so, why? If not, why not?

In the nineteenth century the British jurist, AV Dicey, proposed that the rule of law comprises three main principles:[4] (i) no person can be interfered with or punished by the state except for breaking the law; (ii) no person is above the law and everyone, regardless of their rank or their position within the state itself, is subject to the law; (iii) the freedom guaranteed by the rule of law grows out of judicial decisions constituting the rights of all people.

Scholars have debated whether Dicey's criteria for the rule of law are necessary or sufficient on their own. In practice, the rule of law is subscribed to by most states and so, unsurprisingly, has many different meanings. Brian Tamanaha, a US academic, suggests three formal versions and three substantive versions of the rule of law.[5] Movement along the scale tends to be cumulative. Therefore, countries offering 'thicker' versions of the rule of law tend to incorporate previous positions.

Tamanaha's Alternative Rule-of-Law Formulations

Consider Tamanaha's diagram describing formal and substantive versions of the rule of law:

	Thinner		Thicker
Formal versions	1. **Rule by law** law as an instrument of government action	2. **Formal legality** general, prospective, clear, certain	3. **Democracy + legality** consent determines content of law
Substantive versions	4. **Individual rights** property, contract, privacy, autonomy	5. **Right of dignity and/or justice**	6. **Social welfare** substantive equality, welfare, preservation of community

---

[4] AV Dicey, *Introduction to the Study of Law of the Constitution* [1885] (Boston, MA, Adamant Media Corporation, 2005).

[5] BZ Tamanaha, *On the Rule of Law: History, Politics, Theory* (Cambridge, Cambridge University Press, 2004).

Q1.4 Which formal version of the rule of law is dominant in Western countries?

Q1.5 Which substantive version of the rule of law is dominant in Western countries?

Q1.6 Considering the following paragraphs taken from Magna Carta. What principles associated with the rule of law does each reflect?

> 38. No bailiff for the future shall, upon his own unsupported complaint, put anyone to his 'law', without credible witnesses brought for this purposes.

> 39. No freemen shall be taken or imprisoned or disseised or exiled or in any way destroyed, nor will we go upon him nor send upon him, except by the lawful judgment of his peers or by the law of the land.

> 40. To no one will we sell, to no one will we refuse or delay, right or justice.

Q1.7 In *Ghaidan v Godin-Mendoza*, the House of Lords interpreted the Rent Act 1977 in such a way as to protect homosexual couples. In what way did this reflect the rule of law?

At the beginning of the formal scale is 'rule *by* law', meaning that government acts in accordance with its own laws. This notion of the rule of law is consistent with a totalitarian state. The formal scale moves through to versions linked to democracy, meaning that law is applied by consent. Between these two is the dominant version, formal legality, which means that law is general, prospective, clear and certain, and everyone is equal before the law.

While formal versions of the rule of law describe legal processes, none say anything about the content of law. Substantive versions of the rule of law move from protection of individual rights to property, contract, privacy and autonomy, through to a promising equality, welfare and preservation of community. The mid-range position asserts the individual's right to dignity or justice.

The notion of formal legality, as formulated by Joseph Raz, requires that, in order to comply with the rule of law, rules must be produced by open processes. The law must therefore be clear, accessible and predictable. The rules must also be prospective, not retroactive, meaning that they apply only to behaviour occurring after the law was enacted. Courts must be accessible to ordinary people. The principles of natural justice should be observed and the independence of the judiciary must be guaranteed. The courts should have the power of judicial review and they must be able to control law enforcement. They must also be able to limit the involvement of any agencies that might pervert the law.

Legal System

Legal Traditions

One of four main legal traditions dominate in different countries. These systems are the civil law, common law, socialist and Islamic traditions. Common law systems dominate in English-speaking countries, including, for example, the US, Australia and Hong Kong. Civil law systems are pervasive in continental Europe and have been adopted by countries such as Japan and Russia. Socialist systems are still used in some communist regimes, such as Cuba or North Korea. Many Muslim countries contain elements of Sharia law in their legal systems.

Each kind of legal system has very distinctive features. In civil law systems, the law and procedure is codified and constantly updated. Judges in civil systems are in control of cases. They may interview witnesses, decide what evidence is produced and in what order. During the trial the judge often questions witnesses. Judges may decide cases with juries in very serious cases, but the use of juries is less pervasive in civil law systems. In socialist and Islamic legal systems, judges tend to dominate proceedings.

There is widespread agreement that recognition of the rule of law is intrinsic to a healthy society. This 'health' may not just lie in the fact that the human rights of the individual are recognised. The rule of law may also promote other benefits, including economic benefits. A contentious issue is which legal systems are most effective at promoting social benefits.

Case Study
The Rule of Law

'Economics and the Rule of Law'[6]

Observing the rule of law is a precondition of a state's membership of the international political order, but the social stability it promotes also facilitates economic activity.[7] Until the 1990s the 'Washington consensus' assumed that correct economic policies, for example on budgets and exchange rates, would lead to economic growth. The Asian financial crisis of 1997–98 drove economists to conclude that the context of policymaking, especially the rule of law, was more important. When the Soviet Union collapsed the emergent independent states quickly adopted conventional economic policies. Until that point Daniel Kaufmann, since then the head of the World Bank Institute's Global Governance group followed the consensus, but 'When I went

---

[6] For a more extended exposition see 'Economics and the Rule of Law: Order in the Jungle' *The Economist*, 13 March 2008.

[7] UN General Assembly (GA/L/3346) Links between Commercial Law reform and 'Culture of the Rule of Law' Stressed in General Assembly's Legal Committee (20 October 2008).

to Ukraine, my outlook changed. Problems with governance and the rule
of law were undermining all our efforts.' He worked out that a country's
income per head rose by around 300% when small improvements in governance were made.

Rich countries, except possibly Italy and Greece, score well on rule-
of-law measures while most poor countries do not. Effective governance
institutions, such as accessible courts, are more important than geography
and openness to trade in promoting prosperity. More debateable are the features of the rule of law that are important in achieving this effect.

Some economists suggest that the economic performance of common-
law countries (such as America and Britain) perform better than civil-law
ones (France, Germany and Scandinavia) because they provide more secure
property rights, better shareholder and creditor protection, diverse share
ownership, and tougher disclosure and liability laws. It is suggested that
these factors contribute to growth by improving stock market performance.

Independent judiciary

The Hon Justice Michael Kirby, Speech to the Law Council of Australia, Presidents of Law Associations in Asia Conference, Queensland, 20 March 2005

[T]he essence of a modern democracy is the rule of law … [which] will not
prevail without assuring the law's principal actors—judges and practicing
lawyers and also legal academic—a very high measure of independence of
mind and action.

…

The *Beijing Statement of Principles of the Independence of the Judiciary*
evidences the universality of this concept as a core value of international law.
Almost ten years ago this statement of judicial independence was adopted
by unanimous resolution at the 6th Biennial Conference of Chief Justices of
Asia and the Pacific. The statement was supported by the Chief Justices of
twenty nations. A further twelve signatories have since been added. Despite
the political, social, cultural, and economic differences between these states,
all have agreed that the principle of a strong and independent judiciary is
a common goal of societies that uphold human rights and respect the rule
of law.

…

Despite its important position as a protector of minority rights and individual freedoms, the judiciary is also the weakest arm of government. It is
the branch of government that holds '… neither the sword nor the purse'.
This fact increases the need for vigilance to ensure the strength and vitality
of the institution. Even in countries where the independence of the legal

profession has a long history and appears to be well entrenched, it is easy to take the principle for granted. There are many examples illustrating the fragility of the independence of the legal profession. These examples should be considered, not simply to indulge in censure but to learn from them and to avoid repeating mistakes.

The extent of the challenge is demonstrated in the recently released *2004 Country Reports on Human Rights Practices*, which is compiled by the United States State Department. The report raises concerns over the independence of the legal profession in more than half of the nations whose Chief Justices have endorsed the *Beijing Statement of Principles of the Independence of the Judiciary*. By the same token, in the same period, concerns have been expressed within the Asia-Pacific region over the independence of action of the courts and legal profession in the United States in respect of detainees in Guantanamo Bay. Those concerns have been partly assuaged by the decision of the United States Supreme Court in *Rasul v Bush*, deciding that those retaining the detainees of the 'war on terror' are answerable to the courts and not just to the executive government.

Similarly, the report *Attacks on Justice: the Harassment and Persecution of Judges and Lawyers (2002)*, released by the International Commission of Jurists records reprisals against 315 lawyers and judges, including 38 murders and 5 disappearances in the period covered. Undoubtedly, this report understates the real position. The instances illustrate that a gap exists between the commitment to the theory of legal independence and translation of that commitment into day to day practice.

Recent examples, both within our region and around the world, illustrate just how easily independence can be compromised and how quickly the strength of the judiciary and legal profession can be eroded.

For example, the situation in Nepal is obviously of concern. On 1 February 2005 His Majesty King Gyanendra dismissed the government, assumed direct rule and declared a state of national emergency. Since that date, human rights lawyers have been amongst the leaders and activists who have been detained or placed under house arrest. Sindhu Nath Pyakurel (the former President of the Nepal Bar Association) was reportedly one such detainee. He was ultimately released just two hours before the Supreme Court of Nepal was listed to consider his *habeas corpus* petition. Once again, the importance of the Great Writ for the defence of liberty and the maintenance of the rule of law was demonstrated. The recent royal order establishing the Royal Commission on Corruption Control has also been condemned by the Nepal Bar Association. The Association has said that the establishment of the Commission is contrary to the rule of law and undermines judicial independence. Time will tell whether this is so.

An example outside the Asia/Pacific region, one in which a resolution appears to have been achieved, concerns the Swaziland judicial crisis in

November 2002. That crisis was triggered by the government's rejection of a judgment of the High Court of Appeal. The government claimed that the judges were influenced by 'external forces' in their judgment. The government declined to release certain people who had been granted bail by the court. The crisis led to the resignation of the entire bench of the High Court of Appeal. A fact-finding mission conducted in January 2003 by the International Commission of Jurists concluded that:

> ...threats to judicial independence are deeply rooted and routine in Swaziland and that periodic attacks on the judiciary by the Executive have given way to an Executive attitude that holds the judiciary, the rule of law, and the separation of powers in virtual contempt, in particular when they conflict with entrenched interests.

The crisis was only resolved in August 2004 when a new Prime Minister unequivocally withdrew the government statement that had triggered the crisis. He introduced legislation to reconstitute the High Court of Appeal and to pave the way for the release of all persons who had been granted bail by the courts but who were still incarcerated.

Similarly, direct attacks on judicial independence, also outside the Asia/Pacific region, have been seen in both Venezuela and Ecuador. In Venezuela, the enactment of so-called 'court-packing' legislation has allowed the ruling coalition to expand the size of the Supreme Court by more than half its former number, through the appointment of twelve new Justices to the Court in December 2004. The new Organic Law of the Supreme Court also purported to give the governmental coalition the power to remove judges from the Supreme Court without the two-thirds majority vote required by the Constitution.

In Ecuador, the Congress in a special session called by President Lucio Gutierrez in December 2004, voted to replace 27 of the 31 Supreme Court Justices. The replacement Justices were all selected from political parties that had successfully opposed earlier attempts to impeach the President. This move followed the replacement of the majority of judges on the Electoral Court and Constitutional Court the previous month. It occurred despite the fact that the 1998 Ecuadorian Constitution does not grant Congress the authority to impeach justices and specifically provides that vacancies on the Supreme Court should be filled by the Court, itself a somewhat controversial provision.

Independent associations of lawyers

Associations of lawyers, active in civil society, are often seen as a guarantor and measure of the health of the rule of law within a state. Such associations promote regulatory frameworks that support the independence of lawyers.

In states where violence is common neutrality is an important principle. The relative weakness of legal professional associations and the absence of neutrality principles in professional roles may contribute to the assassination of human rights lawyers in many jurisdictions. In Columbia, for example, there are only 400 human rights lawyers in a population of 170,000 lawyers yet, in 2004, 26 lawyers were murdered there.[8] It may be significant that Columbia is the only country in Latin America without a national representative body for lawyers.

As part of its mission 'to establish conditions under which justice can be maintained, and proclaim as one of their purposes the achievement of international cooperation in promoting and encouraging respect for human rights and fundamental freedoms without distinction as to race, sex, language or religion' the UN has made a declaration on the role of lawyers in society, formulated to:

> assist Member States in their task of promoting and ensuring the proper role of lawyers, should be respected and taken into account by Governments within the framework of their national legislation and practice and should be brought to the attention of lawyers as well as other persons, such as judges, prosecutors, members of the executive and the legislature, and the public in general. These principles shall also apply, as appropriate, to persons who exercise the functions of lawyers without having the formal status of lawyers.[9]

The declaration urges that governments should ensure appropriate education and training, ensuring that lawyers are 'aware of the ideals and ethical duties of the lawyer and of human rights and fundamental freedoms recognized by national and international law', that entry to legal professions be provided to disadvantaged groups and that legal education and professional life should be informed by ethical standards.

Basic Principles on the Role of Lawyers Adopted by the Eighth United Nations Congress on the Prevention of Crime and the Treatment of Offenders, Havana, Cuba, 27 August to 7 September 1990.

Guarantees for the functioning of lawyers

16. Governments shall ensure that lawyers (a) are able to perform all of their professional functions without intimidation, hindrance, harassment or improper interference; (b) are able to travel and to consult with their clients

---

[8] F Gibb, 'The Human Cordon that Protects Human Rights Lawyers' *Times Online*, 15 October 2007, http://business.timesonline.co.uk/tol/business/law/article2665733.ece.

[9] Basic Principles on the Role of Lawyers Adopted by the Eighth United Nations Congress on the Prevention of Crime and the Treatment of Offenders, Havana, Cuba, 27 August–7 September 1990.

freely both within their own country and abroad; and (c) shall not suffer, or be threatened with, prosecution or administrative, economic or other sanctions for any action taken in accordance with recognized professional duties, standards and ethics.

17. Where the security of lawyers is threatened as a result of discharging their functions, they shall be adequately safeguarded by the authorities.

18. Lawyers shall not be identified with their clients or their clients' causes as a result of discharging their functions.

19. No court or administrative authority before whom the right to counsel is recognized shall refuse to recognize the right of a lawyer to appear before it for his or her client unless that lawyer has been disqualified in accordance with national law and practice and in conformity with these principles.

20. Lawyers shall enjoy civil and penal immunity for relevant statements made in good faith in written or oral pleadings or in their professional appearances before a court, tribunal or other legal or administrative authority.

21. It is the duty of the competent authorities to ensure lawyers access to appropriate information, files and documents in their possession or control in sufficient time to enable lawyers to provide effective legal assistance to their clients. Such access should be provided at the earliest appropriate time.

22. Governments shall recognize and respect that all communications and consultations between lawyers and their clients within their professional relationship are confidential.

Freedom of expression and association

23. Lawyers like other citizens are entitled to freedom of expression, belief, association and assembly. In particular, they shall have the right to take part in public discussion of matters concerning the law, the administration of justice and the promotion and protection of human rights and to join or form local, national or international organizations and attend their meetings, without suffering professional restrictions by reason of their lawful action or their membership in a lawful organization. In exercising these rights, lawyers shall always conduct themselves in accordance with the law and the recognized standards and ethics of the legal profession.

Professional associations of lawyers

24. Lawyers shall be entitled to form and join self-governing professional associations to represent their interests, promote their continuing education and training and protect their professional integrity. The executive body of

the professional associations shall be elected by its members and shall exercise its functions without external interference.

25. Professional associations of lawyers shall cooperate with Governments to ensure that everyone has effective and equal access to legal services and that lawyers are able, without improper interference, to counsel and assist their clients in accordance with the law and recognized professional standards and ethics.

Q1.8   Why is the rule of law socially beneficial?

Q1.9   How might the rule of law help the economies of nations to grow?

Q1.10 What kinds of legal system gain the greatest benefits for a society governed by the rule of law?

Legal Systems

Adjudication systems reflect two values: fair dispute resolution and social values, that is, those values shared by a society.[10] In England and Wales the state operates dispute resolution systems to promote the rule of law. These are based on the common law system and adversarial justice.

The Common Law

The common law develops on a case-by-case basis. Judges follow precedents created by senior courts in previous cases. Legislation often codifies previous common law, whereupon judges interpret the will of Parliament in future decisions. Judges therefore play a major role in shaping the law.

In order to ensure fair adjudication, tribunals adopt uniform standards of fairness. There are three main elements: impartial adjudication, rational decision-making and giving a voice to the participants. Written reasons are given for decisions. These formal processes help to generate decisions that people can accept as fair, even if they are adverse. Formality of process protects legal

[10] EE Sward, 'Values, Ideology, and the Evolution of the Adversary System' (1989) 64(2) *Indiana Law Journal* 301, 306.

values. The participation of parties in the process ensures that the process is seen to be fair.

The Adversarial System

The adversarial system of dispute resolution is identified with common law systems. It is based on lawyers putting forward their client's case and the judge deciding who wins. The lawyers are therefore seen as adversaries. Indeed, the common law system, for both civil and criminal matters, is known as the adversarial system. The presentation of conflicting theories and evidence tests factual accounts effectively. Cross-examination, where an advocate questions opposing witnesses, has been described as the 'greatest legal engine ever invented for the discovery of truth'.

The Values of Different Dispute Resolution Systems

The common law system achieves a number of social goods. It generates firm but flexible rules, whether in new areas of law or by interpreting existing legislation, and helps to achieve behavioural change. This is an ongoing process of social adaptation that is arguably achieved much more effectively through judicial decisions than by legislative programmes. It may affect individuals needing to comply with a new rule, or it may affect whole social and economic sectors.

The adversarial system of dispute resolution is identified with common law systems and with a particular set of values. It promotes liberal notions of equality before the law. It is also claimed that the impersonal nature of adversarial processes supports a particular kind of individual dignity and autonomy. The adversarial system allows individuals to assert their rights in a way that affords them maximum freedom. It rewards their proactivity and initiative.

Through their lawyers the parties choose what evidence to present and how they themselves are presented. The judge does not interfere in this process. Because the parties, or their advisors, determine how the case will be presented, they are in a better position to predict outcomes than the judge.

Criticisms of the Adversarial System

Critics of adversarial methods argue that trials are too long and, therefore, expensive. This means that most ordinary people often cannot afford to go to court, at least with the assistance of lawyers. Adversarial trials are sometimes said to be ineffective; a battle between two versions of the truth does not necessarily reveal the truth. In particular, it can be argued that adversarial trials are unfair because the outcome depends too much on the skills of the lawyer.

Alternative Systems

The adversarial system is contrasted with the inquisitorial system used in civil law countries. In such systems, judges have a much more proactive role in directing what evidence needs to be gathered. The parties may suggest directions for the investigation to take, or indicate witnesses to interview, but do not take any of the steps themselves. The lawyers may only see witnesses in court. This is a more co-operative process than the adversarial system. Both adversarial systems and inquisitorial systems have biases that need to be adjusted for. When these are taken into account, the systems are possibly more similar than they appear at first sight.[11]

Q1.11 What are three key features of adversarial and inquisitorial proceedings?

Q1.12 What advantages are claimed for the adversarial trial?

Q1.13 To what extent does the rule of law depend on adversarial justice?

Legal Roles

The Judiciary

Constitutional Role

Judges have a constitutional role within the separation of state powers between legislative, executive and judiciary. The judiciary has a constitutional responsibility for applying the law according to the will of parliament and for controlling any abuse of power by the state. In these tasks, the rule of law is an important yardstick and guide.

In the US judges can strike down primary legislation. This power, surprisingly, does not derive from the US constitution but it was declared, in cases beginning with *Marbury v Madison* (1803),[12] that it flows from the constitution.

---

[11] Ibid, 316.
[12] *Marbury v Madison* (1803) 5 US 137.

In England, constitutional lawyers have treated the court's role in enforcing the rule of law as part of its function in interpreting the will of parliament. It is sometimes argued that English judges might declare an independent constitutional justification of the rule of law if Parliament threatened to undermine it. At present however, the conventional view is that judicial power to control the legislature is limited.

An English Supreme Court declaration that primary legislation is incompatible with the Human Rights Act 1998[13] does not invalidate the legislation, but usually encourages Parliament to make suitable amendments to it.[14] Judges also have an important role in interpreting legislation against the standards of the rule of law. In *R v Secretary of State for the Home Department*, Lord Steyn said that 'unless there is the clearest provision to the contrary, Parliament must be presumed not to legislate contrary to the rule of law. And the rule of law enforces minimum standards of fairness, both substantive and procedural.'[15]

Judicial control of the executive is important and often decisive. In modern times the power of the judiciary to control the executive has been mainly exercised through the mechanism of judicial review. In this way the judges help to control the power of the state and the executive in particular. One of the roles of the judiciary is, therefore, to resist erosion of their powers.

In 2013 a government consultation paper proposed restricting the right to seek judicial review to those who had standing, that is, had a direct involvement in the matter. This would exclude campaigning organisations bringing judicial review cases. It claimed 'that judicial review is hampering economic recovery and growth, and is being used inappropriately as a campaigning or delaying tactic'.[16] The move was controversial and Lord Neuberger,[17] President of the Supreme Court, explained why.

I should mention the Government's recent paper on judicial review in this context. It contains proposals intended to cut down the cost and delay involved in J[udicial] R[eview] applications. The desire to discourage weak applications is understandable, even, laudable, and the desire to reduce delay and expense is plainly right, at least in principle. However, one must be very careful about any proposals whose aim is to cut down the right to JR. The courts have no more important function than that of protecting citizens from the abuses and excesses of the executive—central government, local government, or other public bodies. With the ever-increasing power of Government, which now commands almost

---

[13] Human Rights Act 1988 s 4.

[14] Human Rights Act 1988 s 10.

[15] *R v Secretary of State for the Home Department, ex p Pierson* [1998] AC 539, 581.

[16] A Street, *Judicial Review and the Rule of Law: Who Is in Control* (London, The Constitution Society, 2013), www.consoc.org.uk/wp-content/uploads/2013/12/J1446_Constitution_Society_Judicial_Review_WEB-22.pdf

[17] 'Justice in an Age of Austerity', JUSTICE, Tom Sargant Memorial Annual Lecture 2013 given by Lord Neuberger of Abbotsbury, President of the Supreme Court, on 15 October 2013, paras 37–38. Cited in Street (n 16).

half the country's GDP, this function of calling the executive to account could not more important. I am not suggesting that we have a dysfunctional or ill-intentioned executive, but the more power that a government has, the more likely it is that there will be abuses and excesses which result in injustice to citizens, and the more important it is for the rule of law that such abuses and excesses can be brought before an impartial and experienced judge who can deal with them openly, dispassionately and fairly. While the Government is entitled to look at the way that JR is operating and to propose improvements, we must look at any proposed changes with particular care, because of the importance of maintaining JR, and also bearing in mind that the proposed changes come from the very body which is at the receiving end of JR.

Q1.14 In this extract, is Lord Neuberger arguing that government should not restrict the right of judicial review?

Q1.15 Summarise the arguments why they should be cautious before doing so.

Procedural Role

In common law systems the judge in court traditionally takes a less dominant role than in other systems. This is because the lawyers control the collection and presentation of evidence. It is also because the underlying ethos of the trial in common law countries is often a conflict of two accounts of 'the truth'. Having heard all the factual evidence and the advocates' legal arguments, the judge delivers a verdict covering findings of fact and law. In serious criminal cases, juries are directed on the law by the judge and reach a verdict based on their finding of fact.

Judicial Ethics

Judicial ethics are captured in the Bangalore Principles of Judicial Conduct. The Principles are based on the values of judicial independence, impartiality, integrity, propriety, and competence and diligence. In England and Wales, judges are subject to judicial codes, such as the Supreme Court Guide[18] ('The Guide'). According to this, judicial independence is 'a prerequisite to the rule of law and a fundamental guarantee of a fair trial'.[19]

Judicial independence is supported by the fact that judges may only be

[18] *United Kingdom Supreme Court Guide to Judicial Conduct* (2009).
[19] Ibid, para 1(2)i.

removed from office in limited circumstances, thus making it more difficult to subject them to political pressure. Judges also enjoy immunity from actions in tort or other civil proceedings arising from acts in their judicial role.[20] In common law jurisdictions, judges tend to be chosen from successful practitioners. This addresses concerns that judicial independence might be threatened when judges are trained by the state or work closely with state officials.

To be impartial, judges must have a neutral disposition towards an issue. They must also be independently minded, rationale, dispassionate and able to ignore the opinions of others. English Supreme Court Justices swear a judicial oath, stating: 'I will do right to all manner of people after the laws and usages of this Realm, without fear or favour, affection or ill-will.'[21] Putting the underlying ethos of the rule of law into operation requires that judges are seen to be neutral as well as actually being neutral.

The integrity and propriety of judges are protected by rules against accepting gifts or lending their prestige to advance private interest.[22] They must 'try to avoid situations which might reasonably lower respect for their judicial office, or cast doubt upon their impartiality as judges, or expose them to charges of hypocrisy. They will try to conduct themselves in a way which is consistent with the dignity of their office.'[23] In court they must display polite and neutral behaviour to the parties. In court:

> [T]hey will strive to ensure that no one in Court is exposed to any display of bias or prejudice on grounds such as race, colour, sex, religion, national origin, disability, age, marital status, sexual orientation, social and economic status and other like causes. Care will be taken that arrangements made for and during a hearing do not put people with a disability at a disadvantage.[24]

When they fail to meet these standards judges may be removed from the case.[25]

The Lord Chief Justice is responsible for the training, guidance and deployment of judges. In addition to undergoing any prescribed training, judges have personal responsibility for keeping up to date with practice in their areas of work.[26] The duty of diligence demands steady and careful application to the task at hand.

---

[20] *Sirros v Moore* [1975] QB 118, per Lord Denning, 134.

[21] *United Kingdom Supreme Court Guide to Judicial Conduct* (2009) para 2(2).

[22] Ibid, paras 4(4), 5(3) and 5(4).

[23] Ibid, para 4(2).

[24] Ibid, para 4(3).

[25] *El Farargy v El Farargy* [2007] EWCA Civ 1149, [2007] All ER (D) 248.

[26] *Guide to Judicial Conduct* 2009 (n 21) para 6.

The Lawyers

Lawyers and the Rule of Law

Arguably, the adversarial system is the system that best supports the rule of law based on formal legality. It embodies the institutional separation of powers[27] and the rule of law.[28] Most importantly, within the framework of an adversarial trial, lawyers have the platform to hold the liberal state to its promises of liberty and equality. From this position, the judiciary and legal profession are strongly placed to control government powers and restrict government immunities.[29]

Values of Lawyers in an Adversarial System

The adversarial system dictates the values of lawyers working within it. The adversarial trial of the common law system demands that advocates do their utmost for their clients. This emphasises the value of loyalty. However, while lawyers are advocates for their clients they owe balancing duties to the court. This emphasises the value of independence.

Weber thought that the rational values of lawyers dominated the intellectual system of the law. Once the law is formulated, lawyers develop and pass on the skills and ways of thinking necessary to maintain it. Weber perceived that the independence of lawyers from political and other influence were essential to the autonomy, generality and universality of law as a system. Hazard and Dondi, US legal academics, argue that the effectiveness of the rule of law depends on 'a legal profession sufficiently autonomous to invoke the authority of an independent judiciary'.[30]

Lawyers working in different kinds of legal systems have different degrees of independence. Civil law systems allow lawyers less scope to control proceedings than common law systems do. Communist regimes are often characterised as allowing lawyers very little independence. Adversarial systems place a premium on the lawyer's separation from all influences outside the framework of professional values.

---

[27] See generally TC Halliday and L Karpik, *Lawyers and the Rise of Western Political Liberalism* (Oxford, Clarendon Press, 1997).

[28] TC Halliday and L Karpik 'Politics Matter: A Comparative Theory of Lawyers in the Making of Political Liberalism', in Halliday and Karpik, ibid, 15, 21 and 30.

[29] N MacCormick, 'The Ethics of Legalism' (1989) 2(2) *Ratio Juris* 184.

[30] Hazard and Dondi (n 3) 1.

The lawyer's social role tends to reflect the social system in which it evolved. Consider the following example:

> As expressed by law professors at the University of Havana, 'the first job of a revolutionary lawyer is not to argue that his client is innocent, but rather to determine if his client is guilty and, if so, to seek the sanctions that will best rehabilitate him.' Similarly, a Bulgarian attorney began his defence in a treason trial by noting that: 'in a Socialist state there is no division of duty between the judge, prosecutor, and defence counsel. ... The defence must assist the prosecution to find the objective truth in a case.' In that case, the defence attorney ridiculed his client's defence, and the client was convicted and executed. Sometime later the verdict was found to be erroneous, and the defendant was 'rehabilitated'.[31]

Q1.16 Which formal version of the rule of law does the example illustrate?

Q1.17 What point about the lawyers' role is the author seeking to make?

The Ideology of Advocacy

The dominant belief system of legal professionals in an adversarial setting has been called the ideology of advocacy.[32] It is traceable to foundations laid by Thomas Hobbes in positivist legal theory. In a society of egoistic individuals pursuing their own ends the state provides order. It commands loyalty and provides each individual with the prescribed space to pursue their own ends. This space is governed by rules that, according to William Simon, are 'artificial, impersonal, objective and rational'.[33]

The role of the judge is to interpret the sovereign's intention. The role of the lawyer is to explain to the citizen how this will affect him and to pursue his rights. A number of writers suggest that the ideology of advocacy is based on the twin principles of neutrality and partisanship. The idea behind these two principles is that every individual is entitled to a champion who will take their side against the whole world.

Simon suggests that two other principles sustain the ideology of advocacy. Simon's third principle is procedural justice. This is the idea that the legitimacy of a situation lies in the way it is produced, for example, by a judicial proceeding. According to this idea it is possible to act justly by conforming to procedure. The second principle is professionalism. In this context, it is the

---

[31] M Freedman, 'Are there Public Interest Limits on Lawyers' Advocacy?' (1977) 2 *Journal of the Legal Profession* 47.

[32] WH Simon, 'The Ideology of Advocacy: Procedural Justice and Professional Ethics' (1978) *Wisconsin Law Review* 29.

[33] Ibid, 40

idea that the development of key disciplines should be left to the practitioners of relevant disciplines. This act of delegation rests on the belief that experts are best placed to identify and resolve the ethical dilemmas produced by a complex role.

Most writers on the ideology of advocacy are critical of its implications. They are particularly critical of the fact that the legal mind-set is fundamentally affected by the ideology of advocacy. Therefore, lawyers are adversarial even when the context does not demand it, and potentially against the interests of their clients.

Some critics have sought refinements or adjustments of the ideology of advocacy in codes of conduct and the training of lawyers. Simon argues that these cannot change the underlying basis of the ideology of advocacy. Only deprofessionalisation of advocacy can fundamentally alter the ideology. Today, this seems like less of a fantasy than when Simon first proposed it. In order to explore the implications of the rise and fall of the ideology of advocacy it is necessary to trace its evolution through the legal profession and in the courts.

The Art of Advocacy

There are numerous books about what constitutes good advocacy. Early versions approached advocacy as an art.[34] This suggests that advocacy is often viewed as the expression or application of human creative skill and imagination to the task of presentation in court. The books generally cover the whole process, from pleading cases, presenting evidence, introducing and cross-examining witnesses and making speeches. As this shows, good advocacy is determined by context. It is shaped by the legal system, the culture and the rules of court. The performance of English barristers has always been assessed on their ability to persuade while assisting the judge to reach a just decision.

There are many iconic advocates. This section takes examples from the lives of two: Thomas Erskine and Henry Brougham. These two are often cited as proponents of neutrality and partisanship, respectively. In many respects they also demonstrate some of the qualities required to be an advocate and, indeed, a good lawyer of any kind.

i. Efficiency and Diligence

Being helpful to the court involves assessment of what the circumstances and the case requires. The thorough, honest and skilful presentation of cases saves court time and reduces expense. Roscoe Pound related having seen a record in which 'a boy, asleep in the well of the court, fell and broke his neck. The bar-

---

[34] The Hon Sir Malcolm Hilberry, *Duty and Art in Advocacy* (London, Stevens and Sons, 1946); LP Stryker *The Art of Advocacy: A Plea for the Renaissance of the Trial Lawyer* (London, Simon & Schuster, 1954); R Du Cann, *The Art of the Advocate* (London, Penguin, 1964).

rister speaking at the time was, in the spirit of 'comradely humour', indicted by the Circuit 'for murder with a certain dull instrument, to wit, a long speech of no value'.[35]

Pound's anecdote illustrates the fact that the Bar has its own standards of rhetoric. It also shows how poor advocacy was discouraged by peer pressure. The pressure to be efficient did not mean that the court process was perfunctory. As a visitor from the US noted:

> Patience and thoroughness is the rule of the Bar and the Court; time is never more than a passing consideration and counsel are permitted to exhaust the argument ... no warning light and cutting short as in the US Supreme Court—'Justice is seen to be done.'[36]

In fearlessly representing their client, barristers were required to be politely persistent if the judge did not follow their point. They sometimes had to be politely insistent if the judge was, in their view, wrong in directing the evidence.

ii. Persuasion

Good advocacy is persuasive, potentially to a judge or to a jury. For the judge, the advocate must marshal the legal arguments and present them convincingly, respectfully and without arrogance. The jury may need emotional or psychological anchors as well as rational argument. To do both these things with economy and confidence, while marshalling the evidence and the law, is a complex and demanding set of operations.

The first task of the advocate is to decide the organising theme of the case, to which all the individual points lead. Arnold suggests that Erskine's approach was that:

> In every case he proposed a great leading principle to which all his efforts were referable and subsidiary. ... As the principle thus proposed was founded in truth and justice, whatever might be its application to the particular case, it necessarily gave the whole of his speech and air of honesty and sincerity which a jury could with difficulty resist.[37]

The second is to find a form of presentation that is natural and appealing. With juries it is important to communicate effectively. Thomas Erskine was said to have been particularly successful at this, whereas Brougham was awkward with juries and seldom successful in persuading them. They must make their theme accessible and convey a sense of importance of the issue to be decided. Arnold remarked on Erskine's

---

[35] R Pound, *The Lawyer from Antiquity to Modern Times: With Particular Reference to the Development of Bar Associations in the United States* (St Paul, MN, West Publishing, 1953) 127.
[36] B Hollander, *The English Bar: The Tribute of an American Lawyer* (London, Bowes, 1964).
[37] H Roscoe, *Lives of Eminent British Lawyers* (London, 1830) 381.

ability in a single speech, to direct effective persuasion towards the predisposition of judges and jurors even when these two classes of auditors were differently inclined; the entire harmony of language, thought and purpose which marks all his pleas; and, above all else, his ability to make inescapable the *public* significance of each case for which he accepted a brief.[38]

Erskine's approach is illustrated in an extract the trial of Tom Paine. Erskine concluded a long speech with a parable: Jupiter and the countryman. The tale deals with the importance of tempering power with reason. It is an allegory of the relationship between the state and its citizens:

> You all remember, Gentlemen, the pleasant story in that fable of his respecting the Countryman and Jupiter they were conversing with great freedom and familiarity on the subjects of heaven and earth; the countryman listened with great attention, and acquiesced in the conversation so long as Jupiter tried only to convince him by reason and argument; but the Countryman happening to hint a doubt as to the truth and propriety of something which Jupiter had advanced, he instantly turned round and threatened him with his thunder: No, says the Countryman, if you up with your thunder, I believe you are in the wrong; you are always wrong when you appeal to your thunder; as long as you have reason on your side, I believe you may be right, but I cannot fight against thunder.[39]

In this extract, Erskine gently suggests that the heavy handedness of the state indicates that it has lost the argument, and hence the claim to act legitimately in prosecuting Paine.

Effective advocates use the rules that circumscribe their behaviour to their advantage. For example, the prohibition on venturing an opinion on the innocence of their client is overcome by conveying confidence in their client by their manner.[40] This is arguably much more effective than a hollow and inauthentic verbal expression of faith in a client's innocence.

Evolution of the Ideology of Advocacy in England and Wales

Lawyers have a claim to be agents in the formation of the modern, democratic state. Leading advocates were engaged in social movements in the eighteenth and nineteenth centuries. Indeed, they won some of the important victories in the struggle for civic equality and human rights. Barristers were often campaigners, politicians and lawyers. As the public face of a battle for democracy they could become popular heroes.

---

[38] CC Arnold, 'Lord Thomas Erskine: Modern Advocate' in TW Benson (ed), *Landmark Essays on Rhetorical Criticism* (Davis, CA, Hermagoras Press, 1993) 89, 92.

[39] *The Genuine Trial of Thomas Paine, for a Libel Contained in the Second Part of Rights of Man* (London, Guildhall, 1792), www.constitution.org/tp/trial_of_thomas_paine.html, accessed 23 January 2014.

[40] D Pannick, *Advocates* (Oxford, Oxford University Press 1992) 154.

Lawyers agitated for a legal system that both reflected and could facilitate the social and political changes that they promoted through the causes they supported. Their views on the proper disposition of lawyers towards society, their clients and the courts, influenced the legal professions, the law and lawyers' self-perception. Their stirring phrases continue to be quoted in arguments about the proper role of lawyers. The voices of Thomas Erskine and Henry Brougham were not the only ones heard in this evolution. They did, however, in some memorable instances articulate the core ethic of lawyers. They illustrate how lawyers forced the pace of political progress and helped forge the ideology of advocacy.

Thomas Erskine and the Obligations of Fearless Advocacy

Thomas Erskine (1750–1823) was a barrister from Edinburgh. He was from an aristocratic family that had fallen on hard times. He rose through the Bar to serve briefly as Lord Chancellor (1806–07).[41] Lovat-Fraser says:

> Erskine brought to his profession the dignified qualities and lofty ambition of a great spirit. He did not, with sordid greed, think only of amassing money, and regulate his attendance and exertions according to the fee marked upon his brief. To Erskine, the Bar was a field for noble effort, where he sought the renown that is secured by eloquence and courage, and zeal for justice.[42]

When Erskine first arrived in London he was poor. In his very first case he appeared on the defence team of the Lieutenant Governor of Greenwich Hospital, Thomas Baillie.[43] The hospital had been built for seamen, but the First Lord of the Admiralty, Lord Sandwich, had introduced corrupt officials who were diverting funds. When Baillie objected to this practice, these officials brought a case of criminal libel against him. Baillie instructed a team of lawyers of which Erskine was the most junior.

Three of Erskine's senior counsel urged compromise of the action, but Baillie preferred Erskine's advice to resist the charges. In the trial the Solicitor-General concluded his closing speech against Baillie, and Erskine's three senior counsel all responded. The Solicitor-General was about to close, assuming that Erskine would not speak. Erskine rose and launched a verbal assault on Sandwich. The judge, Lord Mansfield, said that the Lord was not a party before the court, to which Erskine responded:

> [F]or that very reason I will bring him before the court. He has placed these men in the front of the battle, in hopes to escape under their shelter; but I will not join in battle with them; their vices, though screwed up to the highest pitch of human

---

[41] See generally J Hostettler, *Thomas Erskine and Trial by Jury* (Hook, Waterside Press, 2010); Rt Hon Lord Widgery, 'The Compleat Advocate' (1975) 43(6) *Fordham Law Review* 909.

[42] JA Lovat-Fraser, *Erskine* (Cambridge, Cambridge University Press, 1932) x.

[43] Ibid.

depravity, are not of dignity enough to vindicate the combat with me. I will drag him to light who is the dark mover behind the scene of iniquity … if he keeps this injured man suspended, or dares to turn that suspension into a removal, I shall not scruple to declare him an accomplice in their guilt, a shameless oppressor, a disgrace to his rank and a traitor to his trust.[44]

Whether or not Erskine's rhetoric appeals to modern tastes, no one could criticise his commitment and courage. Remember, this was an advocate on his first outing.

Later, Erskine's most notable cases involved defence of radicals and reformers against charges of seditious libel. Sedition was an offence defined in the early 1600s in the Star Chamber. It involved any act that the authorities deemed to be provoking insurrection, but was often used to stifle criticism of the establishment. Seditious libel was constituted by the act of committing the offending words to print.

In 1785 Erskine represented William Shipley, an Anglican priest, who had published *Principles of Government, in a Dialogue between a Gentleman and a Farmer*. This tract advanced radical views on the relationship between the state and citizens. *Principles of Government* was based on a pamphlet Shipley had found at a public meeting, although it turned out to have been written by his brother-in-law.

The Sherriff of Flintshire, a political opponent of Shipley, funded a private prosecution for seditious libel. The Society for Constitutional Information retained Erskine to defend Shipley. The trial judge attempted to bully the jury into a quick conviction on all the charges, but it resisted. Shipley was convicted only of publication and appealed the decision. The appeal court held that the publication was not criminal and Shipley was discharged. The case was instrumental in the passing of the Libel Act 1792, which provided that the decision that a publication is libellous must be left to a jury.

In 1792 Erskine appeared on behalf of Thomas Paine, who was charged with seditious libel following publication of the second part of *Rights of Man*, which the government saw as incitement to revolution. Erskine based his defence of Paine on the argument that a free press leads to stronger and more secure government. Paine was convicted in his absence by a special jury, selected from wealthier property owners. They did not even bother to retire to consider their verdict.

Erskine's friends had advised him not to take the case, and doing so cost him his position as Attorney General to the Prince of Wales, which he had held since 1786. Erskine is frequently quoted on the obligation of barristers to take on causes involving challenges to the state. In 1794, for example, there was great anxiety in government that the campaign for parliamentary reform might spiral into revolution. The government of William Pitt put troops on the

---

[44] Ibid, 9–10.

street, suspended habeas corpus and arrested 12 leading radicals for treason. Erskine was assigned to seven of the cases pro bono, as was the custom in treason trials.

In the first of the trials the jury acquitted the defendant following a seven-hour speech from Erskine on the final day. Joyous crowds outside the court unharnessed Erskine's horses and dragged his carriage through the streets. Erskine appeared in the next two cases, which also failed. The prosecutions, and a large number of other warrants of arrest, were abandoned. Stopping the escalation of the situation into a 'reign of terror' is attributed to Erskine's 'singular skills and resolution'.[45]

Erskine's eminence lent credibility to two key elements of the ideology of advocacy in England. The first was neutrality. At a time when the establishment and the middle classes were anxious that the spirit of revolution would spread to England, it was vital that those agitating for reform could not be cast as radicals.

In the trial of Paine, Erskine went to great lengths to explain to the jury how a loyal Englishman could still support reform. His second cause was jury trial. He had ample reason to trust the good sense and democratic inclinations of ordinary people when the state machinery threatened justice.

The Fearless Advocacy of Henry Brougham

The ethic of advocacy is often predicated on the need for advocates to stand in defiance of the state on behalf of clients. Today it is manifest in the demand for freedom from the influence by the state. This commitment is deep in the culture of the English Bar. An early exponent was Henry Brougham, a Scottish lawyer, Whig politician and social reformer, who joined Lincoln's Inn in 1803.

From 1812, Brougham was a legal adviser to Caroline of Brunswick, the estranged wife of the Prince of Wales and Prince Regent. In 1820, she appointed him her Attorney-General. Caroline was married to George, Prince of Wales, in 1795 although she had not met him previously. They separated and Caroline lived abroad. An investigation was launched into her alleged adultery in 1806 but no evidence was found. In 1820 the Prince of Wales acceded to the throne as George IV and Caroline returned to England, ostensibly as queen.

Caroline became associated with opposition to George, who was an unpopular king. He began divorce proceedings against her and presented evidence of Caroline's adultery to the House of Lords. A bill was introduced to remove Caroline's title. The proceedings lasted 11 weeks, but were tightly controlled to deny Brougham any chance to discredit the king or to mention his mistress, Maria Fitzherbert, whom George had secretly married before he married Caroline. Caroline was cheered by crowds as she went to the House each day.

---

[45] Ibid, xvii.

The bill passed by the narrow margin, but public opinion, and the risk that the bill might fail in the House of Commons, led to its withdrawal. Brougham defended his willingness to expose the king to embarrassment and ridicule. This speech is often quoted in discussions of the ethics of advocacy. It is cited in support of the duty of 'zealous advocacy', originally adopted by the American Bar Association in its model rules. Brougham's explanation of his duty to defend Queen Caroline is a defence of the lawyer's partisan obligation to defy power, at whatever personal or political cost.

The Association of Advocacy and Rights

Advocates such as Brougham and Erskine tied the obligations of advocacy to the discourse of freedom and rights. By the early nineteenth century the foundations of the ideology of advocacy had been laid and cemented, with the Bar as its custodian. Refinements occurred between 1820 and 1850.

Changes to the rules of advocacy were needed. Some barristers took Brougham's oft-quoted expression of counsel's obligation to defend clients by 'all expedient means' too far. There were infamous cases of counsel asserting their client's innocence while being aware of their guilt.[46] This led to restrictions on counsel, outlined below.[47] Nevertheless, the infrastructure, the basic orientation of the advocate to the state, to clients and to courts, remained.

The Standard Conception of the Lawyer's Role

The standard conception of the lawyer's role is derived from an interpretation of the American Bar Association model code by US academics.[48] Their analysis cites the rhetoric of advocates such as Erskine and Brougham as inspirations behind the code (see further chapter four: The Relationship). The 'standard conception' which they propose is based on two overarching principles: neutrality and partisanship.

The principle of neutrality demands that lawyers present cases on behalf of unpopular causes or those they disagree with morally. The principle of partisanship demands that they follow their client's instructions so far as the law allows, even if this produces unjust outcomes. The first two principles of the standard conception are supported by a third, the principle of non-accountability.

The principle of non-accountability suggests that, provided lawyers observe

[46] A Watson, 'Changing Advocacy: Part One' (2001) 165 *Justice of the Peace* 743.

[47] Ibid, attributed to the arguments of William Forsyth in *Hortensius or the Advocate, an Historical Essay* (1849).

[48] See eg ML Schwartz, 'The Professionalism and Accountability of Lawyers' (1978) *California Law Review*, 66; Simon (n 32); D Luban, *Lawyers and Justice: An Ethical Study* (Princeton, NJ, Princeton University Press, 1988).

the principles of partisanship and neutrality, they are absolved of personal moral responsibility for the consequences of actions on behalf of clients. The moral justification for this proposition is that, by pursuing clients' goals, they promote the liberal society, the rule of law and their clients' personal autonomy. Therefore, the role they perform is itself good.

One of the issues posed in legal ethics in recent years is whether lawyers can live a 'good life' on this basis.[49] This means, in classical terms, whether can they live according to independent moral principles while fulfilling their professional role. Some critics of the standard conception of the legal role argue that it mandates lying and cheating and so cannot be consistent with a good life. Others argue that because of the good the role performs, and the limitations it imposes on professional conduct,[50] the standard conception is perfectly consistent with a virtuous life.

The legitimacy of the lawyer's role in an adversarial system is contested. It has been argued that conferring a distinctive 'role morality' on lawyers' legitimises behaviour that is contrary to the effective administration of justice and against the public interest. This is a recurring theme in debates about whether the lawyer's ethical commitment to clients should be balanced by duties other than a duty to the court (see further chapter seven: Third Parties (Non-Clients) and chapter eight: Social Responsibility).

Professionalism and Ethics

Professional practice has a privileged position among occupations because of the 'indeterminacy', or uncertainty, in professional judgement.[51] Indeterminacy gives professional work a craft dimension. The fact that clients are generally unable to judge whether the legal service they receive is good or bad requires the professional to control the situation in the client's interest.[52] Being subject to 'a calling' or vocation requires that an individual is inducted into the values of the professional group.[53]

Professional Values and Virtues

Values are standards influencing choices between courses of action.[54] There are

---

[49] M Bayles, *Professional Ethics* (Belmont, CA, Wadsworth Publishing, 1981) 11.

[50] J Oakley and D Cocking, *Virtue Ethics and Professional Roles* (Cambridge, Cambridge University Press, 2001).

[51] T Johnson, *Professions and Power* (London and Basingstoke, Macmillan, 1972) 43; H Jamous and B Pelloille, 'Changes in the French University Hospital System' in JA Jackson (ed), *Professions and Professionalization* (London, Cambridge University Press, 1970).

[52] D Rueschemeyer, 'Doctors and Lawyers: A Comment on the Theory of the Professions' (1964–65) 1(1) *Canadian Review of Sociology and Anthropology* 17.

[53] Ibid, 227.

[54] N Rescher, *Introduction to Value Theory* (Englewood Cliffs, NJ, Prentice Hall, 1969) 2.

different ways of classifying values. For example, one system identifies three groups: moral values such as fairness, justice and truth; pragmatic values such as thrift, efficiency and health; and aesthetic values such as beauty, softness and warmth. A value system is a collection of consistent and coherent values ranked according to importance. The core professional values of lawyers can be elusive, or even controversial.[55] Some legal professional values may be equally strongly claimed by other professions. Values may be unarticulated, reflect differences of opinion or change over time. Any list of professional core values is likely to be contentious.

Professional leaders often define their terms in office by referring to values. In 2003, the President of the Law Society opined that independence, integrity and confidentiality were the core values for solicitors.[56] In 2007, another President of the Law Society said that solicitors should possess the 'level of honesty, integrity and professionalism expected by the public and members of the profession'.[57] The Code of the International Bar Association emphasises 'the highest standards of honesty and integrity', [58] serving 'the interests of justice', observing the law, maintaining ethical standards[59] and maintaining sufficient independence to allow them to give their clients unbiased advice.[60]

Like any provider of a service, lawyers must ensure that what they offer is valuable. They must help clients negotiate alien legal processes and deliver expertise in a form that is both useful to them and good value. Professionals are assumed to have particular virtues enabling them to engage with clients and help them with their problems. Some virtues, such as honesty and integrity, may seem to be obvious requirements for all professionals. Others may be particularly prioritised by professions demanding a high degree of technical skill. Some demanding tasks carried out by lawyers, such as dispute resolution, may require different kinds of skills and exceptional development of particular virtues.

Professional value systems include a mixture of moral and pragmatic values. During the course of this chapter, values such as independence and neutrality have been identified as values that are particularly associated with legal roles in an adversarial system. Other values arguably include technical competence, diligence, loyalty, empathy, courage and wisdom. This list is not exhaustive. This section sets out the reasons why, in particular circumstances, a lawyer might need each of these.

---

[55] D Nicolson and J Webb, *Professional Legal Ethics* (Oxford, Oxford University Press, 1999) 13–21.

[56] P Williamson, 'When Core Values Matter' [2003] *Young Solicitors Group Magazine*, Issue 21, July, 8.

[57] Solicitors Regulation Authority, *Guidelines on the Assessment of Suitability and Character* (2007).

[58] International Bar Association [1995] *International Bar News*, Summer, 23 rule 1.

[59] Ibid, rule 2.

[60] Ibid, rule 8.

i. Commitment

Professionals have a commitment to their work. This is sometimes called a vocation or calling. Commitment to the vocation involves, for example, a determination to be competent in doing the work the profession performs. It might also involve a sense of satisfaction in seeking the outcomes that can be achieved using law. These kinds of commitment can be described as intrinsic motivation. To be intrinsically motivated means being more interested in the work than in the extrinsic reward, the money or prestige it offers.[61]

ii. Altruism

An aspiration to service is not confined to lawyers or Western culture. In the *Bhagavad Gita*, Lord Krishna says that '[o]ne must perform his prescribed duties as a vocation, keeping in sight the public good'.[62] The key professional value of legal professions in common law countries is the idea of a professional role as 'service'. Altruism does not only involve putting a client's financial interests over one's own, it involves promoting client autonomy.

Professional values reflect client goods, such as a right to self-determination, privacy and protection from harm. The realisation of these values has practical implications. For example, a profession committed to the value of client autonomy promotes client self-determination. It might do this by ensuring that clients make their own moral choices. As we shall see, it also involves helping them make good moral choices. This involves training professionals to present options for clients, to reason with clients about these choices and to facilitate client decisions.

iii. Loyalty

The role assigned to lawyers by the rule of law demands that every individual has their champion. Lawyers are loyal to their client for the duration of the matter in which they are instructed. Elements of this obligation, for example the duty of confidence, extend beyond the conclusion of the matter. Loyalty may be subject to wider social responsibilities, for example a duty not to mislead the court.

Professional loyalty trumps duties to other parties, but not wider duties to the system. Loyalty is, therefore, not an absolute value for lawyers. Alternatives, such as zeal are, for reasons discussed below, even more contentious. This may, to some extent, reflect changing perceptions of the duty of loyalty. While the early stages of professional development reflect the need to ensure

---

[61] Pound (n 35).

[62] OP Dwivedi, 'Ethics for Public Sector Administrators: Education and Training' in RM Thomas (ed), *Teaching Ethics: Government Ethics* (London, HMSO, 1996) 339, 345.

that clients are protected, later stages may be more concerned to recognise their autonomy and to promote their sense of agency.

iv. Empathy

In Schaffer's words, 'The distinctive feature of ethics in a profession is that it speaks to the unequal encounter of two moral persons. Legal ethics 'becomes the study [for lawyers] of what is good … for this other person, over whom I have power'.[63] Understanding what is good for others involves the professional being able to comprehend their clients' perspectives. It does not mean approaching every case by applying one's own view of what is good for others.

Awareness of 'the other' is a key philosophical concept with various, often related meanings. These perhaps begin with John Stuart Mill's consideration of 'other minds', the question of how one can know that other individuals have thoughts and feelings. In contemporary theory, the way in which the idea of 'the other' is used depends on context. It appears in politics, economics and the social sciences, particularly anthropology. It may refer to a category other than that initially considered or something beyond the self.

The term 'other' has also been used to explore different identities, for example between ethnicity and culture.[64] It has been related to gender, for example the idea of woman as 'other' to man. Emanuel Levinas has argued that ethical obligation derives from consideration of the other.[65] He argued that 'the other' helps us to define ourselves. 'The other' provides people with meaningful direction and orientation. Levinas used the term alterity, to describe the entity in contrast to which identity is constructed.[66]

Alterity, the ability to distinguish between the self and non-self, allows us to conceive of the possibility of a different viewpoint. This is the root of the personal capacity for empathy. Professionals may need this capacity for empathy in order to perform their role well. Lawyers, in particular, need empathy in order to represent people who are 'outsiders'. It helps them to understand and present views with which it is difficult to agree or even to sympathise.

v. Courage

Some views of the lawyer and client relationship place a high value on the need for lawyers to demonstrate courage in defending clients' interests. Lawyers are sometimes called on to perform a daunting task—one they might try

[63] TL Schaffer, 'Legal Ethics and the Good Client' (1987) 36 *Catholic University Law Review* 319.

[64] E Said, *Orientalism* (New York, Penguin Classics, 2003).

[65] E Levinas, *Otherwise than Being or Beyond Essence* (trans A Lingis) (Pittsburgh, PA, Duquesne University Press, 1998).

[66] E Levinas, *Alterity and Transcendence* (London, Athlone Press, 1999).

and avoid if it were a personal choice. The duty to a client may demand that they perform it. Think here of Thomas Erskine's first case, where he had to ignore the advice of his senior counsel, and the expectations of the judge, to do what he thought was right for the client.

The Bar Code expresses this more strongly than does the solicitors' code. It states that a barrister must 'promote fearlessly and by all proper lawful means the client's best interests ... without regard to the consequences for any other person (whether to your professional client, employer or any other person'.[67] This suggests that barristers must not be intimidated by officials, even judges, or let the risk of public disapproval affect their actions. Courage may also be required in dealing with clients, for example when delivering advice that is unlikely to be well received.

vi. Wisdom

The various virtues described above demand co-ordination. A good candidate for a co-ordinating virtue is wisdom. Aristotle argued that wise people develop intellectual, emotional and social skills that allow them to put general understanding into practice in different situations. Anthony Kronman argued that practical wisdom was central to any meaningful practice of law.[68] It may be particularly relevant in advising clients as to the most suitable course of action in their circumstances.

vii. Neutrality

The value of neutrality is essential to any judicial role, but is relevant to lawyers in general. Neutrality represents the value of disinterestedness. This enables professionals to take a detached view and to reconcile a pull on their loyalties in more than one direction. The idea of equality before the law means that lawyers must be able to represent morally indefensible individuals without compromising their own personal integrity.

viii. Justice

The status of professions is often attributed to a key good that they deliver to society. Just as the medical profession delivers health, lawyers deliver justice. There are many different meanings of justice and lawyers are associated with procedural justice of a kind delivered by courts. Some lawyers embrace a wider notion of justice to include responsibilities to fairness, to the acces-

---

[67] Bar Standards Board, *The BSB Handbook 2014: Code of Conduct*, rC15.1 and rC15.3.
[68] A Kronman, *The Lost Lawyer: Failing Ideals of the Legal Profession* (Harvard, Belknap Press, 1993) 144.

sibility of legal services or social justice. Others may see justice as tempering their client's ambitions by regard for the interests of non-parties.

ix. Integrity

Having integrity involves having strong moral principles focused on being honest, fair and reliable. Integrity is important in any role, but particularly so when clients are vulnerable and dependent on lawyers to deliver their rights.

x. Independence

Lawyers must serve each client faithfully. They must not, therefore, prioritise any other allegiance, whether to other lawyers, other clients or institution. This includes the state and its agencies, and, on occasions, the judiciary. Neither, however, must the lawyer be the unquestioning servant of clients. They need to maintain a keen sense of the wide range of their responsibilities. They may occasionally need to tell a client that they cannot carry out a particular action because it is unethical.

SRA Code of Conduct 2011 (as amended)

(www.sra.org.uk/solicitors/handbook/code/part2/content.page)

Outcomes

You must achieve these outcomes:

O(1.1) you treat your *clients* fairly;
O(1.2) you provide services to your *clients* in a manner which protects their interests in their matter, subject to the proper administration of justice;
O(1.3) when deciding whether to act, or terminate your instructions, you comply with the law and the Code;
O(1.4) you have the resources, skills and procedures to carry out your *clients'* instructions;
O(1.5) the service you provide to *clients* is competent, delivered in a timely manner and takes account of your *clients'* needs and circumstances;

Q1.18 To what extent does this extract confirm the need for lawyers to possess the virtues of competence, diligence, loyalty, empathy, courage and wisdom in their relationship with clients?

Q1.19 Looking at the remainder of Chapter 1 in the SRA Code of Conduct, how far are these virtues required generally in solicitors' practices?

Conclusion

The lawyer's role is defined by the system which created it and which helped to define the modern liberal state. Lawyers, arguably, serve an important constitutional importance. They are among the few groups in society that can hold the state to account. Other occupations, eg journalists, trade unionists and politicians, may occasionally achieve similar success. Lawyers, however, regularly use state mechanisms, such as the justice system, to control state power. This constitutional role is the basis of their claim to independence from the state and their right to self-governance and self-regulation.

The legal professions are committed to virtuous conduct and high standards of behaviour. Their role in an adversarial system often seems to contradict these commitments. Debates surrounding the immorality of legal roles essentially concern the interpretation of the standard conception of the lawyer's role. This is defined by neutrality, partisanship and non-accountability. Some argue that, if lawyers' ethics are meaningful, the constraints on partisanship must be considerably more significant than 'whatever is legally permitted short of a criminal offence'.

Institutions and Organisations

Introduction

Lawyers' ethics reflect standards of behaviour expected in the conduct of legal work. These standards have evolved over centuries, initially through legislation and the decisions of judges, and later as a result of professional self-regulation. Gradually lawyers took over the task of regulating themselves through programmes of education and the imposition of professional discipline. The recognition of the legal professions by the state is one way of maintaining the independence of lawyers from state interference.

In liberal democracies the development of lawyers' ethics is associated with the development of legal professions. Over the past thirty years some countries, notably England and Wales, Australia and New Zealand, have tried to limit the power of the legal professions. Governments claim that this is to improve the position of consumers of legal services and to increase access to justice. This curbing of power has involved undermining the traditional nature of professions, including their self-regulatory status.

This chapter explores the issue of whether lawyers' ethics are still meaningful. It looks at the conditions and circumstances that led to the development of the legal professions. It also examines the importance of institutions in the development of ethics. It considers whether professional ethics reflect the inherent altruism of professionalised occupations or are a smokescreen for self-interest. Finally, it raises questions about whether ethics remain significant following the Legal Services Act 2007 and the changes it brought about.

Lawyers and Society

The Importance of Theory

It is difficult to explore the role of law and lawyers in society without reference to theory. Various social science disciplines have contributed to our understanding of the place of lawyers in society. In the nineteenth and twentieth centuries lawyers and the legal professions proved of interest to the 'founding fathers' of the new discipline of sociology: Emile Durkheim, Max Weber and Karl Marx. Their work continues to influence theories about lawyers and their position in the modern state.

Law and Lawyers

Marx considered that the culture of the legal profession merely reflected the social relationships of economic production. Because Marx saw the state in capitalist society as an organ of class domination, law, morality and religion were merely 'bourgeois prejudices, behind which lurked in ambush just as many bourgeois interests'.[1] In capitalist society, Marx wrote, 'all of the unproductive classes, civil servants, physicians, lawyers, scholars etc ... obtain for themselves a share of the surplus product, of the capitalist's *revenue*'.[2]

Marx's theory of human development through class struggle predicted that the capitalist class would be overthrown by the revolution of the proletariat or working classes. Communism would eradicate social conflict, the need for law based on property relations and the need for lawyers.

Weber noted that the culture of society was made up of various groups, based on ethnicity, religion or occupation. These comprised sub-cultures within the dominant culture. Weber sought the subjective meaning and purpose that individuals attach to their actions—a method called symbolic interactionism. Weber saw ideas as important determinants of events, and challenged Marx's characterisation of law as merely a reflection of the material interests of the capitalist classes.

Weber acknowledged that society was shaped by the struggle to control society's material resources, but he also considered that intangibles, such as status, were important. Weber argued that social order is maintained by

---

[1] K Marx and F Engels, *Collected Works,* 40 vols (New York, International Publishers, 1976) 6:494–95.

[2] K Marx, *The Grundrisse*, Notebook 4, 1857–22 January 1858 (1857).

the coercion of those controlling the greatest political, economic, and social resources. Class, race and gender are the source of the most persistent struggles. Consensus only arises when groups identify common interests held in opposition to other groups. Weber saw the English Bar as exemplifying the use of status to exert authority and social influence.

Durkheim was interested in law as a phenomenon. For example, he noted how societies tend to develop from punitive legal sanctions to reparation. He was less concerned with lawyers as such, but very interested in professions. In the Middle Ages, lawyers, together with doctors and the clergy, formed a triumvirate of learned professions. By the nineteenth and twentieth centuries the significance of these groupings were of great interest to the new discipline of sociology.

Professions

Theory of Professions

i. Professional Traits

Early analysis of professions tried to identify their common features. These studies suggested that professions have distinctive areas of work, which are technical. They have a professional body which co-ordinates activities, and determines the content and delivery of education and training. They maintain control over members, often via formal disciplinary proceedings.

Early in the twentieth century some theorists attempted to define professions according to their traits. An early attempt, by Flexner, compared the 'unmistakable professions' of law, engineering, literature, painting and music.[3] Later, Greenwood argued that 'full professions' had five traits: systematic theory, authority, community sanction, ethical codes and a professional culture.[4]

Various attempts to identify professional traits followed. Some focused on intangible features, such as controlling esoteric knowledge, mystique, social prestige and autonomy. Others sought more concrete features, for example the stringent entry requirements that professions enforced, their demanding educational programmes and their codes of ethics.[5]

Professions were allowed independence and autonomy by the state. This was because they deployed a socially important and esoteric field of knowledge

---

[3] A Flexner, 'Is Social Work a Profession?', address before the National Conference of Charities and Correction, Baltimore, 17 May 1915.

[4] E Greenwood, 'Attributes of a Profession' [1957] *Social Work*, July, 45.

[5] TJ Johnson, *Professions and Power* (London and Basingstoke, Macmillan, 1972) 23–35; CO Houle, *Continuing Learning in the Professions* (San Francisco and London, Jossey-Bass, 1980); CW Wolfram, *Modern Legal Ethics* (St Paul, MN, West Publishing, 1986); E Schein, *Professional Education: Some New Directions* (New York, McGraw-Hill, 1972); and MD Bayles, *Professional Ethics*, 2nd edn (Belmont, CA, Wadsworth Publishing, 1989) 14.

for the public good. A commitment to behave ethically involved articulating how this role served the public interest. Entrants were socialised into the role through education and training and by the professional community.

By the 1970s, social scientists were more concerned about the effectiveness of professionalism as a means of controlling expert knowledge in the public interest. The English sociologist, Terence Johnson, identified professionalism as one of several alternatives.[6] Others included direct control of professional services by the state, by which is meant the political organisation of a nation. This served to highlight the critical importance of the relationship between professions and the state. This was an issue that had also interested the founding fathers of sociology in the beginning.

ii. Professions and the State

The position that lawyers occupy in society is defined either expressly or tacitly by the state. The state establishes a court system and typically devolves control of it to judges. The control of lawyers by the courts may later give way to control by the legal professions. The way in which these controls develop depends on a number of variables including, crucially, their continuing relationship to the state.

Marx saw the state in capitalist society as an organ of class domination. Law, morality and religion were tools of control for the ruling class. Weber attached more importance to these institutions and their role in creating the conditions for the advent of industrial capitalism.[7] Durkheim focused on how social order was maintained by the state and the political community of secondary groups, such as churches, corporations and professions.

Durkheim observed that none of the groups in the political community dominated the whole, but they counterbalanced each other, and the state. Together they protected the rights of the individual and encouraged moral individualism. Durkheim conceived the role of the state as reminding the secondary groups of their responsibility to the whole. In this role it protected individuals from oppressive action, for example by corporations on employees.

Of these three sociologists, Durkheim held the most benign view of the importance of professions. He considered the state to be the ultimate moral force in society, but recognised that it faced problems in promoting the individual. The main risk was that the state would be either too remote from individuals to understand their needs, or so close that it risked stifling them. The secondary groups, therefore, fulfilled an important intermediary role. They

---

[6] Johnson (n 5) 38.

[7] M Weber, *Economy and Society*, ed G Roth and W Wittich (1968) and for critical summaries see DM Trubek, 'Max Weber on Law and the Rise of Capitalism' (1972) 3 *Wisconsin Law Review* 720 and M Albrow, 'Legal Positivism and Bourgeois Materialism: Max Weber's View of the Sociology of Law' (1975) 2 *British Journal of Law and Society* 14.

provided moral connections between those social practices for which they are responsible and the goods promoted by those practices.[8]

The distinctive way in which professions organise occupational expertise can be contrasted with the approach of corporations. Corporations are hierarchical and bureaucratic, whereas professional organisations are collegiate. Colleagues operate as a close network of autonomous individuals, with freedom to define client problems. Durkheim assumed that social institutions served 'the general needs of the social organism' meaning society generally. Durkheim used the word 'function', rather than 'end' or 'purpose', because he recognised that a result may not be intended. His method, which became known as functionalism, was a dominant theory of professions for most of the twentieth century.

In Durkheim's view, a society based on the division of labour was held together by what he called organic solidarity. Society shaped individual consciousness through beliefs and moral codes. These had logical, functional and historical dimensions. For Durkheim, social order was maintained by people's commitment to common values because they believed them to be right. The democratic state had a responsibility to promote 'moral individualism' as part of a community identity.[9]

Durkheim considered it natural that people with work interests in common would form communities of interest: a 'restricted group, having its special characteristics ... in the midst of general society'.[10] He thought that a moral ethos could only emerge from common understanding and community action to control personal needs. In his view, professions were a model for other occupations to follow. Their commitment to community interest, rather than self-interest,[11] offered a model to improve social cohesion and civil society.

Durkheim believed that the benefits of professions extended beyond the socialisation of individuals. He suggested that the deliberation, reflection and critical spirit they encouraged was critical to the health of democracy. They would, he argued, counterbalance the drift of the modern state towards domination by the market and by state bureaucracy. Leading US sociologists, such as Talcott Parsons and Robert K Merton, continued in Durkheim's footsteps, identifying serving the public good as a key 'function' of professions.

Durkheim recognised that his organic theory of society failed to identify mechanisms for change. Parsons addressed this, focusing on how social values were formed and passed on by families and the education system. He sug-

---

[8] AD MacIntyre, *After Virtue: A Study in Moral Theory* (London, Duckworth, 1985).

[9] MS Cladis, *A Communitarian Defence of Liberalism: Emile Durkheim and Contemporary Social Theory* (Stanford, CA, Stanford University Press, 1992).

[10] E Durkheim *The Division of Labour in Society* [1893] (trans G Simpson) (New York, Free Press, 1933) 14.

[11] E Durkheim, *Professional Ethics and Civic Morals* (trans C Brookfield) (London and New York, Routledge, 1992); R Pound, *The Lawyer from Antiquity to Modern Times: With Particular Reference to the Development of Bar Associations in the United States* (St Paul, MN, West Publishing, 1953) 95.

gested that disturbance in the social system was the mechanism for change. Merton suggested a more critical approach to whether institutions were functional, dysfunctional or non-functional.

Early British attempts to analyse professions adopted a functionalist perspective. In the 1930s Carr-Saunders and Wilson presented professions as a counterweight to state power and a cushion against the fragmentation of the traditional moral order brought about by the division of labour.[12] They emphasised the bonds between practitioners, the civility this promoted and the beneficial impact on social systems.

By the 1980s the functionalist analysis of professions had declined in popularity.[13] It was seen to confuse the existence of institutions with their social benefit. The functionalist view, that society is an organic whole with parts working in harmony, gave way to conflict theories of society. They focused on the role of power in the arrangement of social roles and social organisation.[14] They therefore drew on the approach of Marx in seeing society as comprising a struggle between different groups for power.

iii. Professional Culture

Durkheim's view that professions develop a distinctive culture survived the decline of functionalism. Therefore, it seems obvious that norms of behaviour, rules of manners or 'etiquette' operating at a subconscious level develop in professional groups. The French sociologist Pierre Bourdieu coined the term 'habitus' to describe the taken-for-granted assumptions that are learned and passed on in this way.[15] This theory suggests that professionals develop certain behavioural dispositions that reflect a distinctive culture.

Bourdieu's theory applies at both the professional level and in different fields of practice. At the level of the profession, cultural understandings may, or may not, be reflected in their codes of conduct. In fact, professional etiquette used to be a term commonly used to describe professional conduct rules. Different fields of practice may have different ideas of how a professional role should be performed. Examples of such differences are explored in relation to personal injury and family law litigation (see chapter ten: Litigation and Advocacy and chapter eleven: Settlement).

---

[12] AM Carr-Saunders and PH Wilson, *The Professions* (Oxford, Clarendon Press, 1933).

[13] R Dingwall and P Lewis (eds), *The Sociology of the Professions: Lawyers, Doctors and Others* (London, Macmillan, 1983).

[14] RM Rich, 'Sociological Paradigms and the Sociology of Law: An Overview' in CE Reasons and R Rich (eds), *The Sociology of Law: A Conflict Perspective* (London, Butterworth, 1978) 148–49.

[15] P Bourdieu, *Outline of a Theory of Practice* (Cambridge, Cambridge University Press, 1977).

iv. Professionalisation Theories

Most current accounts of professions build on previous theories but tend to lean more towards conflict theories. They are concerned with the process of 'professionalisation'. Hughes has suggested that professionalisation occurs in chronological stages:

- Selection, training and initiation of members.
- Defining the nature of services provided.
- Obtaining a monopoly for the provision of those services.
- Creating a professional ideology regarding the work.[16]

The US sociologist Magali Sarfatti Larson illustrated the professionalisation process by historical analysis of the ways in which professions in England and the US organised themselves to establish a monopoly over work.[17] Larson's theory of professionalism focuses particularly on the mystery of expert knowledge and technique.

Larson separates knowledge into theoretical and practical components. She suggests that professions' control of knowledge is used to justify closure of both the market to outsiders and to restrict access to the occupation. Later, theory is given higher status and taught in universities. Professions therefore turn control of the production of knowledge into control of the production of their own members.

Larson identifies conditions favouring the establishment of market control. Ideally, to become a profession an occupation should provide an important, universal, yet invisible service. The market should be uncompetitive or protected by a legal monopoly or comprised of a broad and unorganised client base. Ideally, members of the occupation should be independent of the demands of the markets, and of sponsoring elites. Finally, a profession's ideology should be consistent with other dominant ideologies.

Larson suggests that professional culture adapts medieval notions of craft and community to industrial capitalism. Professions promote the values of science in social and economic reform and in professional ethics. Professional socialisation takes standards determined by the elite and attempts to make them part of the *subjectivity* of individuals. In Larson's analysis there is an element of social control inherent in being subject to 'a calling' or vocation.[18]

Abbott covers similar ground to Larson in noting the importance of institutionalisation, education and licensing to professionalism. Having established their expertise and legitimacy, professions seek legal jurisdiction, protection by law, and privileges such as self-regulation. Abbott emphasises the importance of the occupation's ability to construct its work so that it is 'impermeable', that

---

[16] EC Hughes, *Men and Their Work* (London, Collier Macmillan, 1958) 159.

[17] MS Larson, *The Rise of Professionalism: A Sociological Analysis* (Berkeley, CA, University of California Press, 1977).

[18] Ibid, 227.

is, so that outsiders cannot perform it.[19] Professions then control and manage the boundaries of the different jurisdictions. However, as Abbott argued, the prime audience for legal jurisdiction is the state. Only the state has the power to grant monopolies recognised by law, together with powers of self-regulation.

Case Study
The Professionalisation of Attorneys, Barristers, Solicitors and Legal Executives

The process of professionalisation normally requires there to be a body capable of enforcing the rules, but this is not necessarily the case. The American Bar Association (ABA) is a professional body that is different from the norm. The ABA was founded in 1878. It is based in Chicago with a large office in Washington DC. It responds to the problem that the US is a large country with over fifty independent state Bars. The ABA produces model rules of conduct that are widely adopted by state Bars. However, there is no compulsion to follow the model rules. California, for example, has a different code which appears to draw on the ABA code for some, but not all, of its provisions.

In England, barristers, solicitors and legal executives demonstrate quite different paths to becoming professions.[20] In each case the professional body played a different role. Until recently, there was very little legislation regarding the Bar, whereas most of the Law Society's powers were granted by Acts of Parliament. The barristers and solicitors reached a 'settlement' regarding their respective work jurisdictions. Barristers were primarily advocates and solicitors controlled conveyancing. Legal executives, however, did exactly the same work as solicitors but had to work in solicitors' offices.

The exact origins of the English Bar are unclear. A more or less recognisable occupation began to be formed from around 1340 in the Inns of Court in the Holborn area of London. The Inns were probably originally used as student accommodation. The Inn of Inner Temple was established by 1388, and probably expanded in around 1609, when the Crown granted it the former Templar land on condition that it maintained the church.

By Elizabethan times, there were four Inns of Court: Temple, Inner Temple, Lincoln's Inn and Gray's Inn. There were around 3,500 inhabitants of Inner Temple and Gray's alone. The Inns sought to protect the occupational identity of barristers and to distinguish them from other kinds of lawyers. Barristers lived and worked in the Inns and education was provided for students. By the beginning of the nineteenth century entry to an Inn was

---

[19] A Abbott, *The System of Professions: An Essay on the Expert Division of Labour* (Chicago, University of Chicago Press, 1988).

[20] See further M Burrage, *Revolution and the Making of the Contemporary Legal Profession: England, France and the United States* (Oxford, Oxford University Press, 2006).

at the discretion of senior members of the Inn, called benchers. Candidates had to keep five terms, eat six dinners in each and have references from two barristers. It was not until 1872 that the Inns of Court adopted entry examinations.

In 1895 a General Council of the Bar was formed. This was responsible for Bar policy, but was controlled by the Inns. It established rules of etiquette, such as that requiring that a barrister be briefed by a solicitor. It also developed a disciplinary role over the whole Bar. Although the Bar became more centralised, the Inns continued to have substantial responsibilities. It was not until 1966, for example, that the four Inns delegated their authority over training to a Senate of the Inns of Court.

Although most barristers are still based in chambers, they are self-employed, independent practitioners. They typically share a clerk between about twenty barristers and contribute to the expenses of the chambers.

Solicitors professionalised in a quite different way. In the Middle Ages there were many groups of lawyers, besides barristers, working outside courts. Many of these lawyers, particularly attorneys, had offices in the Inns of Court. From the 1500s the Inns' policy of restricting access to the Inns by non-barristers had a damaging effect on the discipline and reputation of attorneys.

In 1739, elite London proctors, attorneys and solicitors formed the Society of Gentleman Practisers in the Courts of Law and Equity ('The Gentleman Practisers') in 1739 to try and raise their status.[21] They were granted a royal charter in 1831 and eventually became the Law Society in 1903.[22]

By 1834, the Law Society initiated its first disciplinary proceedings and begun to collect and publish 'best practice' on issues of etiquette and costs. In a succession of statutes the Law Society gained disciplinary powers over solicitors, including the right to suspend solicitors and strike them from its roll. In 1906 the Law Society sponsored legislation preventing solicitors using client money for their own purposes. In 1941 the Law Society acquired the power to inspect the accounts of practitioners. It also created a compensation fund for clients cheated by solicitors.

The Law Society also took control over entry into the profession. An entry examination for solicitors was introduced in 1836. At the beginning of World War II the pass rate for each examination was only 50 per cent. Trainee solicitors also had to complete five-year articles of clerkship, for which they

---

[21] D Sugarman, 'Bourgeois Collectivism, Professional Power and the Boundaries of the State: The Private and Public Life of the Law Society 1825 to 1914' (1996) 3(1/2) *International Journal of the Legal Profession* 81.

[22] P Reeves, 'Case History—A Look Back to the 18th Century to Find the Origins of the Law Society and the Changes over 150 years' (1995) 92 *The Law Society Gazette*, 22 February.

had to pay a premium to an established practitioner. They received no pay for the duration of these articles.

Barristers and solicitors undertook defined areas of work. These were complementary to each other. Barristers had rights of audience, and the right to conduct advocacy, in all courts. Solicitors had more limited rights of advocacy, broadly confined to lower courts, but could conduct litigation and conveyancing, which barristers could not. Solicitors had to 'instruct' barristers to appear in higher courts by preparing a brief.

The traditional organisation of solicitors is in partnerships. There can be from two to several hundred partners, sharing expenses, liabilities and profits. A significant minority of the profession continue to be sole practitioners.

The final example of professionalisation is the legal executives. In the nineteenth century, solicitors' offices employed large numbers of unqualified clerks. The senior clerks managed other clerks, becoming known as managing clerks. These clerks therefore did exactly the same work as solicitors.

In 1892 the Solicitors Managing Clerks' Association was formed. In 1963 the Institute of Legal Executives (ILEX), a company limited by guarantee, was created. ILEX was granted a royal charter in October 2011. In January 2012 it was relaunched as the Chartered Institute of Legal Executives (CILEX).

The objects of the memorandum and articles of association of ILEX included the regulation of members by ensuring compliance with published standards. The Institute controls its own admission process by examination, although exemptions and a fast track are available for law graduates. Disciplinary hearings for members began around 1968. The Solicitors Disciplinary Tribunal also has jurisdiction to control CILEX members' employment by solicitors.[23]

Q2.1   How did the processes of development of the various English legal professions differ?

Q2.2   What do you think were and are the different challenges facing the four legal professions described in the previous section?

Q2.3   Does the development of the professions of English barristers and solicitors show how legal roles reflect underlying economic systems?

Q2.4   Given their different histories, how might the ethical priorities of barristers and solicitors differ?

---

[23] Solicitors Act 1974 s 43.

Decline of Professionalism

An influential writer on legal professions, the American, Richard Abel, defined professionalism 'as a specific historical formation in which the members of an occupation exercise a substantial degree of control over the market for their services, usually through an occupational association'.[24] Even in the 1980s, Abel suggested that legal 'professionalism', so defined, was in decline.

Abel noted that control included control of the market for legal services and control of the producers of legal services. He argued that the legal professions in England and Wales had begun to lose control of traditional monopolies and the numbers of lawyers qualifying. This inevitably involved a decline of professionalism as defined by Abel.

There are various reasons why professions may have lost power. One reason is that other organisations, like companies, have adopted some of their strategies of market control, such as education, training and selection by merit. However, the decline of professionalism also marks a change in the relations between professions and the state. This appears to be because government is no longer convinced that self-regulation operates in the public interest.

Andrew Abbott writes about the process of professionalisation as one of control of three *jurisdictions*: workplace, public and legal. Each of these jurisdictions has an audience.

Q2.5   What do you think fledgling professions seek in each jurisdiction and how do they convince the relevant audiences?

Q2.6   What is different about the respective claims of barristers, solicitors and legal executives to 'jurisdiction' over the workplace?

Q2.7   What might have changed to undermine professional influence in each jurisdiction?

Alternatives to Professionalism

Johnson emphasised that professions are not simply a type of occupation, but a means of controlling an occupation. He suggests that professionalism is one of three possible forms of control of expert services: collegiate control (pro-

---

[24] RL Abel, 'The Decline of Professionalism?' (1986) 49 *Modern Law Review* 1.

fessionalism), patronage (control by consumers) and mediation (control, for example, by the state). [25]

Larson suggests that being an occupation that tends to be colleague-orientated, rather than client-orientated, is the essence of professionalism.[26] The concept of collegiality is traceable to the Roman *collegia* and was adopted from the medieval craft guilds.[27] Larsson argues that the professional culture of collegiality makes work important to self-identity and self-realisation.

Collegiality has a dramatic impact on the nature of professions. Because of collegiality, status and distinction are more important to professionals than material rewards.[28] Professional socialisation and culture promote a long-term view and a concern to promote the common good.[29]

The spirit of professional collegiality allows rivals to compete against each other yet maintain goodwill and respect for each other.[30] Ihara defines collegiality as support and co-operation between colleagues, a reciprocal respect for colleagues' ability to further professional ends through their knowledge and skills, a commitment to common professional values and goals, a willingness to have confidence in colleagues as responsible autonomous agents, a sense of 'connectedness', or sharing with others the bond of being part of a larger independent whole.[31]

The English Bar has an archetypal collegial structure. Arthurs, for example, observes that:

> For the Canadian legal profession, the real (or imagined) culture of the English bar is the point of reference (not to say reverence). ... Indeed, if there is any legal profession whose culture can be identified with some precision, it is surely this one. Accordingly, in the case of the English bar, culture can be seen as an important vehicle for the transmission of values and the regulation of behaviour.[32]

The key features of Bar collegiality are the organisation of independent practitioners in chambers, contained within Inns, providing physical proximity and identity. This helps to maintain discipline.

Each method of control offers an imperfect way of controlling important knowledge. Collegial regulation takes the form of self-regulation. It could become regulation in an occupation's self-interest. Patronage systems allow powerful clients to define their own needs and the services they require. They

[25] Johnson (n 5).

[26] Larsson (n 17) 226.

[27] Durkheim (n 11) 19.

[28] RL Nelson, DM Trubeck and RL Solomon, 'New Problems and New Paradigms in Studies of the Legal Profession' in *Lawyers' Ideals/Lawyers' Practices: Transformations in the American Legal Profession* (Ithaca, NY, Cornell University Press, 1992) 1, 17.

[29] PF Camenisch, 'On Being a Professional: Morally Speaking' in A Flores (ed), *Professional Ideals* (Belmont, CA, Wadsworth Publishing, 1988) 14.

[30] Pound (n 11) 15.

[31] CK Ihara, 'Collegiality as a Professional Virtue' in Flores (n 29) 56.

[32] HW Arthurs, 'Lawyering in Canada in the 21st Century' (1996) *Windsor Yearbook of Access to Justice* 202, 223.

offer insufficient curbs on improper behaviour by the patron's lawyers and are only available to the rich and powerful.

Communal control, for example by consumer organisations, could emphasise cost at the expense of quality. Direct regulation by the state could be inflexible. It is arguable that systems of control, other than the collegial form, could suppress initiative and occupational responsibility, encouraging legal occupations to act in their own economic interest. Non-collegial ways of controlling occupational expertise reduce the power of the occupation, particularly its independence.

Johnson's typology overlaps with Freidson's three 'logics' for managing the sale and distribution of services (see below).[33] Freidson sees the alternatives to professionalism as perfect competition, where innovation is encouraged and prices kept low, and corporate bureaucracy, where efficient management produces reliable products at reasonable cost.

The problem with perfect competition is that it is very difficult to achieve. Consumers often do not know whether they are getting value for money. This problem is exacerbated with professional services, which are difficult to compare effectively. Bureaucracy is characterised by a hierarchy of authority, rigid division of labour, fixed rules and impersonal relationships.

Liberalised Legal Services Markets

Professions in the Regulatory State

Theories of state regulation suggest a movement from a 'command-and-control' approach, where legislation is used to directly control behaviour, to more subtle strategies. The transition, from a state dependent on delegation of power to groups like professions to a more active regulatory state, began with the introduction of the welfare state.

After the Second World War the UK adopted a welfare state model. It introduced public ownership and direct provision of benefits and services. This involved the state in formulating policy and delivering services. In the 1980s the welfare model was challenged by increasing international economic competition. This rendered welfare states less competitive than those with lean social services and open markets.

Under Margaret Thatcher, the Conservative government returned to a more liberal, market-based approach to the regulation of society. This approach,

---

[33] E Freidson, *Professionalism: The Third Logic* (Oxford: Blackwell Publishers, 2001).

labelled neo-liberalism, involved the state being more directly involved in creating more competitive markets. This model became known as the post-regulatory state.[34]

The key features of the post-regulatory state involve separation of operational from regulatory activities, sometimes involving privatisation, separating purchasers and providers of public services, through policies of contracting out and market testing, and separation of operational from policy tasks within government departments. These objectives are usually achieved by the creation of executive agencies.

Each of these policies shifts the emphasis of control, to a greater or lesser degree, from traditional bureaucratic mechanisms towards instruments of regulation. Either government departments, or other agencies, regulate the provision of services. They set standards, monitor compliance and have enforcement powers. Sometimes they work with existing bodies, such as professions, as co-regulators. The post-regulatory state seeks control of areas of social and economic life which were formerly self-regulatory.

The Market Economy

One of the key aims of neo-liberal economics and the regulatory state is to establish the market economy. This is a system where the prices of goods and services are determined by supply and demand in free price system. Therefore, investment, production and distribution decisions are all dictated by a market that is as unregulated as possible.

The drive towards the establishment of a market economy often involves reducing the size of the state and therefore of welfare provision. Professional arrangements that may increase the cost of services are challenged. The significance of traditional organisational forms, such as professions, are called into question. The market economy establishes corporations as a preferred organisational form and consumerism as a preferred ideology.[35]

Revolutions in Regulation

Common law countries have, under the influence of market ideology, been undergoing a small revolution in the delivery of legal services. This tends to involve a move away from professional self-regulation. At one end of the scale, new procedures increase the involvement of lay people in controlling

---

[34] M Moran, 'The Rise of the Regulatory State in Britain' (2001) 54 *Parliamentary Affairs* 19. C Scott, Regulation in the Age of Governance: The Rise of the Post-Regulatory State' in J Jordana and D Levi-Faur (eds), *The Politics of Regulation: Institutions and Regulatory Reforms in the Age of Governance* (Cheltenham, Edward Elgar Publishing, 2004) 145.

[35] A Giddens, *Modernity and Self-Identity: Self and Society in the Late Modern Age* (Cambridge, Polity Press, 1991).

the delivery of legal services. At the other end of the scale the state establishes new agencies to regulate legal professions. This may involve changes in methods of regulation. New providers may also be admitted to the market to compete with lawyers to deliver legal services.

Among the common law countries England and Wales and Australia have made the strongest moves towards a more competitive and consumerist model for the delivery of legal services. The legal professions in the US and Canada have been most successful in limiting movement towards such a model. Indeed, lawyer groups in the US have brought actions against online legal services on the grounds that they represent the unauthorised practice of law.

England and Wales: The Legal Services Act 2007

The Legal Services Act 2007 (LSA) is the culmination of nearly two decades in which government sought better ways to manage the legal services market. Following a report in 2001 from the Office of Fair Trading, in July 2003 Sir David Clementi was asked to conduct a review of the legal services market. His report, published in December 2004, resulted in changes to existing institutions and new organisations being allowed to compete with lawyers.

Regulatory Objectives of the Act

The regulatory objectives of the LSA are:

- protecting and promoting the public interest;
- supporting the constitutional principle of the rule of law;
- improving access to justice;
- protecting and promoting the interests of consumers;
- promoting competition in the provision of services in the legal sector;
- encouraging an independent, strong, diverse and effective legal profession;
- increasing public understanding of citizens' legal rights and duties;
- promoting and maintaining adherence to the professional principles.

Elliot Freidson identifies three 'logics' for organising expert services, each with its own basic rationale. The logics and their rationales are as follows:

- Perfect competition, where innovation is encouraged and prices kept low.
- Corporate bureaucracy, where efficient management produces reliable products at reasonable cost.
- Professionalism where expert workers are dedicated to doing good work, both for their own satisfaction and for the benefit of others, rather than for their personal financial advantage

E Freidson *The Third Logic* (Oxford, Blackwell Publishers, 2001)

Q2.8   Which of Freidson's logics does each regulatory objective mainly relate to?

Q2.9   What might be the problems of trying to achieve all of the objectives?

The Three Main Measures for Effecting Change

While the LSA contains many measures which have changed the way in which professions operate, three are highly significant. These measures are:

- A requirement for legal professions to separate their representative and regulatory activities.
- The introduction of a Legal Services Board (LSB) to oversee regulatory activity.
- Provision for creation of Alternative Business Structures (ABS) to compete with conventional lawyers.

The LSA introduced a restructuring of the legal services market while preserving the identity of the legal professions.

Separation of Representative and Regulatory Activities

The separation of representative and regulatory activity meant that the professional bodies, like the Bar Council and the Law Society, could not regulate their members directly. They had to set up independent regulators to do so. Under the LSA, the regulatory arms of the professional bodies are 'overseen' by the LSB, a government agency created by the Act.

The professions therefore established an independent regulatory body, separate from the old professional body. For example, The General Council of the Bar established the Bar Standards Board (BSB), The Law Society the Solicitors Regulatory Authority (SRA), and the Chartered Institute of Legal Executives ILEX professional standards (IPS). Each independent regulatory body is approved to regulate a particular profession.[36] The profession, representative body and the independent regulatory body for the eight 'legal professions in England and Wales are set out in the first three columns of Table 1.

i. Regulatory Functions

Legal professionals became 'authorised persons' under the LSA. Regulators can authorise these professionals to undertake any of the six 'reserved legal

---

[36] Legal Service Acts 2007 s 20.

Table 1

Profession	Approved regulators (representative body)	Independent regulatory body Approved regulator (AR) Licensing authority (LA)	Approved regulator (AR) Licensing authority (LA)	Reserved legal activities regulated
Solicitors	Law Society	Solicitors Regulation Authority	AR LA	• The exercise of right of audience • The conduct of litigation • Reserved instrument activities • Probate activities • The administration of oaths
Barristers	Bar Council	Bar Standards Board	AR	• The exercise of right of audience • The conduct of litigation • Reserved instrument activities • Probate activities • The administration of oaths
Legal Executives	Chartered Institute of Legal Executives	ILEX Professional Standards Limited	AR	• The exercise of right of audience • The conduct of litigation • The administration of oaths
Licensed Conveyancers	Council for Licensed Conveyancers (regulatory body for Licensed Conveyancers, no representative body)		AR LA	• Reserved instrument activities • Probate activities • The administration of oaths
Patent Attorneys	Chartered Institute of Patent Attorneys (CIPA)	Intellectual Property Regulation Board (Regulatory body for both CIPA and ITMA)	AR	• The exercise of right of audience • The conduct of litigation • Reserved instrument activities • The administration of oaths
Trade Mark Attorneys	Institute of Trade Mark Attorneys (ITMA)			• The exercise of right of audience • The conduct of litigation • Reserved instrument activities • The administration of oaths
Costs Lawyers	Association of Costs Lawyers	Costs Lawyer Standards Board	AR	• The exercise of right of audience • The conduct of litigation • The administration of oaths
Notaries	Master of the Faculties (regulatory body for Notaries, no representative body)		AR	• Reserved instrument activities • Probate activities • Notarial Activities • The administration of oaths

activities' that the regulator is authorised to regulate, namely advocacy, conduct of litigation, work on reserved instruments, probate work, notarial work and administration of oaths.[37]

Those entitled to carry on these activities are authorised, or exempt, in relation to that activity.[38] Schedule 3 provides a list of such persons, for example a person granted a right of audience by the court in a particular matter. The regulated persons were placed under a statutory duty to comply with the regulatory arrangements of the approved regulator.[39]

The independent regulators can apply to be approved as Licensing Authorities for ABS. They can only regulate ABS in conducting those reserved legal activities the regulator is approved to conduct and such other activities as it is within its scope to license.

ii. Representative Functions

The LSA required that the professional body may only exercise representative functions and must not try to influence the regulatory function.[40]

Creation of the Legal Services Board

The LSB has the obligation to further the regulatory objectives of the Act. It must also ensure that the regulatory agencies it oversees also further these objectives. The LSB must assist in the development of standards in regulation by the approved regulators and in education and training.[41] The LSB's role in maintaining and developing standards introduces scope for conflict and tension between the different agencies and institutions.

Authorisation of Alternative Business Structures

i. Definition

An ABS is a kind of organisation created by the LSA. It is an entity in which a non-authorised person[42] is a manager or a person controlling at least 10% of voting rights.[43]

---

[37] Legal Services Act 2007 s 12(1) and Schedule 2.
[38] Legal Services Act 2007 s 13(2).
[39] Legal Services Act 2007 s 176.
[40] Legal Services Act 2007 ss 27–31 and Ch 5.
[41] Legal Services Act 2007 s 4.
[42] Legal Services Act 2007 s 72.
[43] Legal Services Act 2007 s 72(2).

ii. Licensing

The LSB or an approved regulator may license such bodies to carry out reserved legal activities. A licensed body is one governed by Part 5 of the Act, under which ABS are permitted.[44] Of the approved regulators, only the SRA and the Council for Licensed Conveyancers are approved regulators for ABS.

iii. Impact

In England and Wales, the government wanted ABS to compete with law firms and to force change in the delivery of legal services. On the face of it, this was a successful strategy. The legal business operated by the Co-operative Society entered the top ten legal businesses by gross fees in its first year of operation. Quality Solicitors, a marketing collective of small firms designed to maximise the benefit of television advertising, was formed to compete with ABS by building their own brand. Nevertheless, some traditional firms became ABS so that unqualified family members could be partners, investors or managers in the business.

Achieving the Regulatory Objectives of the Legal Services Act 2007

The Professional Principles

The LSA attempts to achieve a balance between different methods of occupational control. The professional principles identified by the LSA represent the core values of legal professionalism developed over several centuries. They are independence and integrity; proper standards of work; observing the best interests of the client and the duty to the court; and maintaining client confidentiality.

Promoting the Regulatory Objectives

The LSA assumes that the legal professions will continue to promote the regulatory objectives, including the professional principles, associated with professionalism. Promoting competition in the legal services market will be achieved by allowing ABS. This assumes that non-lawyer ownership and management of organisations will promote innovation, particularly in the delivery of legal services using technology. The interests of consumers are promoted both by

---

[44] Legal Services Act 2007 s 71(2).

the LSB[45] and by its Consumer Panel.[46] The LSB must maintain the panel and is bound to consider any representations it makes.[47]

> Q2.10 Who is responsible for achieving the regulatory objectives of the Legal Services Act?

The Delivery of Legal Services

A wide range of organisations deliver legal services. They service different sectors and take a variety of forms. They often have strikingly different business priorities and, therefore, may be expected to have different values.

Private Practice

Organisational Forms

In most jurisdictions the majority of lawyers work in small organisations. The traditional form of operation is either sole practice or partnership with other lawyers belonging to the same profession. Equity partners share profits and are jointly and severally liable for the firm's debts. This is based on the idea that unlimited liability encourages responsibility and independence from external influence.

The partnership arrangement subsists across organisation types, from small firms to extremely large international firms. The classical partnership has a departmental structure and solicitors can carry out all the legal tasks, research, interviewing clients and advocacy. A senior partner usually holds the title managing partner and spends some time dealing with partnership matters. The role is often rotating. There is a low turnover of staff and the atmosphere of the firm is collegial.

Some legal firms serve niche markets, such as criminal law, intellectual property or immigration. The most numerous firms are general practices offering a range of legal services to local populations. In England and Wales

---

[45] Legal Services Act 2007 s 2.
[46] Legal Services Act 2007 s 8.
[47] Legal Services Act 2007 s 10(1).

small firms often serve and are known as 'high street firms'. They may have a core clientele but many of their clients only need lawyers at times of crisis.

Private practices are usually classified as large firms when they have over 80 partners. Large firms became very well established in the United States during the 1900s. They offered business clients high-quality services focused on corporate and commercial work. They were also likely to offer other areas, such as property, litigation and tax. Large firms undertake large-scale transactions, often using multidisciplinary teams involving accountants, economists or architects.

The large US firms had a very distinct form of organisation and culture. They recruited large numbers of lawyers from the best law schools, selecting the most dedicated and entrepreneurial for partnership.[48] The most valuable partners were primarily business getters and holders of the goodwill of corporate clients.[49]

Since the 1970s large firms have become familiar in Australia, Canada and Britain. In the UK, solicitor partnerships were restricted to 20 partners until 1967.[50] Since this ceiling was lifted they have grown massively, dominating legal services provision. The 100 largest firms represent nearly 1% of all solicitors' firms in England and Wales, but account for half the turnover of all private practitioner solicitors.

Ethical Implications

Because of their huge scale, many large law firms have the bureaucratic structure of a corporation. Among the positive ethical impacts of this is that large firms tend to have a democratic and meritocratic environment,[51] providing opportunities for the advancement of women and ethnic minorities. They also take a lead in providing free legal services, *pro bono publico*.

Among the negative impacts of large firms is a move away from collegial assumptions. In many jurisdictions, professions have been encouraged to adopt the corporate form of organisation rather than the collegial form. Many law firms now operate as limited liability partnerships. As a consequence, large firms are often said to have adopted corporate values.

---

[48] M Galanter and T Palay, *Tournament of Lawyers: Transformation of the Big Law Firm* (Chicago, University of Chicago Press, 1991).

[49] K Llewelyn, 'The Bar Specialises: With What Results?' [1933] *Annals of the American Academy of Political and Social Sciences* 167, 176.

[50] Companies Act 1967 s 120(1)(a).

[51] WW Powell, 'Fields of Practice' (1996) 21 *Law and Social Inquiry* 956.

Employed Practice

Many lawyers do not work in private practice, but perform legal work for an employer in either the public or private sectors. These employees are often called 'in-house' lawyers. Professions tend to allow this activity, but still require that the lawyer be subject to the professional code of conduct. The codes usually provide that employed lawyers can only provide legal services for their employer. Exceptions may be made, for example so that employed lawyers can give advice to work colleagues.[52] The code of conduct often provides different rules on some issues for private practitioners and 'in-house' lawyers.

The Impact of the Legal Services Act 2007

Alternative Business Structures

In England and Wales an intended consequence of the LSA was the increased availability of commoditised legal products.[53] This is because large businesses such as supermarkets would be encouraged to enter the market. Increased use of technology would encourage more self-help among consumers. The advantages of ABS, particularly those run by supermarkets, include familiarity to customers, brand confidence and loyalty.

Added to these market advantages of ABS is the power of large-scale advertising, the capacity to invest in new technologies and economies of scale. The threat to certain types of legal work posed by ABS has already materialised. Co-operative Legal Services is already one of the highest grossing law firms in England.

The Impact of Technology

Richard Susskind predicted that non-lawyer capital and management would accelerate the development of commoditised legal services.[54] These, he suggests, will be based on standardisation, systemisation, packaging and commoditisation of legal products. For Susskind, the final stage, commoditisation, is represented by 'an online solution that is made available for direct use by

---

[52] SRA Practice Framework Rules (2011) Rule 4.
[53] Legal Services Board (2009) *LSB Business Plan* 2009/10 (London, Legal Services Board) para 12, www.legalservicesboard.org.uk/news_publications/publications/pdf/business_plan_2009_10.pdf.
[54] R Susskind, *The End of Lawyers? Rethinking the Nature of Legal Services* (Oxford, Oxford University Press, 2008).

the end user, often on a DIY basis'.[55] This would undermine the delivery of traditional 'bespoke' legal services.

Lawyers, Susskind argues, will be unable to resist 'disruptive legal technologies', such as document assembly, personalised alerting, online dispute resolution and open sourcing. Even corporate work could be susceptible to the 'unbundling' of the legal services that technology supports. Accordingly, there will be five types of lawyer in the future. Only a category he calls 'expert trusted advisers' will provide hand-crafted legal solutions. Their work will be a luxury that most clients will not be able to afford and their numbers will be much reduced. 'Enhanced practitioners' will support the delivery of the standard and commoditised packages that are the staple of future legal services.

In Susskind's dystopian future for lawyers, 'the most numerous lawyers, legal knowledge engineers' will create the standardised packages used by the others. 'Legal risk managers' will advise how to avoid legal problems rather than resolve them. Finally, a 'legal hybrid' will emerge, schooled in complementary disciplines aligned to law, comprising project managers, strategy and management consultants, market experts and deal brokers.

Susskind suggests that:

> Whether law firms can survive in this market will depend on the extent to which traditional lawyers are genuinely needed, when they are frankly and dispassionately compared with their emerging competition in the broadest sense, which includes a healthy third sector, entrepreneurial alternative providers, online self-help, and the various other sources of legal guidance that are and will become commonplace.'[56]

One criticism of Susskind's prediction is that he assumes that lawyers will not adapt to using technology in legal work. Most enterprises adopt technology a little ahead of the time that not to do so could be damaging. Susskind himself predicts that there will be an 'incremental revolution [where] lawyers and their clients will change their ways in significant steps rather than huge leaps'.[57]

Another criticism is that Susskind overestimates the ability of computer programming to replace lawyers. This will not happen without fundamental changes in the legal system. Therefore, it is arguable that technology will undoubtedly change legal work in the future, but it seems likely that the need for lawyers will remain.

[55] Ibid, 32.
[56] Ibid, 246.
[57] Ibid, 282.

The Contemporary Role and Significance of Professions

The story of this chapter so far seems to be of the rise and fall of legal professionalism. This assumes that professionalism is only about controlling markets for professional services. While this has been a dominant theory in recent years it may not be the whole story. If a drift towards de-professionalisation of the legal services market is to be arrested, thought needs to be given to whether legal professions serve a continuing purpose. This section considers some theories that suggest a rationale for the continuing presence of professions in delivering legal services.

Institutional Theories

It may be that our conception of professionalism is changing. Recently, sociologists and sociolegal scholars have developed new theories about the role of professions. These theories have focused on the norms of professionalism, including professional ethics, and the institutions that preserve them. A particular issue is the collegial organisation of professions. This may serve to provide different regulatory options to organisational control using outcomes-focused regulation (see chapter three: Regulation and Discipline).

Social science has seen a revival of functionalist perspectives on professions. Neo-functionalist analysis revives the ideas that professions function for the benefit of civil society. It points to the difference between professions' collegial form of organisation and the bureaucratic structure of corporations. Professionals are socialised into professional values, primarily through education and training. One of the aims of this process is to build character strengths and virtues.

Character and Personality

It could be argued that society in general values personality, but that professions continue to focus on a person's character. Personality is superficial. It is more obvious on first meeting. It is in the nature of character that it develops over time, as a result of emotional experience. Weakness of character may be revealed only occasionally at moments of pressure, for example as a lack of fortitude or a propensity to lie.

In employment, strong character may be expressed as loyalty, mutual commitment, the pursuit of long-term goals and delayed gratification for the sake of a future end. It is less clear, however, that increasingly transient employment situations are good for building character. It is arguably important that society nurtures institutions, like professions, that regard character as important.

Promoting Social Change

Sciulli argues that professions' promotion of social change is the essence of their distinctive contribution to society.[58] They provide their services consistently with prevailing standards of truth. They therefore offer society things that corporations do not. They tend to be disinterested contributors to public debate. They also tend to oppose positional power, including their own power over clients. Finally, professions take responsibility for the design of institutions in their area of governance within civil society.

Reflexivity

Reflexivity is a social science theory which originally proposed that the observation of social systems affects the situations observed and the behaviour of individuals. This idea has been influential in explaining how interaction and experience change perception. Giddens suggests that reflexivity is a feature of modernity. It involves constant process of monitoring of social life in the light of new knowledge and experience. The constant search for improvement undercuts traditional habits, customs and institutions.[59]

Personal reflexivity changes a person's values, beliefs, relationships, interests and work. This is a potentially useful insight for regulators. It suggests that interactive strategies will be more successful than others in changing the behaviour of the regulated. Epistemological reflexivity involves the re-examination of the foundations of knowledge in the light of new research findings. It has been identified as a process of self-inquiry, reflection and adaptation.

Professions provide the conditions for the development of reflexivity among their members. They are also able to engage in revising accepted professional knowledge. The development of these functions provides an avenue for professions to serve the public interest that may be more difficult for other regulatory forms.

Building Social Capital

Professions build the social capital of their members. Social capital is repre-

---

[58] D Sciulli 'Continental Sociology of Professions Today: Conceptual Contributions' (2005) 53 *Current Sociology* 915.

[59] Giddens (n 35).

sented by the social bonds between people. Putnam, for example, suggests that high levels of social capital build social reciprocity and trustworthiness, so that people routinely take into account other people's interests when acting. The idea of social capital is also central to the theories of Pierre Bourdieu, whose ideas have been influential in sociolegal studies. Bordieu sees society as constituting various autonomous social spaces or fields, for example politics, law, economy, arts and education.

Actors acquire attitudes and behaviours from practical experience, including the conditions of the field, contributing to deep consciousness, a set of dispositions that Bourdieu called 'habitus'. Social conflicts focus on different kinds of capital. These are economic, cultural, such as social skills and qualifications, and social, such as networks of influence. In the struggle for power within fields, a fourth kind, symbolic capital, for example prestige, can be just as powerful and even decisive. Professions are rich in social capital and deploy it in order to realise social benefit in their areas of expertise.

Conclusion

Professional people are typically members of and regulated by professional bodies. These were initially groups of members of an occupation who took a special interest in protecting the occupation's area of activity and raising its status. The legal profession enjoyed high status which endured during the industrial revolution. This status declined during the twentieth century. With the rise of market-based economic policies, professions fell out of favour. There are now serious questions about what the organisation of lawyers in legal professions brings to the market for legal services.

The possibility of non-lawyer ownership and management of law firms is banned in many countries. In some common law countries, lawyers' monopoly of legal provision is being challenged. The government's plan is to reduce the cost of legal services in the interests of consumers. Part of the strategy is to increase competition between legal services providers by bringing new providers into the legal services market. This threatens to end the traditional dominance of law firms.

Regulation and Discipline

Introduction

This chapter explores the regulation of legal professions. It looks at different theories of regulation before outlining the argument for self-regulation of legal services providers. It then considers ways in which future practitioners are prepared to make ethical choices by legal education and training. It also outlines the regulatory mechanisms used and the place of codes of conduct in ensuring ethical performance. The chapter concludes by outlining the change in regulatory philosophy prompted by the Legal Services Act 2007 (LSA). Traditional methods of regulation are juxtaposed with the regulatory regimes beginning to emerge in response to the Act.

Theories of Regulation

Definition

Regulation is a contested term with at least three current meanings.[1] The first conceives of regulation as a set of authoritative and targeted rules, issued by a public agency or similar body. The second sees regulation as direct state intervention in steering the economy through its agencies, using tools such as contracting or state ownership. The third meaning sees mechanisms of social control, whoever exercises them and whether they are intended to facilitate or control, or not, as regulation. The last of these three meanings would include

---

[1] R Baldwin, C Scott and C Hood, *A Reader on Regulation* (Oxford, Oxford University Press, 1998).

within the definition of regulation anything that might produce effects on behaviour. This could include workplace or other environments.

Regulation Types and Strategies

Government Regulation

i. Command-and-Control Regulation

Command-and-control regulation describes the direct regulation of an industry by the state, usually through legislation. It involves the specification of quality standards (command) with specified sanctions for breach (control). A criticism of a command-and-control approach is that it aims to deter non-compliance rather than to encourage compliance. Its operation is therefore remedial rather than preventative.

A problem with implementing an effective command-and-control regime is that standards need to be specified accurately and on a large scale (eg the level of carbon emission at a factory). A command-and-control regime is less feasible where it is difficult to specify quantitative standards. These various criticisms may contribute to command-and-control approaches being relatively ineffective in changing behaviour in the economic and organisational spheres.

ii. Indirect Government Regulation

Governments can regulate indirectly by inviting bids for franchises or contracts, the terms of which incorporate regulatory objectives. Contractors can also be required to submit to pre-existing quality-control regimes as a term of the contract. The eminent sociologist Max Weber was ambivalent about state bureaucracy impinging on civil society. He saw state interference as an efficient, even necessary, form of organisation, but also as an 'iron cage', inducing conformity and threatening individual freedom.

Types of Self-regulation

i. Self-regulation

Self-regulation is justified by a situation of market failure. An example is where consumers cannot judge the product they are buying. This is usually the case with legal services. This is a situation of information asymmetries, where the producer knows more than the purchaser. Self-regulation is a good solution when private law cannot correct this problem adequately or cheaply enough, or where conventional public regulation is less good or more expensive.[2]

The preference for self-regulation over public regulation largely stems from the expertise held by the regulated sector. Formulating, implementing and amending standards is arguably cheaper for a self-regulatory agency than an external agency. Monitoring and enforcement costs are reduced and borne by the industry, rather than the taxpayer.

There are many concerns about the legitimacy and economic effect of self-regulation. Self-regulatory agencies that are not democratic cannot legitimately represent their membership. The accumulation of too many functions, from rule formation to enforcement for example, offends the principle of the separation of powers. Restrictions on entry to self-regulated industries, and 'rules of etiquette', can restrict the supply of services. This enables those in self-regulated industries to claim higher profits, 'rents', than would be available in a competitive market.

ii. Enforced Self-regulation

Concern that self-regulation can too easily favour the regulated group has led to adjustments in regimes. Schemes whereby industries make their own rules, but have them approved by public agencies, are potentially more efficient and less costly than direct state regulation. Such schemes have been called 'enforced self-regulation'.[3] These regimes are often supported by compliance officers within firms who are under an obligation to report regulatory infractions. Regimes involving state monitoring were originally advocated as a way of dealing with self-regulatory failure.

Enforced self-regulation can be accompanied by strategies to increase competition and reduce rents. Competition between self-regulatory agencies can be sufficient to reduce prices, but this alone is not a solution. Ideally, consumers should be able to purchase the quality they can afford. Unfortunately, if consumers can compare price but not quality, this may force quality to be consistently cut, leading to a 'race to the bottom'. Therefore, some control over quality needs to be exercised. This can be provided by external rating agencies, or by a public agency charged with eliminating anti-competitive practices and maintaining minimum quality standards.

Mixed Regulation

A number of different regulatory regimes can be operated as part of a self-regulatory regime or, more typically, though a government-appointed agency.

---

[2] A Ogus, 'Rethinking Self-Regulation' (1995) 15 *Oxford Journal of Legal Studies* 97.
[3] J Braithwaite, 'Enforced Self-Regulation' (1982) 80 *Michigan Law Review* 1466.

i. Responsive Regulation

Responsive regulation proposes an alternative to the choice between deterrence regimes, punishing after the event, and compliance regimes, involving preventative persuasion. Combined strategies that involve initial persuasion, followed up by deterrent sanctions for recalcitrant offenders, offer a dual approach.[4] This approach also forms part of a wider suite, or pyramid, of strategies, starting with self-regulation but ending with strictly enforced sanctions for non-compliance as a final step.

Compliance regimes can be developed through ongoing relationships between regulators and regulated entities. Their success depends on the transparency and clear communication between the parties.[5] Visits by regulators to regulated organisations check the effectiveness of systems and the outcomes achieved. This may result in recommendations for change, for example to systems. The focus of such visits can also escalate to other processes, such as disciplinary investigations, or to involve other sanctions, such as fines.

There are a number of potential problems with such regimes. Their success depends on a number of factors including the resources available for regulatory activity, the attitudes of regulators and political support for intervention. It is useful if the regulator can have a wide range of sanctions available. If the only sanction is extremely serious it is less likely to be used. However, if the use of sanctions depends on co-operation with the regulator, there is a risk that different sanctions will be applied for the same offence, thus undermining the legitimacy of the regime.

ii. Risk-based Regulation

In 2005 the Hampton Review proposed that regulatory agencies should focus resources on the regulated parties posing the biggest risk that the regulator would not achieve its regulatory objectives. Risk-based strategies assume that there is an evidence base that allows risks to be assessed. This may lead to the risks identified being historic problems rather than prospective ones. There should also be a process of prioritisation of risks at a high level. If transparent systems are in place it is likely that reporting of these priorities will evoke a hostile reaction.

iii. Reflexive Regulation

Reflexive regulation refers to the idea that regulators and the regulated learn from and respond to the experience of regulation. Both adjust their behaviour

---

[4] I Ayres and J Braithwaite, *Responsive Regulation—Transcending the Deregulation Debate* (Oxford, Oxford University Press, 1992).

[5] C Parker, 'Compliance Professionalism and Regulatory Community: The Australian Trade Practices Regime' (1999) 26(2) *Journal of Law & Society* 215.

accordingly, with the regulator taking on board new approaches and strategies according to what works.[6] Mechanisms for this can be seen in proposals for the development of responsive regulation to take account of factors such as the attitudes of regulated parties, the wider regulatory environment and the interplay of regulatory tools.[7] Through a reflexive process, regulators can reassess and redesign regulatory strategy.

Choice of Regulatory System

Self-regulation is often associated with detailed disciplinary rules and codes of conduct. Regulation by public authority tends to be associated with administrative regimes. These may use a range of tools including inspection, audit and advice. These tools can be used in association with regulatory codes, though these may not be as detailed as a professional code of conduct. However, the strategies of mixed regulation can be used in the context of self-regulation. Likewise, a situation of enforced self-regulation could take on the characteristics of a mixed system.

A number of factors bear on the choice of system including the current situation of an industry, the history of performance of that industry and the approach of the state to the issue of regulation. As a generalisation, hierarchical societies are more likely to favour direct government regulation, individualist societies to favour deregulation and light-touch regulation, and egalitarian societies to prefer participatory models.[8]

Regulation of the Legal Profession

Self-regulation

As the legal professional bodies grew in organisation and confidence they took on the task of guaranteeing the behaviour and performance of their members. They therefore exercised disciplinary powers over their members. Effective disciplinary machinery was essential because, without prescription or sanction,

---

[6] S Deakin and C McLaughlin, 'The Regulation of Women's Pay: From Individual Rights to Reflexive Law?' in J Scott, S Dex and H Joshi (eds), *Women and Employment: Changing Lives and New Challenges* (Cheltenham, Edward Elgar, 2008) 313.

[7] R Baldwin and J Black, 'Really Responsive Regulation' (2008) 71(1) *Modern Law Review* 59.

[8] Baldwin et al (n 1) 23.

rules may not provide effective control of the whole membership.[9] Formal powers to discipline members were eventually delegated by the state, and the professions established and operated disciplinary tribunals. The machinery supporting control of the legal profession, including disciplinary, educational and other mechanisms, is known as self-regulation.

When the legal professions first emerged, state regulation of occupations was rudimentary. As professional practice became more sophisticated, it became incomprehensible to outsiders. External regulation was therefore seen as impracticable. With the growth of the regulatory state (see chapter two) the effectiveness of self-regulation was contested. This was partly because professional bodies also represented members' interests, giving them conflicting roles. Therefore, the legal professions in England and Wales currently operate under a regime closer to enforced self-regulation. This is described in more detail later in this chapter.

Regulation of the Right to Practice

Regulation of the right to practice is a fundamental aspect of the professional control of legal markets. The right to practice is protected by statute. It is an offence for an unqualified person to act as a solicitor, 'wilfully pretend to be' a solicitor, or imply that he or she is a solicitor.[10] Under the LSA 'authorised persons' in England and Wales can only undertake the reserved legal activities that their regulator can authorise and which that regulator has authorised them to undertake. Certain areas of work, for example immigration and asylum, can be done by non-lawyers.

Some jurisdictions are open to lawyers from other states operating in their jurisdiction, although they may not be able to do exactly the same things as home-qualified lawyers. Following EU directives in 1989 and 1998, qualified lawyers from EU Member States can practice in other EU jurisdictions under their own title. In England and Wales they must register with the SRA. They can also qualify as a lawyer of their host state provided they fill any gaps in their knowledge and skills. The host state must facilitate this by providing suitable assessments.[11]

---

[9] R Baldwin, 'Why Rules Don't Work' (1990) 53 *Modern Law Review* 321.
[10] Solicitors' Act 1974, ss 20, 21 as amended.
[11] Directive 89/48/EEC.

Preparation for Practice

Socialisation into Professional Values

It is important not to ignore the fact that there are reasons, other than sanctions, why rules work. This is because everybody is socialised into a set of behaviours by family and other institutions. Professions provide occupational socialisation, building on these earlier stages. Membership, identification and peer pressure provided by the professional group as a whole counterbalance workplace pressure to drop standards. Entrants to professions are socialised into values throughout their education and training and beyond. It is important, therefore, to consider whether professional structures, taken as a whole, support ethical performance of member practitioners.

i. Education

Knowledge is the foundation of professional authority. Education and training is the core responsibility of regulation. Institutionalised legal education consolidates, expands and theorises the knowledge base in universities. It is also symbolically important. Because professional knowledge changes, professional education is a lifelong activity. It used to be assumed that professionals acquired wisdom through experience. Nowadays, they are likely to be subject to compulsory continuing professional development programmes. These typically require attendance at a given number of lectures a year as a condition of practice.

The length of education and training signifies the intrinsic difficulty of assimilation and mastery of professional knowledge and skill. Larson suggests that one of the reasons for professional monopolies is so that intending professionals are not dissuaded from investing time, effort and money in education and training. The result is that the education process can be seen as unnecessarily lengthy and complex. Moreover, it is arguable that it pays insufficient attention to moral values. It typically pays professional ethics, arguably one of the fundamental building blocks of professional practice, little attention. This can be attributed to the way in which university legal education developed.

ii. The Curriculum

A method of study based on analysis of cases and precedents evolved in England in the nineteenth century under the influence of a largely Oxford-based elite. The case method involved the systematisation, exposition and analysis of legal doctrine.[12] The popularity of the case method is attributed to the Harvard Law professor Christopher Columbus Langdell, who, in 1887, asserted that 'Law is a science, and that all the available materials of that science are contained in printed books.'[13]

The case method became entrenched in English university law teaching between 1850 and 1907. Its material was 'black letter law', a term derived from the presentation of basic legal principles in bold type in traditional texts.[14] The general approach became universal, although it took different forms in different jurisdictions. In the US the 'Socratic method' required students to state the facts of the case, the outcome and whether it was 'good' law.

The case method is integral to legal positivism, which holds that the legal and the moral are separate realms. Positivism defines 'law' as that material formally enacted by designated authorities. This contrasts with natural law, which suggests that universal principles of morality, religion and justice must be present for norms to be called 'law'. Sugarman argues that the adoption of legal positivism by universities created an area of autonomy between the university, the profession and the state. Practitioners were masters of the relation between law and facts but legal academics 'were masters of the principles of law ... facts and reality were kept at a safe distance'.[15]

From the early 1900s, law became a subject in many provincial universities. It was often developed with local law societies and taught by local practitioners. As a result, these provincial courses took a practical approach.[16] In 1913 the Haldane Commission promoted the combination of theory and practice, excluding social, political or moral context, with support from the academy.[17] In a post-war review of legal education, the president of the Society of Public Teachers of Law said that legal education should be based on precedent, not legislation. Criticising law and discussing law reform was dangerously like sociology, and impinged on the objectivity necessary for legal study.

As legal education developed in the twentieth century, university law schools clung to the scientific pretensions of positivism. By the 1950s the doctrinal approach to legal study was under challenge. A number of legal academics argued that lawyers should know some economics, political science and sociology as well as legal cases. In the 1970s, critics argued that

---

[12] D Sugarman, '"A Hatred of Disorder": Legal Science, Liberalism and Imperialism' in P Fitzpatrick (ed), *Dangerous Supplements: Resistance and Renewal in Jurisprudence* (London, Pluto Press, 1991) 34.

[13] 'Harvard Celebration Speeches: Professor Langdell' (1887) 8 *Law Quarterly Review* 123.

[14] AC Hutchinson, 'Beyond Black-Letterism: Ethics in Law and Legal Education' (1999) 33 *Law Teacher* 301.

[15] Sugarman (n 12) 41.

[16] B Abel-Smith and R Stevens, *Lawyers and the Courts: A Sociological Study of the English Legal System 1750–1965* (London, Heinemann, 1967) 182.

[17] B Hepple, 'The Renewal of the Liberal Law Degree' (1996) 55 *Cambridge Law Journal* 470, 474.

the pedagogy of the case method stimulates competitiveness, orthodoxy and conservatism, turning students away from whatever public service orientations stimulated their interest in law.[18]

Legal positivism fell out of favour with many academics from the 1960s onwards. The professional bodies encouraged the idea that law should be taught 'in context', encouraging a multidisciplinary approach.[19] The evolution of legal studies from the 1960s coincided with the growth of sociolegal research in universities. This involved the empirical investigation of legal phenomena using the methods of the social sciences.

The multidisciplinary approach to law broke the stranglehold of conventional legal study. It was a form of knowledge that was not found in practice but was valuable in law reform, as evidenced by the establishment of the Law Commission in 1965. The adoption of a broader approach to academic legal study began a debate about what legal education was for.

A broad consensus emerged between professional policymakers and university law lecturers that limited the scope of undergraduate legal education. It was only to contribute to professional development by laying the foundations of legal study through substantive core subjects. Study of the legal system, or skills or ethics was not required. This approach helped integrate law schools into a wider university culture based on a liberal ideal and the neutral values of scientific inquiry.

Universities have a liberal ethos in which independence is a key value. Bradney identifies John Henry Newman, the nineteenth-century Roman Catholic cardinal and academic, as an inspiration for this liberal ideal. Newman wished to build a Catholic university for Catholic students. He recognised, however, that he needed to be able to publish free from church interference.

Newman's view of liberal education was that it

> apprehends the great outlines of knowledge, the principles on which it rests, the scale of its parts, its lights and its shades, its great points and its little. ... A habit of mind is formed which lasts through life, of which the attributes are, freedom, equitableness, calmness, moderation and wisdom.[20]

This vision is usually antithetical to vocational or other 'non-academic' values.

Despite the absence of vocational content, legal professions often specify much of the undergraduate law curriculum as a mandatory prerequisite of

---

[18] D Kennedy, 'How the Law School Fails: A Polemic' (1971) 1 *Yale Review Journal of Law and Social Action* 71; CC Stanley, Training for the Hierarchy? Reflections on the British Experience of Legal Education' (1988) 22(2/3) *The Law Teacher* 78; S Matambanadzo, 'Fumbling toward a Critical Legal Pedagogy and Practice' (2006) 4 *Policy Futures in Education* 90.

[19] The Hon Mr Justice Ormrod (Chairman) Report of the Committee on Legal Education (1971) Cmnd 4595 (Ormrod), para 109; ACLEC, para 2.4; and K Economides, 'Legal Ethics— Three Challenges for the Next Millenium' in *Ethical Challenges to Legal Education and Conduct* (Oxford, Hart Publishing, 1998) xxxii.

[20] A Bradney, *Conversations, Choices and Chances: The Liberal Law School in the Twenty-First Century* (Oxford, Hart Publishing, 2003) 32.

progress to vocational qualification. There is no strong rationale for most of the content. Nevertheless, in much of the common law world, further courses and an apprenticeship in practice is required.

Over the past quarter century vocational courses have developed a distinct methodology, integrating skills into practice. They have increasingly required that professional ethics be taught as part of the curriculum. The focus has often been on a few rules of conduct. The result is that nowhere in legal education do professional ethics receive full treatment.

Glasser argued that, as the membership of professions becomes more diverse, and experiences of practice diverge, education would need to provide 'the cement' binding the legal profession together.[21] It might therefore be expected that education and training would play a greater role in professional socialisation. This may suggest a need for programmes traversing the conventional stages of education and training.

Requiring the initial stage to cover ethical materials would have a number of advantages. It would provide a common platform for the vocational stage, where a common understanding of ethics could be assumed. This would enable the vocational stage to adopt more ambitious aims and lay the foundation for higher levels of education and training at the training and post-qualification stages.

The Legal and Education and Training Review for England and Wales, which reported in 2013, came to remarkably mixed conclusions about ethics. Legal and professional ethics was rated one the two most important knowledge areas by barristers solicitors and CILEX members in an online survey conducted for the review. Only contract law and tort, third and fourth respectively, commanded anywhere near the same general consensus.

The Future of Legal Services Education and Training Regulation in England and Wales (June 2013)

Ethics, values and professionalism

4.65 This was rated the most important knowledge area in the LETR online survey, a result which echoed the demand for a greater emphasis on professional ethics and conduct across the qualitative data and stakeholder responses to Discussion Papers. It is also an area that bridges the affective/moral domain and 'habits of mind', as well as the cognitive dimension.

4.66 An increased emphasis on ethics and legal values in LSET would be consistent with the focus of the LSA 2007 regulatory objectives, and the need to develop a more thoughtful and contextual approach to professional obligations,

---

[21] C Glasser, 'The Legal Profession in the 1990s: Images of Change' (1990) 10 *Legal Studies* 1.

particularly where those are expressed via principles-based regulation or OFR rather than detailed rules. It is suggested that all approved regulators review the treatment of ethics and professionalism within their education and training regimes to ensure that the subject is addressed with the prominence and in the depth appropriate to the public profession of law.

4.67 A majority of respondents took the view that ethics and professionalism need to be developed throughout the continuum of education and training. This view is accepted and underpins a number of the final recommendations in this report. The approach taken in Scotland which seeks to develop professionalism as a distinct foundation for both the professional training (PEAT 1) and work-based (PEAT 2) stages of training is also commended, not least for its capacity to link commitments to personal integrity, continuing improvement, public service and diversity to the legal role.

Affective/moral

4.83 The affective and moral dimensions are critical to professional practice, and aspects of them are widely captured in competence frameworks—aside from the purely cognitive dimension of professional ethics and regulation. Independence and integrity are particularly valued in Briefing Paper 1/2012 and 'honesty and integrity' was also a highly-ranked attribute in the LETR online survey ... . Respect for clients and co-workers is also commonly identified, though consumer data suggest that respect for, and empathy with, clients are areas where there are still significant gaps between expectation and reality ... .

...

4.104 It should be noted that, despite the general emphasis placed on legal ethics and professional values, there was no majority support for the introduction of professional ethics as a further Foundation subject for the QLD/GDL. This does not preclude the academic stage from providing an important basis for the study of professional ethics. Hence it is proposed that the QLD/GDL should include outcomes that advance an awareness and understanding of the values embedded in law, legal processes and solutions, and the role of lawyers in advancing those values. Further, it is recommended that some understanding of underlying legal values should be incorporated in the education and training of any authorised person.

4.105 At the same time, institutions should not be required to devote more than the existing 180 credits to any prescribed Foundation subjects. This fits with comparable approaches internationally. It is important to acknowledge that the traditional professions are now a minority career destination for law graduates, and university law schools also have their own legitimate and distinctive objectives for the degree ..., which should be respected.

4.143 Outcomes will reflect the knowledge, skills and understanding required of a practitioner. Aside from the need for domain knowledge, the outcomes must place sufficient emphasis on ethics and professionalism, core communication skills (oral and written communication and, in appropriate contexts, advocacy), business and social awareness, equality and diversity issues, and legal research. This approach highlights the need for a reasonable degree of transparency in knowledge outcomes and therefore for some increase in the specification of the Foundations of Legal Knowledge.

Professionalism and ethics

7.10 The perceived centrality of professionalism and ethics to practise across the regulated workforce is one of the clearest conclusions to be drawn from the LETR research. Legal ethics was rated 'important' or 'somewhat important' by over 90% of survey respondents and was seen as a defining feature of professional service in the qualitative data. A majority of respondents thought that an understanding of legal values, ethics and professionalism needs to be developed throughout legal services education and training. Views differed as to what that might mean in practice. There was no majority support for the introduction of professional ethics as a new Foundation of Legal Knowledge for the QLD/GDL. This does not prevent a basis for the study of professional ethics being provided at the academic stage. There is general support for all authorised persons receiving some education in legal values, as well as the technical 'law on lawyering'.

7.11 Three other factors are also significant. The LSA 2007 regulatory objectives emphasise the centrality of the core ethical standards captured by s 1 LSA 2007 ('professional principles'), as well as a wider notion, reflected across the objectives as a whole, of professional responsibility to society and to the rule of law. The development of OFR has also been seen to require a different approach to education and training in ethical values. Lastly, a greater emphasis on ethics would better align England and Wales to international practice, where a growing number of common law jurisdictions have included some element of ethics, professional governance/regulation and professionalism as part of both initial and continuing education and training in recent years. The impact in the US of the MacCrate statement of professional values, and the introduction of a 'professionalism' requirement across the Law Society of Scotland's PEAT 1 and 2, are influential examples. The PEAT definition of professionalism is particularly commended as a way of capturing the wider commitments of legal professionals to society, addressing:

• the interests of justice and democracy;
• effective and competent legal services on behalf of a client;
• continuing professional education and personal development;
• diversity and public service;
• trust, respect and personal integrity.

iii. Induction into a Community

Many professions require that entrants go through a period of training, like an apprenticeship, before admission. Trainees are usually required to work under the guidance of an established practitioner. They develop the ability to apply their knowledge and the practical skills associated with that area of practice. It is arguable that they also develop relevant attitudes and values through this process.

In addition to apprenticeship, professions may require that entrants acquire experience within the broader professional community. Indeed, Larson argues that community and ethicality are intimately related. It is in the culture of professions that explanations of the origins of practices and norms lie. The possibility of regulation by the community of peers began to be realised with concentrations of lawyers at the Inns of Court. This is a prime example of induction into a discernible ethical community.

As part of the induction into the profession the Inns of Court typically require that students dine in an Inn a number of times before being called to the Bar. It is seen as one of the ways of inducting entrants into the culture of the Bar. In the past, many students resented having to travel to London, and pay for a dinner, just to satisfy what seemed to be a quaint tradition. To many it seemed like an outdated requirement that served no purpose. To the Inns, dining was an important symbolic commitment.

The Inns eventually found an ingenious compromise to the dining requirement. Students are now required to complete twelve 'units' in order to be called to the Bar.[22] These are known as qualifying sessions and are defined as 'educational and collegiate activities arranged by or on behalf of the Inn for the purpose of preparing junior barristers for practice'. These sessions typically include 'dining sessions', with senior practitioners, but need not do so. Nowadays, therefore, it is usual for 'dining' to accompany relevant talks and training workshops. However, even these limited requirements are sometimes resented.[23]

Regulation of Professional Behaviour

Early Systems of Control

In the early days regulation of lawyers was largely by the monarch and through

---

[22] BSB Joining and Inn (https://www.barstandardsboard.org.uk/qualifying-as-a-barrister/bar-professional-training-course/how-to-apply-for-the-bptc/joining-an-inn/).

[23] A Aldridge, 'Barristers' Dinners—A Bit of Fun or One Upper-Class Indulgence Too Many?' *The Guardian*, 12 May 2011.

the courts. The first legislation concerned with the behaviour of lawyers was the Statute of Westminster (1275). This imposed a penalty of imprisonment for one year and a day and disbarment on a lawyer for an act of deception. From 1280 London courts had codes of conduct applying to all practising lawyers. Serjeants practising in the courts swore an oath to uphold the dignity of the city courts. Attorneys charged with breaches of discipline were tried by juries composed of other attorneys.

Mixed Regulatory Controls

The use of different systems of professional regulation persists to the present day. In the early 1990s Wilkins identified four systems that tend to be used in common law jurisdictions.[24] There are the disciplinary controls exercised by legal professions under the supervision of the courts, institutional controls operating in the relevant practice forum (eg a court) legislative controls operated by administrative agencies, and liability controls (eg for negligence claims). All of these tend to operate, to some degree, in different spheres. The balance between them often reflects the effectiveness of each in controlling lawyer behaviour in its particular sphere.

Professional Controls

Self-regulating professions usually control all aspects of professional behaviour, including education and training. Following the collegial principle, professions tend to operate as a heterarchy. This tends to mean that, as far as belonging to the profession is concerned, full members do not have a rank. In contrast to a hierarchy, none of those in a heterarchy are subordinate to others. In theory, the professional standards apply equally to all members, whatever their status and circumstances.

Professional self-regulation usually also includes disciplinary processes for lawyers who have broken disciplinary rules. These typically involve the regulator bringing proceedings before a panel composed of members of the profession. The panels usually have wide powers of discipline, including the power to remove a practitioner's rights to practice. Increasingly, these panels are required to include lay members.

Forum Controls

Most forums in which lawyers practise exercise some control over practitioners. These controls take a variety of forms. Therefore, courts and tribu-

---

[24] D Wilkins, 'Who Should Regulate Lawyers' (1992)105 *Harvard Law Review* 799.

nals may have the power to impose disciplinary sanctions while proceedings are ongoing. However, when effective disciplinary proceedings are in place, judges are more likely to refer lawyers to their professional regulator. It is becoming increasingly common for courts to order that lawyers pay costs to the other side when they have behaved unreasonably in legal proceedings. These 'wasted costs orders' are covered in more detail in chapter seven: Third Parties (Non-Clients).

Legislative Controls

Legislative controls of lawyers tend to be light when self-regulation operates. Increasingly, however, legislation is used to control some legal professions. In England and Wales, the LSA, which created the Legal Services Board (LSB), is a good example of this.

Liability Controls

Lawyers are often liable to either their clients, or to a limited range of third parties, in circumstances where their negligence causes loss. Until 2000, liability for negligence did not extend to advocates presenting cases in court. This immunity was based on two main policy grounds. The first was that to allow clients to sue advocates could lead to the endless rehearing of cases. The second was that the prospect of liability to clients may encourage advocates to put their duty to clients above their duty to the court. The House of Lords dismissed both arguments in the case of *Hall v Simons*.[25]

Ethical Standards and Decision-Making

Codes of Conduct

The ethical standards of practitioners derive from the work they perform. These standards are often systematised and reproduced as a code of conduct. Codes of conduct take various forms. Most codes of conduct appear as a set of rules. These rules aim to prescribe clearly what behaviour is required in different situations. However, conduct rules often have different degrees of force. The language of some provisions requires certain behaviour in given situations, for

---

[25] *Hall v Simons* [2000] 3 All ER 673 (HL); [2002] 1 AC 615.

example where they provide that 'you must' do something. Others are more aspirational, for example 'you should' do something.

The Usefulness of Codes in Making Ethical Decisions

Codes of conduct may make it clear what the rules are, but they do not take all of the effort out of ethical decision-making. Even if they are comprehensive, professional codes cannot answer every question arising in professional work. The rules in different parts of a code of conduct may conflict, leaving doubt about which should prevail. Problems arise where applying a rule produces an outcome considered to be unethical. In these instances, professionals are presented with an ethical dilemma. There are various theories that may be useful in considering how such dilemmas should be resolved.

Ethical Theories

Ethics is a branch of philosophy concerned with how people make good and right decisions on the issues confronting them. Different ethical theories suggest distinct ways of thinking about making such decisions. Four main approaches are considered here. Considering these theories is necessary in order to illustrate the different possibilities for reaching ethical decisions and the intrinsic difficulty of making such decisions. It also shows how ethical decisions may be contestable.

The four theories about how practitioners should approach ethical dilemmas are deontology, consequentialism, virtue ethics and principlism. Deontology is concerned with whether there is a duty to behave in a particular way.[26] Consequentialism advocates that one must consider outcomes before deciding on a course of action. Virtue ethics is based on the proposition that good character is essential to ethical decision-making. Principlism is based on the idea that practical ethical decisions should be based on a small number of universal principles.

It is not suggested that practitioners explicitly use one or more ethical theory in any given situation. In practice, decision-making tends to be intuitive. However, although practitioners may not consciously apply ethical theory, it is useful to be aware of its practical implications.

---

[26] Derived from the ancient Greek *deon*, meaning binding duty (J Pearsall and B Trumble (eds), *The Oxford English Reference Dictionary* (Oxford, New York, Oxford University Press, 1995), and see D Luban, 'Freedom and Constraint in Legal Ethics: Some Mid-Course Corrections to Lawyers and Justice' (1990) 49 *Maryland Law Review* 424, 424–28).

Deontology and Consequentialism

Deontic ethics assumes that certain actions are right in themselves, carrying a duty to act according to principle, irrespective of consequences. For example, Kant proposes that it is wrong to lie, even to a killer seeking the location of an intended victim.[27] This illustrates the weakness of deontology. It is inflexible and may lead to unnecessary harm. Attempting to regulate behaviour by rules of conduct is sometimes referred to as deontology. The ethicality of an act is judged by the extent to which it complies with a rule.

Consequentialism seeks justification for actions by considering results. Act-consequentialism considers the result of each act, while rule-consequentialism appraises the results of general rules requiring or permitting acts.[28] Utilitarianism, the best-known form of consequentialism,[29] values actions aimed at achieving the overall or average well-being of people. This can be measured with reference to intensity, duration, propinquity and extent of benefit.[30]

The weakness of consequentialism is that it can be difficult to apply where the outcomes of a particular action are not obvious. It may therefore be a methodology better suited to calm reflection in the light of complex data. It may be more difficult for a busy practitioner to take a consequentialist approach in their everyday work.

Virtue Ethics

Aretaic, or virtue, ethics are traceable to the ancient Greeks, particularly Aristotle. Virtue ethicists argue that it is the possession of inner traits, or character, that make an individual's actions ethical. Therefore, ethical actions are those that a virtuous person would carry out in a particular situation. As is obvious, this is not particularly helpful to someone who is not sure if they are virtuous, but still wants to do the right thing. Despite this limitation, virtue ethics are potentially useful in determining the profile of ideal professionals and thinking about how to educate them.

To the ancient Greeks, virtues were social goods contributing to a goal, or telos. The human telos was a good society achieved through 'intellectual virtue', the ability to think and reason, and moral actions for their own sake.[31]

---

[27] C Korsgaard, 'Kant on Dealing with Evil' in JP Sterba (ed), *Ethics: The Big Questions* (Oxford, Blackwell Publishing, 1998).

[28] This distinction was made by J Rawls in 'Two Concepts of Rules' (1955) 64 *Philosophical Review* 3. See also Luban (n 26) 438 and R Posner, 'Utilitarianism, Economics and Legal Theory' (1979) 8 *Journal of Legal Studies* 103.

[29] D Nicholson and J Webb, *Professional Legal Ethics: Critical Interrogations* (Oxford, Oxford University Press, 1999) 21–29.

[30] See generally PA Facione, D Scherer and T Attiq, *Ethics and Society* (Englewood Cliffs, NJ, Prentice Hall, 1991).

[31] A Flores, 'What Kind of Person Should a Professional Be?' in A Flores (ed), *Professional Ideals*, (Belmont, CA, Wadsworth Publishing, 1988) 1.

According to Aristotle, virtue becomes a habit. The virtuous individual reacts naturally and morally correctly.[32] Aristotle conceived of virtues as a balance between extreme behaviours. The virtue of courage, for example, lies between cowardice and rashness. Which virtues are selected for a particular purpose depends on the desired end.

Virtues, or 'excellences', are each unique aspects of human potential, the realisation of which make one person more human, or excellent, than another. Some are more relevant for people in certain roles, or in certain situations, than others. Much discussion about professional ethics relates to whether people can be educated and trained to be virtuous and, if so, how. Is it enough that people understand ethical obligations or do they also need to develop certain capacities, such as empathy?

Research conducted by the University of Birmingham Centre for Character and Virtues asked four groups, namely undergraduates, vocational course students, solicitors and barristers, to select 'six personal character strengths from a list of 24 [see Table 3.1] and, later, from the same list of 24, to select six character strengths they associated with the "ideal" lawyer'. It is not clear from this whether participants were asked to identify strengths that they thought they possessed or that they thought were generally important. The report of the research describes these as 'self-reported character strengths', suggesting that it is the former.

Q3.1   What do you think might be the point of comparing one's own character strengths with those of an ideal lawyer.

Q3.2   Which rank order of six character strengths do you think are most important to you personally, most important to society and most important in a lawyer

Q3.3   How do you explain any differences between the rank orders?

Q3.4   Comparing your six character strengths with those set out towards the end of chapter one under 'Professional Values and Virtues', are there any important character strengths missing from this list?

Q3.5   What character strengths do you think you need to develop to be a lawyer?

---

[32] J Hospers, *Human Conduct: Problems of Ethics* (San Diego, CA, Harcourt Brace Jovanovich, 1982) 5–9.

Table 3.1

	Personal	Society	Lawyer
Appreciation of beauty			
Bravery			
Creativity			
Curiosity			
Fairness			
Forgiveness			
Gratitude			
Honesty			
Hope			
Humour			
Judgement			
Kindness			
Leadership			
Love			
Love of learning			
Modesty			
Perseverance			
Perspective			
Prudence			
Self-regulation			
Social intelligence			
Spirituality			
Teamwork			
Zest			

The Birmingham study went on to consider the results

> **J Arthur, K Kristjansson, H Thomas, M Holdsworth,**
> **LB Confalonieri, T Qiu, *Virtuous Character for the***
> ***Practice of Law* (Birmingham, Jubilee Centre for Character and**
> **Virtues, University of Birmingham, 2014)**
>
> **4.1.2.1 Personal virtues**
>
> Table 3 shows fairness, honesty, humour and perseverance as the most common
> personal virtues self-reported in all four respondent groups. Kindness and curiosity

completed the six most commonly selected personal virtues for undergraduate students, while LPC/BPTC respondents identified curiosity and teamwork within their six. Of note was the finding that judgement was identified by both solicitors (whose six items also included kindness) and barristers (whose six items also included love of learning).

4.1.2.2 Virtues of the 'Ideal' Lawyer

Table 4 shows the six virtues of the 'ideal' lawyer most commonly selected by respondents [the table shows a reasonably strong consensus across undergraduates, vocational course students, solicitors and barristers. In declining order of importance the virtues identified were judgement, perseverance, perspective, fairness, social intelligence and leadership].

These findings show a greater concentration of choices than for personal virtues. As with the personal virtues, fairness and perseverance were among the most identified six virtues across the four groups with judgement and perspective also in the most identified six virtues for all four groups.

That undergraduates and LPC/BPTC students identified judgement as a leading virtue of the 'ideal' lawyer but that it was not in the top six personal virtues, while solicitors and barristers both identified it in their top six personal virtues and in the virtues of the 'ideal' lawyer, suggests that judgement is recognised as a central virtue for lawyers but one developed in practice rather than possessed at an early stage of their careers as legal professionals.

For all groups, the top six items now account for a greater percentage of all choices and represent 64% and 67% of all choices by experienced lawyers. There is also greater agreement about the top six virtues of the 'ideal' lawyer than was the case when identifying their personal values. This is particularly apparent with the choice of judgement and honesty by experienced lawyers as they were selected as top six virtues by 84% of solicitors and 93% of barristers. Bravery appears in the top six character strengths for an 'ideal' lawyer from the perspective of barristers, while teamwork is valued by solicitors; this difference may reflect the nature of their respective roles. ... What stands out from the comparison of the self-reported personal virtues and the ideal virtues is the greater correlation, across the career stages, in the virtues ascribed to the 'ideal' lawyer than in the self-reported virtues.'

Q3.6   Why might there be a greater correlation between the virtues of an ideal lawyer than between self-reported virtues?

Q3.7   Why might perceptions of the ideal lawyer's virtues depend on the context of respondents' work?

Principlism

Principlism is based on the idea that ethical conduct can be judged against a few, key criteria. An influential text by Beauchamp and Childress, *Principles of Biomedical Ethics*, provides a standard theoretical framework for analysing dilemmas arising in medical ethics,[33] but also claims wider applicability.

The four guiding principles are: autonomy (the right of an individual to make his or her own choice), beneficence (doing good and acting with the best interest of the other in mind), non-maleficence (not doing harm), and justice (achieving fairness and equality among individuals). These principles are intended to provide a practical framework for ethical decision-making in pressured circumstances.

There are various criticisms of principlism. First, the selected principles may not reflect a universal consensus. The four principles selected by Beauchamp and Childress may represent dominant values in Western society, but not elsewhere. The prioritisation of moral autonomy, for example, reflects the individualistic values of the West, whereas other societies may value community and other principles, such as respect and purity, more highly.[34]

The second criticism of principlism is that the four key principles provide no way of resolving conflicts between them. The third is that, because they are so broad, the key principles provide little practical help with actual decision-making. For example, even if we assume that the informed consent of a client shows respect for autonomy, there need to be several subsidiary procedures and principles in place to specify what this means.[35]

While acting for Company A, lawyer B discovers that it is engaged in activity that could result in environmental damage to a particular locality and possibly injury to people in that locality. Lawyer B's code of conduct provides that he can only break client confidentiality in order to prevent serious injury to identifiable persons.

Q3.8   How might ethical theories be applied in helping B reach an ethical decision?

Q3.9   Would your answer differ if B's professional code of conduct provided that lawyers should not breach client confidentiality under any circumstances?

---

[33] TL Beauchamp and JF Childress, *Principles of Biomedical Ethics*, 4th edn (New York, Oxford University Press, 2001) 12.

[34] T Walker, 'What Principlism Misses' (2009) 35 *Journal of Medical Ethics* 229.

[35] RB Davis, 'The Principlism Debate: A Critical Overview' (1995) 20 *Journal of Medicine and Philosophy* 85.

> Q3.10 How helpful do you think ethical theory is in reaching ethical decisions?

Ethical Discretion

Lawyers usually follow their code of conduct when making ethical decisions. To do otherwise would invite disciplinary proceedings by their professional body. William Simon argued that this is too limited an ambition.[36] He thought that lawyers should exercise their own judgement and discretion in deciding what clients to represent and how to represent them. This is contrary to the standard conception of the lawyer's role, although, Simon would argue, it is more likely to achieve an ethical outcome.

Using Simon's approach, lawyers would act with the overarching aim of seeking to do justice. They would be required to consider the merits of a client's claim relative to those of opposing parties and other potential clients.[37] They might consider the resources available to each side in deciding what behaviour is justified. When deciding how to represent a client, weighing these considerations, the lawyer could sometimes to go beyond the letter of the law, but sometimes not even use it to its full extent.

Under Simon's 'discretionary' approach, rules of conduct would be seen as rebuttable presumptions. They would be regarded as instructions to behave in a certain way unless the circumstances suggest that the values relevant to the rule would not be served by doing so. The advantage of such an approach is that it avoids over-reliance on rules and engages the professional's moral capacity. It is not inconsistent with having codes, but it does change their nature. Within such a framework, codes operate as advisory rather than mandatory requirements.

> Q3.11 What are the advantages and disadvantages of requiring lawyers to exercise discretion, rather than just follow rules, when making ethical decisions?

There have been many suggestions for strengthening the ethical components of legal education. The report produced by the University of Birmingham Centre for Character and Virtues highlighted four priorities. First, it said, more time is needed for ethics education in undergraduate courses and in vocational training.[38] Second, law students need to embrace a range of ethical theories,

---

[36] W Simon, *'Ethical Discretion in Lawyering'* (1988) 101 *Harvard Law Review* 1083.
[37] Ibid, 1090.
[38] J Arthur, K Kristjansson, H Thomas, M Holdsworth, LB Confalonieri, and T Qiu, *Virtuous*

including virtue ethics, to make sense of the moral nuances of being a good lawyer. Third, it favoured featuring models of ethical character, reasoning and action in education as much as those bringing commercial success. Fourth, it recommended that greater attention be given to informal learning in workplace culture, including opportunities for reflection on ethics in the workplace.

Disciplinary Processes

Disciplinary proceedings were one area that was not really affected by the LSA. The Act merely required that disciplinary tribunals be independent, although the different legal professions must financially support their own tribunals.

Status

In England and Wales, the main legal professions have separate disciplinary tribunals, the Solicitors Disciplinary Tribunal (SDT) and the Bar's Disciplinary Tribunal, the latter administered by the the Bar Tribunals and Administration Service. These bodies enjoy a high degree of independence. While parties have a right of appeal to a Divisional Court of the High Court, and thence to the Court of Appeal, the unique expertise of the lawyers' disciplinary procedures in dealing with professional misconduct is recognised and respected.

In *Bolton v The Law Society*[39] a lawyer was convicted of misconduct, short of outright dishonesty, and suspended from practice for two years. He appealed to the Divisional Court, which quashed the sentence and fined him instead. On appeal, the Court of Appeal implicitly criticised this decision.

The Court of Appeal in *Bolton* held that The Law Society is the body best fitted to determine the appropriate punishment for misconduct by members of the legal profession and appellate courts should not be quick to interfere with sentences passed by the SDT. While the court had been wrong to interfere with the tribunal's decision, it would be oppressive to reinstate the suspension because of the lapse of time between the offence and this appeal.

Character for the Practice of Law (Birmingham, Jubilee Centre for Character and Virtues, University of Birmingham, 2014).
[39] *Bolton v The Law Society* [1994] 1 WLR 512.

Purpose

Where professionals are guilty of a significant breach of professional rules, they can be subject to professional disciplinary proceedings. In *Bolton v The Law Society* the Court of Appeal set out the fundamental principle and purposes of the imposition of sanctions by the Tribunal. Sir Thomas Bingham, then Master of the Rolls, said:

> Any solicitor who is shown to have discharged his professional duties with anything less than complete integrity, probity and trustworthiness must expect severe sanctions to be imposed upon him by the Solicitors Disciplinary Tribunal.

> ... a penalty may be visited on a solicitor ... in order to punish him for what he has done and to deter any other solicitor tempted to behave in the same way...

> ... to be sure that the offender does not have the opportunity to repeat the offence; and ... the most fundamental of all: to maintain the reputation of the solicitors› profession as one in which every member, of whatever standing, may be trusted to the ends of the earth ... a member of the public ... is ordinarily entitled to expect that the solicitor will be a person whose trustworthiness is not, and never has been, seriously in question. Otherwise, the whole profession, and the public as a whole, is injured. A profession's most valuable asset is its collective reputation and the confidence which that inspires.

Process

Infractions are usually investigated by the regulator, but cases are heard by an independent body. Different tribunals have different rules of procedure, but they tend to follow the format of adversarial proceedings. Decision-making follows a judicial process. Having decided that the accused party is guilty of a breach, the tribunal has to decide an appropriate sentence. This may require that a number of factors be considered. The criteria that follow are taken from the guidance given to those serving on Bar tribunals.[40]

Step 1

Consider the following checklist of relevant factors:

- Individual facts of the case—breaches of the Handbook will differ significantly. The panel is entitled to form a view based on the individual facts of each case.
- Assessing the seriousness of the breach—How serious is the breach? Where does the breach sit on the scale of seriousness?

---

[40] The Bar Tribunals and Arbitration Service, *Sentencing Guidance: Breaches of the BSB Handbook* (http://www.tbtas.org.uk/wp-content/uploads/2014/06/Sentencing-Guidance-2014.pdf).

- Culpability—How culpable is the defendant for the breach? Did the breach arise from planned or intentional actions?
- Actual harm or the risk of harm—What was the outcome of the breach? Did the breach involve actual harm or the risk of harm? Does the breach impact the general reputation of the bar? Is there harm to the public as a result of the breach?
- Aggravating and mitigating factors.
- Personal circumstances of the individual barrister.
- Previous disciplinary/professional record—Is the barrister of previous good professional standing?
- Reflect on any equality and diversity factors within the case and the panel's commitment to the Equality Act 2010.

Step 2—Look up the offence/breach within the Guidance (Part 2).

Step 3—Decide whether to reduce, stay at or increase the sentence in the circumstances of the case.

Step 4—Decide whether a concurrent or consecutive sentence would be appropriate.

Step 5—Give your reasons.

> Q3.12 Are the Bar guidelines a suitable guide to sentencing in cases involving other legal professionals?

Sanctions

Disciplinary tribunals typically exercise a wide range of powers, including the right to impose sanctions. For example, under the Solicitors Act 1974 section 47, the SDT has the power to make 'such order as it thinks fit', including:

striking a solicitor off the roll

suspension from practice indefinitely or for a fixed period

the payment of a penalty

the imposition of conditions on the issue of a practising certificate

exclusion from legal aid work permanently or for a fixed period

the issue of a reprimand

an order for payment of costs[41]

---

[41] Solicitors' Act 1974 s 47.

Penalties used to be limited to a fine of up to £5,000 for each established allegation, but the limit was lifted by the LSA. The fines imposed by the SDT still appear to be relatively low.

Analysis of a year of disciplinary cases in 2008[42] showed strong correlations between:

- misuse of client money and being struck off;
- dishonesty and being struck off;
- dishonesty and being fined;
- practising without being a recognised body and being suspended;
- breaches of the solicitors' publicity code and being reprimanded;
- failure to give proper advice/information/representation and being reprimanded;
- breaches of the solicitors' account rules and being fined.

In *SRA v Dennison* the Court of Appeal held that striking off was appropriate for all but less serious cases of dishonesty even if, as here, client money was not involved.[43] The test for dishonesty is that laid down in *Twinsectra Ltd v Yardley and others*,[44] where it was held that to be dishonest a solicitor must have acted dishonestly by the ordinary standards of reasonable and honest people. He/she also had to be aware that, by those standards, he/she was acting dishonestly. Most cases involving intentional misuse of client money result in striking off.

Consider the cases of Respondent A and Respondent B.

Respondent A

A was a solicitor and former president of his local Law Society. He was convicted of voyeurism under the Sexual Offences Act 2003. He was charged under section 67(1) of the Act under which a person commits an offence if—

(a) for the purpose of obtaining sexual gratification, he observes another person doing a private act, and

(b) he knows that the other person does not consent to being observed for his sexual gratification.

There had been no physical contact involved in the offence, no exposure and no involvement of a minor. In the magistrates' court A was sentenced to four months imprisonment suspended for two years. He was required to attend a sex offender programme for two years and to register as a sex offender.

---

[42] A Boon, A Whyte and A Sherr, *The Disciplinary Processes of the Legal Profession* (unpublished report).

[43] *SRA v Dennison* [2012] EWCA Civ 421; (2012) 162 NLJ 542

[44] *Twinsectra Ltd v Yardley and others* [2002] UKHL 12.

He received testimonials from a senior partner in the firm where he worked and a promise of workplace supervision following the proceedings. He also received testimonials from some clients.

Respondent B

B was retiring from practice and was recently divorced. He wished to claim monies due under an endowment policy. In error the insurance company sent B a form that also required his wife's signature, even though it seemed she was not a beneficiary under the policy. B attended his ex-wife's home to find that she was not there. It was his last day at work and he was going on a post-retirement walking holiday the next day. He therefore put his wife's name in the space provided for his wife's signature and returned the form to the insurance company. He attached a post-it note to the form explaining what he had done and why. The insurance company paid out the monies. The matter came to light when B's ex-wife was going through his papers. She reported the matter to the police, but the CPS declined to take action. She then went to the Law Society.

Q3.13 Is A's case one that should be brought before the SDT? Why?

Q3.14 Is A guilty of conduct unbefitting a solicitor or of bringing the profession into disrepute?

Q3.15 Assuming A is found guilty, using relevant sentencing guidelines, what sanction would you apply?

Q3.16 Is B's case one that should be brought before the SDT? Why?

Q3.17 Would you find B guilty of dishonesty?

Q3.18 Assuming B is found guilty, using relevant sentencing guidelines, what sanction would you apply?

Inspection and Intervention

In addition to the power to prosecute cases of indiscipline before the SDT, the SRA can inspect and if necessary intervene in solicitors' practices. The powers contained in the Solicitors Act 1974 include the power to require production of solicitors' accounts and production of documents.[45] The powers of intervention arise, for example, where the Law Society suspects dishonesty, in the event of the bankruptcy of a solicitor or where it seems a solicitor has abandoned his practice.

---

[45] Solicitors Act 1974 ss 32 and 34.

Intervention usually involves closing down the firm, although this is done in such a way as to protect client interests as far as possible. Where any losses are not covered by the defaulting solicitor's insurance, clients may be able to claim from the Solicitors Indemnity Fund.

The Legal Services Act 2007

Background to the Act

In England and Wales the last decades of the twentieth century saw government shift the system of legal services regulation towards direct government regulation with the professed aim of promoting competition and reflecting better the interests of consumers.[46] Sir David Clementi was asked to review the regulatory framework for legal services and to prepare a report. His specific brief in considering reform was to:

(a) consider what regulatory framework would best promote competition, innovation and the public and consumer interest in an efficient, effective and independent legal sector; and

(b) recommend a framework which will be independent in representing the public and consumer interest, comprehensive, accountable, consistent, flexible, transparent, and no more restrictive or burdensome than is clearly justified.

Clementi reported in 2004.[47] His wide-ranging recommendations were outlined in chapter two. This chapter deals with his proposals for professional regulation and the impact that the subsequent Act, the LSA, had on regulation. Clementi saw advantages in retaining elements of self-regulation. For example, he did not think that vesting regulatory control in a state agency, rather than professions, was a good idea. Further, he considered that the disciplinary processes were working well.

Clementi advised that the legal professions should operate under an 'oversight regulator', to control regulation. He also recommended that professional regulation should operate independently of the professional bodies. This led to the separation of the representative and regulatory functions of the profes-

---

[46] N Semple, RG Pearce and RN Knake, 'Taxonomy of Lawyer Regulation: How Contrasting Theories of Regulation Explain the Divergent Regulatory Regimes in Australia, England and Wales and North America' (2013) 16(2) *Legal Ethics* 258.

[47] Sir David Clementi, *Review of the Regulatory Framework for Legal Services in England and Wales*, (London, Department for Constitutional Affairs, 2004) ch B, para 23.

sional bodies and to the establishment of the LSB in order to oversee the regulatory function.

Regulatory Structure

Section 29 of the LSA provided that the LSB should not interfere with the representative functions of the professional bodies, but it was also charged by a sub-section with ensuring:

(a) that the exercise of an approved regulator's regulatory functions is not prejudiced by its representative functions, or

(b) that decisions relating to the exercise of an approved regulator's regulatory functions are, so far as reasonably practicable, taken independently from decisions relating to the exercise of its representative functions.

The result of this was that the new 'regulatory arm' of each of the professions looked to the LSB for regulatory guidance. The regulator's own former professional body had to be kept at arm's length. The regulator could only listen to its views as it would with any other stakeholder, for example through its responses to public consultations. The LSA provided a list of regulatory objectives which the LSB and the approved regulators were bound to pursue and promote.

Legal Services Act 2007

The regulatory objectives

(1) In this Act a reference to 'the regulatory objectives' is a reference to the objectives of—

(a) protecting and promoting the public interest;
(b) supporting the constitutional principle of the rule of law;
(c) improving access to justice;
(d) protecting and promoting the interests of consumers;
(e) promoting competition in the provision of services within subsection (2);
(f) encouraging an independent, strong, diverse and effective legal profession;
(g) increasing public understanding of the citizen's legal rights and duties;
(h) promoting and maintaining adherence to the professional principles.

(2) The services within this subsection are services such as are provided by authorised persons (including services which do not involve the carrying on of activities which are reserved legal activities).

(3) The 'professional principles' are—

(a) that authorised persons should act with independence and integrity,
(b) that authorised persons should maintain proper standards of work,

(c) that authorised persons should act in the best interests of their clients,

(d) that persons who exercise before any court a right of audience, or conduct litigation in relation to proceedings in any court, by virtue of being authorised persons should comply with their duty to the court to act with independence in the interests of justice, and

(e) that the affairs of clients should be kept confidential.

(4) In this section 'authorised persons' means authorised persons in relation to activities which are reserved legal activities.

Regulatory Philosophy

Best Regulatory Practice

Under section 28 of the LSA approved regulators were required to have regard to:

(a) the principles under which regulatory activities should be transparent, accountable, proportionate, consistent and targeted only at cases in which action is needed, and

(b) any other principle appearing to it to represent the best regulatory practice.

Regulatory Method

Principles-Based Regulation

Before the LSA the regulatory method favoured by government was called principles-based regulation (PBR). Rather than the detailed codes of conduct favoured by professions, PBR worked from high-level principles which organisations were supposed to follow and achieve. It was used in the financial services industry and was considered to be a method of regulation that responded to the description in section 28 of the LSA.

The LSB championed a move away from rule-based regulation to PBR. The SRA was steered towards PBR by two reports for the Law Society, by Lord Hunt of Wirrall on regulation generally, and by Nick Smedley on the regulation of large firms, both of which recommended its use. In 2011 the SRA adopted a rulebook focused on high-level principles.

SRA Principles 2011

1. SRA Principles

These are mandatory *Principles* which apply to all.

You must:

1. uphold the rule of law and the proper administration of justice;
2. act with integrity;
3. not allow your independence to be compromised;
4. act in the best interests of each client;
5. provide a proper standard of service to your clients;
6. behave in a way that maintains the trust the public places in you and in the provision of legal services;
7. comply with your legal and regulatory obligations and deal with your regulators and ombudsmen in an open, timely and co-operative manner;
8. run your business or carry out your role in the business effectively and in accordance with proper governance and sound financial and risk management principles;
9. run your business or carry out your role in the business in a way that encourages equality of opportunity and respect for diversity; and
10. protect client money and assets.

Q3.19 To what extent do the principles of the SRA Code of Conduct reflect legal professional goals or would they be relevant to any business?

Q3.20 To what extent do the principles reflect the regulatory objectives of the LSA?

The Bar also revised its rulebook in 2014, adopting a similar set of high-level principles, which it called core duties.

Bar Standards Board Code of Conduct 2014

B. The Core Duties

CD1. You must observe your duty to the court in the administration of justice.
CD2. You must act in the best interests of each client.
CD3. You must act with honesty and integrity.
CD4. You must maintain your independence.
CD5. You must not behave in a way which is likely to diminish the trust and confidence which the public places in you or in the profession.
CD6. You must keep the affairs of each client confidential.
CD7. You must provide a competent standard of work and service to each client.
CD8. You must not discriminate unlawfully against any person.

CD9. You must be open and co-operative with your regulators.

CD10. You must take reasonable steps to manage your practice, or carry out your role within your practice, competently and in such a way as to achieve compliance with your legal and regulatory obligations.

Q3.21 What are the similarities and differences between the SRA principles and the BSB core duties?

Q3.22 Can you suggest reasons for any differences?

Entity Regulation

Much of the change in the new regulatory regime was driven by the Law Society's decision to be a regulator for ABS. The LSA required ABS to have a Head of Legal Practice and a Head of Finance and Administration, among whose duties was to report any breach of the licence in their area of responsibility.[48] The SRA 'rebranded' these posts Compliance Officer for Legal Practice (COLP) and Compliance Officer for Finance and Administration (COFA), and required solicitors firms, as well as ABS, to appoint such officers.

The SRA also promised to develop relationships with regulated entities. Occasional visits would occur to monitor progress. This arguably gives managers and those responsible for behaviour within organisations a good incentive to ensure that there is a culture of ethical compliance. Some writers have referred to the organisation of a business to provide support for good behaviour as 'ethical infrastructure'. The risk, of course, is that where a few managers become responsible for ethical conduct, ordinary employees may feel less responsibility.

Administrative Sanctions

The LSA amended the Solicitors Act 1974 by adding section 44(D).[49] The new section allowed the Law Society to issue a rebuke or to fine solicitors or their employees for breaches of the Act or of the professional rules without referring them to the SDT. The LSA also allowed the LSB to provide for approved regulators to fine ABS. Astonishingly, the levels of fine set by the LSB for this purpose were £250 million for an ABS and £50 million for an employee of an ABS.

The discrepancy between the levels of fine available to the SRA seemed

---

[48] Legal Services Act 2007 ss 91–92.
[49] Legal Services Act 2007 s 177 and Schedule 16.

grossly unfavourable to ABS, but in practice the difference was likely to be to the disadvantage of solicitors. In 2013 the SRA consulted on proposals to increase its powers to levy fines on solicitors, and asked for views on maximum fines between £10,000 and £100,000. As the consultation paper observed, the lower level set on solicitors' fines meant that the SRA would need to refer more serious cases to the SDT. This would force solicitors into a position where they would be paying costs that ABS would not incur.

Outcomes-Focused Regulation

The Law Society's decision to pursue regulatory control of ABS also led to the 2007 Code of Conduct being amended in 2009 to make this right explicit. The need to regulate ABS led to a shift from the regulation of individuals to the regulation of entities, the organisations in which they work. Entity regulation requires that regulators exercise regulatory control of all those working in entities, professionals and non-professionals.

An entity regulator, for example the SRA, could therefore be regulating an entity that may, or may not, include members of the profession of which it is also the approved regulator. The SRA decided to regulate solicitors and ABS using the same code of conduct. This decision underpinned a move away from rules designed to regulate the behaviour of individual solicitors to a focus on goals that an organisation might expect to achieve.

One of the main aims of focusing on high-level principles was to get away from the 'rule-based' approach traditionally used by professions. The idea was that professional organisations should focus on the desired 'outcomes' of regulation rather than follow rules. After the financial crisis of 2008 PBR was rebranded as 'outcomes-focused regulation' (OFR).

When the SRA introduced its new handbook in 2011 it contained the high-level principles and the outcomes to be achieved. However, it also included indicative behaviours. It was not mandatory for entities or solicitors to follow the indicative behaviours, though following them may demonstrate that the outcome has been achieved. They operate as a kind of default position for achieving the outcomes. It is arguable that this is an example of 'situational ethics'—circumstances where there may be better or worse ways of satisfying an overarching principle.

The first chapter of the SRA Code, concerned with client care, has sixteen outcomes that must be achieved. The first outcome of Chapter 1 (Outcome 1.1) specifies that 'you treat your clients fairly'. There are other outcomes that might also require treating clients fairly. There are also several indicative behaviours suggesting what 'treating fairly' may involve in practice. For example, Indicative Behaviour 1.1 is 'agreeing an appropriate level of service with your client, for example the type and frequency of communications'.

Comparing Conduct Rules and Outcomes-Focused Regulation
Solicitors Code of Conduct 2007, rule 2.02(2)

You must, both at the outset and, as necessary, during the course of the matter:

(a) agree an appropriate level of service;

(b) explain your responsibilities;

(c) explain the client's responsibilities;

(d) ensure that the client is given, in writing, the name and status of the person dealing with the matter and the name of the person responsible for its overall supervision; and

(e) explain any limitations or conditions resulting from your relationship with a third party (for example a funder, fee sharer or introducer) which affect the steps you can take on the client's behalf.

Under the SRA Code of Conduct, these rules become principles, outcomes and indicative behaviours. Arguably, the following are relevant:

SRA Code of Conduct 2011 (as amended)

PRINCIPLE: [You must] provide a proper standard of service to your clients

OUTCOME: O(1.5) the service you provide to clients is competent, delivered in a timely manner and takes account of your clients' needs and circumstances;

SAMPLE INDICATIVE BEHAVIOURS:

IB(1.5) explaining any limitations or conditions on what you can do for the client, for example, because of the way the client's matter is funded;

IB(1.6) in taking instructions and during the course of the retainer, having proper regard to your client's mental capacity or other vulnerability, such as incapacity or duress;

IB(1.7) considering whether you should decline to act or cease to act because you cannot act in the client's best interests;

Q3.23 What is the feature of rule 2.02(2) that gives the provisions the quality of rules?

Q3.24 What might be the advantages for practitioners in using either conventional professional conduct rules or outcomes-based regulation?

Q3.25 To what extent does outcomes-focused regulation increase the use of a lawyer's ethical discretion as advocated by William Simon?

Q3.26 Indicative behaviours could function as rules if they were differently expressed. Indicative Behaviour 1.7 is 'considering whether you should decline to act or cease to act because you cannot act in the *client's* best interests'. How could this be expressed as a rule?

Q3.27 What would be the advantages and disadvantages of using a rule or an indicative behaviour?

The Shift in Professional Regulation: An Overview

Changes in the regulation of the legal services market have stimulated a number of changes in regulation. These can be represented in tabular form (see Table 3.2). Each of these changes has been mentioned in the present chapter.

Table 3.2 The different emphases of rule-based and outcomes-based regulation

Old	New
Profession-controlled	Co-regulation
Individual	Entity
Rules	Principles
Infractions	Outcomes
Observance	Discretion
Acts	Indicative behaviours
Investigation	Accreditation
Professional responsibility	Compliance
Disciplinary process	Administrative sanction
Professional community	Ethical infrastructure
Heterarchy	Hierarchy
Deontological	Situational

Source: A Boon, 'Professionalism under the Legal Services Act 2007' (2011) 17(3) *International Journal of the Legal Profession* 195.

Q3.28 Which developments can be taken as evidence of each transition detailed in Table 3.1?

Q3.29 How far do old and new methods of regulation respond to the requirement of LSA section 28, which requires that 'regulatory activities should be transparent, accountable, proportionate, consistent and targeted only at cases in which action is needed'?

The changes brought about by the LSA are symptomatic of changing attitudes towards professions in general and, possibly, the legal profession in particular. This is exemplified in a challenge to a new scheme of quality assurance for criminal advocates. The scheme started as an initiative of the Legal Services Commission, at the time responsible for legal aid, which was apparently concerned about reports of low standards of criminal advocacy. At the instigation of the LSB, the scheme was developed by the regulators for the Bar, solicitors and legal executives. The core involves judicial assessment of advocates' performance in actual criminal trials.

The Quality Assurance Scheme for Advocates (QASA) strikes at the core of legal professionalism. It imposes external assessment of professional standards in a core legal activity. It also assesses performance in an area that has always been seen as key to the rationale of the rule of law, criminal defence. Four barristers sought judicial review of the LSB's decision to approve the QASA scheme.

Among its various roles the LSB must approve regulatory changes proposed by the approved regulators. In exercising this role it must ensure that the regulatory objectives are met and the better regulation principles are put into effect. The way in which these responsibilities are put into effect was illustrated when the QASA litigation reached the Court of Appeal. The barristers challenged the LSB's approval of the scheme.

THE QUEEN ON THE APPLICATION OF (1) KATHERINE LUMSDON (2) RUFUS TAYLOR (3) DAVID HOWKER QC (4) CHRISTOPHER HEWERTSON Appellants
- and -
LEGAL SERVICES BOARD Respondent
- and -
(1) GENERAL COUNCIL OF THE BAR (acting by the BAR STANDARDS BOARD) (2) SOLICITORS REGULATION AUTHORITY (3) ILEX PROFESSIONAL STANDARDS (4) LAW SOCIETY OF ENGLAND AND WALES Interested Parties

The Master of the Rolls

...

8. If an approved regulator makes an application under paragraph 20 of Schedule 4 to approve an alteration or alterations of its regulatory arrangements, then the LSB must deal with such application in accordance with paragraphs 21–27 of that Schedule. Paragraph 25 provides:

(3) The Board may refuse the application only if it is satisfied that—
    (a) granting the application would be prejudicial to the regulatory objectives,
    (b) granting the application would be contrary to any provision made by or by virtue of this Act or any other enactment or would result in any of the designation requirements ceasing to be satisfied in relation to the approved regulator,
    (c) granting the application would be contrary to the public interest ...

...

17. Ms Rose advances three principal submissions. The first is that QASA is unlawful in particular because the cumulative effect of ten particular elements of the scheme is to undermine the independence of advocates by exposing them to pressures which will tend to deter them from representing their clients effectively. The second is that the LSB failed properly to consider whether QASA would expose the advocate to such pressures. The third is that it misdirected itself in only considering whether QASA would *actually* undermine the independence of the advocate: it should also have considered whether it would give rise to a *perceived* threat to the independence of the advocate.

...

18. Ms Rose makes it clear that the vice in QASA is not in judicial evaluation per se, but in the cumulative effect of ten particular elements of the scheme. These elements are: (i) the scheme is to operate in the context of criminal trials, in which the importance of the independence of (particularly) the defence advocate from pressure applied by the judge is at its highest; (ii) if the advocate fails the assessment, he or she will be prohibited from practising criminal advocacy either at all or at the selected level; (iii) advocates are required to be assessed in the first two (or three) consecutive trials undertaken at their selected level; (iv) only two or, at most, three assessments are undertaken, giving very great significance to and increasing the pressure of each individual assessment; (v) assessments by a single judge may be sufficient to lead to a finding that the advocate is incompetent to practise; (vi) the assessment is conducted against very detailed performance indicators, many of which are highly subjective, and thereby increase the risk of inconsistent or unfair assessment; (vii) some of the matters against which the judge is required to assess the advocate depend on the judge's perception or inference of matters which are privileged or outside the knowledge of the judge; (viii) advocates are required to notify the judge of their requirement for assessment *before* the trial commences; (ix) advocates are not required to inform their client that they are being assessed, nor even that they have been assessed as incompetent in defending their client; and (x) non-disclosure of the assessment appears to be an essential feature of the scheme: if an advocate were required to inform his or her client of the assessment in advance, a significant number of

clients, if properly advised, would be likely to object to being represented by that advocate.

19. Before we consider the ten elements on which Ms Rose relies, we should make some preliminary observations. First, assessing whether a scheme is compatible with the regulatory objectives and whether it is most appropriate for meeting those objectives calls for an exercise of judgment on the part of the LSB. This is not a hard-edged question. The regulatory objectives are not tightly defined. That is not surprising since, despite their fundamental importance, they are broad and to some extent aspirational objectives. That is evident from the language of section 1(1) viz '(a) *protecting and promoting* the public interest; (b) *supporting* the constitutional principle of the rule of law; (c) *improving* access to justice; (d) *protecting and promoting* the interests of the consumer; *promoting* competition...; (f) *encouraging* an independent...legal profession; (g) *increasing* public understanding of the citizen's legal rights and duties; (h) *promoting and maintaining* adherence to the professional principles' (emphasis added). Moreover, whether these aspirations are achieved by a scheme is a question for the LSB and not the court. Section 3(2)(b) requires the LSB to act in a way which *it* considers most appropriate for the purpose of meeting the regulatory objectives. Section 3(3)(a) requires it to have regard to the principles under which regulatory activities should be 'transparent, accountable, proportionate, consistent and targeted only at cases in which action is needed'.

20. Secondly, the independence of the advocate is clearly an important relevant consideration. But it is not the only one. The 'regulatory objectives' include 'protecting and promoting the public interest', and promoting and maintaining adherence to professional principles, which include 'that authorised persons should maintain proper standards of work'. It is in the public interest that criminal advocates should not only be independent, but also that they should be competent. Lord Hobhouse said in *Medcalf* that it was fundamental to a just and fair judicial system that there be available to a litigant 'competent and independent legal representation'. Competence is no less important than independence. The LSB is required to act in a way which is compatible with *all* of the regulatory objectives and which it considers most appropriate for the purpose of meeting *all* of the objectives. The very diverse character of the objectives may require a weighing exercise to be undertaken. As the Divisional Court said at para 56 of its judgment, the Act does not establish an order of priorities between the regulatory objectives, nor between the professional principles. For the most part they will be in harmony with each other, but where they are not, the regulators have to carry out a balancing exercise between them.

...

31. But the issue is not whether QASA undermines the independence of the advocate, but whether the LSB acted in breach of its statutory duty in relation to the question of the independence of the advocate. This is an important distinction to which we have already drawn attention. The statutory obligation of the LSB is more nuanced and complex than merely to consider whether the scheme is

likely to undermine the independence of the advocate. First, the obligation is not an unqualified obligation to safeguard or not to undermine the independence of the advocate. Rather, it is 'so far as is reasonably practicable' to act in a way which is compatible with the regulatory objectives and which it considers most appropriate for the purpose of meeting those objectives. It has to be satisfied that granting the application will not be prejudicial to the regulatory objectives which include not only encouraging 'an independent, strong, diverse and effective legal profession', but all the other objectives. These include protecting and promoting the public interest, supporting the constitutional principle of the rule of law, improving access to justice, protecting and promoting the interests of consumers as well as promoting and maintaining adherence to the 'professional principles'.

Q3.30 Can the LSB and the approved regulators achieve all the regulatory objectives?

Q3.31 Based on this extract are regulators supposed to (i) balance regulatory objectives, (ii) prioritise some over others or (iii) apply regulatory objectives as the context requires?

Q3.32 In your opinion is QASA a threat to the rule of law or does it strengthen it by improving the competence of advocates?

Conclusion

The regulation of the legal profession has developed from supervision by courts (forum controls) to self-regulation by largely independent legal professions. In the last thirty years the state has significantly reined in self-regulation, culminating in the LSA. This introduced changes in regulatory structure by the creation of a LSB and the separation of the regulatory and representative functions of professional bodies.

The LSA opened the way for ABS to operate in the legal services market. ABS employ lawyers to conduct reserved legal work and to supervise delivery of other legal services by non-lawyers. Existing regulators became regulators of ABS, leading to significant changes in regulatory practice. The SRA recognised that to regulate ABS, it would have to find a way of regulating personnel within the organisations who were not regulated as 'approved persons'. These others might include non-lawyer managers, lawyers belonging to other professions and non-qualified employees.

The decision to regulate both ABS and individual practitioners with a single rule-book had a knock-on impact on the form of regulation. The adoption of a method of regulation called outcomes-focused regulation introduced high-level principles and outcomes that had to be observed. Taken together, changes in the regulation of lawyers represent a significant change in attitudes towards professions and traditional forms of regulation. They may even represent significant steps towards the regulation of the legal services market by a state bureaucracy.

Part II

Clients

4

The Relationship

Introduction

The relationship between lawyers and clients is the primary focus of professional ethics. The duties owed to clients are both broad and deep. The most basic obligation that the lawyer owes his or her client is competent delivery of the required service. Clients typically have little idea about how well their lawyer conducts their matter. There are potentially several dimensions to competent performance. The main component is technical expertise in law and procedure.

Another component in the relationship between lawyers and clients is the quality of service. The growth of the consumerist society has made client experience an increasingly important aspect of the service delivered. A good 'interpersonal experience' may, however, serve to obscure poor technical competence. It is debatable, however, whether the level of service provided by lawyers is an ethical issue.

Focus on competence and service often tends to cloud more fundamental questions. One of these relates to decision-making in the lawyer–client relationship. At the most basic level, the question is: 'Who is in charge?' If the client wants the lawyer to do something the lawyer considers immoral, must the lawyer comply? These questions raise issues about how lawyers reconcile their wider duties, to third parties and to the system of justice, with obligations to clients.

Foundations of the Lawyer–Client Relationship

Legal Basis

The lawyer–client relationship reflects aspects of agency, contract and trust. In a contractual relationship a client gets the service agreed upon. An agency relationship is one in which the agent is given a task and then carries it out in the way they think best. The trust relationship is sometimes imposed when a party in a vulnerable position vests confidence and reliance in another party, who is then held to what are called fiduciary obligations.

Fiduciary obligations arise in different kinds of situations, usually where a person holds money or property for the benefit of another. A party can be vulnerable, however, simply because of a lack of understanding about a situation. In economics this is sometimes described as a situation of 'information asymmetry', where one party to a transaction knows much more than the other. This can lead to a situation of market failure. This is an appropriate circumstance for regulatory intervention.

The traditional solution to information asymmetry between lawyers and clients is to treat the relationship, or aspects of it, as fiduciary. This imposes an exacting standard of behaviour on the party in the trustee role to act only for the other party's benefit. What is less clear is whether, and if so how, the same high standard applies equally to aspects of the relationship not involving money or property.

It seems fair to conclude that the basic relationship between lawyer and client is usually seen as contractual, but once employed the lawyer has a broad scope of action and discretion about how to do the job, much like an agent. The courts have also imposed fiduciary obligations on lawyers, meaning that they must act solely in the interests of another party. This gives rise to a fiduciary obligation on the part of the person in a situation of trust. Different legal professions emphasise different aspects of the relationship with clients.

> **Homepage of the website of Law Society of New South Wales, Australia**
> **Solicitors' Duties to Clients**
>
> In our legal system, the solicitor–client relationship has long been recognised as a fiduciary relationship. The term 'fiduciary' means trust, so in a fiduciary relationship one person (the client) places his or her confidence, good faith, reliance and trust in another (the solicitor), whose advice is sought in some matter.

What are the duties?

A fiduciary relationship creates many legal duties for the person in whom the trust has been placed. Generally this person must act in the best interests of the other. In relation to their clients, solicitors must:

- act honestly and fairly in a client's best interests
- act with due skill and diligence, reasonable promptness and courtesy
- maintain a client's confidences
- avoid conflicts of interest
- communicate effectively and promptly with clients
- follow a client's lawful instructions.

(www.lawsociety.com.au/community/thelawyerclientrelationship/
Solicitorsdutiestoclients/index.htm)

The prelude to Chapter 1 of the SRA Code of Conduct: Client Care, states 'Your relationship with your *client* is a contractual one which carries with it legal, as well as conduct, obligations. This chapter focuses on your obligations in conduct.'

In England and Wales, the relationship between lawyers and clients has been considered by the courts, but without a conclusive conclusion as to its legal basis. In *Hilton v Barker Booth & Eastwood*[1] the House of Lords held that a solicitor's duty to the client was 'primarily contractual' but it was also a fiduciary relationship. The fiduciary relationship could be 'moulded and informed' by the terms of the contract but its fundamental basis could not be modified.

The Lawyer's Obligations

Before looking in more detail at the nature of the lawyer–client relationship as represented in codes of conduct, it is necessary to explore the underlying requirements. The main aspects are loyalty, competence, diligence and service.

Loyalty

Loyalty is the fundamental requirement of a lawyer's obligations to his or her clients. It underpins the duty to maintain client confidences and not to allow

---

[1] *Hilton v Barker Booth & Eastwood* [2005] 1 All ER 651, particularly paras 28 and 38.

conflicts of interest, both of which are dealt with in succeeding chapters. A solicitor's obligation to make full disclosure of all matters known to him/her that are relevant to the client's interest, and the duty to respect the client's confidences, can be seen as an example of loyalty. What constitutes loyalty in the context of the lawyer–client relationship is the subject of much of the remainder of this chapter.

Competence

Competence, in simple terms, means the ability to perform a task or do a job properly. It can also mean someone who is qualified to do so. It is a term that is particularly relevant in legal education, which has become focused on the elements, skills and knowledge contributing to the capacity to practice. Professionals are usually subject to rules requiring that they undergo continuing professional development once in practice. This often requires either completing a given number of hours of lectures, or completing a record of education and training. The grant of practising certificates is often made subject to demonstrating completion of the requirements.

Legal practice has, in most legal sectors, moved towards increasing specialisation. It has for some time be mooted that it would be a more efficient use of time spent in education and training if the period to basic qualification were shorter, but that additional training were required to undertake certain activities. An example of this is the higher rights of audience regime for solicitors. On qualification solicitors can undertake advocacy in lower courts, but they require additional certification to appear as advocates in higher courts.

The Quality Assurance Scheme for Advocates applies a similar principle to those wishing to undertake criminal advocacy. In order to move from basic advocacy in the lower courts, criminal advocates must undergo training and, ultimately, assessment by a judge. The Legal Education and Training Review was expected to recommend an extension of the post-qualification specialisation regime, but its proposals in this respect were modest.

One of the basic problems in the market for legal services is that clients cannot assess the quality of performance of their lawyers. This is the underlying rationale of professionalism, which subjects lawyers to an obligation of trust in relation to clients. It is unclear how far trust is justified. One piece of research that sought to explore the relationship between competence and service looked at 'quality and cost' assessments. This explored a method of evaluating the delivery of legal aid services under the government's contracting regime.[2]

The quality and cost research found that peer review of the quality of casework did not necessarily equate with the results of client satisfaction sur-

---

[2] R Moorhead, A Sherr and A Paterson, 'What Clients Know: Client Perspectives and Legal Competence' (2003) 10(1) *International Journal of the Legal Profession* 5.

veys. However, the discrepancy was apparently greater when lawyers were, unknowingly, faced with model clients. These presented fake problems and recounted in detail the advice they received for analysis by peer reviewers. This methodology recorded relatively high levels of satisfaction for model clients.

The model clients in the quality and cost research were relatively happy with the lawyers they saw. For example, over 80 per cent of advisers were said to have given adequate time to the interview and to have understood the client's problem. Peer review of the advice given by lawyers in interview, and their follow-up, revealed that poor-quality advice, either inaccurate or incomplete, was given in 16 out of 40 client interviews. In one scenario advisers failed to ask to see a credit agreement that was central to the problem presented. In another, only 'touchy feely' advice, devoid of necessary legal content, was provided.

Codes of conduct often make specific reference to competence. The Bar core duties, for example, provide that barristers must provide a competent standard of work and service to each client.[3] They may also include requirements that professionals do not take on matters that they do not have the time, capacity or skill to handle.[4]

Diligence

Diligence means giving a client's matter the skill and the level of care and attention that ensures that their rights are protected and their aims achieved or advanced. It conveys a sense of conscientiousness, thoroughness and rigour. To say that diligence is central to the lawyer–client relationship underlines the fact that loyalty does not just involve a capacity to perform. It requires a capacity to perform well. There are various examples of the application of diligence in the lawyer–client relationship.

Although the term diligence was briefly used in earlier editions of the solicitors' code and the code of the American Bar Association, it is not commonly used to describe the lawyer's duty. It is, however, implicitly reflected in specific parts of the codes. The Bar code provides that barristers must not accept instructions to undertake any task for which they do not have enough time to prepare or which they cannot discharge in the time requested, or in any event within a reasonable time.[5] Excessive delay can be a cause of complaint and of disciplinary action.

---

[3] Bar Standards Board, *The BSB Handbook 2014: Code of Conduct*, CD 7.
[4] Ibid, r 4.4R(1) and (2).
[5] Ibid, r 4.4R(3) and (4).

Service

In economics, a service is an intangible and exhaustible benefit delivered to a consumer. In retailing, service refers to the quality of the interaction with customers. It refers to the suitability of methods of delivery, focusing on issues such as convenience and comfort. It may embrace issues such as the attentiveness, politeness and helpfulness of staff. Attention to the service dimension of professional work has increased with the growth of consumerism in society.

The idea that solicitors should be concerned with the service they provide began to gain prominence in the 1990s with the introduction of the idea of 'client care'. One of the motives behind the idea was reducing the level of complaints about solicitors. The client care regime specified that solicitors had to have in place internal complaint procedures. It also required that clients be given information about using these procedures and the costs involved.

The idea of service now permeates the solicitors' code of conduct. For example, the SRA Principles state that: 'you must ... provide a proper standard of service to your *clients*'[6] and 'protect *client* money and *assets*'.[7] The first section of the SRA Code of Conduct is entitled 'You and Your Client'. The first chapter, the only chapter dealing with the nature of relationships with clients, is called 'Client Care'.

SRA Code of Conduct 2014 (Version 13) Chapter 1: Client Care

This chapter is about providing a proper standard of service, which takes into account the individual needs and circumstances of each *client*. This includes providing *clients* with the information they need to make informed decisions about the services they need, how these will be delivered and how much they will cost. This will enable you and your *client* to understand each other's expectations and responsibilities. This chapter is also about ensuring that if *clients* are not happy with the service they have received they know how to make a *complaint* and that all *complaints* are dealt with promptly and fairly.

Outcomes

You must achieve these outcomes:

O(1.1)   you treat your clients fairly;
O(1.2)   you provide services to your clients in a manner which protects their interests in their matter, subject to the proper administration of justice;
...
O(1.4)   you have the resources, skills and procedures to carry out your clients' instructions;

---

[6] Solicitors Regulation Authority, *SRA Code of Conduct*, Principle 5.
[7] Solicitors Regulation Authority, *SRA Code of Conduct*, Principle 10.

...

O(1.5) the service you provide to clients is competent, delivered in a timely manner and takes account of your clients' needs and circumstances;

...

O(1.10) clients are informed in writing, both at the time of engagement and at the conclusion of your complaints procedure, of their right to complain to the Legal Ombudsman, the time frame for doing so and full details of how to contact the Legal Ombudsman;

...

O(1.12) clients are in a position to make informed decisions about the services they need, how their matter will be handled and the options available to them;

...

O(1.16) you inform current clients if you discover any act or omission which could give rise to a claim by them against you.

These outcomes can be compared with various relevant measures of quality revealed by the research into clients' reactions to their lawyers referred to earlier.[8] These include:

- the extent to which clients are satisfied with the overall handling of the case;
- promptness;
- interest in the client's problem, and whether they were listened to;
- understanding and remembering the facts of a case;
- honesty;
- willingness to explain matters and keep the client informed;
- attentiveness;
- explaining the necessary legal steps;
- predicting how long the case would take;
- a reluctance to give home visits;
- the use of multiple advisers and, where they are used, the failure to advise clients properly on their use;
- the handling of complaints;
- confidence in advocacy and negotiations and robust advice.

Q4.1 To what extent do the SRA Code provisions relating to clients reflect the issues that apparently concern clients?

---

[8] Moorhead, Sherr and Paterson (n 2).

Theory of the Lawyer–Client Relationship

The Standard Conception of the Lawyer's Role

As outlined in chapter one, a lawyer's obligations are defined by the institutions of the legal system in a liberal and democratic state. The rationale for such a state is to promote the welfare and autonomy of citizens. The governing principle of this effort is the rule of law. The operation of the rule of law takes different forms. In the Anglo-American tradition it takes the form of an adversarial system. This sets the tone of the relationship between lawyers and their clients.

Analysis of the rules of the US legal profession has led scholars to conclude that these institutions give rise to a standard conception of the lawyer's role. Two overarching principles, ie neutrality and partisanship, define the performance of this role; these are central both to the issue of who lawyers should accept as clients and what they are entitled to do on their behalf.

The Principle of Neutrality

Observance of the principle of neutrality requires that lawyers adopt a detached stance in relation to the morality of their client and their client's case. The lawyer's role is to advance that case whatever view he or she may have of it, even if he or she finds the client or case morally repugnant. The justification for this 'standard conception' of the lawyer's role is that it reinforces the notion of equality before the law, itself a social good, particularly in a society of pluralistic values.

Another aspect of neutrality is common to many professions, and probably supports neutrality in client selection. It is the idea that professional people should be emotionally detached from their clients. If they are too involved, the fear is that, when analysing their client's case, they will not see the whole picture objectively. They will therefore be unable to offer wise advice.

The Principle of Partisanship

The obligation of partisanship was mainly based on a provision in the American Bar Association model rules. This required that attorneys act 'zealously, within the bounds of the law'[9] and to 'not intentionally fail to seek the lawful

---

[9] American Bar Association, *Model Code of Professional Responsibility* (1969) Canon 7.

objectives' of clients.[10] This was assumed to require lawyers to pursue the legal but immoral objectives of their clients.

The Principle of Non-Accountability

The third pillar of the standard conception is the principle of non-accountability. This principle operates to ensure that lawyers following the dictates of their role are not morally responsible for the consequences. These consequences could obviously be serious, for example if a lawyer successfully represents someone he or she suspects of being a murderer and the acquitted defendant subsequently commits a murder.

Thomas Erskine and Henry Brougham are often quoted as examples of the origin and implications of the standard conception. Which of these quotations is a defence of neutrality and which is a defence of partisanship?

I will forever, at all hazards, assert the dignity, independence, and integrity of the English bar, without which impartial justice, the most valuable part of the English constitution, can have no existence. From the moment that any advocate can be permitted to say that he will or will not stand between the Crown and the subject arraigned in the court where he daily sits to practice, from that moment the liberties of England are at an end. If the advocate refuses to defend from what he may think of the charge or of the defence, he assumes the character of the judge; nay, he assumes it before the hour of judgment; and in proportion to his rank and reputation, puts the heavy influence of perhaps a mistaken opinion into the scale against the accused, in whose favour the benevolent principle of English law makes all presumptions, and which commands the very judge to be his counsel.[11] (Thomas Erskine)

An advocate, in the discharge of his duty, knows but one person in all the world, and that person is his client. To save that client by all means, and expedients, and at all hazards and costs to other persons, and among them, to himself, is his first and only duty; and in performing this duty he must not regard the alarm, the torments, the destruction which he may bring upon others. Separating the duty of a patriot from that of an advocate, he must go on reckless of consequences, though it should be his unhappy fate to involve his country in confusion.[12] (Henry Brougham)

---

[10] Ibid, Disciplinary Rule 7-101(A)(1).

[11] J Hostettler, *Thomas Erskine and Trial by Jury* (Hook, Waterside Press, 2010) 93.

[12] *Trial of Queen Caroline* (ed J Nightingale (1821)) quoted in ME Frankel, 'The Search for Truth: An Umpireal View' (1975) 123 *University of Pennsylvania Law Review* 1031, 1036; and GC Hazard, 'The Future of Legal Ethics' (1991) 100 *Yale Law Journal* 1239, 1239.

> Q4.2   In what ways are the views expressed in these quotations consistent with the rule of law based on formal legality?

Formation of the Lawyer–Client Relationship

The main manifestation of neutrality in the lawyer–client relationship relates to client selection. Observance of the neutrality principle would mean that the lawyer must not judge either the client personally or the moral nature of his/her cause. Putting into operation the philosophy of the rule of law requires that every citizen with a legal problem has a right to a champion. This is a hotly contested notion. Many academics argue that lawyers should not be obliged to represent causes they do not agree with.[13]

It is argued that ethical neutrality is the correct disposition for lawyers in modern, diverse, competitive societies because neutrality facilitates pluralism.[14] Neutrality needs to underpin institutions as well as the practices and procedures for selecting officials, judges and governments. The habit of neutrality is also essential in maintaining an appropriate professional relationship with clients. Maintaining a scrupulous professional detachment enables lawyers to also observe their wider duties.

Abrogating neutrality weakens the justification for partisanship. If all people are not entitled to partisan advice, why should a few people have that right? The logic of a system based on formal legality and a society of plural values is that all citizens should have representation in principle, even if their cause is not one that a particular lawyer approves of. Lawyers must be both neutral and partisan if society is to derive the political benefit that resolving disputes through the legal system offers.[15]

Two Fictional Examples of Lawyers, Clients and Neutrality

Harper Lee's novel *To Kill a Mockingbird* is set in Alabama in the 1930s. In a deeply racist community a white lawyer, Atticus Finch, is assigned to defend Tom Robinson, a black man accused of rape. During the course of

---

[13] A Hutchinson, 'Taking it Personally: Legal Ethics and Client Selection' (1998) 1(2) *Legal Ethics* 168

[14] T Dare, 'Mere Zeal, Hyper-Zeal and the Ethical Obligations of Lawyers' (2004) 7(1) *Legal Ethics* 24.

[15] D Markovits, *A Modern Legal Ethics: Adversary Advocacy in a Democratic Age* (Princeton, NJ, Princeton University Press, 2009).

the trial Atticus and his family are subjected to intimidation, but he calmly sticks to his task and does his best for his client. Atticus proves that his client could not have committed the crime but Robinson is still convicted. Atticus was voted the greatest film hero by the American Film Institute in 2003, but Monroe Freedman argues that he should not be seen as a role model. 'He is not the admirable figure he is made out to be: appointed counsel to an unpopular defendant, Atticus admits that he had hoped "to get through life without a case of this kind" (p 98). He excuses the leader of a lynch mob as "basically a good man" who "just has his blind spots along with the rest of us" (p 173). He sees that "one of these days we're going to pay the bill" for racism, but hopes that payment, and so justice for black people, will not come during his children's life times (pp. 243–44).'[16]

In his book *Lawyers and Justice: An Ethical Study* David Luban argues that 'nothing permits a lawyer to discard her discretion or relieves her of the necessity of asking whether a client's project is worthy of a decent person's service'. He illustrates this proposition with a tale of Abraham Lincoln, who practised law in Springfield in the nineteenth century. Lincoln, having heard a client describe to him a morally dubious claim, is said to have advised the client:

> Yes, we can doubtless gain your case for you; we can set a whole neighborhood at loggerheads; we can distress a widowed mother and her six fatherless children and thereby get you six hundred dollars to which you seem to have a legal claim, but which rightfully belongs, it appears to me, as much to the woman and her children as it does to you. You must remember that some things legally right are not morally right. We shall not take your case, but will give you a little advice for which we will charge you nothing. You seem to be a sprightly, energetic man; we would advise you to try your hand at making six hundred dollars in some other way.[17]

Q4.3   To what extent does *To Kill a Mockingbird* illustrate the standard conception of the lawyer's role and the principle of neutrality in client selection?

Q4.4   Does *To Kill a Mockingbird* show that upholding the lawyer's duty to the rule of law cannot be left to anti-discrimination measures covering client selection?

Q4.5   Does Lincoln act consistently with the lawyers' role as defined under the rule of law?

---

[16] T Dare, 'Lawyers, Ethics and To Kill a Mockingbird' (2001) 25(1) *Philosophy and Literature* 127.

[17] D Luban, *Lawyers and Justice: An Ethical Study* (Princeton, NJ, Princeton University Press, 1988) 174.

> Q4.6 Does Lincoln act consistently with the standard conception of the lawyers' role?
>
> Q4.7 Do you agree or disagree with Lincoln's position?

Neutrality in the Codes

Barristers

Operation of the principle of neutrality is most clearly demonstrated in the 'cab-rank rule' of English barristers. Under this rule, barristers must accept any brief or instructions in any field in which they profess to practice. This goes beyond an obligation not to discriminate. It is specifically focused on the situation where a client has done something so morally outrageous that popular opinion is roused against them.

BSB Code of Conduct 2014

Core Duty: You must not discriminate unlawfully against any person [CD8].

Chapter 3: You and Your Client

The 'cab-rank' rule

rC29 If you receive instructions from a professional client, and you are:

.1 a self-employed barrister instructed by a professional client;

and the instructions are appropriate taking into account the experience, seniority and/or field of practice of yourself or (as appropriate) of the named authorised individual you must, subject to Rule C30 below, accept the instructions addressed specifically to you, irrespective of:

> .a the identity of the client;
> .b the nature of the case to which the instructions relate;
> .c whether the client is paying privately or is publicly funded; and
> .d any belief or opinion which you may have formed as to the character, reputation, cause, conduct, guilt or innocence of the client.

rC30 The cab rank Rule C29 does not apply if:

.1 you are required to refuse to accept the instructions pursuant to Rule C21; or
.2 accepting the instructions would require you or the named authorised individual to do something other than in the course of their ordinary working time or to cancel a commitment already in their diary; or
.3 the potential liability for professional negligence in respect of the particular matter could exceed the level of professional indemnity insurance which is reasonably available and likely to be available in the market for you to accept; or

---

.4 you are a Queen's Counsel, and the acceptance of the instructions would require you to act without a junior in circumstances where you reasonably consider that the interests of the client require that a junior should also be instructed; or

.5 accepting the instructions would require you to do any foreign work; or

.6 accepting the instructions would require you to act for a foreign lawyer (other than a European lawyer, a lawyer from a country that is a member of EFTA, a solicitor or barrister of Northern Ireland or a solicitor or advocate under the law of Scotland); or

.7 the professional client:

   .a is not accepting liability for your fees; or

   .b is named on the List of Defaulting Solicitors; or

   .c is instructing you as a lay client and not in their capacity as a professional client; or

.8 you have not been offered a proper fee for your services (except that you shall not be entitled to refuse to accept instructions on this ground if you have not made or responded to any fee proposal within a reasonable time after receiving the instructions); or

.9 except where you are to be paid directly by (i) the Legal Aid Agency as part of the Community Legal Service or the Criminal Defence Service or (ii) the Crown Prosecution Service:

   .a your fees have not been agreed (except that you shall not be entitled to refuse to accept instructions on this ground if you have not taken reasonable steps to agree fees within a reasonable time after receiving the instructions);

   .b having required your fees to be paid before you accept the instructions, those fees have not been paid;

   .c accepting the instructions would require you to act other than on (A) the Standard Contractual Terms for the Supply of Legal Services by Barristers to Authorised Persons 2012 as published on the Bar Council's website; or (B) if you publish standard terms of work, on those standard terms of work.

Q4.8   Are the exceptions to the cab rank rule justified?

Q4.9   Given the exceptions, is the rule worth retaining?

The neutrality principle may be seen to be particularly important in the case of the Bar. The ready availability of dispassionate advice and advocacy is part of the fundamental rationale of the split profession supporting an independent bar. It has been criticised as outdated in research funded by the Legal Services Board (LSB).[18] The LSB consultants argued that the rule dated from a time when lawyers' moral accountability for the actions of clients was more

---

[18] J Flood and M Hvvid, 'The Cab Rank Rule: Its Meaning and Purpose in the New Legal Services Market', https://research.legalservicesboard.org.uk/wp-content/media/Cab-Rank-Rule_final-2013.pdf.

significant. Nowadays, they said, the cult of celebrity may have increased the publicity value of 'immoral clients' removing the need for any rule.

In their report the LSB consultants criticised the large number of exceptions to cab rank rule. These currently number nine, including a right to refuse on the grounds of lack of competence or when a proper fee is not offered.[19] The LSB consultants also said that there was no evidence that the cab rank rule is either meaningful or enforced. This was despite the fact that they had found a 2006 case in which a barrister was fined £1,000 for breach of the cab rank rule. He was a regional chairman of the Lawyer's Christian Fellowship who refused a brief to act for an immigrant who claimed asylum on the grounds of his homosexuality.

In a response to the consultants on behalf of the Bar Council Sir Sydney Kentridge pointed out that the absence of enforcement could be taken as evidence of compliance, rather than redundancy.[20] A response by three barristers commissioned by the BSB focused on a large number of errors and misconceptions in the consultants' report.[21]

Solicitors

English solicitors are not explicitly subject to any obligation of neutrality in client selection. They must not discriminate unlawfully in deciding whether to act for clients.[22] It is sometimes reported that solicitors feel that they should accept cases from unpopular clients or from clients with whom they disagree on a moral issue connected with representation. There are also examples of solicitors either refusing clients because they do not like what they represent or refusing clients in a particular kind of matter.

An example of refusal to represent an individual arose when the head of a noted civil rights solicitors' firm said that he would refuse to represent General Pinochet, a former South American dictator accused of human rights abuses.[23] The refusal to represent a defendant on a point of principle is illustrated by criminal defence firms who claim a policy of not defending men on rape charges who want to raise the defence of consent.

---

[19] BSB Rules of Conduct, rC30.

[20] S Kentridge, *The Cab Rank Rule: A Response to the Report Commissioned by the Legal Services Board*, http://live.barcouncil.netxtra.net/media/203452/sir_sydney_kentridge_crr_response.pdf, 12.

[21] M Mclaren, C Ulyatt and C Knowles, *The 'Cab Rank Rule': A Fresh View*, https://www.barstandardsboard.org.uk/media/1460590/bsb_cab_rank_rule_paper_28_2_13_v6__final_.pdf.

[22] Solicitors Regulation Authority, *SRA Code of Conduct 2011*, Indicative Behaviour 2.5, http://www.sra.org.uk/solicitors/handbook/code/content.page (accessed 5 December 2012).

[23] A Boon, 'Cause Lawyers in a Cold Climate' in S Sheingold and A Sarat (eds), *Cause Lawyering and the State in a Global Era* (Oxford, Oxford University Press, 2001) 143.

SRA Code of Conduct 2011 (as amended)

Chapter 2: Equality and Diversity

You must achieve these outcomes:

O(2.1) you do not discriminate unlawfully, or victimise or harass anyone, in the course of your professional dealings

Acting in the following way(s) may tend to show that you have not achieved these outcomes and therefore not complied with the Principles:

IB(2.4) being subject to any decision of a court or tribunal of the UK, that you have committed, or are to be treated as having committed, an unlawful act of discrimination;

IB(2.5) discriminating unlawfully when accepting or refusing instructions to act for a client.

Q4.10   In what way is non-discrimination different from neutrality in client selection, as exemplified in the cab-rank rule?

Q4.11   Should barristers abandon the cab rank principle, should solicitors adopt neutrality in client selection or should the present arrangement be preserved?

Q4.12   Draft a rule of conduct expressing what you would consider to be an appropriate representation of a solicitors' obligation to neutrality in client selection.

Q4.13   What kinds of defendant may not get the solicitors of their choice? Does it matter?

Q4.14   What are the arguments for and against solicitors observing a cab-rank rule?

The Nature of the Lawyer–Client Relationship

Models of Professional Relationship

Models of the professional relationship can be placed on a spectrum reflecting the degree of client autonomy they allow and promote. The lowest level of client autonomy is found in the paternalistic model. This is consistent with the assumptions of professionalism and a traditional approach to the professional relationship. Paternalism assumes that lawyers determine client needs and how to meet them. A participatory model arguably represents a more modern approach. It assumes that lawyers and clients work out ends, and possibly means, together and that key decisions are based on lawyers' advice.

A further step away from paternalism is represented by a model aimed at promoting client autonomy. Under this model the lawyer becomes a means of promoting the client's idea of his own good. It envisages that the lawyer will implement the client's moral choices. Finally, there is a model of the lawyer–client relationship that promotes client empowerment. This envisages that lawyers enable clients to use the law to their own ends, carrying out for themselves actions usually performed by lawyers. This enables clients to make their own moral choices

None of these models is expressly sanctioned by the legal professions and it is unclear whether one consistently operates in practice. When the professions revamped their professional courses in the 1990s the participatory model was promoted in most curricula. Codes of conduct tend not to refer to the nature of the lawyer–client relationship. They may deal with it obliquely by indicating what it is the lawyer's obligation to do for clients or, perhaps, how they are to do it.

Q4.15 Which model of the lawyer–client relationship is reflected in the extract earlier in this chapter in which Abraham Lincoln advises his client?

Q4.16 What is likely to happen within each of the models if the client suggests to their lawyer that they have a purpose in seeking advice that the lawyer considers immoral but which is not illegal.

Consider extracts from the US and English professional codes.

American Bar Association Model Rules of Professional Conduct 1983 (as amended)

Rule 1.3: Diligence

Client–Lawyer Relationship

Rule 1.3 Diligence

A lawyer shall act with reasonable diligence and promptness in representing a client.

Client–Lawyer Relationship

Rule 1.3 Diligence—Comment

[1] A lawyer should pursue a matter on behalf of a client despite opposition, obstruction or personal inconvenience to the lawyer, and take whatever lawful and ethical measures are required to vindicate a client's cause or endeavor. A lawyer must also act with commitment and dedication to the interests of the client and with zeal in advocacy upon the client's behalf. A lawyer is not bound, however, to press for every advantage that might be realized for a client. For example, a lawyer may have authority to exercise professional discretion in determining the means by which a matter should be pursued. See Rule 1.2. The lawyer's duty to act with reasonable diligence does not require the use of offensive tactics or preclude the treating of all persons involved in the legal process with courtesy and respect.

SRA Code of Conduct

Principle 4: act in the best interests of each client;

Principle 5: provide a proper standard of service to your clients;

Outcomes: O(1.2) you provide services to your clients in a manner which protects their interests in their matter, subject to the proper administration of justice;

…

O(1.12) clients are in a position to make informed decisions about the services they need, how their matter will be handled and the options available to them;

Indicative Behaviours: IB(1.1) agreeing an appropriate level of service with your client, for example the type and frequency of communications;

IB(1.2) explaining your responsibilities and those of the client;

…

IB(1.5) explaining any limitations or conditions on what you can do for the client, for example, because of the way the client's matter is funded;

Q4.17 Which code best describes what clients can expect from their lawyers by way of performance?

Q4.18 Which model of the lawyer–client relationship is reflected in these extracts from the codes?

Q4.19 Are these extracts relevant to the issue of who is in charge of decision-making in the lawyer–client relationship?

Partisanship

Interpreting the Obligation of Partisanship

An extreme view of the obligation of partisanship in criminal advocacy was advanced by Monroe Freedman. He argued that the best way to prevent the state from overpowering the liberty of subjects was for there to be an independent Bar, prepared to challenge government action as zealously and effectively as possible.[24] This, he argued, required defence advocates to discredit witnesses known to be telling the truth, allow their witnesses to give perjured testimony, and to advise clients in a way that enabled them to give perjured evidence.

Others argue that partisanship only gives permission for acts that are legal, but morally dubious, such as taking advantage of loopholes in the law, mistakes by the other side or grey areas in legal ethics.[25] Wendel argues that partisanship is not based on fidelity to clients, but on fidelity to law.[26] This means that lawyers' ethical duties are performed by providing that which clients are entitled to in law, rather than by delivering every advantage that the law allows. This view suggests that, like judges, lawyers have an underlying obligation to support the rule of law. This includes a responsibility not to exploit the indeterminacy of law.[27]

Dare argues that the obligation of partisanship only entitles clients to a level of commitment he calls 'mere zeal', rather than 'hyper zeal'.[28] Mere zeal, Dare suggests, is desirable, whereas hyper-zeal is to blame for the worst excesses of lawyer behaviour, such as those described by Freedman. The idea that the level of zeal of a lawyer might vary depending on circumstances has some appeal. Therefore, criminal defence might justify stronger partisanship, whereas in civil litigation it would be weaker. There is some empirical evidence of such variations. In family disputes, for example, the conventional wisdom is that lawyers should not inflame the situation or assert a case that is not legally defensible.

The idea of a varied obligation of partisanship in litigation raises the issue

---

[24] MH Freedman, 'Are There Public Interest Limits on Lawyers' Advocacy' (1977) *Journal of the Legal Profession* 47, 54.

[25] G Postema, 'Moral Responsibility in Professional Ethics' (1980) 55 *New York University Law Review* 63.

[26] WB Wendel, *Lawyers and Fidelity to Law* (Princeton, NJ and Oxford, Princeton University Press, 2010).

[27] Ibid, and BZ Tamanaha, *On the Rule of Law: History, Politics, Theory* (Cambridge, Cambridge University Press, 2004).

[28] Dare (n 14).

of what ethos is appropriate in transaction work. It is arguable that lawyers should be more co-operative and more aware of public interest considerations when acting for clients whose liberty is not at stake. Nevertheless, there is no suggestion in the codes of conduct of England and Wales that different levels of commitment apply.

The Representative Obligation

This section explores the extent of the lawyer's obligation of partisanship. It does so by considering whether there is an obligation or a permission, conferred by the role, or the codes of conduct, tó pursue a client's wishes with which the lawyer does not agree.

Partisanship in Law

The law recognises some obligation to pursue client wishes and legal rights, even where a lawyer does not think it fair or reasonable to do so.[29] Legal practice does recognise, after all, the idea that clients give their lawyers 'instructions' on the handling of their matters. This, of course, does not necessarily determine how the instructions are carried out. This may well depend on the circumstances of representation.

In the context of advocacy, it is well established that the lawyer owes a duty to the court which limits the partisan obligation of the lawyer to the client. This means that there are real, practical constraints on what the lawyers can do for their clients. This duty to the court is usually thought to be limited to a duty not to mislead, which is considered in more detail in chapter ten. Nevertheless, in *R v Farooqi*[30] Lord Judge CJ reserved a wide area of discretion and responsibility to the advocate:

> Something of a myth about the meaning of the client's 'instructions' has developed. As we have said, the client does not conduct the case. The advocate is not the client's mouthpiece, obliged to conduct the case in accordance with whatever the client, or when the advocate is a barrister, the solicitor 'instructs' him. In short, the advocate is bound to advance the defendant's case on the basis that what his client tells him is the truth, but save for well-established principles, like the personal responsibility of the defendant to enter his own plea, and to make his own decision whether to give evidence, and perhaps whether a witness who appears to be able to

---

[29] *Griffiths v Dawson* [1993] FL 315.
[30] *R v Farooqi* [2013] EWCA Crim 1649.

give relevant admissible evidence favourable to the defendant should or should not be called, the advocate, and the advocate alone remains responsible for the forensic decisions and strategy.

This dictum applies specifically to the conduct of advocates, but it is consistent with the views of many lawyers concerning their responsibilities in their relationships with clients. It is a paternalistic view, somewhat at odds with the notion that the law promotes the autonomy of the individual. It may grow less prevalent with increasing domination of the culture of consumerism.

Partisanship in the Codes of Lawyers

Historically, partisanship is most strongly represented in the ABA Model Rules of Conduct. Luban referred to the Model Rules as imposing an obligation to 'maximize the likelihood that the client's objectives will be attained'.[31] The Model Rules have been modified since the versions that gave rise to the standard conception. Nevertheless, the current ABA Model Code still provides that '[a] lawyer shall not intentionally fail to seek the lawful objectives of his client through reasonably available means permitted by law and the Disciplinary Rules'.[32]

The position under the ABA Model Rules contrasts with the position in England and Wales. The duty in both the solicitors' and barristers' codes is to act in a client's best interests. A rule in the Bar Code of Conduct evoking a sense of partisanship requires barristers to 'promote fearlessly and by all proper and lawful means the client's best interests'.[33] Otherwise, the Bar Code takes a fairly paternalistic line on defining the client's best interests.

Consistent with *R v Farooqi*, the Bar Code of Conduct warns barristers that they must not permit their professional client, employer or any other person to limit their discretion in deciding how a client's best interests are served.[34] It is not clear whether the reference to 'any other person' includes the client. Rule rC21.5 provides, however, that: 'You must not accept instructions to act in a particular matter if ... your instructions seek to limit your ordinary authority or discretion in the conduct of proceedings in court.' This probably excludes the client's input to decision-making, apart from on those limited grounds indicated in *R v Farooqi*.

The SRA Code of Conduct also states that they have a duty to act in their clients' best interests.[35] Apart from protecting these interests, the nearest any

---

[31] D Luban, 'Partnership, Betrayal and Autonomy in the Lawyer/Client Relationship' (1990) 90 *Columbia Law Review* 1004 and *Lawyers and Justice* (Princeton, NJ, Princeton University Press, 1998). See also chapter one: Roles and Values.

[32] ABA Model Rules 2007, above, DR 7-101(A)1.

[33] *Bar Code of Conduct 2014*, r C15(1).

[34] Ibid, r C15(4).

[35] Solicitors Regulation Authority, *SRA Code of Conduct 2011*, Principle 4.

outcome comes to an obligation of partisanship is Outcome 11.12. This provides that the outcome to be achieved is that 'clients are in a position to make informed decisions about the services they need, how their matter will be handled and the options available to them'. This is not inconsistent with partisanship, but does not require it. It is also quite consistent with paternalism.

The nature of the US and English obligations are different. Luban observes, that 'the American model is loyalty to the client's wishes and not his interests'.[36] The English obligation as expressed in the codes is consistent with the reverse.

Problem Question

A lawyer advises B that his claim is likely to fail and that a substantial order for costs may be made against him. B says that he feels so strongly about his matter that, as an issue of principle, he wants to pursue his claim, even if he becomes bankrupt in the process.

Q4.20 What would the lawyer's duty to his client be under: (a) the ABA Model Rules, and (b) the SRA Code of Conduct?

Q4.21 What considerations, if any, do you think the lawyer should take into account in considering whether to follow B's instructions?

Partisanship in Practice

Empirical research into the lawyer–client relationship suggests that clients with power who are 'repeat players' in the legal process exercise more control of the relationship than 'one-shotters', clients who only see a lawyer in a legal crisis. Evidence from practice suggests that lawyers often try to mediate their client's more extreme demands and, depending on the type of case, seek 'reasonable solutions' to their problems.[37]

In preparation for and during litigation, lawyers manage client expectations from the first meeting, often by emphasising that the client's perception of what would represent justice in their own circumstances is not necessarily the view that the law would take. This process of expectation management is usually considerably facilitated by warnings about the cost of testing the approach of the court on the issue in doubt. Lawyers typically, therefore, try

---

[36] D Luban, 'The Sources of Legal Ethics' (1984) 48 *Rabels Zeitschift* 262.

[37] S Macaulay, 'Lawyers and Consumer Protection Laws (1979) 14 *Law and Society Review* 115.

to encourage clients to adopt a 'realistic' view of their matter and promote a positive attitude towards compromise and settlement.

The Limits of Loyalty

One of the most serious issues in the professional ethics of lawyers is the limit of loyalty to clients. Lawyers cannot pursue client instructions that require illegal conduct by the lawyer or conduct specifically forbidden by professional rules. A good example is where the conduct requires action involving a breach of the duty not to mislead the court.

Despite the fact that lawyers cannot be involved in illegality there may be circumstances where, if they follow a particular course of action, justice may not be done. This raises a fundamental issue in relation to the ethical principle of client autonomy. Crudely expressed: who is in charge—the lawyer or the client? Or, if the relationship is more complex than such a question implies: who bears the moral responsibility for lawyers' actions on behalf of their clients?

Who's in Charge?

Under the standard conception of the lawyer's role the principle of non-accountability means that lawyers are not legally, professionally or morally accountable for the ends achieved. In theory, a lawyer should assist a client to achieve a purpose about which said lawyer would otherwise have moral qualms. Critics of the standard conception argue that it commits lawyers to pursuing their client's whims, and possibly their immoral ends. Such a conclusion is sometimes said to place a lawyer in the position of a 'hired gun' rather than that of an independent moral agent.

The representation of the client's case is usually a more complex interaction. It results from a kind of negotiation with the lawyer in which the client's interpretation of their facts and circumstances are filtered through the lawyer's technical lens. In this process, the lawyer is as dependent on the client's picture of their circumstances as the client is reliant on the lawyer's legal interpretation of them.

Even though, in reality, clients' immoral ends may be deflected by lawyers, there remains an issue about what happens when this does not occur. Once all the negotiation is done, who is ultimately in charge of decision-making? This is where the four main models of lawyer–client relationship, ie paternalism, participation, autonomy and empowerment, interact with ethical principles to define the limits of professional responsibility for client goals. There are a number of situations that may be thought to pose ethical problems for lawyers. The limits of legitimate action can be explored by looking at these situations.

Four Situations at the Ethical Margins

Representing the Guilty

One of the key challenges for professional ethics is explaining how lawyers can be allowed to represent parties they know are guilty or suspect of being guilty. The starting point is the rule of law. The rule of law decrees that parties are innocent until found guilty; in the meantime they are entitled to proper representation. The consequence of lawyers' ethical duties is that they must not deliberately mislead the court in presenting the case. Therefore, how can a lawyer represent a client they know or suspect to be guilty on a not-guilty plea? This question needs to be broken down before it can be answered.

i. Knowledge of Guilt

Representation of a client known to be guilty was dealt with explicitly in the Bar Written Standards for Professional Work, which, though superseded by the 2014 Code, are still relevant on most points. Barristers who have received an admission of guilt are entitled to advise a client to enter a plea of not guilty and to present the defence. They are told to:

> bear the following points clearly in mind:
>
> (a) that every punishable crime is a breach of common or statute law committed by a person of sound mind and understanding;
> (b) that the issue in a criminal trial is always whether the defendant is guilty of the offence charged, never whether he is innocent;
> (c) that the burden of proof rests on the prosecution.[38]

A confession of guilt from a client does not 'release the barrister from his imperative duty to do all that he honourably can for his client'.[39] It does, however, impose very strict limitations on the conduct of the defence. Having heard a confession, a barrister must not allow the court to gain the wrong impression of the grounds of the defence. This means that no alternative perpetrator can be implicated, or false evidence, such as an alibi, called. The barrister cannot,

---

[38] Bar Standards Board, *Written Standards for the Conduct of Professional Work*, para.12.1, https://www.barstandardsboard.org.uk/regulatory-requirements/the-old-code-of-conduct/written-standards-for-the-conduct-of-professional-work/.

[39] Ibid, para.12.2.

whether or not the defendant gives evidence, set up an affirmative case of innocence that is inconsistent with the confession made to him.[40]

Acting consistently with the obligation to do all that he honourably can do for the client, a barrister can object to the competence of the court, to the form of the indictment, to the admissibility of any evidence or to the evidence admitted. The defence barrister is also entitled to test the evidence given by individual witnesses and to argue that the evidence taken as a whole is insufficient to amount to proof that the defendant is guilty of the offence charged. The Written Standards pronounce that '[f]urther than this he ought not to go'.[41]

ii. Suspicion of Guilt

In circumstances where a lawyer suspects that a client is guilty the situation is more ambiguous. On the face of it, the lawyer is entitled to take the client at face value and not pre-judge the situation. In any such circumstances, however, a lawyer should point out inconsistencies in a client's proposed evidence. If a client insists that they are telling the truth, the lawyer arguably has an obligation to present that case and to explain or challenge any evidence that is inconsistent with the client's version.

If, under questioning, the client changes his/her account, the lawyer's suspicion may harden into a belief that the client is guilty. There may come a point where this is a certainty. It is arguable that a lawyer could not present the case in such circumstances without knowingly misleading the court. In most circumstances, this situation is unlikely to be reached. For the proper functioning of the justice system, in the absence of a confession, it is best if a lawyer is entitled to assume innocence, whatever the evidence stacked against his/her client.

iii. Summary

In summary, barristers can represent on a not-guilty plea by requiring that the prosecution proves that the defendant is guilty of the offence as charged. This neatly reconciles the duty of loyalty to clients with the obligation to the court. It illustrates how the Legal Services Act and the professional codes can claim a role for lawyers in the administration of justice. It is a relatively clear and well-established position that distinguishes lawyers, as professionals, from technicians who merely deliver the service clients pay for. Other situations may be less clear cut.

---

[40] Ibid, para.12.3.
[41] Ibid, para.12.5.

Advising on Illegality

A relatively common problem for lawyers arises where a client seeks advice on a situation where a proposed action may involve breaking the law. The client's purpose in seeking advice may be to better understand the risks and consequences of their proposed action, or to identify other ways of achieving the same thing. Can the lawyer give advice on the basis that nothing has happened yet? Should they refuse to advise, warn parties likely to be affected or counsel against any action?

Pepper gives, by way of illustration, two situations where clients may seek advice about breaking the law.[42] In one, a lawyer is asked about the legal consequences for someone who participates in consensual euthanasia where their parent is known to be terminally ill and in immense pain. Because assisting suicide is illegal, Pepper suggests, the lawyer should be cautious in advising. Two principles are uppermost. The first is that the proposed criminal conduct has consequences for third parties. The second is that lawyers should not provide advice which may assist in the commission of an offence.

The example of assisted suicide teases out several issues in counselling illegality. For example, the issue may not be presented in a way that suggests the client intends unilateral action. The client may, for example, appear to be seeking advice about the possibility of a court-sanctioned suicide. A further problem arises if the third-party element is taken away. If, say, the client is contemplating his own suicide, in circumstances where this would be illegal, the issue becomes one of the client's autonomy versus their intention to break the law. This tends to illustrate Pepper's conclusion. The variety of situations that can arise, and the different contexts in which they arise, make it difficult to formulate clear rules or guidelines.

Pepper's second example relates to a lawyer advising on drafting a contract. The client asks what the consequences would be if he breaks the contract in three years' time. In the scenario, the lawyer knows that the client will break the contract if the financial consequences are favourable. Pepper argues that in civil cases, such as contract or tort, breaches of the law are not prohibited, but merely invite financial sanctions. This view would be contested by many contract lawyers, but it is promoted by economic theories of law.[43] Pepper concludes that advice on the financial consequences of this kind of 'unlawful' conduct is ethical.

Pepper speculates that full legal advice on the financial consequences of breach of contract might include reference to matters that invite debate. He argues that the advice could refer to factors not constituting *legal* knowledge, for example the existence of court backlogs. These might encourage another

---

[42] SL Pepper, 'Counselling at the Limit of the Law: An Exercise in the Jurisprudence and Ethics of Lawyering' (1995) 104 *Yale Law Journal* 1545.
[43] Symposium (2005) 8 *Legal Ethics* 87.

contracting party to accept a lesser sum in damages than the claim is worth. It might be argued that it is bad public policy that lawyers encourage breach of contract on non-legal grounds. On the other hand, full advice would presumably include countervailing arguments, such as the damage to trust and reputation involved in an 'efficient' breach of contract.

Pepper suggests a number of principles that can be applied to situations where lawyers are asked to advise whether proposed actions are legal. The first consideration that lawyers should bear in mind, he argues, is that clients have a right to know the law. The second is that lawyers have a moral obligation to counsel clients, even when they suspect that the clients might try to circumvent the law. The third is that lawyers' legal assistance is bounded by law; lawyers should not help clients to break the law. They should consider a number of factors regarding the impact of the conduct to which the advice may give rise.

Pepper acknowledges that the kinds of distinctions involved in counselling clients who propose breaking the law potentially involve complex decision-making. The factors Pepper indicates might be relevant include:

- the distinction between criminal and civil law;
- conduct wrong in itself and conduct 'merely' prohibited;
- the extent to which the particular law is enforced;
- whether the query relates to procedural rules, substantive law or the enforcement of law (eg where a criminal client seeks information relating to police procedures which might be known to a lawyer);
- whether the information is in the public or private sphere;
- whether the lawyer or client initiated the discussion of the particular issue;
- the likelihood that the information will assist unlawful conduct.

Finally, Pepper argues, in addition to using technical aids to decision-making, lawyers must self-consciously balance the good of providing access to law with their obligations as a lawyer. The principles for counselling illegality fall well short of a definitive guide to ethical decision-making. Client confidentiality means that, except in a few exceptional cases, such as suspected money-laundering or imminent threats to a third party's safety, advice is confidential. It is doubtful that many clients divulge determination to carry out an illegal act when seeking general advice.

To some extent, counselling on the consequences of breaking the law is part of a lawyer's role, even though there is a suspicion that the advice may lead a client to cause harm. Clients should be warned that lawyers cannot promise to maintain confidentiality if the court demands to know what advice was given (see further chapter eight: Social Responsibility). Performing the task ethically demands considerable skill and sensitivity. When a lawyer advises a client what the consequences of particular action are, it is the client's choice whether or not to follow that advice. If the client breaks the law, it is their own conscious act, not that of the lawyer.

Facilitating Illegality

Facilitating illegality occurs in situations where an action is not illegal in itself, but the law could not be broken without an action by a lawyer. This situation is distinguishable from counselling on illegality, where the illegal conduct could happen anyway. A simple example was given in the old *Guide to the Professional Conduct of Solicitors*. The situation described was one where a client asked a solicitor only to instruct a barrister from a particular racial group. The act of instructing a barrister was not illegal, but the instruction to exclude a racial group was a breach of the Race Relations Act 1976. The rule, since 1995, is that a solicitor must try to persuade a client to modify discriminatory instructions, but must otherwise cease to act.[44]

In other circumstances, the action itself may be perfectly innocent in ordinary circumstances, but there may be factors that could or should alert a lawyer to a risk of wrongdoing. Lawyers tend not to be held responsible, legally or morally, for legal actions that might enable client wrongs. It has been argued that they should be. This argument is particularly well illustrated by the case of Lehman Brothers Holdings Inc (see further chapter eight).

Participating in Client's Perceived Immorality

A distinction must be made between counselling illegality and participating in a client's perceived immorality. The idea of participating in immorality envisages a lawyer asked to do something for a client which is perfectly legal but which the lawyer personally disagrees with on moral grounds. Wasserstrom proposed a number of examples that exposed the issues.[45] These were hot topics at the time but now seem somewhat dated. Wasserstrom's first example was: should a lawyer draft a will for a client to disinherit a child because he opposed the war in Vietnam? The second was: should a lawyer represent a corporation which manufactures harmful substances such as tobacco?

Wasserstrom assumes that acting for a vindictive testator or a tobacco company would be immoral. While both propositions can be disputed, the point is that many people would consider the clients to be immoral or have an immoral purpose. Is a lawyer taking that view entitled to decline instructions?

Disappointingly, Wasserstrom comes to no conclusion on the questions he poses. He believes that the 'role differentiated way of approaching matters' would incline many lawyers to act for the clients, against their convictions. His argument is that they should confront the moral dilemmas such action involves, rather than simply taking refuge in the requirements of the role.

Wasserstrom's examples suggest a clear distinction between two different

---

[44] *The Guide to the Professional Conduct of Solicitors*, 8th edn (1999) rule 7.02, para 4(c).
[45] R Wasserstrom, 'Lawyers as Professionals; Some Moral Issues' (1975–76) 5 *Human Rights* 1.

kinds of situation. The first situation arises when the moral issue is obvious from the outset, because of the identity of the client or the task initially identified. Knowing that the client is a tobacco company, for example, is an issue of client selection and not of client loyalty or partisanship. The answer to this kind of problem depends on the profession's position on neutrality. The Bar's position is that the client should be represented. Solicitors can, in principle, reject clients on what might appear to be moral grounds. So, for example, a firm identified with representing clients in the health industry might refuse to represent a tobacco company.

The vindictive testator is a more difficult example because it is not clear at what stage the issue about the disinherited son becomes clear. The lawyer refusing the instructions before agreeing is one case. It is a different issue when the problem is discovered several months into the matter. The issue then is whether lawyers should have a disposition of neutrality towards moral issues, or whether they can cease representing a client if a moral issue arises once representation commences.

The problem of the emerging moral issue is clearly illustrated by the Solicitors' Code. While solicitors are not obliged to represent clients, the rules make it more difficult to get rid of them once representation begins. Therefore, IB.1.26 is a presumption against 'ceasing to act for a client without good reason and without providing reasonable notice'. The moot point is what constitutes a 'good reason'. It seems arguable that the issue would need to be fairly serious before falling out over a moral dimension of a client's case would be deemed sufficient.

Building on Wasserstrom's analysis, Simon proposes a 'professional duty of reflective judgement' requiring evaluation of client goals to see if they will promote justice.[46] Even in an adversary context, Simon argues, the interests of justice should take priority for the lawyer. It is clear that Simon is thinking primarily of the powerful corporate client in putting forward this view. It may be, for example, that a lawyer acting on behalf of a large corporation should not plead limitation rules if, by so doing, a poor person is unable to enforce a debt which undoubtedly is owing to them.

Simon's proposition is that the lawyer should not lend assistance to the client who wants to use procedural rules or technical devices to defeat, rather than promote, the interests of justice. This example demonstrates an approach seeking to achieve substantive rather than procedural justice. Simon is not alone in promoting a responsibility for this kind of 'morally engaged activism' by lawyers.[47] Such a position is arguably beyond the current scope of a professional ethics for lawyers. It is antithetical to the formal legality version of the rule of law. In particular it requires lawyers to balance social justice claims.

---

[46] WH Simon, 'Ethical Discretion in Lawyering' (1988) 101 *Harvard Law Review* 1083.
[47] D Nicolson, 'Afterword: In Defence of Contextually Sensitive Moral Activism' (2004) 7 *Legal Ethics* 269, 270.

The potential scope of an ethic of substantive justice is unclear. The issue is not whether lawyers can reject clients because they disagree with them, but whether they can, or should be able to, terminate representation on that ground. Lawyers can try and dissuade a client from tactics that they consider underhand, but if the action is legal, should they withdraw because consequences may be unjust?

Moral sensibilities are obviously relative, but lawyers probably need a fairly robust and pragmatic approach to moral issues. This is reflected in the practice of a Manchester solicitor who, as part of his practice, regularly gets drivers charged with driving over the legal alcohol limit acquitted on technicalities. Morally, he cannot square this with his conscience but, he writes, 'ethically I can. I am a lawyer and my job is to give my clients the best defence I can.' However he claims he also takes his clients to one side to 'give them a polite ticking off ... and advise them not [to] transgress again'.[48] Whether this improves the lawyer's moral position is moot.

If lawyers were to morally censor their clients' actions they could be accused of adopting an unacceptably paternalistic attitude towards them. This is not to deny that there may be a moral issue on which all lawyers might refuse to continue, terminating representation. To require excessive deliberation over every issue on which a lawyer might have a moral qualm would arguably encourage over-sensitivity. There are various practical reasons why this would not be a good policy for the profession to pursue, particularly against a standard such as promotion of the rule of law or administration of justice.

If lawyers were to terminate representation when they decided that a client or their goals were immoral, appointing new lawyers and acquainting them with the case would cost time and money. Meanwhile the possibly legitimate action that the client seeks may cease to be relevant through delay. This would raise the issue of who should be responsible for the additional costs and open up the morally sensitive lawyer to the risk of being sued for negligence. It would hardly be in the interests of the administration of justice if withdrawal of representation were a frequent occurrence.

A Theory of Client Loyalty

Dinnerstein suggests that it is unclear why any client, corporate or otherwise, would engage the services of lawyers seeking to limit their autonomy, impose their values upon them and deny 'them the opportunity ... to seek vindication of hypothetically legal interests'.[49] The essential truth of this statement hints

---

[48] *Guardian*, 27 January 2006.
[49] RD Dinerstein, 'Client-Centered Counselling: Reappraisal and Refinement' (1990) 32 *Arizona Law Review* 501, 558.

at the very real difficulty in limiting the loyalty of lawyers to clients beyond that which is necessary.

Academics are right to explore the possibility of defining those limits, and the possibility of finding rules that would make the legal role more morally defensible. The reality, however, is that such quests are likely to fail because they impose an impractical burden on legal business.

It is necessary that lawyers do not actively participate in a client's criminality. This hardly needs stating, since both lawyer and client would face criminal charges and the lawyer would probably be struck off. There is probably no conduct limitation on advising clients in such a way that they can avoid legal charges. This is so even if the client achieves their desired result and the outcome remains morally wrong.

There is no ethical responsibility not to perform a task that may, but may not, facilitate illegality. Some models of the lawyer and client relationship envisage responsibility to counsel a client against any action that may result in illegality. Ultimately, the main constraint on what lawyers do for clients is the character of the lawyer and the model of the lawyer and client relationship in use.

Considering the various situations outlined above, the most defensible is the participatory model. This engages lawyers in considering the moral defensibility of client goals and provides them with an opportunity to dissuade clients from taking actions they disagree with. This throws into sharp relief the difficulty with other options. For example, the paternalistic model means that the client's interests are probably not explored and may be ignored. The client autonomy model involves the lawyer acting purely as a hired gun without any opportunity to restrain a client's wilder impulses. The client empowerment model potentially absolves the lawyer of any responsibility for outcomes.

Evaluation

Critique of the Standard Conception

The standard conception of the lawyers' role attracted much criticism in the US, Canada and UK. Critics argue that lawyers should not have to act against their moral conscience. Such critics suggest that neutrality is unnecessary because even the most reprehensible client will usually find someone to act for them. If not, professions should establish panels of lawyers willing to act for these pariahs.[50]

---

[50] Nicolson (n 47).

Critics also suggest that, while partisanship may be justified in criminal defence, it is not justified when lawyers work in other contexts, such as negotiating contracts. They claim that lawyers' ethics are dominated by the 'ideology of advocacy' and that the 'adversary system excuse' is used to justify adversarial behaviour beyond the realms of the adversary system.[51]

Justification of the Standard Conception

Other academics have attempted to justify the standard conception of the lawyer's role. Monroe Freedman argued that the lawyers' role in constraining the power of the state justified lawyers in taking extreme measures to defend clients.[52] Freedman's position was challenged by Noonan, who thought that the standard conception was justified, but not in Freedman's terms.[53] Noonan argued that the lawyer's function as advocate is to promote a wise and informed decision of the case. The role is therefore to assist the judge in making an impartial, wise and informed decision and to seek to establish the truth, and, where conviction results, a sentence proportionate to the crime.[54]

Standard Conception or Misconception?

In the debate following the formulation of the standard conception, some commentators pointed out that the professional codes did not mandate or justify some of the extreme actions attributed to it. Indeed, Schneyer pointed out that the American Bar Association Model Code did not condone neutrality or partisanship, and in fact forbade some of the examples of partisan behaviour cited by critics of the standard conception.[55]

The formal position in England and Wales tends more towards Noonan's view of the purpose of the system than Freedman's. Language limiting partisanship permeates the solicitors' and barristers' codes of conduct. The SRA Code of Conduct stresses that any conflict between principles should be resolved in a way that 'serves the public interest in the particular circumstances, especially the public interest in the proper administration of justice'.[56] It stresses that

---

[51] D Luban, 'The Adversary System Excuse' in D Luban (ed), *The Good Lawyer: Lawyers' Roles and Lawyers' Ethics* (Totowa, NJ, Rowman & Allanheld, 1983).

[52] See particularly M Freedman, 'Professional Responsibility of the Criminal Defence Lawyer: The Three Hardest Questions' (1966) 64 *Michigan Law Review* 1469.

[53] J Noonan, 'The Purposes of Advocacy and the Limits of Confidentiality' (1966) 64 *Michigan Law Review* 1485.

[54] A Ashworth, 'Ethics and Criminal Justice' in R Cranston (ed), *Legal Ethics and Professional Responsibility* (Oxford, Clarendon Press, 1995) 146.

[55] T Schneyer, 'Moral Philosophy's Standard Misconception of Legal Ethics' (1984) *Wisconsin Law Review* 1529.

[56] Solicitors Regulation Authority, *SRA Code of Conduct 2011*, The Principles.

solicitors should 'uphold the rule of law and the proper administration of justice, act with integrity and not allow your independence to be compromised'.[57] Upholding the rule of law arguably means being 'morally blind' regarding the client and his purposes.

The preamble to the SRA Code of Conduct preserves solicitors' discretion in interpreting the provisions, thereby providing considerable latitude to avoid immoral action. The Bar Code contains similar admonitions against dishonesty or discreditable behaviour, actions prejudicial to the administration of justice and conduct likely to diminish public confidence in the legal profession.[58] Even within an adversarial system, therefore, legal roles find justification in the need 'to administer and to facilitate the operation of law'.[59]

Alternatives to the Standard Conception

It is in relation to the lawyer–client relationship that we see the implications of William Simon's argument that lawyers should have more moral autonomy in making ethical decisions.[60] He says that they should have 'discretion to disobey' when partisanship produces immoral consequences. Luban argues that they should act as if the 'adversary system excuse' was not available to them.[61] Postema argues that lawyers should exercise 'engaged moral judgement' in deciding what it is legitimate to do for clients.[62]

Postema sees aspects of the standard conception as a 'recourse role'. This means that lawyers have the recourse of not acting in accordance with their role in a few extreme situations. The role expands or contracts depending on the underlying institutional objectives the role is designed to serve, with lawyers having discretion to disobey their code of ethics when the rule contradicts the objectives of the role.[63]

Some critics of the standard conception have advocated degrees of deprofessionalisation of roles. These range from Simon's consideration of the abandonment of a neutral professional role to making it an institutional rather than a personal responsibility. This, it seems, could produce the exact opposite of what Simon argues for. In a fully deprofessionalised market, where legal services are treated like any other service, lawyers could negotiate with clients

---

[57] Ibid, r 1.

[58] Bar Code of Conduct 2014 gC25.

[59] TW Giegerich, 'The Lawyer's Moral Paradox' (1979) 6 *Duke Law Journal* 1335.

[60] W Simon, 'Ethical Discretion in Lawyering' (1988) 101 *Harvard Law Review* 1083.

[61] Luban, 'The Adversary System Excuse' (n 51) and D Nicholson, 'In Defence of Contextually Sensitive Moral Activism' (2004) 7(2) *Legal Ethics* 269–75.

[62] GJ Postema, 'Moral Responsibility in Professional Ethics' (1980) 55 *New York University Law Review* 63, 83; RS Tur, 'The Doctor's Defense' (2002) 69 *Mount Sinai Journal of Medicine* 317, 327.

[63] S Kadish and M Kadish, *Discretion to Disobey* (Stanford, CA, Stanford University Press, 1973) 31.

as to what level of service and commitment they would provide. The client could buy the lawyer's commitment to his immoral goals. This approach is arguably more consistent with a consumerist than a professional approach to regulation.

Q4.22 Should lawyers be able to decide whether to accept cases?

Q4.23 Should they be able to decide how to pursue client's rights?

Q4.24 Would it be more satisfactory if lawyers acted according to ordinary morality or should we recognise that lawyers have a distinct morality?

Q4.25 What limits, if any, do Freedman, Wendel and Dare place on partisanship?

Q4.26 Can a legal ethics based on the standard conception of the lawyer's role provide a satisfactory foundation for the behaviour of legal professionals?

Conclusion

It is a strange fact that a lawyer's responsibility to his or her clients is relatively ill-defined. It is, however, hotly debated in the literature. Much of the discussion revolves around the standard conception of the lawyer's role, which is largely based on an analysis of the American Bar Association's Model Rules. This is often assumed to mandate that a lawyer must carry out what he or she perceives to be a client's immoral instructions. There may be some limited circumstances where lawyers are bound to pursue a client's instructions with which they do not agree on moral grounds. In reality such situations may be rare.

Conflicts of Interest

The duty to avoid conflicts of interest is a very specific manifestation of the obligation of loyalty. Such conflicts potentially take various forms. They include conflicts between the lawyer's own interests, between different clients' interests, and between clients' and third parties' interests. A core duty of both of the main legal professions in England and Wales is to serve the best interests of each client.[1] This means that while they are able to have many clients at one time, lawyers cannot simultaneously represent two clients whose interests are opposed. This restriction does not necessarily apply when two clients' interests conflict but the timeframe for handling their matters does not overlap.

One of the most significant potential conflicts of interest between lawyers and clients concerns the fees that lawyers charge. This particular conflict is unavoidable and so various measures are taken to control it. It is also a very specific focus of professional conduct rules. The emphasis in the rules has been to require increasing transparency in anticipating, setting out and charging fees. This is an area that courts routinely regulate, by imposing assessments of fees on the parties. Through this process, courts seek to ensure that the allocation and amount of fees are as fair as possible.

The Scope and Impact of Conflict of Interest Rules

Context

An interest can be defined as a benefit or advantage that a person may wish to assert or protect. A conflict of interest therefore arises without either party asserting a right to take their benefit or advantage. The fact that they may

---

[1] Bar Standards Board, *The BSB Handbook 2014: Code of Conduct* CD6, SRA CD2.

seek to assert or protect such a benefit or advantage gives rise to the conflict of interests. A client's interests may conflict with those of his lawyer or with those of the lawyer's other clients.

In solicitor–client conflict situations it does not necessarily matter that the lawyer would not, in fact, act in his own interests. The conflict is inherent in the situation, such that it would not be possible to know whether the lawyer was acting in their client's best interests or not. Where such a conflict exists between a lawyer and a client the lawyer can only act in limited circumstances. Where such a conflict situation exists between parties the lawyer may only act for both of the parties in limited circumstances.

The SRA Code of Conduct deals with conflicts of interest in Chapter 3. It distinguishes conflicts of interest arising between solicitors and their current clients ('own interest conflict') and between two or more current *clients* ('client conflict'). Some outcomes apply to both types of situation while others apply to only one. The relevant outcome in both cases is for the lawyer not to act. This outcome is often, however, not clear cut.

One of the most obvious conflict of interest situations that must be managed is agreeing and charging fees. Thus, a fairly heavy concentration of outcomes and indicative behaviours in Chapter 1 of the SRA Code of Conduct is directed towards this issue. The BSB Code of Conduct contains several rules touching on the issue of conflicts of interest in Chapter 3: You and Your Client.

Bar Standards Board Code of Conduct 2014

oC12 BSB authorised persons do not accept instructions from clients where there is a conflict between their own interests and the clients' or where there is a conflict between one or more clients except when permitted in this Handbook.

gC37 Rules C15 and C16 are expressed in terms of the interests of each client. This is because you may only accept instructions to act for more than one client if you are able to act in the best interests of each client as if that client were your only client, as CD2 requires of you. See further Rule C17 on the circumstances when you are obliged to advise your client to seek other legal representation and Rules C21.2 and C21.3 on conflicts of interest and the guidance to those rules at gC69.

rC21 You must not accept instructions to act in a particular matter if:

.1 due to any existing or previous instructions you are not able to fulfil your obligation to act in the best interests of the prospective client; or

.2 there is a conflict of interest between your own personal interests and the interests of the prospective client in respect of the particular matter; or

.3 there is a conflict of interest between the prospective client and one or more of your former or existing clients in respect of the particular matter unless all of the clients who have an interest in the particular matter give their informed consent to your acting in such circumstances; or

.4 there is a real risk that information confidential to another former or existing client, or any other person to whom you owe duties of confidence, may be relevant to the matter, such that if, obliged to maintain confidentiality, you could not act in the best interests of the prospective client, and the former or existing client or person to whom you owe that duty does not give informed consent to disclosure of that confidential information

Q5.1 Can you identify what kind of conflict of interest each rule covers?

Q5.2 Why do you think confidentiality is mentioned in these rules?

Lawyer and Client Conflicts of Interest

Background

Common law lawyers can enter a range of transactions with clients. These include business ventures, selling to or buying from a client, and lending to or borrowing from a client. These are all situations where some kind of conflict of interest might seem inevitable. Where a conflict of interest is established the court will prevent a lawyer from benefiting from the arrangement. If a client can show that harm would result, an injunction might be granted to prevent a lawyer acting.

In most transactions the lawyer can act or continue to act if the client gives informed consent. Consent can only be informed if the lawyer has disclosed all material facts[2] and has shown that the client had fully understood the arrangement.[3]

The SRA Handbook defines own-interest conflicts of interest as 'any situation where your duty to act in the best interests of any *client* in relation to a matter conflicts, or there is a significant risk that it may conflict, with your own interests in relation to that or a related matter'.[4]

Outcome 3.4 in Chapter 3 on Conflicts of Interests in the SRA Code of Conduct stipulates that 'you do not act if there is an own interest conflict or a significant risk of an own interest conflict'. Some of the conflict situations

---

[2] *McMaster v Byrne* [1952] 1 All ER 1362.

[3] *Hanson v Lorenz Jones* [1986] NLJ Rep 1088.

[4] *SRA Handbook 2011*, Glossary.

are dealt with in Chapter 1 of the SRA Code of Conduct, as an issue of client care, rather than as an issue of potential conflict of interest under Chapter 3.

Avoidable Conflict Situations

Divided Loyalty

Some conflicts of interest are not obvious. Therefore, a lawyer's loyalty may be divided between clients and others who offer that lawyer some advantage. Examples are well established in the literature. One is where lawyers attach too much importance to relationships with opponent professionals or court officials. In such cases they may prize these relationships too highly and not pursue their own client's interests sufficiently vigorously. This can be seen as a failure to be sufficiently adversarial when required.

A similar situation is where lawyers are over-dependent on repeat work from a client. They, might, for example, have close ties with the local police, one of their partners being an ex-policeman. They might handle divorces and conveyances for officers working in the local police station. Arrested suspects who know of these circumstances and arrangements might wonder whether a solicitor advising them would advise a course of action that might upset those arrangements. The risk of such conflict may not be specifically identified in codes, but could be covered by principles and duties referring to clients' best interests and maintaining independence.

Publishing

A potential conflict situation arises when a solicitor proposes publishing details of a client's case. Because of the confidentiality issue the client should receive independent advice before agreeing to publication. The lawyer must also consider whether they can comply with their obligations of independence and integrity in completing the work. They may also consider whether publication will prejudice the reputation of the profession.

Gifts and Financial Benefits

Another example of potential conflicts of interest arises in relation to gifts from clients to their lawyers. Surprisingly, this is not dealt with in Chapter 3 but in Chapter 1: Client Care. The relevant indicative behaviour IB.1.9 is 'refusing to act where your client proposes to make a gift of significant value to you or a member of your family, or a member of your firm or their family, unless the client takes independent legal advice'. It is not clear which outcome in Chapter 1 this relates to, although it would relate reasonably comfortably to Outcome 3.4 (see above).

Holding an Office Creating a Risk of Conflict

The rules on conflicts of interest in the 2007 Code of Conduct stated that a solicitor must decline to act for a client where the solicitor, or a partner, employee or relative, held an office giving rise to a significant risk of a conflict of interest, where the public might reasonably conclude that the solicitor, or his firm, had been able to make use of the office or appointment for the advantage of the client or where the ability to advise the client properly and impartially was inhibited.[5]

These situations all related to conflicts in one way or another, albeit the middle rule reflected concern about perceptions of conflicts. The guidance for the rule gave examples of relevant offices as local councillor, judge, coroner and member of the police authority. Solicitors were told to consider whether the duties or interests of such a public role conflicted with their ability to provide a client with independent advice.

The nearest relevant provision in the current SRA Code of Conduct is in Chapter 11: Relations with Third Parties. Presumably relating to an outcome about not taking advantage of third parties, IB(11.10) is 'taking unfair advantage of a public office held by you, or a member of your family, or a member of your firm or their family'. Therefore the emphasis in the code has shifted from a possible conflict of interest to taking unfair advantage.

Business Ventures

A surprisingly common situation of conflict of interest arises where a client is contemplating a business venture from which their solicitor might benefit. The problem lies in identifying a 'significant risk' of conflict of interest, in which case the outcome would suggest that the solicitor does not act. Under the first relevant indicative behaviour, IB.3.8, the presumption is that a solicitor will not meet the outcome against own-interest conflicts when 'in a personal capacity, selling to or buying from, lending to or borrowing from a client, unless the client has obtained independent legal advice'. This presumably means that the client must also give informed consent, although no formal requirements for this process are specified in the Handbook.

Interestingly, the situation where a client is considering investing in a business owned by their solicitor is dealt with separately. IB.3.9 suggests that 'advising a client to invest in a business, in which you have an interest which

---

[5] SRA Code of Conduct 2011, Rule 3.05 and Guidance, paras 64–66.

affects your ability to provide impartial advice' may indicate that a solicitor has not achieved the outcomes.[6]

Even if it were expressed as a rule, IB.3.9 would be a little short of an absolute prohibition. This is because of the ambiguity introduced by the last part of the sentence. This might be interpreted to mean that having an interest inevitably prevents a solicitor from giving impartial advice. It could also be interpreted to mean that it is alright to advise the client to invest where the solicitor is satisfied that his interest will not affect the impartiality of his advice. In the context it is likely that the former meaning is intended. This interpretation is reinforced by the absence of any provision for informed consent. These outcomes and behaviours can be compared with rules aimed at achieving similar results in the American Bar Association Model Rules.

**American Bar Association
Model Rules of Professional Conduct**

Rule 1.8: Current Clients: Specific Rules

Client–Lawyer Relationship

Rule 1.8 Conflict of Interest: Current Clients: Specific Rules

(a) A lawyer shall not enter into a business transaction with a client or knowingly acquire an ownership, possessory, security or other pecuniary interest adverse to a client unless:

(1) the transaction and terms on which the lawyer acquires the interest are fair and reasonable to the client and are fully disclosed and transmitted in writing in a manner that can be reasonably understood by the client;
(2) the client is advised in writing of the desirability of seeking and is given a reasonable opportunity to seek the advice of independent legal counsel on the transaction; and
(3) the client gives informed consent, in a writing signed by the client, to the essential terms of the transaction and the lawyer's role in the transaction, including whether the lawyer is representing the client in the transaction.

Q5.3   Can you identify differences between the US and English rules?

Q5.4   Do the US and English rules seek to achieve broadly the same result?

Q5.5   Do you think outcomes or rules are more suited to this area of regulation?

---

[6] Ibid, Indicative Behaviour 3.9.

Personal Relationships with Clients

Personal relationships, especially sexual relationships, between lawyers and clients raise a number of ethical issues. First, there is an issue whether, in the circumstances, there is an abuse of authority or power, particularly if the client is emotionally vulnerable. Secondly, there are ongoing ethical issues relating to the representation. For example, can either lawyer or client be frank in their professional dealings? Can the lawyer put aside his or her personal feelings in pursuing the client's best interests?

In the 1990s there was considerable pressure to introduce a rule that solicitors should not continue to act if they entered a sexual relationship with a client.[7] This led to an amendment to the SRA *Guide to the Professional Conduct of Solicitors* in the form of rule 12.09, which stated that 'A solicitor must not abuse the solicitor/client fiduciary relationship by taking advantage of the client.'

To the guidance, which began 'A solicitor must not abuse his or her position to exploit a client by taking advantage of a client's age, inexperience, ill-health or want of education or business experience' were added the words 'or emotional or other vulnerability'. The following clause was also added to the guidance: 'Whilst it would not necessarily be so, it may be an abuse of the solicitor/client fiduciary relationship for a solicitor to enter into a sexual relationship with a client.'

The Solicitors' Code of Conduct 2007 apparently weakened what had gone before. It stated that solicitors in a sexual relationship with a client must 'consider' whether this impaired the ability to act in the best interests of the client.[8] This did not seem to deal adequately with the risk of abuse of power by lawyers in relationships with clients.

The Solicitors' Code of Conduct has taken another step backward on the issue of lawyer–client sexual relationships. The risks attached to such relationships are not mentioned and the rules and warnings replaced by less explicit outcomes and indicative behaviours.

Therefore, Outcome 3.2 in the chapter on conflicts requires that systems and controls for identifying own-interest conflicts require consideration of whether a personal relationship would prevent a firm acting in a client's best interests. Such systems must also enable the firm to identify if any client is vulnerable. This does not help, of course, if the firm is blind to the issue or if a relationship between a lawyer and client develops after screening has taken place.

The indicative behaviours for Chapter 1 of the Solicitors' Code of Conduct are equally oblique in tackling the issue of sexual relationships between

---

[7] 'Courting Clients' [1995] *The Lawyer*, 10 March, www.thelawyer.com/courting-clients/84265. article.

[8] *Solicitors Code of Conduct 2007*, Guidance to Rule 3, para 49.

lawyer and client. IB.1.6 refers to solicitors, 'in taking instructions and during the course of the retainer, having proper regard to your client's mental capacity or other vulnerability, such as incapacity or duress'. IB.1.7 is 'considering whether you should decline to act or cease to act because you cannot act in the client's best interests'.

The provisions in the current code would only seem relevant to sexual relationships between lawyers and clients if the history of previous codes is taken into account. It seems unclear whether a solicitor in a sexual relationship with a client would currently be regarded as at risk of conflict of interest.

Claims and Complaints

Solicitors are required to facilitate client claims and complaints even though it is against their own interests to do so. Therefore IB.1.12 requires solicitors to consider whether they should advise clients to obtain independent advice when they discover that they have made a mistake which might give the client a legal claim against them.[9] It is difficult to think of circumstances where it would not be right to advise clients of their right to take legal advice where a solicitor has made mistakes causing them loss.

There are two outcomes in Chapter 1 relating to complaints. The first is O.1.9 which requires that '[c]lients are informed in writing at the outset of their matter of their right to complain and how complaints can be made'. The second, O.1.10, specifies that '[c]lients are informed in writing, both at the time of engagement and at the conclusion of your complaints procedure, of their right to complain to the Legal Ombudsman, the time frame for doing so and full details of how to contact the Legal Ombudsman'. These are supported by three indicative behaviours relating to complaints, eg IB.1.22, which specifies in some detail the kind of complaints procedure firms should have.

Commissions, Introductions and Referrals

i. Introductions and Commissions

Receiving commissions on introducing client business to a company is a potential breach of Principle 3, which refers to not letting independence be compromised. The availability of a commission may influence a solicitor to recommend one company over another, rather than considering the client's best interests under Principle 4. An extract on this issue from the relevant chapter of the SRA Code of Conduct appears below.

---

[9] SRA Code of Conduct 2011, Indicative Behaviour 1.12.

ii. Referrals

In addition to receiving payments for referring work to others, lawyers may also be in a conflict-of-interest situation when they pay a fee to another when receiving work. If a solicitor has paid another party, a so-called 'claims farmer', a fee in order to handle the client's case, there is also a risk of a conflict of interest. This could arise if the solicitor owes the referring party some obligation that cuts across the duty to the client. This could arise, for example, if the referrer charges the client a fee that they are not legally obliged to pay and the solicitor does not advise them of this.

The Law Society was always opposed to allowing solicitors to get work by paying referral fees. It was under pressure, including from some solicitors, to permit such payments. In 2001 the Office of Fair Trading (OFT) concluded that the ban was obstructing the development of an online market for introductions and was disadvantageous to solicitors.[10] Noting that a Law Society Regulation Review Working Party was considering reforming restrictions on cold calling, the report welcomed 'indications that this restriction might soon be abolished'.[11]

In 2002 two motions before the Law Society Council called for the abolition of the Law Society's Introduction and Referral Code but both were narrowly defeated. Although there was some relaxation of the rules, perceived abuses in personal injury cases led to a ban for such claims. Referral fees are still permitted in other kinds of claim. A small case study illustrating potential problems is included in this chapter ('the miners' costs scandal'). Under IB.1.4 a solicitor must explain 'any arrangements, such as fee sharing or referral agreements, which are relevant to the client's instructions'.

SRA Handbook 2014 (version 10)

Chapter 1: Client care

O(1.15) you properly account to clients for any financial benefit you receive as a result of your instructions;

IB(1.20) where you receive a financial benefit as a result of acting for a client, either:

(a) paying it to the client;
(b) offsetting it against your fees; or
(c) keeping it only where you can justify keeping it, you have told the client the amount of the benefit (or an approximation if you do not know the exact amount) and the client has agreed that you can keep it;

---

[10] Director General of Fair Trading, *Competition in Professions* (2001) Report 328, 14.
[11] *Financial Times*, 2 January 2001, 1.

6: Your client and introductions to third parties

There may be circumstances in which you wish to refer your *clients* to third parties, perhaps to another *lawyer* or a financial services provider. This chapter describes the conduct duties which arise in respect of such introductions. It is important that you retain your independence when recommending third parties to your *client* and that you act in the *client's* best interests.

You must achieve these outcomes:

O(6.1) whenever you recommend that a *client* uses a particular *person* or business, your recommendation is in the best interests of the *client* and does not compromise your independence;

O(6.2) *clients* are fully informed of any financial or other interest which you have in referring the *client* to another *person* or business;

O(6.3) *clients* are in a position to make informed decisions about how to pursue their matter;

IB(6.2) any referral to a third party that can only offer products from one source is made only after the client has been informed of this limitation;

Bar Standards Board Code of Conduct 2014

rC82 If you have a material commercial interest in an organisation which is proposing to refer a matter to you, you must:
.1 tell the client in writing about your interest in that organisation before you accept such instructions;
.2 make a clear agreement with that organisation or other public statement about how relevant issues, such as conflicts of interest, will be dealt with; and
.3 keep a record of referrals received from any such organisation for review by the Bar Standards Board on reasonable request.

Q5.6 Is there a good reason in principle for distinguishing between gifts and other financial benefits a solicitor might receive, apart from fees, from acting for a client.

Q5.7 Should lawyers ever be able to receive a commission or other payment for recommending particular financial or other products to clients?

Q5.8 What safeguards on such a practice would be reasonable?

Q5.9 How can the issue of cross-selling of services or financial products be managed effectively within ABS so as not to infringe outcomes relating to introduction and referral?

Q5.10 Can lawyers ever recommend another business to a client unless they have thoroughly investigated the relevant market?

Q5.11 Does an obligation to inform a client of an interest a lawyer has in another business provide sufficient client protection?

Unavoidable Conflict Situations

Charging Fees

The charging of fees to clients is an obvious area where the interests of lawyers clash with those of clients. A lawyer's interests lie in being very well remunerated conflicts with her client's interests in paying as little as possible for the legal services he receives. Yet, the calculation of fees is one of the areas in the lawyer–client relationship where the information asymmetry between lawyers and clients is most pronounced.

A traditional way of controlling any propensity in lawyers to exploit the information asymmetry regarding costs is the intrinsic motivation associated with professionalism. Another way is to find methods of charging that are transparent, understandable and least open to exploitation. Nevertheless, we might also expect that this is an area of relatively heavy regulation.

Costs

In England and Wales costs are the amounts, including lawyers' fees and outgoings (disbursements), incurred in conducting litigation. The general principle is that 'costs follow the event'. At the end of the case, therefore, the judge usually orders that the losing party pays the winner's costs (*inter partes* costs). Such an order is based on the indemnity principle, meaning that the paying party is not liable for more than the receiving party had agreed to pay their own lawyer.

The losing side in litigation usually pays costs on the standard basis, ie what is reasonable between the parties. A more generous basis, the indemnity basis, usually applies between solicitor and clients, including work the client requested which was not necessary. When costs are awarded in proceedings they are then either agreed between the parties or assessed by the court. Any costs awarded against the other side reduce, and may eliminate, the lawyers' fee charged to his client (solicitor and own-client costs).

One of the aims of the Civil Procedure Rules 1998 was to control costs by increasing the case-management powers of judges. This was intended to cut down on unnecessary work. The CPR also formalised rules relating to wasted costs orders, so that lawyers guilty of improper, unreasonable or negligent acts or omissions could be penalised whether or not their client was ultimately successful. Such orders can be made as the case progresses, so that the controlling effect on lawyers can be increased.

In cases where legal aid is available, no charge is usually made to the client. If lawyers have a legal aid contract, they have a budget that they have discretion to expend. As the availability of legal aid has declined, government has sought other ways to encourage access to justice. The main measures have been to allow contingency-type fees. Where a contingency fee applies, lawyers only get paid if they win the case (the contingency).

The usual arrangement with a contingency fee is that the lawyer is paid an additional fee from the damages recovered by the successful client. There are two main types of agreement. One is a conditional fee agreement and the other is a damages-based agreement. This means that various methods of calculating fees are available. They include time-based charging, fixed fees and the two types of contingency fee arrangement.

The sum charged in time-based charging and conditional fee agreements relate to the amount of work done. Fixed fees are based on an agreed rate for a job. The sum charged in a damages-based agreement is a percentage of the sum recovered. It may, therefore, bear no relation to the amount of work done. The nature of these different arrangements and the challenges they pose for regulation are now considered.

Methods of Determining Fees

i. Time-Based Charging

The traditional method for calculating lawyers' fees, in both litigation and for transaction work, is time-based charging. Using this method, lawyers record the time they spend on a case. This is multiplied by a rate of charge dependent on their level of experience and expertise. This is not a foolproof method for controlling fees. There are no officially fixed rates, so lawyers can charge what the market will bear.

It is often argued that fees based on hourly rates encourage overcharging. Hourly paid fees provide an incentive for a lawyer to do unnecessary work or simply to work more slowly and inefficiently, confident that he or she will be paid whatever the outcome. A Law Society committee on litigation observed that '[e]xperience shows that, given a free rein, lawyers (who are normally paid by the hour) will tend to do too much rather than too little work, with not always sufficient regard to the relevance of what they are producing'.[12] Hourly charging may also inhibit innovation, such as increased use of new technology.

One of the ways that such costs are controlled is through assessment by courts or other third parties. This is fairly routine in litigation, where the loser is usually ordered to pay the winner's fair and reasonable costs. Outside of

[12] The Law Society, *Group Actions Made Easier* (London, The Law Society, 1995) 3.

litigation the Legal Ombudsman has taken on the responsibility of determining the fairness of sums charged.

It is difficult to know how common overcharging is when lawyers are charging by the hour. Analysis by the Law Society of 7,455 complaints about solicitors to the Legal Ombudsman in 2011–12, showed that 8.50 per cent concerned deficient costs information and 8.60 per cent were about excessive costs.[13] Clients complained that itemised bills were misleading. Items such as postage, printing or travel costs were treated as disbursements, whereas these are strictly overheads that should be covered by the hourly rate.

In 2013–14 nearly 8 per cent of the 7,630 cases handled by the Legal Ombudsman related to fees.[14] This amounts to around 611 cases. In 234 cases it was informally agreed that fees be limited to a specified amount and in a further 166 cases the Ombudsman reached that decision.

ii. Fixed Fees

Fixed fees may anticipate the amount of work done but are capped at the agreed amount. They are becoming increasingly common where clients have the power to dictate terms to their lawyers. Therefore, commercial clients and state agencies may seek to agree a rate for work before instructing solicitors. Court rules are increasingly specifying fixed rates of costs recoverable for completing certain stages of litigation.

Fixed fees may not be commonly available to most clients, but are becoming more familiar in highly competitive areas of work. Therefore, it not unusual to see a fixed fee for conveyancing advertised. The obvious problem with fixed fees for inexperienced consumers of legal services is that the provider may use inexperienced staff or cut corners. The level of competence, degree of diligence and quality of service may suffer and mistakes may be more likely.

iii. Conditional Fees

English law was opposed to contingency-type fee arrangements, but a type of contingency fee, called a conditional fee agreement (CFA), was permitted under the Courts and Legal Services Act 1990 and introduced in 1996, mainly for personal injury cases. The principle was that a lawyer entering such an agreement with a client would only be paid if they won. However, if they won they could charge an 'uplift' on their costs calculated on a conventional time-charging basis.

The maximum uplift allowed in a personal injury CFA was 100 per cent,

---

[13] The Law Society, 'Complaints to the Legal Ombudsman', 13 December 2012, www.lawsociety.org.uk/advice/articles/complaints-to-the-legal-ombudsman/, based on data not reproduced in the *Office for Legal Complaints Annual Report and Accounts 2011–2012* (TSO, 2012).

[14] Legal Ombudsman, *Complaints Data 2013–2014*, www.legalombudsman.org.uk/research-decisions/complaints-data-previous.html.

and the percentage of uplift actually charged was to depend on the degree of risk presented by the case. The client's risk of losing the case and being liable for the other side's costs was to be covered by after-the-event (ATE) insurance.

Conditional fee agreements demonstrate the difficulty of deciding who should bear the burden of lawyers' costs incentives. Initially, the success fees and ATE insurance premiums were paid by claimants, then by defendants. This change was perceived to have encouraged a 'litigation explosion' by making claimants almost free from risk. Under the latest CFA regime such costs are again borne by claimants. Therefore, the fees of a successful claimant's lawyers are usually partly paid by the defendant (the basic costs calculated on a time charge basis) and by the claimant (the percentage uplift on basic costs).

iv. Damages-Based Agreements

A fully fledged contingency agreement was permitted from 1 April 2013 for litigation and arbitration proceedings in England and Wales.[15] Damages-based agreements (DBAs) regulations[16] allow lawyers to conduct litigation for a share of damages. The percentage of damages the lawyer is allowed to take varies from up to 25 per cent in personal injury and clinical negligence claims, up to 35 per cent in employment tribunal cases and up to 50 per cent in most other types of claim.

The regulations do not require that the contingency fee reflects the risk involved in supporting the proceedings, but the agreement must set out the reason for setting the percentage.[17] The only sums recoverable from a successful client are the 'payment', the agreed, capped percentage recovery and disbursements. These do not include counsel fees, which must be paid from solicitors' profit costs. In the event the case is lost the lawyer is only entitled to recover non-counsel disbursements from the client. Lawyers are not allowed to combine a DBA with another method of charging.[18]

A losing defendant's costs liability under a DBA are based on a formula known as the 'Ontario model'. The claimant's costs based on hours, rates, proportionality and reasonableness of the charges are paid by the defendant. If the contingency fee charged by the claimant's lawyer is higher than this, which they would normally be, the claimant pays the shortfall from his damages.

If the agreed contingency fee is lower than the figure arrived at through a traditional costs assessment, the defendant only has to pay the lower amount. Where DBAs are unenforceable, for example because of a breach of the regulations, the defendant is not liable for costs, even if he is liable for damages. Lawyers are not liable for their losing client's costs unless they have agreed to indemnify their client for such liability to their opponent.

---

[15] Legal Aid, Sentencing and Punishment of Offenders Act 2012 s 45.
[16] The Damages-Based Agreements Regulations (2013).
[17] Ibid, Regulation 3c.
[18] Ibid, Regulation 4.

Ethical Considerations in the Methods of Determining Fees Compared

Hourly-based charges tends to be trusted by clients.[19] They are transparent and can be easily explained and understood[20] although, arguably, less so than contingency fees.[21] The use of automated time recording systems limits the scope for abuse by over-recording and allows for detailed checking. Lawyers have an incentive to do the work properly because they will be paid for the hours spent.

Since the risks of legal proceedings are taken by clients the lawyer charging on an hourly basis has no incentive to favour early settlement or continuing to trial. The advice they tender can therefore be based purely on their client's interests, rather than their own interests. Lawyers charging on a time basis do, however, have an incentive to recommend acceptance of the other side's high costs, where their client is paying them, so that they can charge similarly high fees for their own work.

Lawyers who have agreed to a fixed fee for work have an incentive to do less work than is necessary. In litigation, because they will receive the same fee if the case settles or goes to trial, they have an incentive to settle the case early.

Lawyers paid under a CFA have various incentives to behaviour that is against their client's interests. They have a strong incentive to recommend settlements that undervalue a claim so as to avoid a risk of losing and not being paid. They have an incentive to over-work because their fee is partly based on time charging. Finally, they have an incentive to over-estimate the degree of risk involved in the case funded by a CFA, so as to as to justify a high uplift.

Lawyers operating under a contingency fee face different incentives and temptations. Contingency-type arrangements do, at least, provide lawyers with some incentive to diligently purse the case because their remuneration depends on success.[22] However, they may sometimes be tempted to under-settle. This is because they take a percentage of damages, irrespective of effort on their part. In some cases, refusing a settlement and continuing for a relatively small increase in damages may not be attractive. In fact, their ideal scenario may be to agree a high contingency fee and to settle the case before they have to do a lot of work. The temptation to act against their client's interests is to recommend acceptance of an early and inadequate offer of settlement.

In addition to the incentives to act against client interests, the different types of fee arrangements sometimes pose other ethical challenges on lawyers.

---

[19] A Woolley, 'Evaluating Value: A Historical Case Study of the Capacity of Alternative Billing Methods to Reform Unethical Hourly Billing' (2005) 12(3) *International Journal of the Legal Profession* 339.

[20] D Webb, 'Killing Time: A Limited Defence of Time-Cost Billing' (2010) 13(1) *Legal Ethics* 39, 57.

[21] R Moorhead, 'Filthy Lucre: Lawyers' Fees and Lawyers' Ethics—What Is Wrong with Informed Consent' (2011) 31(3) *Legal Studies* 345.

[22] CW Wolfram, *Modern Legal Ethics* (St Paul, MN, West Publishing, 1996) 526.

For example, hourly-based charging and the ordinary costs rule puts clients under pressure to settle cases. Insurance against paying the other side's costs removes this pressure. In contrast, contingency-type arrangements may put excessive financial pressure on lawyers to win a case. This may encourage them to engage in unethical conduct, for example by breaking their duty to the court in order to win the case.

One of the hidden ethical issues in the new contingency-based funding regimes is the problem of access to justice. Lawyers are perfectly entitled to refuse to accept a case because they do not want to accept the risk of losing and not being paid. This means that clients with winnable cases, for which legal aid would formerly have been available, may not find lawyers.

Table 5.1 Summary of successful claimants' costs bases in litigation

	Calculation	Recoverability from defendant	Contribution by successful client	Unethical behaviour incentivised
Time based	Hours worked	Standard basis	Solicitor and own client costs	Over-working
Fixed fee	Agreed rate for job	As agreed (on indemnity principle)	None	Corner cutting
Conditional fee	Hours worked + uplift	Standard basis	Uplift	Over-estimating risk Under-settling
Damages based	Percentage of damages	Standard basis	Difference between standard basis and contingency fee	Agreeing high percentage fee Settling early Under-settling

Q5.12 Which kinds of arrangements would tend to lead to claimants keeping a larger proportion of the damages?

Q5.13 Should lawyers doing work on a conditional-fee or contingency-fee basis have a duty to accept some risky cases so as to increase access to justice?

The Long-Term Trend

In the longer time we may expect a greater use of fixed-fee arrangements. These are already effectively in place for legal aid and are forced on lawyers by institutional clients. We might also expect increasing use of funding methods that encourage lawyers to financially support their client's cases. This adds to the overall volume of costs, typically at the expense of either claimants or defendants. This is likely to prompt constant searching for new mechanisms of control and adjustments to the rules of recovery.

The policy of liberalising the litigation-costs regime provides incentives for lawyers to take risks. It may encourage high-value and risky claims. The defendant's liability for costs will not increase and may decrease if the DBA agreed fee is less than the costs calculated in the traditional way. The impact on lawyers' conduct of these developments is debatable.

Lord Ackner thought that 'the lawyer with a financial stake in the outcome of litigation has a concern to win the case which may distort the advice he gives and may even tempt him into unethical conduct'.[23] Lord Allen, a non-lawyer, put the contrary view, that they look 'rather different if one is just an ordinary person who is not poor enough for legal aid and not rich enough to embark upon litigation with equanimity. ... To people like me it seems that at last there is some prospect of access to justice becoming more open.'[24]

Regulation

The development of the litigation funding regime in the UK has become more diverse and less restrictive. This reflects a pattern of lighter regulation of fee regimes and the amount of fees, but tighter regulation of the process of agreement. This is consistent with the trend towards recognising the autonomy of the client and their right to make their own decisions, good or bad.

SRA Code of Conduct 2014 Version

You must achieve these outcomes:

O(1.1) you treat your clients fairly

O(1.13) clients receive the best possible information, both at the time of engagement and when appropriate as their matter progresses, about the likely overall cost of their matter;

O(1.14) clients are informed of their right to challenge or complain about your

---

[23] *HL Debs*, 1613, 1 November 1994, col 789.
[24] *HL Debs*, 12 June 1995, col 1560.

bill and the circumstances in which they may be liable to pay interest on an unpaid bill;

Fee arrangements with your client

IB(1.13) discussing whether the potential outcomes of the client's matter are likely to justify the expense or risk involved, including any risk of having to pay someone else's legal fees;

IB(1.14) clearly explaining your fees and if and when they are likely to change;

IB(1.15) warning about any other payments for which the client may be responsible;

IB(1.16) discussing how the client will pay, including whether public funding may be available, whether the client has insurance that might cover the fees, and whether the fees may be paid by someone else such as a trade union;

IB(1.17) where you are acting for a client under a fee arrangement governed by statute, such as a conditional fee agreement, giving the client all relevant information relating to that arrangement;

IB(1.18) where you are acting for a publicly funded client explaining how their publicly funded status affects the costs;

IB(1.19) providing the information in a clear and accessible form which is appropriate to the needs and circumstances of the client;

IB(1.27) entering into unlawful fee arrangements such as an unlawful contingency fee;

Q5.14 What Outcomes and Indicative Behaviours would you suggest for regulating the setting of contingency fees?

Case Study
The Miners' Costs Scandal

The miners' costs scandal was a toxic mix of some of the issues considered so far in this chapter. These include overcharging, referral arrangements and abuse of conditional fee arrangements (CFAs). The context was the establishment in the 1990s of two compensation schemes for coalminers. One scheme was for those suffering from vibration white finger (VWF), a condition caused by using vibrating tools. The other was for sufferers from conditions such as chronic bronchitis and emphysema, known collectively as chronic obstructive pulmonary disease (COPD), caused by work in dusty conditions.

The schemes were inundated with claims and the compensation paid out far outstripped industry estimates of its liability. Parliament initially became involved because of the massive cost of the schemes and the suspicion of fraud. Further investigation found no evidence of fraud but did raise some questions about the conduct of solicitors representing the miners. The schemes established required claims to be submitted, following which investigations took place and a decision made about the level of compensation based on scales established and agreed between the former employers and 'lead firms' among the solicitors.

Apparently, as far as the solicitors were concerned, there was little work involved. Miners' unions often vetted and presented cases for forwarding under the scheme. Some solicitors also received claims from claims management companies, which specialised in advertising for and recruiting personal injury clients. A large number of firms were involved in processing claims under the schemes. The scheme paid scale fees to solicitors for cases submitted under the scheme where payments were made to miners.

Members of the House of Lords became angry when it was revealed that some solicitors were making additional charges under CFAs. The solicitors justified this on the grounds that not all cases were successful and, where they failed, they were not paid. This risk, they claimed justified the use of CFAs. The Law Society resisted pressure to intervene for some years. It argued that there was nothing wrong in principle with deducting additional fees. Nevertheless, the Parliamentary Under-Secretary for Coal Health wrote personally to panel firms asking them to confirm that they had not been making additional charges.

A further complication was the standard payments made by solicitors to claims management companies as expenses for vetting cases and conducting investigations. These were declared by a High Court judge to be payments for referrals. Payments as a reward for referrals were banned at the time under the Law Society's Introduction and Referral Code, and it transpired that some miners had been charged a fee for bringing their claim. Members of parliament, particularly in the House of Lords, encouraged miners in their home constituencies to complain. In July 2003 the Law Society made an announcement in the *The Gazette* warning solicitors that payments made to claims management companies could amount to referral fees in breach of the introduction and referral code.[25]

Eventually, investigations took place at some of the firms. This revealed abuse far beyond that which had been suspected. It included deductions that amounted to contingency fees and payment of what were effectively referral fees to trade union and claims management companies. In a few extreme

---

[25] 'Introductions and Referrals' [2003] *Law Society Gazette*, 18 July, www.lawgazette.co.uk/news/title-19.

cases, solicitors had set up claims management companies themselves and were making payments to them from miners' compensation.

In a written answer to the House of Commons it was announced that 115 solicitors in 25 firms would be referred to the Solicitors Disciplinary Tribunal in connection with the miners' costs scandal.[26] Hearings of cases began in 2006 and ended in 2010. Three solicitors were struck off and three suspended for periods of between six months and four years. A further 47 solicitors were fined. The largest fine was £25,000 with most fines being £10,000 or under. Six solicitors were reprimanded. A handful of cases were either not pursued or the allegations were withdrawn. Of the solicitors charged, regulatory settlement agreements were entered into by the SRA with three firms covering 16 solicitors in these firms. These recorded acceptance of the charges and agreed sanctions such as a reprimand and payment of costs.

The solicitors who were struck off had allowed serious solicitor and own-client conflicts of interest to arise so that they could not act or did not act in the best interests of their client. These included:

• Setting up claims management companies and collecting referral fees from clients on behalf of these companies.
• Making payments to claims management companies and trade unions for administration or investigation that were actually referral fees
• Using bogus and unenforceable CFAs to collect fees over and above the scale charges payable to lawyers under the Coal Health schemes.
• Responding to the Under-Secretary for Coal Health's letter asking about additional payments by falsely claiming that none were deducted from miners' compensation.

In these cases striking off was accompanied by findings of dishonesty accompanying one or more of these charges.

For a more details including consideration of one of the cases brought to the Solicitors Disciplinary Tribunal, see further A Boon and A Whyte, 'Icarus Falls: The Coal Health Scandal' (2012) 15(2) *Legal Ethics* 277.

Q5.15 In what ways might regulation have prevented the miners' costs scandal?

Q5.16 Which outcomes and indicative behaviours in the current SRA Code of Conduct would be relevant to infractions arising in the coal health scandal?

---

[26] *Hansard*, 19 May 2009.

Clients with Conflicting Interests

Context

It may be useful to return to the definition of an interest as a benefit or advantage that a person may wish to assert or protect. How a benefit or advantage is defined is crucial to the issue of what constitutes a conflict of interest. A classic example is the position between divorcing couples. It is usual for a solicitor to represent a husband and wife while they are married. On most issues they will probably have a common interest, although there may be situations where the solicitor would be wise to suggest that one or the other seeks independent advice.

When a married couple divorces or separates their interests may suddenly and dramatically diverge. Therefore, the couple's solicitor cannot continue to act for both parties because he cannot act in the best interests of both. If the solicitor decides to act for one of the parties, the other may well think that they have lost a benefit or advantage relative to their former partner.

The English courts have indicated that deciding whether to continue acting for clients when they divorce is a matter of professional judgement for the lawyer.[27] This may be unproblematic in situations where the lawyer has a strong relationship with one party and barely knows the other. Where the lawyer is close to both parties it might seem fairer if the solicitor declines to act for either. This is, however, a situation in which the lawyer arguably owes a continuing duty of loyalty to both parties. It is not, for example, purely a problem of reconciling the duty of disclosure and the duty of confidentiality (see chapter six: Confidentiality and Privilege).

It may be that not all interests, so defined, are protected by rules against lawyers acting in conflict-of-interest situations. For example, strict conflict-of-interest rules could be used by parties to litigation or transactions to prevent certain lawyers from acting against them. It may be, however, that client A knows that lawyer B will be a very good advocate against his interest, but client A may be unable to prevent lawyer B acting for a competitor.

While the general principles of conflict of interest are common across legal professions, details often diverge. The situation where the interest of a present client could conflict with the interest of a past client tends to be dealt with differently in different jurisdictions. In the US, for example, such a situation is usually treated as a conflict of interest. In England and Wales it tends to be treated as a potential confidentiality problem. There is therefore no absolute

---

[27] *Royal Bank of Scotland v Etridge* [1998] 4 All ER 705.

prohibition on acting in such situations in England and Wales provided the past client's confidentiality can be protected in relation to the present client.

Regulatory Approach

There are different ways of classifying client conflicts of interest. The SRA Handbook defines a client conflict of interest for the purposes of Chapter 3 of the SRA Code of Conduct as 'any situation where you owe separate duties to act in the best interests of two or more *clients* in relation to the same or related matters, and those duties conflict, or there is a significant risk that those duties may conflict'.[28] This definition, by suggesting that a client conflict of interest can only arise in the context of 'the same or related matters', excludes the possibility that a continuing duty of loyalty arises. This approach can be contrasted with that of the American Bar Association in its model rules (see the end of this chapter).

Same Matter Conflicts of Interest

A lawyer cannot satisfy the requirement of acting in clients' best interests if they were to act for clients with competing interests in relation to the same matter. It is obvious that lawyers cannot act for both sides in either litigation or most transaction work. There are, however, some situations where, for practical or financial reasons, a risk of conflict of interest is accepted, or managed, to a degree. As well as constituting exceptions, these are cases in which the difficulties inherent in conflict-of-interest situations are illustrated.

Litigation

It is not uncommon for lawyers to be instructed to act for co-defendants on criminal charges. This is often because it is cheaper when legally aided defendants face the same charges and have the same defence. Where one of the co-defendants changes his plea or defence the potential for a conflict of interest arises between the parties. This is certainly the case where a 'cut-throat defence' is adopted. This is where one defendant gives testimony on his/her own behalf, usually blaming the co-defendant for the crime.

Where there is a cut-throat defence the lawyers previously instructed by the defendants must cease to act for one of them; they can no longer act in the best interests of both. It is arguable that they should cease to act for both. This is because they probably have collected relevant information from the

---

[28] *SRA Handbook*, Glossary.

defendant they have ceased to act for. They cannot use this because it would breach their former client's confidentiality.[29] Therefore, they cannot act in their remaining client's best interests.

Acting for several parties with a common interest can also occur in civil litigation, but it is possible that their interests may diverge, revealing a conflict. Say, for example, that a lawyer is acting for the beneficiaries of a trust. The beneficiaries have an interest in common if the action is to establish the validity of a trust. There is, however, a conflict of interest if the action concerns their relative entitlements to remaining trust funds.

A slightly different problem is posed by multi-party actions, which are called class actions in the US. Such actions have typically been against drug manufacturers whose products have caused injuries or birth defects. These often involve hundreds or even thousands of claimants with a common cause of action using one lawyer. The EU has been keen to encourage such action, particularly for consumer complaints. Usually, individual consumer claims are too small for individuals to pursue. Class actions make such claims viable.[30]

The problem in these kinds of action is not that the claimants' substantive interests diverge; they all have an interest in receiving compensation for their injuries. There can, however, be practical problems, such as defining the class. Class actions can also cause lawyers problems when it comes to acting in the clients' best interests. These arise because the lawyer cannot attend to relationships with all the clients. They may even find it difficult to get instructions. Because there are so many claimants, it is likely that views on simple issues, whether to accept an offer in settlement for example, will diverge. This, on a small scale, presents a conflict-of-interest problem.

Transactions

Lawyers should not normally act for more than one party to a transaction where the interests of the parties conflict.[31] An exception to this proposition is made in the case of the transfer of land, conveyancing, despite the fact that it is a transaction in which such conflicts of interest can arise. The most common example occurs routinely. This is because building societies and other mortgage lenders use the property that purchasers are buying as security for the mortgage loan.

If the purchaser defaults on mortgage payments the property may need to be sold in order to recoup the amount that has not been paid off. In order to reduce costs to purchasers, building societies generally ask the purchaser's

---

[29] See chapter eight and *R v Ataou* [1988] 1 QB 798.
[30] BFY Chee, 'EU to Pave Way for Class Actions against Cartels', Reuters, http://uk.reuters.com/article/2013/06/06/uk-eu-classactions-idUKBRE95514R20130606.
[31] *Hilton v Barker Booth & Eastwood* [2005] UKHL 8.

solicitors to confirm that they are conveying good title to the purchaser and, generally, that the transaction is low risk. There is no necessary conflict of interest in this situation, but solicitors do need to consider the nature of the duty owed to the mortgage lender in that situation.

In the 1990s, in particular, the easy availability of mortgages encouraged fraud. Clients routinely borrowed more money than they needed to buy a property and spent the balance. Mortgage lenders sometimes found that they could not recover their loan by selling the property. If the solicitor knew things about the borrower that affected the risk the lender was taking, the lender had a good argument that the solicitor caused any loss.[32] The strength of this argument depends, of course, on what the solicitor was asked to do by the lender. The requirements for acting for lenders and borrowers/buyers are now fairly specific.

The 'Substantial Common Interest' Exception and 'Competing for the Same Objective' Exception

The SRA Handbook provides two specific exceptions to the general rule against acting in situations of conflict of interest. It states that, in circumstances where there is a significant risk of conflict between the interests of two or more clients, 'you must not act for all or both of them unless the matter falls within the scope of the limited exceptions set out at Outcomes 3.6 or 3.7'.[33] The two exceptions are where clients have a substantial common interest in the outcome or where they are competing for the same objective.

In deciding whether to act in the limited circumstances, 'the overriding consideration is whether the best interests of each client can be served by the same lawyer acting and whether the benefits to the clients outweigh the risks'.[34]

i. Substantial Common Interest

Solicitors can potentially act in a situation of apparent client conflict where the clients have a substantially common interest in relation to a matter or a particular aspect of it, provided they can comply with Outcome 3.6. This requires that:

- the solicitor has explained the relevant issues and risks to the clients; and
- the solicitor has a reasonable belief that the clients understand the issues and risks; and
- all clients have given informed consent in writing to the solicitor acting.

The solicitor must then be satisfied that it is reasonable to act for all the clients

---

[32] *National Home Loans Corporation v Giffen Couch & Archer* [1997] 3 All ER 808.
[33] See also *SRA Code of Conduct*, Chapter 3, Outcome 3.5.
[34] Ibid, Chapter 3, Preamble.

and that it is in their best interests. Finally, the solicitor must be satisfied that the benefits of acting for the clients outweigh the risks.[35] Unlike the situation where clients are competing for a common objective, the substantial common interest exception is not limited to commercial clients.

It is possible to envisage a commercial situation that might fall within this exception. Suppose two companies are bidding for a contract under a two-stage process. At the first stage potential bidders have to show that they meet the criteria for bidding. At the second stage they enter a competitive bidding process. Here, it would be conceivable that the same solicitor could act for both companies at the first stage but not at the second stage.

A situation of substantially common interest within the exception does not, however, exist where the clients' interests in the end result are different. Examples given in the code include a partner buying out the interest of another partner in their joint business or a seller transferring a property to a buyer.[36]

ii. Competing for the Same Objective

The second exception allowing a solicitor to represent clients in a potential conflict situation arises under Outcome 3.7. This covers situations where clients are competing for the same objective. An indicative behaviour indicates that the outcomes directed at avoiding conflicts of interest are more likely to be met where clients are sophisticated users of legal services.[37] There is, however, nothing in the way that the outcomes are framed that restricts them in this way.

Outcome 3.7 might arguably apply to the second stage in the bidding example given in the previous section. In such circumstances, solicitors can act if they have explained the relevant issues to the clients and where they have a reasonable belief that the clients understand those issues and risks. The clients must then confirm in writing that they want the solicitors to act, knowing that they are competing with other clients for the same objective.

Clients competing for the same objective are likely to be undertaking an activity such as bidding for a franchise. In such a situation it might be convenient for a solicitor to perform investigations (due diligence) for both parties, but not be involved in the bidding process. They are not likely to be met where a solicitor is acting for two private purchasers, eg two buyers competing to buy a residential property.[38]

When solicitors act for clients competing for the same objective, no individual within the firm can act for more than one client in the matter unless the clients specifically agree otherwise. Nor can one person be responsible for

---

[35] Ibid, Chapter 3, Outcome 3.6.
[36] Ibid, Indicative Behaviour 3.11.
[37] Ibid, Indicative Behaviour 3.6.
[38] Ibid, Indicative Behaviour 3.13.

supervising the work of different individuals working on the different clients' matters. Notwithstanding these safeguards the solicitor must still be satisfied that it is reasonable to act for all the clients and that the benefits to them outweigh the risks.[39]

SRA Code of Conduct (as amended)

O(3.5) you do not act if there is a client conflict, or a significant risk of a client conflict, unless the circumstances set out in Outcomes 3.6 or 3.7 apply.

IB(3.7) acting for clients who are the lender and borrower on the grant of a mortgage of land only where:

(a) the mortgage is a standard mortgage (i.e. one provided in the normal course of the lender's activities, where a significant part of the lender's activities consists of lending and the mortgage is on standard terms) of property to be used as the borrower's private residence;
(b) you are satisfied that it is reasonable and in the clients' best interests for you to act; and
(c) the certificate of title required by the lender is in the form approved by the [Law] Society and the Council of Mortgage Lenders.

Q5.17 Is the situation where a solicitor acts for both mortgage lender and borrower in conveyancing transactions a situation of substantial common interest?

Q5.18 Does the existence of IB 3.7 mean that acting for a purchaser and a mortgage lender in the circumstances set out in in paragraphs (a)–(c) does not present a significant risk of a client conflict?

Systems for Detecting Conflicts of Interest

The SRA Code of Conduct places great emphasis on detecting potential conflicts of interest and the decision-making that then takes place before the client is accepted. Systems of detection for both own-interest conflicts and potential client conflicts must be appropriate to the size and complexity of the firm and the nature of the work undertaken. Nevertheless, the Outcomes require that all firms of solicitors, even sole practitioners, must have them.

Having identified potential conflicts of interest, the decision-making process should consider whether the ability of the solicitor or anyone else in the firm is impaired by financial interests, personal relationships or public office

---

[39] Ibid, Chapter 3, Outcome 3.7.

held.[40] In considering client conflicts solicitors should decide whether negotiation between clients may be required and if so whether there is imbalance in bargaining power or vulnerability in one of the clients.[41] These factors may point to a need for separate representation.

American Bar Association
Model Rules of Professional Conduct

Rule 1.7: Conflict of Interest: Current Clients

Client–Lawyer Relationship

Rule 1.7 Conflict of Interest: Current Clients

(a) Except as provided in paragraph (b), a lawyer shall not represent a client if the representation involves a concurrent conflict of interest. A concurrent conflict of interest exists if:
- (1) the representation of one client will be directly adverse to another client; or
- (2) there is a significant risk that the representation of one or more clients will be materially limited by the lawyer's responsibilities to another client, a former client or a third person or by a personal interest of the lawyer.

(b) Notwithstanding the existence of a concurrent conflict of interest under paragraph (a), a lawyer may represent a client if:
- (1) the lawyer reasonably believes that the lawyer will be able to provide competent and diligent representation to each affected client;
- (2) the representation is not prohibited by law;
- (3) the representation does not involve the assertion of a claim by one client against another client represented by the lawyer in the same litigation or other proceeding before a tribunal; and
- (4) each affected client gives informed consent, confirmed in writing.

Q5.19 Are the English or US rules on concurrent client conflicts generally more restrictive?

Q5.20 Which jurisdiction gives greater flexibility on the issue of informed consent to conflicts of interest between current clients?

---

[40] Ibid, Chapter 3, Outcome 3.2.
[41] Ibid, Chapter 3, Outcome 3.3.

Conflict of Interests between Clients in Different Matters

In England and Wales, conflict rules apply to current clients. The issue of whether lawyers can act against former clients in an unrelated matter is treated as an issue of confidentiality rather than an issue of conflict of interest.[42] On the face of it, the US rules on conflicts of interest look stricter. They define two situations of conflict of interest that would be issues of confidentiality in England and Wales.

The first situation in the ABA Model Rules of Conduct conflicts of interest can arise where lawyers propose acting against former clients for new clients in 'the same or a substantially related matter in which that person's interests are materially adverse to the interests of the former client'. This rule only bites in relation to the 'same or substantially related matters', so the impact depends on how a 'substantially related matter' is defined. Presumably, satellite litigation would be caught, whereas a matter that was ostensibly different, but was in fact the continuation of a 'trade war' between corporations, would be more debatable.

American Bar Association
Model Rules of Professional Conduct

Rule 1.9: Duties to Former Clients

Client–Lawyer Relationship

Rule 1.9 Duties to Former Clients

(a) A lawyer who has formerly represented a client in a matter shall not thereafter represent another person in the same or a substantially related matter in which that person's interests are materially adverse to the interests of the former client unless the former client gives informed consent, confirmed in writing.

(b) A lawyer shall not knowingly represent a person in the same or a substantially related matter in which a firm with which the lawyer formerly was associated had previously represented a client

> (1) whose interests are materially adverse to that person; and
> (2) about whom the lawyer had acquired information protected by Rules 1.6 and 1.9(c) that is material to the matter;

unless the former client gives informed consent, confirmed in writing.

---

[42] *Rakusen v Ellis Munday and Clarke* [1912] 1 Ch 831.

Q5.21 How do you think *Rakusen v Ellis Munday and Clarke* (see chapter five: Conflicts of Interest, footnote 42) or *Bolkiah v KPMG* (see chapter six: Confidentiality and Privilege) would be decided applying these rules?

Q5.22 How would you define 'the same or a substantially related matter'?

The second situation covered in the ABA Model Rules is a so-called 'imputa-tion' of conflict of interests. It covers the situation arising in the English case *Re A Firm of Solicitors*.[43] In that case a solicitor (Y) moved from Firm A to Firm B. Later, Firm B was instructed to act for the defendant in a patent case brought by X Co, a former client of Firm A. X Co was refused an injunction to prevent Firm B acting. The court was anxious to protect the freedom of the claimant to instruct a solicitor of its choice. Firm B showed that Y held no relevant information about X Co. There was no reasonable prospect of a conflict between the two clients.

Rule 1.10: Imputation of Conflicts of Interest: General Rule

Client–Lawyer Relationship

Rule 1.10 Imputation of Conflicts of Interest: General Rule

(a) While lawyers are associated in a firm, none of them shall knowingly represent a client when any one of them practicing alone would be prohibited from doing so by Rules 1.7 or 1.9, unless

  (1) the prohibition is based on a personal interest of the disqualified lawyer and does not present a significant risk of materially limiting the representation of the client by the remaining lawyers in the firm; or

  (2) the prohibition is based upon Rule 1.9(a) or (b) and arises out of the disqualified lawyer's association with a prior firm, and

    (i) the disqualified lawyer is timely screened from any participation in the matter and is apportioned no part of the fee therefrom;

    (ii) written notice is promptly given to any affected former client to enable the former client to ascertain compliance with the provisions of this Rule, which shall include a description of the screening procedures employed; a statement of the firm's and of the screened lawyer's compliance with these Rules; a statement that review may be available before a tribunal; and an agreement by the firm to respond promptly to any written inquiries or objections by the former client about the screening procedures;

---

[43] *Re A Firm of Solicitors* [1995] 3 All ER 482.

Q5.23 Applying these rules, how would *Re A Firm of Solicitors* be decided?

Q5.24 Based on the extracts in this section, how do the ABA model rules on conflict of interest differ from the English rules?

Conclusion

The need to avoid conflicts of interests is central to the notion of client loyalty. Avoiding conflicts between a lawyer and his/her client is not always possible. Therefore, the areas in which such conflicts generally arise, over fees for example, tend to be the focus of more detailed rules. Such rules sometimes permit judicious management of such conflicts, possibly by allowing clients to give informed consent. The conditions for giving consent must, however, also be carefully managed.

It is also necessary to regulate potential conflicts between the interests of clients. Lawyers often serve several masters but they cannot do so effectively if they cannot do their best for them in every situation. It may also be possible for inter-client conflicts to be managed. The methods for achieving this partly depend on how they are defined. If a potential conflict is defined as an issue of confidentiality, the solution may be to control information rather than to prevent representation. This possibility is considered in the next chapter.

6

Confidentiality and Privilege

The lawyer's duty of confidentiality is the foundation of the basis of trust in his/her relationship with clients. It means that a lawyer should not say anything about a client, even to confirm that they are acting for them, without the client's express permission. The lawyer's obligation of confidentiality is recognised in and protected by law. The duty of confidentiality is recognised by the courts and protected by legal professional privilege (LPP).

When it applies, LPP ensures that neither lawyer nor client can be required by the courts to give evidence about what has passed between them. This veil of secrecy ensures that clients can tell their lawyer everything they know about their problems. This should ensure that clients receive legal advice that takes account of all relevant factors, including any weaknesses in the client's position.

Theory of Client Confidence

Professionals and Confidences

The acceptance of a duty of confidence is the norm amongst professionals generally. Most professions are put in situations where exceptions have to be made to the duty of confidentiality. In the case of doctors, for example, exceptions are made for information that must be reported by law or in the public interest. Therefore, doctors receive special guidance on reporting concerns about patients to the Driver and Vehicle Licensing Agency, reporting gunshot and knife wounds, and disclosing information about serious communicable diseases.[1]

The General Position at Common Law

A common law duty of confidence applies to situations beyond the duty owed by lawyers to clients. The origin of the general duty of confidence is obscure. Some early, isolated cases demonstrate the courts' willingness to protect a right to confidence,[2] but the modern law dates from around the mid-nineteenth century.[3] It protects information divulged in confidence in many situations, and is implied when it is the reasonable expectation of those involved in a communication.

The conditions in which confidences will be protected, whether by injunction, an order for account or an award of damages, have been judicially defined as follows:

> First, the information itself ... must 'have the necessary quality of confidence about it'. Secondly, that information must have been communicated in circumstances importing an obligation of confidence. Thirdly, there must have been an unauthorised use of the information to the detriment of the party communicating it.[4]

The classic case of breach of confidence involves a claimant's confidential information, such as a trade secret, being used inconsistently with its confidential nature by a defendant, who received it in circumstances where she had agreed, or ought to have appreciated, that it was confidential.[5] A simple example of the classic case is *Seager v Copydex*.[6] There the defendants used details of an unpatented invention revealed in a negotiation to purchase a similar, patented invention, to produce a similar product. This was held to be a breach of confidence.

The broad principle enunciated by the Court of Appeal in *Seager v Copydex*, is that a party using confidential information, obtained directly or indirectly from another party, without their express or implied consent, is guilty of infringing the other party's rights. It was said that the obligation does not depend on an implied contract but on the broad principle of equity that he who has received information in confidence shall not take unfair advantage of it without obtaining his consent. For the conscience of recipients to be affected, they must have agreed, or must know, that the information is confidential.

---

[1] General Medical Council, *Confidentiality: Guidance for Doctors* (London, GMC, 2009).

[2] *Duke of Queensberry v Shebbeare* (1758) 2 Eden 329.

[3] *Prince Albert v Strange* (1849) 2 De G & Sm 652 on Appeal 1 Mac & G 25 and see further *Halsbury's Laws* vol 8(1) paras 401–06.

[4] *Coco v AN Clark (Engineers) Ltd* [1968] FSR 415, [1969] RPC 41 per Megarry J, 47.

[5] *Attorney-General v Guardian Newspapers Ltd (No 2)* [1990] 1 AC 109 , per Lord Goff, 281.

[6] *Seager v Copydex Ltd. No 1* [1967] 1 WLR 973.

Other cases treat an obligation of confidence as arising as either an implied contractual obligation or an equitable obligation.[7]

There is no right of confidence over information that is public knowledge. When information is mixed, being partly public and partly private, then the recipient must take special care to use only the material that is in the public domain. There is a public interest in the disclosure of some information in breach of confidence. This can operate as a defence to actions. In general situations the duty of confidentiality can be outweighed by a countervailing public interest requiring disclosure of the information.[8] This is sometimes referred to as a public interest in revealing iniquity.

Lawyer and Client Confidences

The Absolute Nature of Client and Lawyer Confidences

The obligation of confidentiality that exists between lawyer and client is fundamental to the relationship. This was well established by the eighteenth century. In *Annesley v Anglesey*, for example, it was said that: (1) a 'gentleman of character' does not disclose his client's secrets; (2) an attorney identifies with his client, and it would be 'contrary to the rules of natural justice and equity' for an individual to betray himself; (3) attorneys are necessary for the conduct of business, and business would be destroyed if attorneys were to disclose their communications with their clients.[9]

The lawyer's duty of confidence, however, extends beyond the business field to cover all their legally related work. It requires that lawyers make no unauthorised revelations about the client or their case produced as a result of the lawyer–client relationship. Typically, the duty is absolute and permanent. Even after the relationship ends, the duty of silence persists. Breaches of confidence are likely to be regarded as serious violations that would usually result in disciplinary proceedings and severe sanctions.

One example of the absolute nature of client confidences is that lawyers can never tell the police if a client confesses to having committed a crime. In the much-quoted and much-criticised US case of *State v Macumber*[10] two lawyers were prevented from testifying in a capital murder trial in Arizona. Their evidence would have been that their deceased client had confessed the murder to them. The deceased's legal privilege trumped the rights of a potentially innocent defendant and the state's interest in the administration of justice.

---

[7] *Robb v Green* [1895] 2 QB 315.
[8] *Attorney General v Observer Ltd and other respondents* [1990] 1 AC 109.
[9] *Annesley v Anglesey* 17 How St Tr 1140, 1223–226, 1241 (Ex, 1743); JT Noonan 'The Purposes of Advocacy and the Limits of Confidentiality' (1966) 64 *Michigan Law Review* 1485.
[10] *State v Macumber* 112 Arizona 569,544 PZd 1084 (1976).

Rationale for Protecting Client Confidences

Practical Rationale

On the face of it, the professional duty of respecting confidences seems easy to justify in very practical terms. Without an expectation of confidentiality it would be impossible to advise or represent someone. Therefore,

> to enable him successfully to perform the duties of his office, that the law has considered it the wisest policy to encourage and sanction this confidence, by requiring that on such facts the mouth of the attorney shall be forever sealed.[11]

Surprisingly, the proposition that clients would not consult lawyers who gossip about their affairs has been doubted. Cranston thought that most clients were ignorant of their rights, asking whether 'empirical evidence would lend any support to the rationale of encouraging client disclosure'.[12] Cranston's claim seems doubtful, although there is little empirical evidence either way. If, for example, criminal clients are ignorant of their position, lawyers are arguably under an obligation to inform them of it. It is probably true, however, that many clients are not fully aware of the nuances of the rules on confidentiality.

Research by Zacharias found a low correlation between client frankness and knowledge of rules on confidentiality.[13] Although there are criticisms of the design of such studies, practitioners would probably agree with Zacharias's conclusion that 'in routine cases, attorney–client confidentiality is uncontroversial'. This is probably because most clients who seek advice on commercial, criminal or highly personal matters assume the confidentiality of the information they provide.

Professional Rationale

The duty of confidentiality is consistent with other general ethical duties of lawyers. It is central to the obligation to act in the client's best interest and not to profit personally from client information. It is also connected to rules against acting where there is a conflict of interest between clients. In some circumstances acting for a client could involve breaching the confidentiality of past clients. This possibility has to be controlled.

---

[11] *Hatton v Robinson* 31 Mass (12 Pick) 416 (1834) per Chief Justice Lemuel Shaw, Supreme Judicial Court of Massachusetts, 422.

[12] R Cranston (ed), *Legal Ethics and Professional Responsibility*, (Oxford, Clarendon Press, 1995) 9.

[13] FC Zacharias, 'Rethinking Confidentiality' (1989) 74 *Iowa Law Review* 351.

System Rationale

It is necessary that clients are frank with their lawyers if they are to receive the best advice and most appropriate representation. It is arguable, therefore, that the rationale for protecting confidences is justified by the need to uphold the rule of law and the proper administration of justice. It is also arguable that confidentiality is necessary because lawyers in possession of the best information will produce the arguments that lead to the correct decisions. This idea of using proper processes to produce decisions is intrinsic to upholding the rule of law and the administration of justice.

i. Rule of Law

The lawyer's role is to support the rule of law by ensuring that all individuals can enjoy their rights. To achieve this the law must be blind to ethnicity, gender, status or other distinguishing characteristic. For lawyers to uphold this promise they must be able to understand their client's best interests, including what their client would wish for themselves. This protects individual legal rights, by ensuring that offenders have the best defence available on the true facts.[14] In *Three Rivers DC v Bank of England*, one of the leading cases on the right of clients to protect confidential information, Lord Scott stated that he subscribed to 'the rule of law rationale' even though it meant that cases would sometimes be decided in ignorance of relevant evidence.[15] An extended extract from Lord Scott's judgement appears below.

ii. Administration of Justice

In the leading House of Lords case on the confidentiality of client information Lord Millett said:

> It is of overriding importance for the proper administration of justice that a client should be able to have complete confidence that what he tells his lawyer will remain secret. This is a matter of perception as well as substance. It is of the highest importance to the administration of justice that a solicitor or other person in possession of confidential and privileged information should not act in any way that might appear to put that information at risk of coming into the hands of someone with an adverse interest.[16]

---

[14] See below, *R v Derby Magistrates' Court, ex parte B* [1996] AC 487 and *B v Auckland District Law Society* [2004]4 All ER 269, *D v NSPCC* [1977] 1 All ER 589, 606.

[15] *Three Rivers DC v Bank of England*, para 34, citing *Zuckerman's Civil Procedure* (2003) paras 15.8–15.10.

[16] *Bolkiah v KPMG* [1999] 1 All ER 517, 528.

Client Autonomy

A right of confidentiality is central to the idea of personal autonomy. An ideal of modern, liberal societies is that people can enjoy and enforce their rights. This includes privacy, a 'right' that is increasingly protected under the Human Rights Act.[17] Article 8 of the European Convention on Human Rights provides that everyone has the right to respect for his private and family life, his home and his correspondence.[18] Article 8 goes on to provide that:

> There shall be no interference by a public authority with the exercise of this right except … in the interests of national security, public safety or the economic well-being of the country, for the prevention of disorder or crime, for the protection of health or morals, or for the protection of the rights and freedoms of others.

In a complex modern society legal rights may not be understood by individuals, or realised, without the assistance of a lawyer. The lawyer is seen as being an extension of the client; their interests are the same, 'this identity of lawyer and client provides the moral foundation for an absolute privilege. … If we regard them as constituting one conceptual unit then, *ex hypothesi*, no "communication", as such, has been made.'[19] Article 8 is a reminder that the circumstances in which the state should interfere with the individual's right to privacy, including their private correspondence, are exceptional.

For information and privacy to be secure the relationship between citizens and advisers must be built on trust. This is recognised by the American Bar Association Model Code, which states that:

> A fundamental principle in the client–lawyer relationship is that, in the absence of the client's informed consent, the lawyer must not reveal information relating to the representation. … This contributes to the trust that is the hallmark of the client–lawyer relationship.[20]

Client autonomy is reflected in the notion that the lawyer does for clients what they could legally do for themselves. Autonomy is supported by the idea that the lawyer client relationship is essentially contractual. In most circumstances the betrayal of client confidence would not only be a breach of trust, it would also be a breach of contract.

---

[17] *Morgan Grenfell v Special Commissioners of the IR* [2002] UKHL 21; *R v Sec of State for the Home Dept, ex parte Daly* [2001] UKHL 26.

[18] Human Rights Act (1998) Schedule 1.

[19] A Paizes, 'Towards a Broader Balancing of Interests: Exploring the Theoretical Foundations of the Legal Professional Privilege' (1989) 109 *South African Law Journal* 109, 120, cited by HL Ho, 'Legal Professional Privilege and the Integrity of Legal Representation' (2006) 9 *Legal Ethics* 163, 180.

[20] *ABA Model Rules of Professional Conduct* 2004 rule 1.6, Comment 2.

Case Study
A Breach of Confidence[21]

JK Rowling, the author of the Harry Potter novels, sued Soho law firm Russells for breach of confidence after a partner's indiscretion led to her being identified as the crime writer 'Robert Galbraith', author of a new book called *The Cuckoo's Calling*.

The partner, Chris Gossage, had told his wife's best friend, Judith Callegari, who had then tweeted the information to a *Sunday Times* journalist. The story became front-page news. The news caused huge sales of the book, but it had not been Rowling's intention to use her celebrity to promote *The Cuckoo's Calling*.

At a court hearing to confirm settlement of the case counsel for Russells offered its 'sincere apologies to the claimant for breach of the claimant's confidence'. It promised that the breach was the only confidential information revealed to a third party and undertook that no further disclosures would be made. The firm had made a 'substantial donation' to The Soldier's Charity by way of damages and would pay the author's legal costs.

In a statement to the court Rowling's solicitor, Jenny Afia, a partner at Schillings, said the writer was 'angry and distressed that her confidences had been betrayed and this was very much aggravated by repeated speculation that the leak had, in fact, been a carefully co-ordinated publicity stunt by her, her agent and her publishers designed to increase sales'. Rowling, it was said, was 'left dismayed and distressed by such a fundamental breach of trust'.

Russells had reported the matter to the SRA. A spokesman for the SRA said that firms were obliged to report breaches of confidentiality and that it was 'aware of the issue'.

Q6.1   The SRA decided not to refer the case to the Solicitors Disciplinary Tribunal. Using its power of administrative sanction it issued a written rebuke to Mr Gossage and ordered him to pay a financial penalty of £1,000.[22] Consider whether this decision is consistent with the requirement of the Legal Services Act section 28 that 'regulatory activities should be transparent, accountable, proportionate, consistent and targeted only at cases in which action is needed'.

Q6.2   Would a lawyer be able to do her job properly if she were not bound by a duty of confidentiality?

---

[21] 'JK Rowling Wins Breach of Confidence Damages' [2013] *Solicitors Journal*, 31 July, www.solicitorsjournal.com/news/regulation/conduct/jk-rowling-wins-breach-confidence-damages.

[22] www.sra.org.uk/consumers/solicitor-check/274860.article?Decision-1.

Rationale for Limiting Confidentiality

Declining Adversarial Ethos in Civil Litigation

In England and Wales both criminal proceedings and most civil proceedings are adversarial. The adversarial ethos of civil litigation is being tempered by the development of Civil Procedure Rules designed to enhance co-operation. This may undermine the justification for preserving confidences. If the main aim of the system is the administration of justice, it is arguable that courts must be aware of as much information as possible. There is less tolerance for the rights of a client, for example, when it means that evidence of child abuse or unlawfully siphoning off money from a pension fund may be kept from the court.

A body of academic opinion suggests that the law, and the rules of legal practice, should protect the innocent third party from injury rather than the perpetrator.[23] The lay public may also wonder why an institution should work so hard to protect the guilty, potentially at the expense of the innocent, as in *State v Macumber*. Critics of secrecy argue that lawyers' attitude to confidentiality becomes 'ritualistic and universal', encouraging 'a kind of moral blindness to the real issues of potential conflict and abuse'.[24]

Lawyer Self-Interest

Confidentiality can be regarded as protecting lawyers' pockets because it increases their appeal to clients. It arguably enhances their social status by conferring importance and legitimacy on legal roles. It also protects lawyers from criticism by hiding from public scrutiny dubious activities which some academics argue are encouraged by lawyers' neutral and partisan role.[25] Lawyers are accused of using confidentiality selfishly because they abandon it once it is against their self-interest.

An example of having their cake and eating it arises when lawyers are sued by their clients for malpractice. In these circumstances lawyers claim that the right to confidentiality is necessarily breached; they need to reveal details of the case to defend themselves. This seems an unfair criticism of lawyers. It is as understandable as it is necessary that lawyers would wish the facts to be considered in such cases. Such an example certainly does not justify abolishing or restricting confidentiality.

---

[23] R Wasserstrom, 'Lawyers as Professionals; Some Moral Issues' (1975–76) 5 *Human Rights* 1; W Simon, 'Ethical Discretion in Lawyering' (1988) 101 *Harvard Law Review* 1083, 1142; DR Fischel, 'Lawyers and Confidentiality' (1998) 65 *University of Chicago Law Review* 1; D Nicolson and J Webb, *Professional Legal Ethics: Critical Interrogations* (Oxford, Oxford University Press, 1999) ch 9; and Ho (n 19).

[24] C Wolfram, *Modern Legal Ethics* (St Paul, MN, West Publishing, 1996) 246.

[25] Nicolson and Webb (n 23) 255.

A more difficult example is where the obligation of confidentiality obstructs lawyers from gaining new kinds of work. Some law firms have public relations and lobbying sections. The main lobbyists' association, the Association of Professional Political Consultants, was referred to the competition authorities by a law firm. The Association had tried to gain exclusive access to government agencies for its members.[26] Law firms complained that they could not join the Association because it required members to disclose clients involved in political lobbying. This, the firm said, would be a breach of their client's confidentiality.

The Public Interest

The public interest in protecting confidential information in the hands of lawyers is arguably balanced by an interest in disclosure in certain circumstances. For example, if a lawyer has information that suggests that a client's activity will result in social harm of some kind, should they be under a responsibility to report this? As we shall see in chapter eight, such responsibilities do exist, but they are closely circumscribed. Obviously, over-zealous pursuit of any whistle-blowing responsibility undermines the values protected by allowing information secrecy. It is important, therefore, that the limits of confidentiality and privilege are well defined and understood and that any exceptions are clear. The limits of confidentiality are to some extent defined by LLP.

Legal Professional Privilege

Context

Legal professional privilege exists to protect the confidentiality of certain, but not all, communications between lawyer and client. Where it is found to exist it is, as will be seen, absolute. Where it does not exist a client may still be protected by the lawyer's duty of confidentiality. However, there are circumstances, described in chapter eight, where the court may order a lawyer or client to give evidence regarding a communication not protected by LPP.

Legal professional privilege is seen as a fundamental guarantee of the right to a fair trial under Article 6 of the European Convention on Human Rights.

---

[26] N Goswami, 'Lobbyists in Bid to "Ban" Law Firms from Govt Work' [2007] *The Lawyer*, 10 September.

The European Court of Human Rights has held that the various elements comprise the rights of the defence, equality of arms, the right of access to the courts, and the right of access to lawyers in civil and criminal proceedings. Each of these elements may be infringed if lawyers are unable to carry out their task of advising, defending and representing their clients satisfactorily as a consequence of the invasion of privilege.

Definition

Both a solicitor's duty of confidentiality and LPP were recognised and developed by common law. Legal professional privilege now has a statutory basis in the Police and Criminal Evidence Act 1984 section 10(1). This defines legal professional privilege as:

(a) communications between a professional legal adviser and his client or any person representing his client made in connection with the giving of legal advice to the client;

(b) communications between a professional legal adviser and his client or any person representing his client or between such an adviser or his client or any such representative and any other person made in connection with or in contemplation of legal proceedings and for the purposes of such proceedings; and

(c) items enclosed with or referred to in such communications and made—

(i) in connection with the giving of legal advice; or
(ii) in connection with or in contemplation of legal proceedings and for the purposes of such proceedings, when they are in the possession of a person who is entitled to possession of them.

(2) Items held with the intention of furthering a criminal purpose are not items subject to legal privilege.'

Legal Advice Privilege

Under section 10(1)(a) legal advice privilege relates only to communications between lawyers and clients that are intended to be confidential and for the purpose of obtaining advice. The privilege can only be claimed by the client. The lawyer is not able to claim that a communication with a client is privileged if the client wants to make it public. The courts have come to recognise legal advice privilege as fundamental to the administration of justice.

The House of Lords decision in *R v Derby Magistrates' Court, ex parte B*[27]

---

[27] *R v Derby Magistrates' Court, ex parte B* [1995] 4 All ER 526.

concerned a claim to disclose advice to another party that might have proved or disproved the guilt of a defendant in a criminal case. It was decided that the public interest in protecting privilege overrode the interest in doing justice in a particular case. It was important that clients could take legal advice secure in the knowledge that they could disclose everything to their lawyer. Therefore, once the existence of privilege was established it should be absolute.

Establishing the existence of privilege is not automatic. The communication must be for the purpose of giving legal advice. What constitutes legal advice is given a broad interpretation. In *Three Rivers District Council & Others v Governor and Company of the Bank of England (No 6)*[28] Baroness Hale observed that:

'legal advice is not confined to telling the client the law; it must include advice as to what should prudently and sensibly be done in the relevant legal context'. ... [t]here will always be borderline cases in which it is difficult to decide whether there is or is not a 'legal' context. But much will depend upon whether it is one in which it is reasonable for the client to consult the special professional knowledge and skills of a lawyer, so that the lawyer will be able to give the client sound advice as to what he should do, and just as importantly what he should not do, and how to do it.[29]

The *Three Rivers* case did impose a significant restriction on legal advice privilege. It does not cover all communications between a lawyer and the employees of a corporate client. Whether an employee is one of the smaller category of employees considered to be representative of the client for the purpose of LPP is a question of fact in each case. Otherwise, the *Three Rivers* case gave rather wide scope to legal advice privilege. This scope was called into question when the case went before the Court of Appeal. Lord Phillips had queried why legal advice privilege should apply to conveyancing matters. Were legal advice privilege not to apply to transactions generally, it would come very close to covering the same ground as litigation privilege.

Accountants consider that legal advice privilege distorts competition between them and lawyers when dealing with tax work. An example arose in relation to the Finance Act 2004. This provided a statutory framework for disclosure of tax avoidance schemes (DOTAS). Solicitors who provide services relating to specified taxes come within the ambit of the regime because of the definition of a 'promoter' set out in the Finance Act 2004 section 307.

The requirement to make a disclosure is subject to section 314 of the Act. This provides that nothing in Part 7 of the Finance Act 2004 requires disclosure of privileged information. The Chair of the Consultative Committee of Tax Bodies considered that lawyers had an unfair advantage over accountants. The regime requiring disclosure of certain types of tax schemes was subject to

[28] *Three Rivers District Council & Others v Governor and Company of the Bank of England (No 6)* [2004] 3 All ER 168 (Court of Appeal) and [2005] 1 AC 610 (House of Lords).
[29] Ibid, para 62.

LPP and, to that extent, did not apply to lawyers. They called, unsuccessfully, on the government to remedy this.[30]

Litigation Privilege

Litigation privilege covers communications between lawyers and clients but also, potentially, communications outside of the client–solicitor relationship. It relates to documents or verbal communications for the dominant purpose of litigation. This might include, for example, obtaining advice on prospective litigation, obtaining or collecting evidence or collecting information which may assist in obtaining evidence.

The communications covered are defined very broadly in the Police and Criminal Evidence Act 1984 (PACE) section 10(1)(b). They include communications between the lawyer and third parties and between the client and third parties and between these and 'any other person'. All of these communications are covered provided they are for the purpose of preparing or engaging in actual or contemplated proceedings.

Exceptions to LPP

i. Children Act 1989

Litigation privilege is thought not to apply to expert and other reports produced for purposes connected with cases brought under the Children Act 1989. The Act is concerned with securing the welfare of children and allocating responsibility for their care between parents, local authorities and other bodies. The exception is clearly justified for reports and other material produced by independent experts or by the Children and Family Court Advisory and Support Service, which is attached to family courts. This service advises courts regarding care proceedings or the arrangements for children whose parents have separated.

The rationale for denying litigation privilege to materials produced in Children Act proceedings lies in the fact that they are considered investigative rather than adversarial. This policy finds expression in the Family Proceedings Rules 1991 rule 4.23, which provides that documents normally treated as confidential can be disclosed to all parties, *guardians ad litem* and welfare officers. It is less obvious why parties should not retain privilege in reports they have commissioned themselves.

---

[30] R Baldwin, K Malleson, M Carr, and S Spicer, 'Scoping Study for the Regulatory Review of Legal Services' (Lord Chancellor's Department, March 2003) 154 *New Law Journal* 1463, 1511 and (October 2004) 154 *New Law Journal* 1608.

The signature case for party reports not being covered by litigation privilege in Children Act cases is *Re L*.[31] An expert report commissioned by a mother, a drug addict, had concluded that she had administered methadone to her child. The House of Lords held that the report should be disclosed to the police service, which was considering prosecution. Some reservations about these conclusions were expressed in the judgments and the issue remains debatable.

ii. Waiver

Clients can waive their right to the protection to both kinds of LPP. They can waive litigation privilege accidentally, for example where their lawyers disclose part of an expert report.[32] The principle is that disclosure cannot be selective and must be fair. Therefore, if privilege is waived for one document, disclosure of relevant background material may be ordered. No implied waiver operates when documents are mistakenly disclosed. In fact the recipient is obliged to return the document and not use it in litigation.[33]

iii. Items Required by the Regulator

The SRA and the BSB both claim the right to inspect the records and documents of parties they regulate. Despite some authority that LPP does not apply in such circumstances,[34] it is not entirely clear that this is a correct interpretation of their powers.[35] Unless statute provides an exception, it is safer to assume that disclosure to a regulator could be withheld and challenged on grounds of privilege.

In exceptional circumstances it may be in a party's best interests voluntarily to disclose privileged documents to a regulator. In order to reduce the risk of disclosure leading to a general waiver of privilege, documents should be sent with a covering letter. This should make it clear that the communication is privileged and that it is provided for a limited purpose and on strict terms as to confidentiality. The letter should state that disclosure does not constitute waiver of privilege. Finally, it should specify that any material provided should be destroyed or returned by the regulator in due course.

---

[31] *In re L (A Minor) (Police Investigation: Privilege)* [1997] AC 16.
[32] *Clough v Tameside and Glossop Health Authority* [1998] 2 All ER 971.
[33] *English & American Insurance Co Ltd v Herbert Smith* [1988] FSR 232.
[34] *Parry-Jones v Law Society* [1969] 1 Ch 1.
[35] *R v Special Commissioner and Another, Ex P Morgan Grenfell & Co Ltd* [2003] 1 AC 563.

Communications and Items Enclosed with or Referred to in Privileged Communications

Under PACE section 10(1)(c) items enclosed with privileged communications may be covered if the communication is protected. However, those items must have been 'made' for purposes covered by either of the privileges. Items do not become privileged simply by being enclosed with privileged communications.

Who Is a Lawyer for the Purpose of Legal Professional Privilege?

Legal advice privilege applies only to legal advice provided by legal advisers. In *Prudential PLC and Prudential (Gibraltar) Ltd v Special Commissioner of Income Tax and Philip Pandolfo (HM Inspector of Taxes)*[36] the House of Lords held that, notwithstanding the recognition of regulators by the Legal Services Act, specific legislative authority was required before legal advice given by a non-lawyer, such as an accountant, could attract legal advice privilege.

This raises the issue of whether approved persons under the Legal Services Act are deemed to be 'lawyers'. Fortunately, the Legal Services Act anticipated this problem by providing that, in addition to solicitors and barristers, other authorised persons could be covered when carrying out relevant reserved activities.

Legal Services Act 2007

Section 190: Legal professional privilege

(1) Subsection (2) applies where an individual ("P") who is not a barrister or solicitor—

(a) provides advocacy services as an authorised person in relation to the exercise of rights of audience,

(b) provides litigation services as an authorised person in relation to the conduct of litigation,

(c) provides conveyancing services as an authorised person in relation to reserved instrument activities, or

(d) provides probate services as an authorised person in relation to probate activities.

(2) Any communication, document, material or information relating to the provision of the services in question is privileged from disclosure in like manner as if P had at all material times been acting as P's client's solicitor.

(3) Subsection (4) applies where—

---

[36] *Prudential PLC and Prudential (Gibraltar) Ltd v Special Commissioner of Income Tax and Philip Pandolfo (HM Inspector of Taxes)* [2013] 2 AC 185.

(a) a licensed body provides services to a client, and
(b) the individual ("E") through whom the body provides those services—
  (i) is a relevant lawyer, or
  (ii) acts at the direction and under the supervision of a relevant lawyer ("the supervisor").

(4) Any communication, document, material or information relating to the provision of the services in question is privileged from disclosure only if, and to the extent that, it would have been privileged from disclosure if—

(a) the services had been provided by E or, if E is not a relevant lawyer, by the supervisor, and
(b) at all material times the client had been the client of E or, if E is not a relevant lawyer, of the supervisor.

Q6.3   To whom does section 190 extend LPP?
Q6.4   Who benefits from LPP and in what way?
Q6.5   Who and what does legal advice privilege cover?
Q6.6   Who and what might litigation privilege cover?

Confidentiality and Legal Professional Privilege

Similarities

There are similarities between confidentiality and LPP. The main one is that they are both directed to protecting clients' right to keep their information confidential and are mutually reinforcing. There could be no LPP without a prior obligation of confidentiality. Therefore a claim for privilege cannot be made for information already in the public domain.

Lawyers' commitment to confidentiality is protected by recognition of LPP. Legal professional privilege overlaps with and reinforces lawyer and client confidentiality by protecting clients' secrets from disclosure to courts or other authorities. Therefore, in England and Wales, the principle exemplified in *State v Macumber* is illustrated in the case of *R v Ataou* (see below, chapter eight).

The underlying rationale of recognition and protection of confidentiality and privilege tends to be similar. It is generally based on the right to receive wise counsel and the necessity of protected communication to encourage full disclosure. Both legal advice privilege and litigation privilege cover items, such as documents, created under their ambit. Since LPP exists for the benefit of clients they, but not their lawyers, can waive their right to confidentiality and LPP.

Differences

It is important to recognise that the confidentiality of communications between clients and their lawyer is not coextensive with legal advice privilege. Confidentiality is an obligation imposed on the lawyer regarding all communications with clients, including any material passing between them, providing they are in the nature of confidences. Legal advice privilege applies specifically to legal advice. The communications covered by confidentiality are therefore more extensive than those covered by legal advice privilege.

Another practical difference between confidentiality and LPP is that, whether or not legal advice privilege applies, the duty of confidence does; professionals do not gossip about what their clients may have told them whether or not that information is privileged. Because confidentiality is all-encompassing, professional codes of conduct only need refer to a duty of confidentiality. They tend not to refer to LPP.

Where LPP is found to exist, neither lawyer nor client will be required to give evidence about what has passed between them. Where a court denies a client's claim to LPP, and orders their lawyer to provide information or documents that are nevertheless confidential, in theory the lawyer must comply. If they disclose part of a privileged document, for example, this may be treated as an implied waiver of privilege in the remainder of the document. The court may then order disclosure of the whole document.

There are also potential differences between confidentiality and LPP in how a client may lose them. For example, a client may lose a right to confidentiality by suing his solicitor. The client may have implicitly waived his right to confidentiality and solicitor may be able to produce in evidence material that is relevant to the subject matter of the claim, for example relating to their instructions from the client. A client may lose his right to LPP in a criminal trial, for example by asserting circumstances that give a false impression of the case.

***Three Rivers District Council and Others v Governor and Company of the Bank of England (No 6)* [2004] UKHL 48, [2005] 1 AC 610 (edited)**

A bank (BCCI) collapsed, causing losses to its creditors. The government established a public inquiry under the chairmanship of Lord Bingham. The Bank of England, the regulator of BCCI, established a Unit to handle the Bank's evidence to the inquiry. Following the inquiry, BCCI creditors brought an action against the Bank of England claiming damages for misfeasance in public office relating to its regulation of BCCI.

The claimants sought disclosure of evidence collected by the Unit, including communications between the Unit and the Bank of England's solicitors Freshfields. The Court of Appeal held that the communications were not covered by legal advice privilege on the grounds that it had been prepared for 'presentational' purposes rather than for the purpose of obtaining legal advice. This meant it was for 'the dominant purpose of putting relevant factual material before the inquiry in an orderly and attractive fashion'. It was not prepared 'for the dominant purpose of taking legal advice upon such material' and so could not attract LPP.

The professional bodies were granted leave to intervene in the litigation. In argument to their Lordships counsel for the appellants suggested that the Court of Appeal had approached the case as if there was little justification for LPP beyond the scope of litigation. On that basis the Court of Appeal sought to closely confine it. For the Bar Council it was suggested that privilege was a 'fundamental human right'. Would the House of Lords choose between these extremes or choose another course?

Lord Scott of Foscote reviewed the history of legal advice privilege and the approach of courts in other common law jurisdictions:

> 34 None of these judicial dicta tie the justification for legal advice privilege to the conduct of litigation. They recognise that in the complex world in which we live there are a multitude of reasons why individuals, whether humble or powerful, or corporations, whether large or small, may need to seek the advice or assistance of lawyers in connection with their affairs; they recognise that the seeking and giving of this advice so that the clients may achieve an orderly arrangement of their affairs is strongly in the public interest; they recognise that in order for the advice to bring about that desirable result it is essential that the full and complete facts are placed before the lawyers who are to give it; and they recognise that unless the clients can be assured that what they tell their lawyers will not be disclosed by the lawyers without their (the clients') consent, there will be cases in which the requisite candour will be absent. It is obviously true that in very many cases clients would have no inhibitions in providing their lawyers with all the facts and information the lawyers might need whether or not there were the absolute assurance of non-disclosure that the present law of privilege provides. But the dicta to which I have referred all have in common the idea that it is necessary in our society, a society in which the restraining and controlling framework is built upon a belief in the rule of law, that communications between clients and lawyers, whereby the clients are hoping for the assistance of the lawyers' legal skills in the management of their (the clients') affairs, should be secure against the possibility of any scrutiny from others, whether the police, the executive, business competitors, inquisitive busybodies or anyone else (see also paras 15.8 to 15.10 of *Zuckerman's Civil Procedure* (2003) where the author refers to the

rationale underlying legal advice privilege as 'the rule of law rationale'). I, for my part, subscribe to this idea. It justifies, in my opinion, the retention of legal advice privilege in our law, notwithstanding that as a result cases may sometimes have to be decided in ignorance of relevant probative material.

35 Legal advice privilege should, in my opinion, be given a scope that reflects the policy reasons that justify its presence in our law. In my respectful opinion, the approach of the Court of Appeal in the Three Rivers (No 6) judgment [2004] QB 916 has failed to do so. The Court of Appeal has restricted the scope of legal advice privilege to material constituting or recording communications between clients and lawyers seeking or giving advice about the clients' legal rights and obligations. It has excluded legal advice sought or given for presentational purposes (see para 13 above). The particular issue to be decided under the disclosure application of 1 August 2003 was whether advice that related to the presentation of material to the inquiry qualified for legal advice privilege. In holding that it did not, the Court of Appeal, at pp 930–931, para 26, distinguished between a lawyer–client relationship 'formed for the purpose of obtaining advice or assistance in relation to rights and liabilities' and a lawyer–client relationship where 'the dominant purpose is not the obtaining of advice and assistance in relation to legal rights and obligations'. In relation to the former, 'broad protection will be given to communications passing between solicitor and client in the course of that relationship'; in relation to the latter, a similar broad protection could not be claimed.

36 The authorities on which the Court of Appeal founded their approach were all concerned with private law rights and obligations. ... It is clear, however, that whatever view may be taken of the presentational advice point, legal advice privilege must cover also advice and assistance in relation to public law rights, liabilities and obligations. I understood Mr Pollock in his submissions to your Lordships to accept that that was so.

37 In my opinion, the impossibility of a principled exclusion from legal advice privilege of communications between lawyer and client relating to the client's public law rights, liabilities and obligations is conclusive of the narrow issue in this appeal. One of the main purposes of the inquiry was to examine whether in relation to BCCI the Bank had properly discharged its public law duties of supervision imposed by the Banking Acts. The Bank was naturally anxious that the inquiry's conclusions should be as favourable as possible or, to put the point in reverse, that the inquiry's criticisms of the Bank should be as limited as possible. Every public inquiry conducts its proceedings and expresses its conclusions under the shadow of potential judicial review. The inquiry's procedures may be judicially reviewed if they are perceived to be unfair. The inquiry's conclusions may be judicially reviewed if they are thought to be unsustainable in the light of the evidence the inquiry has received. Presentational advice or assistance given by lawyers to parties whose conduct may be the subject of criticism by the inquiry is advice or assistance that may serve to avoid the need to invoke public law remedies. It would be—or should be—readily accepted that, once an inquiry's conclusions have been reached and communicated to the sponsors of

the inquiry, advice from lawyers to someone criticised as to whether a public law remedy might be available to quash the critical conclusions would be advice that qualified for legal advice privilege. It makes no sense at all, in my opinion, to withhold the protection of that privilege from presentational advice given by the lawyers for the purpose of preventing that criticism from being made in the first place.

38 In *Balabel v Air India* [1988] Ch 317 Taylor LJ (as he then was) said that for the purposes of attracting legal advice privilege—

> '...legal advice is not confined to telling the client the law; it must include advice as to what should prudently and sensibly be done in the relevant legal context' (p 330).

I would venture to draw attention to Taylor LJ's reference to 'the relevant legal context'. That there must be a 'relevant legal context' in order for the advice to attract legal professional privilege should not be in doubt. Taylor LJ said, at p 331, that—

> '...to extend privilege without limit to all solicitor and client communication upon matters within the ordinary business of a solicitor and referable to that relationship [would be] too wide'.

This remark is, in my respectful opinion, plainly correct. If a solicitor becomes the client's 'man of business', and some solicitors do, responsible for advising the client on all matters of business, including investment policy, finance policy and other business matters, the advice may lack a relevant legal context. There is, in my opinion, no way of avoiding difficulty in deciding in marginal cases whether the seeking of advice from or the giving of advice by lawyers does or does not take place in a relevant legal context so as to attract legal advice privilege. In cases of doubt the judge called upon to make the decision should ask whether the advice relates to the rights, liabilities, obligations or remedies of the client either under private law or under public law. If it does not, then, in my opinion, legal advice privilege would not apply. If it does so relate then, in my opinion, the judge should ask himself whether the communication falls within the policy underlying the justification for legal advice privilege in our law. Is the occasion on which the communication takes place and is the purpose for which it takes place such as to make it reasonable to expect the privilege to apply? The criterion must, in my opinion, be an objective one.

It was held that communications between the Bank's inquiry unit and its lawyers regarding presentation of its case to the inquiry were privileged. They were for the purpose of persuading it that the bank of England had discharged its public law obligations under the Banking Acts, that its actions were not deserving of criticism and that they had been reasonable.

Q6.7   Can you summarise briefly the difference between the approach of the Court of Appeal and the House of Lords to the scope of legal advice privilege?

Q6.8   What kind of advice given by a lawyer might not be covered by legal advice privilege?

Q6.9   On the basis of Lord Scott's justification for LPP, should communications between employed lawyers, so called 'in-house' lawyers, and their employers be covered by legal advice privilege?

Confidentiality and Litigation Privilege

Litigation privilege covers communications and material passing between lawyers and clients for the purposes of preparing for litigation. It is therefore likely to substantially overlap with legal advice privilege. There may, however, be communications between them not covered by legal advice privilege that would be covered by litigation privilege. An important difference between legal advice privilege and litigation privilege is that the latter also covers third parties that the lawyer or client may communicate with for the purpose of preparing for litigation.

The Limitations of LPP

For present purposes it is only necessary to establish what LPP is and how it relates to the duty of confidentiality. It will be recognised that LPP is formal recognition by the state of the fundamental importance of the right of the individual to keep his or her personal information secret. Despite the importance and scope of LPP it is not absolute. There are exceptions to LPP for activities that threaten the administration of justice or the security of the state. These exceptions require that lawyers balance obligations to clients with wider social obligations. The legal basis of LPP and exceptions to it are therefore set out in chapter eight: Social Responsibility.

Q6.10 What are the differences between confidentiality and legal advice privilege?

Q6.11 With regard to the JK Rowling case (above) why might LPP be irrelevant in protecting the true identity of Robert Galbraith?

A Critique of LPP

Philosophers have queried the morality of some of the consequences of the duty of lawyers to protect client secrets. In the nineteenth century Jeremy Bentham considered that privilege could only protect the guilty; the innocent had nothing to fear. This is a surprising attitude given Bentham's generally more critical view of the way the criminal justice system actually worked.[37] Nevertheless, some commentators remain sceptical when lawyers claim that privilege and confidentiality belong to the client and not the lawyer. Lawyers benefit from the legal protection gained, particularly from legal privilege, which applies only to lawyers and their clients. Legal privilege is a 'valuable product' that lawyers, and no other professionals, can sell to their clients.

The Regulatory Regime on Confidentiality

Confidentiality in the Solicitors' Codes of Conduct

The SRA Code of Conduct dedicates Chapter 4 to confidentiality and disclosure. The introduction to the chapter confirms that the duty of confidentiality 'continues despite the end of the retainer and even after the death of the client'. It also states that 'all members of the firm or in-house practice, including support staff, consultants and locums, owe a duty of confidentiality to your clients'. This means that entities and individuals could be disciplined or fined for breaches of confidentiality.

The main Outcome in the code reflecting this position is Outcome 4.1 which states that 'you keep the affairs of clients confidential unless disclosure is required or permitted by law or the client consents'. This shows that there are three potential exceptions to the duty of confidentiality. These are disclosures required by law, disclosures permitted by law and disclosures to which clients have consented.

Breach of Confidence Required by Law

Aspects of client's affairs may be exempted by statute from the duty of client confidentiality.[38] The clearest examples are responsibilities placed on various

---

[37] J Bowring (ed), *The Works of Jeremy Bentham*, vol 7 (New York, Russel & Russel, 1962) 474–75.
[38] *Solicitors Code of Conduct 2007* Guidance note 11.

business people, including lawyers, to report any suspicions that clients may be involved in money-laundering or terrorist activity. This is a clear example that cuts across a lawyer's duty of confidentiality owed to clients.

Lawyers reporting suspicious activity under the relevant statutes are also prevented from telling their clients that they have reported a suspicion in this way. This cuts across the lawyer's duty to disclose to the client all information relevant to their matter. These obligations are considered further in chapter eight: Social Responsibility.

Breach of Confidence Permitted by Law

The intended scope of the outcome relating to disclosure permitted by law is unclear. Statutes usually require rather than permit certain behaviour. The idea of disclosure permitted by law is therefore more likely to refer to instances at common law where lawyers are not liable or are not punished in other ways if they reveal client confidences.

It is often assumed that lawyers can disclose clients' confidential information in order to prevent harm to third parties. An authority that is often referred to in this context is the US case *Tarasoff v Regents of the University of California.*[39] A student, P, told a therapist employed by the defendants that he intended to kill a fellow student. The therapist warned campus police who detained but did not hold P. The defendants were held liable in negligence for failing to prevent the subsequent murder taking place.

A US case is weak authority for suggesting that English lawyers have a duty or permission to break client confidence in order to avoid harm to third parties. However, in the old *Guide to the Professional Conduct of Solicitors* Rule 16.02 stated that confidence could be broken in 'certain exceptional circumstances'. Guidance note 3 stated that these circumstances included where a solicitor believed it was 'necessary to prevent the client or a third party committing a criminal act that the solicitor believes on reasonable grounds is likely to result in serious bodily harm'. Another circumstance was to prevent serious threats to the mental or physical health of a child, including a child client.

Similar provisions to those in the *Guide* do not appear in the SRA Code of Conduct. The closest it comes is an exception to the duty of *disclosure* under IB 4.4 where there is a risk of serious mental or physical injury (see below). Guidance that once appeared in past codes is rather weak authority for the proposition that such as an exception to confidentiality exists. It is difficult to imagine a solicitor being disciplined for such a breach of confidence if it were shown to have prevented serious harm occurring.

---

[39] *Tarasoff v Regents of the University of California* (1976) 131 Cal Rpter 14.

Client Consent to Disclosure

In most circumstances a client can consent to her lawyer breaching the duty of confidence. The SRA Code of Conduct contains two examples of circumstances in which it might not occur to solicitors that consent is required. Therefore, the Code reminds them the outcomes might not be complied with if they disclose the content of a will on the death of a client unless consent is provided by the personal representatives for the content to be released (IB 4.6). The code also mentions that solicitors could breach confidence when they disclose details of client bills to third parties, such as debt factoring companies, in relation to the collection of book debts, unless the client has consented (IB 4.7).

The Confidentiality of Past Clients and the Duty of Disclosure to Present Clients

Maintaining the obligation of confidentiality is complicated by the duty of disclosure imposed on solicitors. This is a very particular manifestation of the duty of loyalty. It is expressed in Outcome 4.2, which is that 'any individual who is advising a *client* makes that *client* aware of all information material to that retainer of which the individual has personal knowledge'. Moreover, Outcome 4.3 requires that 'you ensure that where your duty of confidentiality to one *client* comes into conflict with your duty of disclosure to another *client*, your duty of confidentiality takes precedence'.

Since acting concurrently for two clients with conflicting interests would be a clear conflict of interest (see the previous chapter) the main problem that this refers to is solicitors acting sequentially for clients with conflicting interests. This is confirmed by the introduction to the chapter on confidentiality in the SRA Code of Conduct, which suggests that this is intended to include information related to past clients. It states that: 'The duty of confidentiality to all clients must be reconciled with the duty of disclosure to clients. This duty of disclosure is limited to information of which you are aware which is material to your client's matter.'

General Exceptions to the Duty of Disclosure

Despite the fact that the outcome on disclosure is expressed in absolute terms, one of the Indicative Behaviours in Chapter 4 suggests that there are exceptions to the duty to disclose all relevant information to present clients.

SRA Code of Conduct 2011 (as amended)

O(4.2) any individual who is advising a client makes that client aware of all information material to that retainer of which the individual has personal knowledge

Acting in the following way(s) may tend to show that you have achieved these outcomes and therefore complied with the *Principles*:

IB(4.4) Where you are an individual who has responsibility for acting for a *client* or supervising a *client's* matter, you disclose to the *client* all information material to the *client's* matter of which you are personally aware, except when:

(a) the *client* gives specific informed consent to non-disclosure or a different standard of disclosure arises;

(b) there is evidence that serious physical or mental injury will be caused to a person(s) if the information is disclosed to the *client*;

(c) legal restrictions effectively prohibit you from passing the information to the *client*, such as the provisions in the money-laundering and anti-terrorism legislation;

(d) it is obvious that privileged documents have been mistakenly disclosed to you;

(e) you come into possession of information relating to state security or intelligence matters to which the Official Secrets Act 1989 applies;

Q6.12 Can you give a concrete example of how each exemption from the disclosure requirement could apply?

The exceptions to the duty to disclose information to clients is reasonably clear. Given the apparent importance attached to disclosure, however, some of these provisions may be considered controversial. For example, how can a client consent to non-disclosure under exception (a) when he cannot be told what information the solicitor holds?

As regards exception (d), it is well established that lawyers must return privileged documents unread. Where they do not realise that they are privileged and they read them in error, the position is less clear. In fairness to the other party they may not be able to act in the matter. It is less clear how, if they read them, they can be relieved of their obligation to disclose the content to their client.

It is not clear where exception (b) comes from. It may assume that the 'the physical or mental injury' referred to would result from a crime that would be likely to be committed by the client if information is disclosed to them. If the lawyer was implicated in the crime, legal advice privilege would not apply (see chapter eight: Social Responsibility) and this would, on some authority, negate confidentiality. If, however, possible harm would not result from a crime, how is non-disclosure to a client justified?

Of course, it is open to a solicitor to decide not to act for a client in one of the IB 4.4 situations where the circumstances are clear at the outset. However, that is not what IB 4.4 says. What it presents are *exceptions* to the principle of disclosure of material facts to clients.

Information Barriers Securing the Confidentiality of Past Clients

As we saw in the last section, the SRA Code of Conduct Outcome 4.3 requires that 'you ensure that where your duty of confidentiality to one *client* comes into conflict with your duty of disclosure to another *client*, your duty of confidentiality takes precedence'. The introduction to the chapter on confidentiality says that acting may still be possible. It envisages a situation where the information about the past client is not known to the solicitor handling the matter even though it is held by the solicitor's firm.

The SRA Code of Conduct states that:

> You should not continue to act for a *client* for whom you cannot disclose material information, except in very limited circumstances, where safeguards are in place. Such situations often also give rise to a *conflict of interests* which is discussed in Chapter 3.

The circumstances envisaged in the code reflect practice in large City of London law firms. These firms consider that they have rigorous systems for dealing with past client confidentiality. When they were asked to act for a client to whom they have a duty to disclose information confidential to past clients, they erect an information barrier within the firm. This prevents information held by the firm leaking to the solicitor or team dealing with the present matter.

The case of *Bolkiah v KPMG* threatened to undermine the use of information barriers by large commercial firms.[40] In that case the accountancy firm KPMG had worked for a Government of Brunei agency chaired by Prince Jefri. The firm had also acted for Prince Jefri in a personal capacity. Later, the Government of Brunei asked KPMG to investigate the agency's affairs. Prince Jefri had ceased to work for the agency and was no longer a client of KPMG. He sought an injunction to prevent KPMG working on the matter.

The House of Lords held that a former client had to consent to their former professional adviser acting in a matter where they held confidential information material to the new matter. The practice of City of London law firms of

---

[40] *Bolkiah v KPMG* [1999] 1 All ER 517.

erecting information barriers within firms to safeguard such information were potentially inadequate. Clients had to be informed of the arrangements and to consent to their former adviser acting.

The present outcomes in the SRA Code of Conduct relating to the competing obligations of confidentiality and disclosure derive from rules introduced in response to *Bolkiah*. They were produced by a working party of City of London solicitors. They first appeared as rules in the Solicitors' Code of Conduct 2007.

SRA Code of Conduct 2011 (as amended)

O(4.4) you do not act for A in a matter where A has an interest adverse to B, and B is a *client* for whom you hold confidential information which is material to A in that matter, unless the confidential information can be protected by the use of safeguards, and:

(a) you reasonably believe that A is aware of, and understands, the relevant issues and gives informed consent;

(b) either:

    (i) B gives informed consent and you agree with B the safeguards to protect B's information; or

    (ii) where this is not possible, you put in place effective safeguards including information barriers which comply with the common law; and

(c) it is reasonable in all the circumstances to act for A with such safeguards in place;

O(4.5) you have effective systems and controls in place to enable you to identify risks to *client* confidentiality and to mitigate those risks.

Indicative Behaviours

Acting in the following way(s) may tend to show that you have achieved these outcomes and therefore complied with the *Principles*:

IB(4.1) your systems and controls for identifying risks to *client* confidentiality are appropriate to the size and complexity of the *firm* or *in-house practice* and the nature of the work undertaken, and enable you to assess all the relevant circumstances;

IB(4.2) you comply with the law in respect of your fiduciary duties in relation to confidentiality and disclosure;

IB(4.3) you only outsource services when you are satisfied that the provider has taken all appropriate steps to ensure that your *clients'* confidential information will be protected;

IB(4.5) not acting for A where B is a *client* for whom you hold confidential information which is material to A unless the confidential information can be protected.

Q6.13 Why might commercial clients wish to consent to their former lawyers acting for a competitor?

Q6.14 Under Outcome 4.4 can a firm act for a client (A) if it holds material
information on a past client (B) and B will not consent to the firm
acting?

The Limitations of Information Barriers

Notes to Chapter 4 in the SRA Code of Conduct allude to circumstances to
be wary of and others where erecting effective barriers may be problematic.
The notes suggest that protecting confidential information may be difficult
following mergers of firms or where solicitors move between firms. The notes
also suggest that effective safeguards and information barriers may be difficult
to implement in small firms or where the physical structure or layout of the
firm prevent separation of staff.

Bizarrely, the notes to Chapter 4 say that the fact that clients are not sophisticated users of legal services would make it difficult to implement effective
safeguards. This is clearly irrelevant to that issue, although it may be relevant to
whether they could give informed consent to breaches of their confidentiality.

Since *Bolkiah* there have been numerous cases where clients have brought
actions to prevent former solicitors acting for clients entitled to disclosure of
the former client's confidential information. In many of these cases the courts
have approved arrangements where they are satisfied that the former client's
information is secure, notwithstanding that the former client does not consent
to their former lawyers acting. In others they have refused.

Georgian American Alloys Inc v White and Case LLP
[2014] EWHC 94 (Comm)

The claimant companies (G) sought a permanent injunction to restrain the
defendant law firm (W) from acting for or advising a client (P) in proceedings which he had brought in the Commercial Court. W had initially
provided advice to P in a dispute with G's owners over an alleged joint
venture. Believing that dispute to be settled, W had then agreed to act for G
in implementing a corporate restructuring. Subsequently, when the original
dispute re-emerged and a related dispute arose over the alleged breach by
G's owners of an oral agreement, W agreed to represent P. It decided that
there was no conflict of interest and put in place ethical screens to keep
separate its representation of G and P. Nevertheless, G sought the injunction
on the ground that there was a risk that, in the commercial proceedings, W

might use confidential information it had obtained when it had acted during the corporate restructuring.

Held: The applicant had discharged the burden of showing that W possessed confidential information which he had not consented to being disclosed and that the information was or might be relevant to the new matter in which the interest of the other client was or might be adverse to his own. The court should intervene unless it was satisfied that there was no real risk of disclosure, and it should restrain the solicitor from acting for the second client unless it was satisfied that all effective measures had been taken to ensure that no disclosure would occur (*Bolkiah v KPMG* [1999] 1 All ER 517 (HL); [1999] 2 AC 222 applied).

In the instant case, the information which G had imparted to W was all confidential information which the latter was under a duty not to disclose; G had not consented to its disclosure; G's interests were adversely affected by reason of their owners being adversely affected by P's action; and the information was relevant because W's knowledge of the assets of G's owners could be of significant use for enforcement purposes and could assist on issues of credibility.

There had been a real risk of disclosure in the period before the introduction of the ethical screens. There was a real risk that the confidential information came into the possession of some of W's team representing P and that use of that information, at least inadvertently, had been or would be made in the Commercial Court action. Accordingly, G were entitled to the injunction they sought and W would be enjoined from acting for P in the Commercial Court action.

Q6.15 In what way does conflict of interest and confidentiality overlap in this case?

Q6.16 Could the case have been decided as a conflict-of-interest case?

Confidentiality in the Bar Codes of Conduct

The Bar Code of Conduct recognises a duty of confidentiality to both present and to previous clients. However, barristers do not, on the face of it, have to deal with the organisational complexity of practice arrangements that solicitors have. As independent practitioners they are not assumed to know what other members of chambers may know about mutual clients. Therefore, the only confidential knowledge of former clients they need worry about is their own. These circumstances will not survive barristers becoming part of organisations offering litigation services.

The Bar Standards Board Code of Conduct 2014

Core duties

CD6 You must keep the affairs of each client confidential [CD6].

Rules

rC5 Your duty to the court does not require you to act in breach of your duty to keep the affairs of each client confidential.

rC15.5 you must protect the confidentiality of each client's affairs, except for such disclosures as are required or permitted by law or to which you client gives informed consent.

rC21 You must not accept instructions to act in a particular matter if:

.4 there is a real risk that information confidential to another former or existing client, or any other person to whom you owe duties of confidence, may be relevant to the matter, such that if, obliged to maintain confidentiality, you could not act in the best interests of the prospective client, and the former or existing client or person to whom you owe that duty does not give informed consent to disclosure of that confidential information.

rC26 You may cease to act on a matter on which you are instructed and return your instructions if:

.6 you become aware of confidential or privileged information or documents of another person which relate to the matter on which you are instructed;

Guidance

gC43 Rule C15.5 acknowledges that your duty of confidentiality is subject to an exception if disclosure is required or permitted by law. For example, you may be obliged to disclose certain matters by the Proceeds of Crime Act 2002. Disclosure in those circumstances would not amount to a breach of CD6 or Rule C15.5 In other circumstances, you may only make disclosure of confidential information where

your client gives informed consent to the disclosure. See the Guidance to Rule C21 at gC68 for an example of circumstances where it may be appropriate for you to seek such consent.

gC69 Rules C21.2, C21.3 and C21.4 are intended to reflect the law on conflict of interests and confidentiality and what is required of you by your duty to act in the client's best interests (CD2), independently (CD4), and maintaining client confidentiality (CD6). You are prohibited from acting where there is a conflict of interest between your own personal interests and the interests of a prospective client. However, where there is a conflict of interest between an existing client or clients and a prospective client or clients or two or more prospective clients, you may be entitled to accept instructions or to continue to act on a particular matter where you have fully disclosed to the relevant clients and prospective clients (as appropriate) the extent and nature of the conflict; they have each provided their informed consent to you acting; and you are able to act in the best interests of each client and independently as required by CD2 and CD4.

Q6.17 Is it possible to disclose the extent and nature of a conflict of interest (gC69) without compromising a client's confidentiality?

It will be clear that rC21.4 does not impose the same obligation as the SRA Code does in relation to disclosure. There is no obligation to divulge the confidential information of previous clients if it is material to the interest of a present client. What the BSB Code does say is that a barrister cannot act where he thinks that he could not act in the new client's best interests without revealing that information. This appears to be different; it seems to allow the barrister discretion to determine the relevance of the information to the issue of whether he can still act in the client's best interests.

Duncan v Duncan[41] (Court of Appeal (Civil Division))

A wife (W) took proceedings for financial provision ('ancillary relief') against her husband (H). She was represented by a barrister (B). B had appeared for H in ancillary relief proceedings arising out of his first marriage. B was alerted to this a day before the case appeared in court. H consented to B acting for W. H then appealed against the decision on the ground that he had not fully known what he was consenting to. On appeal the judge found for H and set aside the order for ancillary relief, ordered a rehearing and made a costs order against W. The judge cited three examples when B's cross-examination of H suggested an inescapable conflict of interest.

W appealed to the Court of Appeal. She argued that there had been no conflict of interest. H argued that before he consented to B acting for his wife B should have disclosed information he had as a result of having previously acted on his behalf, including the skeleton arguments he had prepared for use in those previous proceedings.

Held: H's complaint was that B's cross-examination had taken him by surprise. It was inconsistent with the case that B had advanced on H's behalf in the previous proceedings. H could not point to any specific misuse of confidential information. The examples relied on by the judge which allegedly demonstrated a conflict of interest were incapable of demonstrating that B had inappropriately used any confidential information when representing W.

The skeleton arguments from the previous proceedings were irrelevant

---

[41] *Duncan v Duncan* [2013] EWCA Civ 1407; [2014] 2 FLR 624; [2014] Fam Law 289.

and had no evidential weight. They were based on instructions given to B by H in that previous case and merely constituted written advocacy. There was no opportunity for B to use them to advance W's case, and there was no suggestion by H that B had done so. The judge had wrongly concluded that there was an inescapable conflict of interest and the original decision should stand.

Q6.18 What do you think that B should have done had he realised when receiving instructions that he had previously acted for H?

Q6.19 Did the courts address the right question by asking whether confidential information had been used to undermine H's case?

Q6.20 Should the issue have been whether H's confidential information was material to the issue in the present case?

Q6.21 Leaving aside the issue of consent, would this have been a breach of confidentiality under the SRA Code of Conduct?

Q6.22 Based on the facts and findings provided, would you have found a conflict of interest in this case?

Conclusion

The confidentiality of client communications is a promise of most professions, but, because of LPP, it is a promise only lawyers can fully deliver. Even for lawyers the promise is qualified. Legal professional privilege ensures that lawyers are generally not required to surrender their clients' secrets in the courts. The privilege in various kinds of legal communication is protected, even when injustice may result. Such consequences are, however, carefully considered. In a number of situations courts are reluctant to recognise that privilege applies. The primary category is where privilege is used as a cloak for criminality.

Part III

Others

7

Third Parties (Non-Clients)

Introduction

A third party is usually someone outside of a defined relationship between people. This chapter deals with individual third parties, identifiable persons outside of the lawyer–client relationship. This could include other lawyers, the parties they represent and witnesses appearing in cases. Constraints on lawyer behaviour in all of these interactions potentially impinge on what lawyers can do for clients. While a lawyer's obligations to clients seem obvious and natural, it is less obvious what obligations are owed to non-clients and, indeed, why they should be owed.

In some situations lawyers owe duties to specific third parties. Such obligations may be very clear in certain contexts. Therefore, for example, lawyers may be expected to treat judges with respect. They may also be expected to extend courtesy to other professionals they are dealing with. How far this goes is likely to be less clear. This illustrates that obligations to third parties may be easier to impose when a third party is clearly in view. Obligations become less obvious to define as parties become more removed.

The degree of responsibility to third parties sometimes does not appear to be based on clear, unifying principles. It is not even clear, for example, that lawyers owe a general duty to be fair to third parties, particularly when this would cut across obligations to clients. Yet there are numerous examples of lawyers being criticised or sanctioned for their conduct in relation to third parties. There are also cases where they are charged but escape sanction. What these examples tend to show is that lawyers do not always have to be fair.

Theory of Lawyer–Third Party Relationships

The constraints that relationships with third parties impose may come from a variety of sources. For example, constraints may be imposed on what lawyers can do for clients by the government, by the courts or even by powerful third parties. These are considered in the next chapter. This chapter considers various conduct constraints imposed on lawyers to benefit individual third parties.

Early stages in the development of professional ethics tend to emphasise duties to clients. The later stages begin to pay more explicit attention to the rights of third parties. This is explained by the fact that the adversarial disposition traces back to the rule of law, which places an emphasis on the rights of the individual and the value of personal autonomy. As society and professions evolve, the right of the individual to assert and defend their rights is balanced with greater sensitivity to the competing claims of others to personal autonomy.

The promise of the liberal state is for an individual to assert their own rights, or interests, provided this does not impinge on the legitimate rights of others. To assert the rights of clients often creates conflict with the rights or interests of others. It is important to consider whether this is justified. In considering the justification for causing harm to others it is also necessary to recognise that the advocacy of rights is a distinctly legal discourse.

Other social science disciplines suggest various reasons for being sensitive to the interests of others. Early theories in the social sciences proposed that human beings evolved by co-operation.[1] Social behaviour regarded as virtuous often springs from co-operative impulses.[2] Despite the individualistic nature of capitalist societies, business depends on high levels of trust to support investment and financial market trading. Key intermediaries, such as lawyers, must be trustworthy if transactions are to take place at the volume and intensity that capitalist economies require. The need for co-operation and trust in social and business life places constraints on purely selfish activity.

For the good of society, co-operation is generally formalised in rules of behaviour, norms, so that we know what to expect of others. This builds trust in social structures. The standards defined by law often incorporate these standards. Reasonableness and fairness are obvious examples. It is therefore logical to expect that lawyers will temper their pursuit of selfish client goals with regard for the rights and interests of others.

---

[1] P Kropotkin, *Mutual Aid: A Factor of Evolution* [1902] (Forgotten Books, 2008).
[2] M Ridley, *The Origins of Virtue: Human Instincts and the Evolution of Cooperation* (New York, Penguin Books, 1996).

Mechanisms for Controlling Behaviour towards Third Parties

Although in principle it seems desirable that there should be constraints on lawyers' behaviour it is less clear what standards should apply and when. Then there is the issue of what is and what is not within the scope of any such duty. For example, if lawyers are under an obligation to treat others fairly, it means that they may not be able to take advantage of an opposing lawyer's ignorance or take advantage of any bargaining leverage their client has in a situation. It is not clear how desirable, or feasible, it is to regulate behaviour in such circumstances.

The difficulty of defining obligations to third parties at a high level of principle is partly because different standards apply in different situations. As in the law of torts, the issue of whose interests a lawyer must consider is raised in any discussion about lawyer obligations to third parties. Ethical obligations may vary depending on the context in which the relationship arises and the degree of proximity between the lawyer and the third party. As in tort law, proximity may be created by the reliance a third party is entitled to place in the lawyer in a particular situation.

Codes of conduct are often non-specific about the kinds of duty owed by third parties. In fact, lawyers' obligations to third parties are better explored by examining how they are defined across the range of regulatory mechanisms. These include legal liability controls and forum controls, for example courts. Each of these mechanisms imposes responsibilities on third parties or limits what lawyers can do for clients. They may have different degrees of success when it comes to enforcement. Having identified what alternative regulatory mechanisms can and cannot achieve it is easier to understand the limits of lawyers' responsibility to third parties in the codes of conduct.

Liability Controls

Liability as a Kind of Regulation

Threat of civil liability is seen as a kind of regulatory control. It is seldom discussed as an ethics issue because liability usually results from a negligence claim. It therefore does not involve conscious behaviour and ethical thought. Liability can also be an inefficient regulatory mechanism. It depends on prospective claimants acting when they have suffered harm. Liability controls are, however, a relevant regulatory issue. Significantly, liability in negligence potentially reflects on the competence of practitioners. Moreover, because of the financial implications, notable cases of lawyers' liability often command significant attention among practitioners.

Accepted Obligations

It is in the nature of professional obligations that they are often recognised by the courts despite the lack of a firm legal basis. Therefore, for example, responsibility will be based on reliance rather than contract. If a lawyer promises to do something, that obligation may be enforced even though there was no contractual responsibility to perform. Such promises, known as undertakings, are considered in more detail in chapter twelve: Commercial Practice.

Imposed Obligations

The idea that lawyers might be liable to parties other than to their client is relatively recent.

Negligence Liability

The harm caused to third party interests by lawyers tends to be financial loss. Courts have been concerned to limit liability for 'pure economic loss' independent of physical damage. This reluctance has broken down in a few distinct categories potentially relevant to lawyers. The imposition of obligations on lawyers in these situations may affect thinking about the scope of professional responsibility to third parties.

i. Negligent Misstatements

Hedley Byrne v Heller[3] was a breakthrough case in claims for negligently caused economic loss. A bank was asked to provide a credit reference for a customer by a third party. In reliance on the reference the third party suffered loss and sued the bank in negligence. The House of Lords held that, in circumstances where it was being asked to exercise its special skill, the bank owed a duty to exercise due care even though it was not liable in contract. In order to claim this protection, the third party must be the intended recipient of the statement, they must have specified why the information was required and they must rely on the statement for the purpose for which it was provided.[4]

---

[3] *Hedley Byrne & Co Ltd v Heller & Partners Ltd* [1964] AC 465.
[4] *Caparo Industries Plc v Dickman and Others* [1990] 2 WLR 358.

ii. Negligent Breach of Undertaking

An undertaking is a promise to do something or to refrain from doing something. Lawyers may offer undertakings in litigation and in non-contentious matters. Breach of an undertaking given to a third party may be actionable in negligence. In *Al-Kandari v Brown*,[5] for example, solicitors in a matrimonial matter released a passport to their client, in breach of their undertaking, allowing him to take his children out of the jurisdiction. The solicitors were successfully sued in negligence by the wife.

iii. Negligence Causing Loss to Beneficiaries

In *Ross v Caunters*[6] it was held that a law firm owed a duty of care to an intended beneficiary (B) under a will. B could not take her share because the firm had not warned the testator that the witnessing of the will by a spouse of a beneficiary would invalidate their share. This principle has gradually been extended. In *White v Jones*[7] the beneficiary established a claim in negligence when a solicitor failed to draw up a will before the testator client died. In *Carr-Glynn v Frearsons*[8] solicitors negligently failed to serve notice severing a joint interest in real property before the testatrix died. They became liable to a beneficiary who would have been entitled to the severed share had they done so.

iv. Negligence Causing Loss to Unrepresented Third Parties

Lawyers offering free advice to unrepresented parties can be liable in negligence if the advice is acted upon and loss is caused.[9] Liability can be avoided in such situations if the third party is advised to obtain independent advice.[10]

v. Negligence causing loss to witnesses

Witnesses relying on the gratuitous advice of lawyers are generally in the same position as unrepresented third parties. They can sue the lawyer offering the advice if they act on it and suffer loss.[11]

vi. Negligence towards Victims of Crime

A duty on professionals to warn prospective victims of crime threatened by

[5] *Al-Kandari v Brown* [1988] 1 All ER 833.
[6] *Ross v Caunters* [1980] Ch 297.
[7] *White v Jones* [1995] 1 All ER 691.
[8] *Carr-Glynn v Frearsons* [1998] 4 All ER 225.
[9] *Dean v Allin & Watts* [2001] All ER (D) 288, J Ross 151 NLJ 960 (29 June 2001).
[10] *Hemmens v Wilson Browne* [1995] Ch 223.
[11] *Law Society Gazette*, 1 September 2005, 4.

clients was upheld in the US case *Tarasoff v Regents of the University of California*.[12] There are several difficulties with the case, in which a student had confessed to a university employee that he intended to murder a fellow student. It is an American authority, so only a persuasive precedent. The professional involved was a campus therapist. The action was against the university and the campus police had apprehended and released the assailant. Nevertheless, it is plausible that professionals receiving information about the risk of harm to others from their client could be liable.

Palmer v Tees Health Authority [2000] PIQR P1

The claimant's daughter, R, was abducted, sexually assaulted and murdered by A. For two years prior to the murder A had been in the care of a hospital for which the defendants were responsible. Negligence in the care and treatment of A was alleged, including causing or permitting him to be discharged from hospital when he should not have been. The claimant claimed damages. The defendant applied to strike out the statement of claim as disclosing no cause of action. It argued that it owed no duty of care to R or to the claimant. At first instance it was not disputed that the injuries to R and the claimant were arguably foreseeable, but Gage J. held that there was no sufficient proximity between the defendant and R or the claimant. It was not fair, just and reasonable to impose a duty of care on the defendant. The claimant appealed to the Court of Appeal.

Held, dismissing the appeal ... 'that it was appropriate to strike out actions on the grounds that, in law, proximity was not established. The critical decision was that of *Hill* [*Hill v Chief Constable of West Yorkshire* [1989] AC 53], where it was held that police officers do not owe a general duty of care to the public at large to apprehend unknown criminals, nor to individual members of the public unless such failure creates an exceptional additional risk and there is a proximity between the officers and the potential victim] the crucial point being that in that as in the instant case there was no relationship between the defendant and the victim. An additional reason why in this case it was at least necessary for the victim to be identifiable (although it might not be sufficient) to establish proximity was that the most effective way of providing protection would be to give a warning to the victim, his or her parents or social services so that some protective measure could be made. It was a relevant consideration in approaching the question of proximity to ask what the defendant could have done to avoid the danger, if the suggested precautions, *i.e.* committal under section 3 of the Mental Health Act, or treatment were likely to be of doubtful effectiveness, and the

---

[12] *Tarasoff v Regents of the University of California* [1976] 131 *Cal Rpter* 14. See further chapter six: Confidentiality and Privilege.

most effective precaution could not be taken as the defendant did not know whom to warn.'

Q7.1   Does this dictum suggest that a lawyer could be held liable for failing to warn a potential victim of a risk of physical harm?

Q7.2   On what grounds might the position of a lawyer be distinguished from that of a medical practitioner receiving notice of intention to do harm?

Q7.3   What considerations and what interests are weighed in the balance in deciding issues of liability in cases such as *Tarasoff* and *Palmer*?

Q7.4   Is the absence of any clear duty in law to avoid harm to others a reason not to impose ethical responsibilities on professionals?

Forum Controls

The different forums in which lawyers work or appear may impose obligations on lawyers. The most obvious limitations and expectations are imposed by the rules of litigation or under the inherent jurisdiction of the court. These duties may be owed to other parties or to witnesses. Alternatively, they may be expressed as a more general duty, for example the duty not to mislead the court. Enforcement of general duties may, incidentally, benefit third party opponents.

The courts have an inherent jurisdiction over lawyers working in them. The courts can impose responsibilities between lawyers and between parties. In *Myers v Elman* the House of Lords said that solicitors must conduct litigation with due propriety so as to promote the cause of justice.[13] Their Lordships said that there were separate jurisdictions to discipline solicitors appearing before them or to make an order for wasted costs against them. A disciplinary finding required serious professional misconduct but a wasted costs order did not. Conversely, there may be circumstances where a court finds improper conduct but no wasted costs.[14] It may then refer the lawyer to the regulator and legal aid authorities if appropriate.

[13] *Myers v Elman* [1940] AC 282.
[14] *Re A barrister (wasted costs order) (No 1of 1991)* [1993] QB 293.

Judicial Control of Litigation Conduct

The conduct of litigation is controlled by detailed rules describing what must be done by the parties and when. In civil cases the process is governed by the Civil Procedure Rules 1999 (CPR). Under the CPR judges have an obligation of 'active case management' in more serious claims. Apart from ensuring that lawyers follow the rules of court, judges may also ensure that they follow the spirit of the rules. In *Ernst & Young v Butte Mining Co*[15] the claimants were supposed to prepare an order setting aside a judgment in default obtained by their client and giving the defendant leave to counterclaim. In order to deny the defendant's counterclaim they filed notice discontinuing the action. This was held to be an abuse of process.

The proposition that lawyers will not be allowed to take an unconscionable advantage of the other side is demonstrated by the practice of the courts when privileged papers are disclosed in error. The general expectation is that, if lawyers realise that a mistake has been made, they must return the material without reading it. If they do read it, to prevent prejudice to the opposing party, an injunction may be granted restraining them from acting.[16]

The obligation of lawyers to be fair to opponents is particularly marked in dealings with unrepresented parties. Lawyers must point out procedural errors that may be advantageous to their client or themselves.[17] They must also be particularly wary of intimidating unrepresented parties, for example with concerns about costs.[18]

As noted in chapter five, the losing party in litigation is usually ordered by the court to pay the other side's costs on the standard basis, that is, what is reasonable between the parties. Parties can be punished by orders for costs and, in some cases, their lawyers can be ordered to pay costs. In serious cases lawyers may also be referred to their regulator by judges. It is possible that disciplinary proceedings against the lawyer may then be brought.

Wasted Costs Orders

Irrespective of the outcome of litigation, a court has the power to make a wasted costs order against lawyers. Wasted costs orders compensate a party for work done or expenses incurred unnecessarily by the conduct of the opposing lawyer. Before an order is made the courts must be satisfied that these costs are the result of 'any improper, unreasonable or negligent act or

---

[15] *Ernst & Young v Butte Mining Co* [1997] 2 All ER 471.

[16] *Ablitt v Mills & Reeve (A Firm) and Another* ChD, *The Times* 24 October 1995; *English & American Insurance Co Ltd & Others v Herbert Smith* [1988] FSR 232; ChD 1987; (1987) NLJ 148.

[17] *Haiselden v P & O Properties* [1998] All ER 180 (D).

[18] *Gee v Shell UK Ltd* [2002] EWCA Civ 1479.

omission on the part of any legal or other representative or any employee of such representative'.[19]

The jurisdiction to award costs against lawyers arises in civil and criminal cases.[20] In the civil courts the wasted costs jurisdiction is now governed by the CPR Part 46.8. The rules provide that where lawyers are charged, the court must give them a reasonable opportunity to make written submissions or, if the legal representative prefers, to attend a hearing before it makes such an order.[21] Clients may be informed that an order may be made or has been made against their lawyer.[22]

The CPR rules on wasted costs follow pre-existing case law. This is still relevant to understanding how the courts exercise their powers. The leading case, *Ridehalgh v. Horsefield and another*,[23] established that both advocates and litigators could be ordered to pay wasted costs. It also provided a three-stage test, which became the basis of the jurisdiction in CPR Rule 5.5.

CPR Practice Direction 46—Costs Special Cases:
Personal liability of legal representative for costs—wasted costs orders: rule 46.8,
Practice Direction 46: Costs Special Cases, para 5.5

5.5 It is appropriate for the court to make a wasted costs order against a legal representative, only if—

(a) the legal representative has acted improperly, unreasonably or negligently;

(b) the legal representative's conduct has caused a party to incur unnecessary costs, or has meant that costs incurred by a party prior to the improper, unreasonable or negligent act or omission have been wasted;

(c) it is just in all the circumstances to order the legal representative to compensate that party for the whole or part of those costs.

5.6 The court will give directions about the procedure to be followed in each case in order to ensure that the issues are dealt with in a way which is fair and as simple and summary as the circumstances permit.

5.7 As a general rule the court will consider whether to make a wasted costs order in two stages—

(a) at the first stage the court must be satisfied—
    (i) that it has before it evidence or other material which, if unanswered, would be likely to lead to a wasted costs order being made; and

---

[19] Supreme Court Act 1981 (now known as the Senior Courts Act) s 51(7).
[20] Ibid, s 51(6).
[21] CPR rule 46.8(2).
[22] CPR rule 46.8(4).
[23] *Ridehalgh v Horsefield and anor* [1994] Ch 205; *Orchard v SE Electricity Board* [1987] 1 All ER 95 (CA); [1987] QB 565 (CA).

> (ii) the wasted costs proceedings are justified notwithstanding the likely costs involved;
>
> (b) at the second stage, the court will consider, after giving the legal representative an opportunity to make representations in writing or at a hearing, whether it is appropriate to make a wasted costs order in accordance with paragraph 5.5 above.
>
> **5.8** The court may proceed to the second stage described in paragraph 5.7 without first adjourning the hearing if it is satisfied that the legal representative has already had a reasonable opportunity to make representations.

Q7.5   Who is liable to satisfy a wasted costs order?

Q7.6   What arguments are there for dealing with wasted costs issues at the time they occur rather than waiting for the end of the case?

The Three-Stage Test

i. Improper, Unreasonable or Negligent Acts

In *Ridehalgh v Horsefield and another* the words 'improper, unreasonable and negligent' were held to be intended to have their ordinary meanings. 'Improper' means conduct amounting to a significant breach of a substantial duty imposed by a relevant code of professional conduct or considered improper by the profession; 'unreasonable' is likely to be vexatious or harassing conduct; and 'negligent' is failure to reach a competent professional standard.

In *Ridehalgh v Horsefield and another* it was made clear that helping a party to bring a hopeless case is not usually unreasonable conduct.[24] This is because the courts do not want to discourage lawyers from bringing difficult cases.[25] Lawyers may be penalised, however, in circumstances where no reasonably competent legal adviser would have evaluated the chance of success as being such as to justify continuing with proceedings.[26] For a wasted costs order to be made on the grounds of unreasonableness, the legal representative must lend assistance to proceedings amounting to an abuse of process or the duty to the court.[27]

---

[24] Ibid, per Lord Bingham, 863a; *Locke v Camberwell HA* [1991] Med LR 249; and *C v C* [1994] 2 FLR 34.

[25] *Southcombe & Anor v One Step Beyond* [2008] EWHC 3231 (Ch).

[26] *Dempsey v Johnstone* [2003] All ER (D) 515.

[27] *Mitchells Solicitors—In a Matter of Costs Order v Funkwerk Information Technologies York Ltd* 2008 WL 924960.

***Tolstoy v Aldington* [1996] PNLR 335**

A firm of solicitors, who acted free of charge for T in a case which was struck out as an abuse of process, appealed against a costs order made under the Supreme Court Act 1981 section 51(1) and section 51(3) in favour of A, by which they were ordered to pay 60 per cent of A's costs. A sought confirmation of the original order, contending also that it should have been made as a wasted costs order under section 51(6) and section 51(7) of the 1981 Act. A argued that the solicitors' conduct had been improper and unreasonable, even though they had acted on a pro bono basis.

Held, dismissing the appeal, that the action amounted to an abuse of process. Although acting without a fee in a hopeless case could not on its own justify a wasted costs order, taking account of all the facts and circumstances of the case, there had been a lack of propriety in the conduct of the litigation which showed that the solicitor had failed to act reasonably in pursuing the action.

Rose LJ (at p 346)

> The proper discharge of that duty must, as it seems to me, depend on the circumstances of the particular case. The background to the present litigation was unusual in a number of respects. The plaintiff was not initially sued in the libel proceedings; he was joined as co-defendant at his own request. The trial took two months, so the costs, like the damages awarded by the jury, were enormous. Count Tolstoy had not and still has not the means or, apparently, the intention to satisfy either. I set out at the beginning of this judgment the course of subsequent events. The appellant solicitors knew of all these matters. They chose to act for the plaintiff without fee. More than four years after the trial, without a letter before action and without applying for, or apparently considering applying for, legal aid they issued proceedings on the plaintiff's behalf. The action was a collateral attack on the decision of a court of competent jurisdiction which, it is conceded, was *prima facie* an abuse. There was no, or so little, evidence of fraud and perjury that the proceedings were struck out as 'utterly hopeless' and an abuse of process under Order 18, rule 19. The pleading was signed by counsel, 'surprisingly' as the judge found. I am astonished, though it is right that I should emphasise that no submissions on behalf of the counsel in question have been made in the course of these proceedings. Counsel's role, however, did not exonerate the solicitors from their obligation to exercise their own independent judgment to consider whether the claim could properly be pursued; they were not entitled to follow counsel blindly. ... They had to apply their 'own expert professional mind' to the substance of the advice received.

Q7.7   Given that the courts are not prone to penalise lawyers for bringing hopeless cases, what factors might have made this case different?

Q7.8   Could a wasted costs order have been made against counsel?

ii. Causation

Before making an order the court must be satisfied that, but for the conduct complained of, the applicant would not have incurred the costs in question.[28] In *Koo Golden East Mongolia v Bank of Nova Scotia*[29] a claim for wasted costs was dismissed because a party had not refused to pay costs yet to be assessed. The applicant could not demonstrate any loss.

iii. Whether it Is Just in All the Circumstances to Make an Order

Wasted costs orders are a discretionary remedy and the court must consider whether it is just in all the circumstances to make an order. In *Medcalf v Mardell*[30] the House of Lords declined to make a wasted costs order against barristers who had made baseless fraud allegations in the claim. The barristers claimed that the client was unwilling to waive professional privilege and so they could not prove that they had credible evidence of fraud as required by the code of conduct. The majority held that the barristers had to have the benefit of the doubt and quashed the wasted costs order.

The courts have shown reluctance to make an order when it is perceived that the application for wasted costs is a tactic to pressurise the other side to withdraw a claim.[31] There have been similar suspicions that wasted costs may be a new form of satellite litigation aimed at prolonging disputes. An order may also be refused if it will have disproportionate effect it will have for a legal representative, for example bankruptcy.[32]

Although there have been many cases the general reluctance to make wasted costs orders may be due to the fact that the jurisdiction is summary and parties often have other avenues for redress. In cases of negligence or professional conduct, for example, separate court proceedings for negligence or disciplinary proceedings are a viable alternative.[33]

Witnesses

The kinds of person who appear as witnesses vary greatly. They can be victims of crime, witnesses to crimes or other events, or technical experts. In both criminal and civil cases witnesses are important third parties. They are an obvious example of people, apart from their clients, to whom lawyers may owe responsibilities. This is possibly most obvious in the case of advocates. They have the task of striking a balance between treating witnesses for the

---

[28] *Brown & anor v Bennett and others* [2002] 2 All ER 273.
[29] *Koo Golden East Mongolia v Bank of Nova Scotia* [2008] EWHC 1120 (QB).
[30] *Medcalf v Mardell* [2002] 3 All ER 721; [2002] UKHL 27; [2003] 1 AC 120.
[31] *Orchard v South Eastern Electricity Board* [1987] 1 All ER 95 (CA); [1987] QB 565.
[32] *R (on the application of Hide) v Staffordshire County Council* [2007] EWHC 2441 (Admin).
[33] *Harley v McDonald* [2001] 2 WLR 1749, paras 49–54.

other side with respect and casting doubt on their evidence when their client's case requires it.

The Bar has developed various longstanding conventions concerned with maintaining a balance between duties to clients and to witnesses. Restrictions on the treatment of witnesses have appeared in past versions of codes of conduct and are represented in the current code in Chapter 1, 'You and the Court', under the heading 'Not abusing your role as an advocate'.

Bar Standards Board Code of Conduct 2014

Not abusing your role as an advocate

rC7 Where you are acting as an advocate, your duty not to abuse your role includes the following obligations:

.1 you must not make statements or ask questions merely to insult, humiliate or annoy a witness or any other person;

.2 you must not make a serious allegation against a witness whom you have had an opportunity to cross-examine unless you have given that witness a chance to answer the allegation in cross-examination;

.3 you must not make a serious allegation against any person, or suggest that a person is guilty of a crime with which your client is charged unless:

.a you have reasonable grounds for the allegation; and

.b the allegation is relevant to your client's case or the credibility of a witness; and

.c where the allegation relates to a third party, you avoid naming them in open court unless this is reasonably necessary.

.4 you must not put forward to the court a personal opinion of the facts or the law unless you are invited or required to do so by the court or by law.

Q7.9 Can you give examples of how each of these rules could be breached by a barrister?

Q7.10 Is there any reason why these kinds of restrictions should be restricted to situations where barristers are acting as advocates?

Despite the various restrictions in the Bar Code of Conduct, advocates are generally given considerable leeway in how they cross-examine opposing witnesses. They are taught to use closed questions, permitting only 'yes' or 'no' answers and to not allow the witness to embellish their answers. The advocate can use various strategies to trip up and mislead the witness. A witness who shows any confusion or uncertainty may be accused of lying.

The approach lawyers take to cross-examination can appear bullying and intimidating. It is justified because some witnesses, inevitably, are glib liars. It is not possible to tell the liar from the truth-teller unless their evidence is rigorously tested. Some take this rationale to an extreme. Freedman, for example, argued that almost any tactic to discredit an honest witness was legitimate in criminal defence. As rC7 demonstrates, in England and Wales this is not the case. There are, however, categories of witness who are afforded special protection. These include victims of alleged rape and sexual offences and child victims.

In cases involving these vulnerable witnesses lawyers are often accused of exploiting that vulnerability for the advantage of clients. The tactics include confusing cross-examination. This can include, for example, the use of tag questions, where the question follows a statement, such as 'He didn't touch you, did he?' These are said to be particularly confusing for children. Another controversial practice is the repeated cross-examination of rape victims, on behalf of multiple defendants, where the victim is repeatedly accused of lying.

Lawyers may use doubts, inconstancies or uncertainties in witness responses to cross-examination to suggest that the evidence given is unreliable. These practices of lawyers in criminal trials have become controversial, with some victims allegedly too scared of the ordeal of cross-examination to give evidence. This situation has been seen as contrary to the proper administration of justice.

Increasingly, the procedural criterion applied is that the procedures in place should allow witnesses to give their best evidence. Special rules and guidelines have been developed for use by courts dealing with vulnerable witnesses. Lawyers have to comply, restricting what they would otherwise do for their client. The nature of these restrictions can be seen in the guidelines produced for prosecutors.

Crown Prosecution Service
Interim Guidelines on Prosecuting Cases of Child Sexual Abuse
(www.cps.gov.uk/consultations/csa_consultation.html#a16)

Support given to victims and witnesses in court

…

90. The Court of Appeal has addressed restrictions on cross-examination:

where there is a risk of a child acquiescing to leading questions (*R v Barker* (2010); and on 'putting your case' to a child (*R v Wills* [2011] and *R v Edwards*). As the Court of Appeal observed in Wills, 'Some of the most effective cross-examination is conducted without long and complicated questions being posed in a leading or "tagged" manner'.

91. Where limits are 'necessary and appropriate', the Court of Appeal in *Wills* stated that:
* limitations on questioning must be clearly defined;
* the judge has a duty to ensure that limitations are complied with;
* the judge should explain limitations to jury and reasons for them;
* if the advocate fails to comply with limitations, the judge should give relevant directions to the jury when that occurs; and
* instead of commenting on inconsistencies during cross-examination, the advocate/judge may point out important inconsistencies after (instead of during) the witness's evidence, following discussion with the advocates. The judge should be alert to alleged inconsistencies that are not in fact inconsistent, or are trivial.

92. As set out in paragraph 89 above, in multi-defendant cases the judge should be asked to consider whether repeat cross-examination on similar points should be restricted. Being accused of lying, particularly if repeated, may cause the witness to give inaccurate answers or to agree simply to bring questioning to an end. It may also have a longer term damaging impact on the child or young person. If such a challenge is essential, it should be addressed separately, in simple language, at the end of cross-examination.

Q7.11   Are these restrictions on cross-examination fair or do they threaten the right to a fair trial?

The protection offered to witnesses generally has increased. A recent example of this is a proposal by the Director of Public Prosecutions that witnesses generally be better informed before they give evidence in court.

Case Study
The Protection of Victims and Witnesses

The issue of how victims and witnesses are treated in the justice system has been controversial for years. It was brought to public attention again 2014 when two women from the north-west of England killed themselves having given evidence in rape trials. In the second incident police failed to persuade Tracey Shelvey, a 41-year-old mother of one, not to jump from the top of a car park in the middle of Manchester. A few days previously, the jury in a second trial had failed to convict a man of raping her and two other women.
    The case followed an earlier case in which violinist Frances Andrade

killed herself during the trial of Michael Brewer, a choirmaster later convicted of sexually assaulting her when she was a pupil at a music school in
Manchester. Andrade had criticised the police for providing her with inadequate support and, following a gruelling cross-examination, was reported to
have said that she felt as if she had been 'raped all over again'.

Following the Shelvey case Sir Peter Fahy, the Greater Manchester police
chief, and the local crime commissioner called for fundamental changes to
the treatment of vulnerable witnesses in court and a rethink of the adversarial justice system. Rather than putting pressure on the victim, he said,
'The focus should be more on the ways in which we can control this type of
offender.'[34] The crime commissioner said that '[t]he court process is a brutal
one, and the fact that we have had at least two people in Greater Manchester
alone who have taken their lives after going through this ordeal is of grave
concern. ... We need to ensure that victims and witnesses are surrounded
by support from when they report to police, throughout the investigation,
the court process and—critically—after trial is over, whether the accused is
found guilty or innocent.'[35]

Criticism of the adversarial process was not limited to cases of sexual
abuse. In 2013 Nigella Lawson, a famous TV cook, had been a witness in a
case brought against two former personal assistants by Charles Saatchi, her
former husband. She claimed her experience as a witness against the former
employees had been 'mortifying' and said she had been 'maliciously vilified
without the right to respond'.

Following the Shelvey case Alison Saunders, director of public prosecutions, announced that the Crown Prosecution Service was undertaking a
consultation on new guidelines on helping witnesses. Rather than waiting to
get to court before finding out what they would face, prosecutors would be
instructed to inform witnesses when:

- the general nature of the defence case, for example in cases of mistaken
identification, consent, self-defence or lack of intent;
- material such as social services reports, medical or counselling records,
had been disclosed to the defence;
- the judge had given the defence permission to cross-examine a witness
on their alleged bad character or sexual history.

Saunders justified the move by saying that 'The law is not a game and the
court process is not about ambushing the witness. ... Some people might
think these guidelines go too far, but I don't. They are intended to help

---

[34] H Pidd and F Perraudin, 'Police chief calls for rape cases rethink after woman's death',
The Guardian, 4 February 2014, www.theguardian.com/society/2014/feb/04/greater-manchester-
police-rape-cases.
[35] Ibid.

witnesses give their best evidence and make sure that everyone has their rights acknowledged. We have not had guidance like this before and it is overdue.'[36] Saunders said that '[a]sking someone to come to court without any idea of what they face in the witness box does not seem fair to me. ... To stand up in a formal setting and to be asked sometimes difficult and personal questions in front of a court full of strangers is a very big ask. In coming to court to give evidence, victims and witnesses are performing an important public service and I think we can assist them better.'

Tony Cross QC, chairman of the Criminal Bar Association, said that '[t]he general idea is very laudable but defence and prosecution barristers will find many of the proposals dangerous and impractical. ... There are real evidential concerns, including a risk of rehearsing witnesses. ... Our system of justice demands that the first time a witness hears the detail of the defence case is when it is put to them in court, so the jury see their reaction.'[37] Cross added that the requirements would risk prosecutors becoming witnesses in the trial they were briefed to prosecute and the whole trial having to start again. The new procedures would also be demanding for CPS lawyers, who would have to ensure that conversations with victims and witnesses were scrupulously recorded to reduce the chance of disputes in court.

Q7.12 Do these proposals adequately address the problems identified as the reasons for introducing them?

Q7.13 Why do you think the DPP may have introduced them?

Q7.14 Who should be responsible for defining the limits of what advocates should do on behalf of clients?

The Limits of Forum Controls

Besides the law of negligence and the courts' inherent control of litigation lawyers owe limited obligations to third parties. In *Re Schuppan (A Bankrupt)* (1996)[38] a bankrupt (S) objected to a solicitor for one of their petitioning creditors being appointed to act for their trustee in bankruptcy. S argued that the solicitor would be prejudiced against him, in part because S had sued him

---

[36] A Hill, 'DPP Proposes New Guidelines to Help Victims and Witnesses in Court', *The Guardian*, 19 January 2015 (http://www.theguardian.com/law/2015/jan/19/cps-new-guidelines-victims-witnesses-court-trials)

[37] D Barratt, 'Rape victims will be warned of defence lawyer tactics under new guidelines', *The Telegraph*, 19 January 2015, www.telegraph.co.uk/news/uknews/crime/11353540/Rape-victims-will-be-warned-of-defence-lawyer-tactics-under-new-guidelines.html.

[38] *Re Schuppan (A Bankrupt)* [1996] 2 All ER 664.

for slander! The court was unsympathetic to S and allowed the solicitor to act subject to a few modest restrictions. This decision reflects a generally robust attitude by courts to restricting lawyers when parties feel that the circumstances of representation prejudice their interests.

British Sky Broadcasting Plc v Virgin Media Communications Ltd (formerly NTL Communications Ltd) [2008] EWHC 1283 (Ch)

The applicant television broadcaster (B) applied for an order to prohibit the inspection of confidential documents by solicitors advising the respondent broadcaster (V). B and V were involved in various proceedings against each other that generally concerned access to television channels. As part of the instant proceedings, B was required to disclose highly confidential documents concerning its business practices. B applied for an order to restrict access to such documents by three named solicitors who were advising V in the instant proceedings, and also advising V in a separate hearing against B. B submitted, relying on *Bolkiah v KPMG* [1999] 1 All ER 517 (HL); [1999] 2 AC 222, that if the solicitors inspected the documents, then it would subsequently be impossible for them to put that information out of their minds. The information could then be misused for V's benefit in the separate matter.

Application refused. The duty to preserve confidentiality was unqualified and called for a strict test in order to give effect to the policy on which professional legal privilege was based. However, such a policy did not apply to a case where documents were disclosed in the course of disclosure by one adversary in proceedings to another. *Bolkiah* was therefore distinguished, there being no general duty of confidence between adversaries in litigation. Any such duties as did exist were imposed by the rules of court or by such confidentiality undertakings as opposing parties were prepared to give. In addition, there was no risk of subliminal or inadvertent use of the confidential material by V's solicitors. The parallel proceedings in question concerned judicial review and V no longer intended to adduce further evidence. V's solicitors were well aware of their obligations not to use or deploy material obtained on disclosure, and B were adequately protected by the Rules of the Supreme Court and the additional safeguard that would be imposed by the confidentiality undertakings that the solicitors in question were prepared to enter into.

Q7.15 Do you think confidentiality undertaking are very effective in circumstances such as those described in this case?

Q7.16 Since the courts are not prepared to protect opposing parties' confidentiality in these kinds of circumstances should codes of conduct do so?

Q7.17 What form might a conduct rule protecting information disclosed to adversaries in litigation take?

Other Third Parties Affected by Proceedings

i. Children as Third Parties

Some proceedings involve third parties who may be indirectly involved but not represented. The obvious case is children who are not separately represented in proceedings that affect them, such as divorce or guardianship proceedings. The Children Act 1989 created an exception to legal privilege, whereby expert reports, and possibly other documents bearing on the welfare of children, were required to be disclosed (see further chapter six: Confidentiality and Privilege). This could involve lawyers acting against the wishes of client parents or guardians and in favour of a third party, the child. This is a relatively rare example of an obligation imposed on lawyers for the benefit of third parties.

Conduct Controls

The new codes of conduct for solicitors and barristers contain high-level but non-specific core duties and principles. None are directed towards third parties, although some might be interpreted as carrying responsibilities to third parties.

SRA principles	BSB core duties
1. uphold the rule of law and the proper administration of justice; 2. act with integrity; 3. not allow your independence to be compromised; 4. act in the best interests of each client; 5. provide a proper standard of service to your clients; 6. behave in a way that maintains the trust the public places in you and in the provision of legal services;	CD1 You must observe your duty to the court in the administration of justice CD2 You must act in the best interests of each client CD3 You must act with honesty and integrity CD4 You must maintain your independence CD5 You must not behave in a way which is likely to diminish the trust and confidence which the public places in you or in the profession

Q7.18 Which core duties and principles suggest client obligations, which system obligations and which third party obligations.

Q7.19 How, might it be argued, are third parties protected by any of these high level statements of principles and duties?

Third Party Obligations in the Codes

High-level principles and core duties are not very helpful in defining the extent of duties to third parties. It is therefore necessary to look to the codes for specific examples. The detail here is also often sparse. This is illustrated by the current Bar Code of Conduct, which produces some longstanding rules against certain behaviours as examples of the duty to act with honesty and integrity.

Bar Standards Board Code of Conduct 2014

rC9 Your duty to act with honesty and integrity under CD3 includes the following requirements:

.1 you must not knowingly or recklessly mislead or attempt to mislead anyone;

.2 you must not draft any statement of case, witness statement, affidavit or other document containing:

    .a any statement of fact or contention which is not supported by your client or by your instructions;

    .b any contention which you do not consider to be properly arguable;

    .c any allegation of fraud, unless you have clear instructions to allege fraud and you have reasonably credible material which establishes an arguable case of fraud;

    .d (in the case of a witness statement or affidavit) any statement of fact other than the evidence which you reasonably believe the witness would give if the witness were giving evidence orally;

.3 you must not encourage a witness to give evidence which is misleading or untruthful;

.4 you must not rehearse, practise with or coach a witness in respect of their evidence;

.5 unless you have the permission of the representative for the opposing side or of the court, you must not communicate with any witness (including your client) about the case while the witness is giving evidence;

Q7.20 Give three examples of how third parties would directly or indirectly benefit from these rules?

Previous codes of conduct of English legal professions have contained more explicit recognition of third party rights, at the expense of client rights, than the present versions do. As noted in the previous chapter, *The Guide to the Professional Conduct of Solicitors* included a statement that information could be revealed if it was necessary 'to prevent the client or a third party committing a criminal act that the solicitor believes on reasonable grounds is likely to result in serious bodily harm'.[39] This guidance had no basis in the Solicitors Practice Rules so its authority was dubious. The guidance gave permission to break confidence, so did not impose a positive duty to warn a potential victim of physical violence.

The current codes of conduct devote fairly limited attention to obligations to third parties. Section four of the SRA Code, which is titled 'You and Others', contains two parts. The second is devoted to controlling the relationship between SRA-regulated businesses and separate businesses they may run. The first part, 'Relations with Third Parties', ostensibly covers all the relevant outcomes and behaviours for dealing with third parties.

The chapter covering relations with third parties in the SRA Code, Chapter 11, contains only four outcomes. The first outcome is general, representing an obligation not to take unfair advantage. The others relate to very specific situations, undertakings and dealing with multi-parties (sometimes called contract races) in the sale of property. The last is really nothing to do with obligations to third parties. The indicative behaviours for the chapter suggest that these outcomes are intended to have fairly limited scope.

SRA Code of Conduct 2011 (as amended)

Chapter 11: Relations with third parties

O(11.1) you do not take unfair advantage of third parties in either your professional or personal capacity;

O(11.2) you perform all undertakings given by you within an agreed timescale or within a reasonable amount of time;

O(11.3) where you act for a seller of land, you inform all buyers immediately of the seller's intention to deal with more than one buyer;

O(11.4) you properly administer oaths, affirmations or declarations where you are authorised to do so.

Indicative behaviours

Acting in the following way(s) may tend to show that you have achieved these outcomes and therefore complied with the *Principles*:

---

[39] N Taylor (ed), *The Guide to the Professional Conduct of Solicitors* (London, Law Society, 1999) Rule 16.02, Circumstances which override confidentiality, Guidance note 3.

IB(11.1) providing sufficient time and information to enable the costs in any matter to be agreed;

IB(11.2) returning documents or money sent subject to an express condition if you are unable to comply with that condition;

IB(11.3) returning documents or money on demand if they are sent on condition that they are held to the sender's order;

IB(11.4) ensuring that you do not communicate with another party when you are aware that the other party has retained a *lawyer* in a matter, except:

(a) to request the name and address of the other party's *lawyer*; or

(b) the other party's *lawyer* consents to you communicating with the *client*; or

(c) where there are exceptional circumstances;

IB(11.5) maintaining an effective system which records when *undertakings* have been given and when they have been discharged;

IB(11.6) where an *undertaking* is given which is dependent upon the happening of a future event and it becomes apparent the future event will not occur, notifying the recipient of this.

Acting in the following way(s) may tend to show that you have not achieved these outcomes and therefore not complied with the *Principles*:

IB(11.7) taking unfair advantage of an opposing party's lack of legal knowledge where they have not instructed a *lawyer*;

IB(11.8) demanding anything for yourself or on behalf of your *client*, that is not legally recoverable, such as when you are instructed to collect a simple debt, demanding from the debtor the cost of the letter of claim since it cannot be said at that stage that such a cost is legally recoverable;

IB(11.9) using your professional status or qualification to take unfair advantage of another *person* in order to advance your personal interests;

IB(11.10) taking unfair advantage of a public office held by you, or a member of your family, or a member of your *firm* or their family.

Q7.21 To what extent does Chapter 11 suggest any obligation to avoid harm to unidentified third parties?

Q7.22 To what extent does Chapter 11 suggest that solicitors have any responsibility to avoid harm to identified third parties?

General Obligation of Fairness?

The highest duty owed by solicitors to third parties in the SRA Code is a general obligation not to take unfair advantage of others. It seems likely that this is intended to set a lower standard than would be set by an outcome such as 'treating others fairly' or even of 'not treating them unfairly'.

Not taking unfair advantage could cover a very wide range of situations, but the intended scope of coverage may be suggested by the indicative behaviours. These are very narrowly drawn in general, referring only to not taking advantage of lay third parties' lack of legal knowledge. This gives very little clue regarding the boundaries of not taking unfair advantage.

The Bar Code of Conduct 2014 has no particular focus on lay third parties. Any non-client focus within the rules tends to be directed toward the duties a barrister owes to the court. These duties, for example covering the treatment of witnesses, are dealt with in the chapter on advocacy. Of course, third parties are often the beneficiaries of such duties, because they tend to support reasonable conduct, openness and fairness, in the conduct of litigation.

This general orientation of the Bar Code to the court also applies to the rules in Chapter 2, Behaving Ethically. One rule, rC9.1, however, imposes a very obvious constraint on dealings with third parties. It provides that barristers should not knowingly, or recklessly, mislead, or attempt to mislead, anyone. This is quite an onerous obligation because it is owed to 'anyone' and it is close to an obligation of candour, or total openness. This broad scope may be unintended. It is not obvious that a duty of candour is supported by the guidance to Chapter 2.

Etiquette

Professional etiquette used to be a popular term for professional conduct rules. This may be because, far more than today, professional rules were concerned with the kinds of work that lawyers in particular professional groups could and could not do. This understanding of the role of etiquette is classically illustrated in the 'settlement' of work activity between the English Bar and the solicitors' profession. Before the introduction of professional access and public access, barristers would only accept instructions from a solicitor. This was essentially a rule of etiquette but it was regarded as an ethical principle. Rules of etiquette continue to be reflected in the new Bar Code.

BSB Code of Conduct 2014

oC17 Clients and BSB authorised persons and authorised (non-BSB) individuals and BSB regulated managers are clear about the circumstances in which instructions may not be accepted or may or must be returned.

gC49 Your duty to comply with Rule C17 may require you to advise your client that in their best interests they should be represented by:

.1 a different advocate or legal representative, whether more senior or more junior than you, or with different experience from yours;

.2 more than one advocate or legal representative;

.3 fewer advocates or legal representatives than have been instructed; or

.4 in the case where you are acting through a professional client, different solicitors.

gC50 Specific rules apply where you are acting on a public access basis, which oblige you to consider whether solicitors should also be instructed.

The importance of etiquette as defining work roles has been relegated in importance by government's attempt to remove differences between professionals. As part of this change professions have been encouraged to do away with any behaviour that could be seen as a restrictive practice, meaning an arrangement between workers to exclude competitors or reduce competition. A possible casualty of this change in emphasis may have been the downgrading of the importance of behaviour between professionals.

The idea of etiquette as manners is obviously relevant to the ways in which professionals treat third parties. This kind of etiquette helps identify the norms of behaviour that apply in a particular social situation. It may define what behaviour is acceptable between lawyers. The legal professions in England and Wales tend not to include this kind of material in their codes of conduct. It is more common in other jurisdictions, eg Canada.

**Law Society of Upper Canada
Rule of Professional Conduct 2014**

Chapter 5—Relationship to the Administration of Justice

Courtesy

5.1-5

A lawyer shall be courteous, civil, and act in good faith to the tribunal and with all persons with whom the lawyer has dealings.

[Amended—October 2014]

Commentary

[1] Legal contempt of court and the professional obligation outlined here are not identical, and a consistent pattern of rude, provocative, or disruptive conduct by the lawyer, even though unpunished as contempt, may constitute professional misconduct

Q7.23 Why might it be beneficial to include behavioural standards in codes of conduct?

Q7.24 Should a lawyer's failure to meet prescribed standards of behaviour lead to disciplinary proceedings?

It is arguable that the maintenance of civil relations between professionals and others is an important aspect of maintaining an appropriate professional culture. Traditionally, professional culture is based on the idea of collegiality. This means that members of a profession share a commitment towards a group and common goal that transcends their workplace commitment to an organisation. Therefore, their relationship as professional colleagues is one of mutual respect for each other's ability. The collegial ideal is that members of professions share equal standing as a member of the professional group.

Maintaining and promoting the commitment to collegiality is, arguably, a key component of professional responsibility (see further chapter nine: Professional Responsibility). Dodek reports that the Chief Justice of Ontario, and the head of the Law Society of Upper Canada, formed the Chief Justice of Ontario's Advisory Committee on Professionalism in response to a perceived growing 'lack of civility among lawyers'.[40] Among the products of these kinds of initiative are various publications intended to help define and improve expectations of professional behaviour between colleagues.

The Principles of Professionalism for Advocacy and Principles of Civility for Advocates (Toronto, The Advocates' Society, Institute for Civility and Professionalism, 2009)

An Advocate's Duty *to* Opposing Counsel

1. The proper administration of justice requires the orderly and civil conduct of proceedings. Advocates should, at all times, act with civility in accordance

---

[40] A Dodek, 'An Education and Apprenticeship in Civility: Correspondent's Report from Canada' (www.lsuc.on.ca/media/definingprofessoct2001revjune2002.pdf).

with the *Principles of Civility for Advocates*. They should engage with opposing counsel in a civil manner even when faced with challenging issues, conflict and disagreement.

2. Discussion about opposing counsel with others, including clients and the court, is permitted. Reasoned criticism based on evidence of a lawyer's incompetence or unprofessional acts may be made. Conversely, ill-considered or uninformed comments about opposing counsel should not be made.

3. Advocates should extend professional courtesies to opposing counsel. Such courtesies include extending assistance, to which opposing counsel are not entitled by law, that does not prejudice their own client.

For the collegial aspirations of professions to succeed it is important that there is a culture of mutual respect. The professional disposition should be able to separate hot disputes at work from personal relations with fellow professionals. This may seem to go without saying, but there are examples of professional behaviour that suggest that more work could be done to define suitable conduct between professionals.

***Iqbal v Mansoor*, Court of Appeal (Civil Division)**
[2013] EWCA Civ 149

Sir Terence Etherton C, Rix and Lewison LJJ
5 March 2013

Rix LJ: The background to this litigation can be found in my judgment in this court in *Iqbal v Dean Manson Solicitors (No 1)* [2011] EWCA Civ 123; [2011] CP Rep 26. In summary, Mr Iqbal had until 31 March 2006 been employed as a part-time assistant solicitor by Dean Manson. They must have been pleased with him because they offered him full-time employment, but he declined. Some years after he had left their employment and started his own firm under the name of Ahmads' Solicitors of Putney, he had been engaged by a Mr Butt, whom Dean Manson sued in January 2009 in the Leeds County Court as alleged guarantor of the fees of their former clients, Mr and Mrs Tahir. Dean Manson appear to have become enraged at this opposition. They wrote to Mr Iqbal three letters, the second and third of which were also copied to Leeds County Court, in which they accused him of having intentionally taken Mr Butt's instructions in order to settle scores because of a personal vendetta against the firm. They said that he had been summarily dismissed from the firm for insubordination and reckless conduct. They accused him of poaching clients and inciting them to initiate malicious complaints. They said that he suffered from a conflict of interest because he had worked on the files of Mr and Mrs Tahir when he had been with the firm. They told him to advise Mr Butt to pay their claim. They accused him of breach of immigration laws and of professional misconduct in forming a partnership with a Mr Sajjid Ali, whom they said had no permission to remain and work in the United Kingdom.

This attack led Mr Iqbal to issue proceedings against Dean Manson in March 2009 in the Croydon County Court for harassment, pursuant to the Protection from Harassment Act 1997 (see below). He claimed an interim injunction to restrain Dean Manson from further acts of harassment aimed at damaging his professional and personal integrity.

The judge was perhaps concerned, and rightly so, not to set up every complaint between lawyers as to the conduct of litigation as arguably a matter of harassment within the Act. It must be rare indeed that such complaints, even if in the heat of battle they go too far, could arguably fall foul of the Act. However, in my judgment, these three letters, particularly when viewed in the light of each other, and especially the last two, arguably amount to a deliberate attack on the professional and personal integrity of Mr Iqbal, in an attempt to pressurise him, by his exposure to his client and/or the court, into declining to act for Mr Butt or else into advising Mr Butt to meet the demands of Dean Manson. It cannot, at any rate arguably, assist Dean Manson that such letters were written in the context of litigation and in an attempt to improve their position in that litigation, or in an attempt to raise even serious and proper concerns as to possible conflicts of interest. Arguably, the letters go way beyond such concerns. Indeed, Mr Brown conceded in argument that if the above was, even arguably, the view which could be taken of these letters, as distinct from the view of them which he submitted was the correct one, namely that they were simply and solely raising legitimate queries as to conflicts of interest between Mr Iqbal and his client and as to breach of confidence between Mr Iqbal and Dean Manson, then Mr Iqbal's claim could not be struck out ...

In sum, in my judgment, each of these letters does, when considered side by side, arguably evidence a campaign of harassment against Mr Iqbal. They are arguably capable of causing alarm or distress. They are arguably unreasonable, or oppressive and unreasonable, or oppressive and unacceptable, or genuinely offensive and unacceptable. Arguably, they go beyond annoyances or irritations, and beyond the ordinary banter and badinage of life. A professional man's integrity is the lifeblood of his vocation. If it is deliberately and wrongly attacked, whether out of personal self-interest or malice, a potential claim lies under the Act."

I also said (with reference to Dean Manson's defence):

'Whatever the hardships involved in litigation, it is not the occasion for irrelevant and abusive dirt to be thrown as part of a malicious campaign. Just as even the freedom of the press may be abused in a rare case (*Thomas v News Group Newspapers Ltd* [2001] EWCA Civ 1233; [2002] EMLR 4; Times, July 25, 2001), so even litigation, whose natural contentiousness also requires its own freedom of speech, can exceptionally be abused. I would, however, equally deplore satellite litigation.'

...

The Court of Appeal was not, however, considering the Protection from Harassment case. On this occasion the appellant was appealing against the dismissal of his claim for libel against the respondent firm of solicitors. It was held, dismissing the appeal, that there was absolute privilege from suit in defamation for witness evidence given in the course of proceedings. The test of whether statements qualified for privilege was not whether they were relevant to the proceedings, but whether they could be said to 'make no reference at all to the subject matter of the proceedings'. Therefore, an allegation that he had changed his practising address to avoid due service of process, may have weakly referred to the subject matter of the claim, but it did so.

...

Protection from Harassment Act 1997 section 1: Prohibition of harassment.

(1) A person must not pursue a course of conduct—

(a) which amounts to harassment of another, and
(b) which he knows or ought to know amounts to harassment of the other.

(2) For the purposes of this section, the person whose course of conduct is in question ought to know that it amounts to harassment of another if a reasonable person in possession of the same information would think the course of conduct amounted to harassment of the other.

(3) Subsection (1) does not apply to a course of conduct if the person who pursued it shows—

(a) that it was pursued for the purpose of preventing or detecting crime,
(b) that it was pursued under any enactment or rule of law or to comply with any condition or requirement imposed by any person under any enactment, or
(c) that in the particular circumstances the pursuit of the course of conduct was reasonable.

2 Offence of harassment.

(1) A person who pursues a course of conduct in breach of section 1 is guilty of an offence.

(2) A person guilty of an offence under this section is liable on summary conviction to imprisonment for a term not exceeding six months, or a fine not exceeding level 5 on the standard scale, or both.

...

According to the Court of Appeal judgment, Dean Manson had also referred Mr Iqbal to the SRA for conflict of interest and breach of confidentiality. The SRA declined to take any action. They had also obtained a default costs assessment for over £80,000 against Mr Iqbal which, it was said, threatened to bankrupt him.

Q7.25 What responsibilities, on the evidence of *Iqbal v Mansoor*, do legal professionals owe each other?

Q7.26 Was either side's conduct in this case collegial?

Q7.27 What kind of regulatory mechanism might have prevented the conflict described in the judgment?

Conclusion

Any obligation that a lawyer owes to third parties potentially cuts across the duty owed to clients. It is perhaps for this reason that third party duties do not figure very significantly in codes of conduct. The highest duty, not to take unfair advantage, is fairly narrow. There are, however, forum responsibilities imposed on lawyers in favour of third parties. Lawyers can be disciplined or penalised by wasted costs orders where they do not respect third party rights. Again, the circumstances where this may occur can be fairly narrow.

It sometimes appears that lawyers have to be complicit in an abuse of process before they can be penalised for subjecting a third party to their client's hopeless case. There is still less authority in the codes for breaching client confidentiality to prevent serious physical or financial harm to others resulting from the risk of client misconduct. Because of the rules on confidentiality and LPP there are significant difficulties in imposing such responsibilities. Consequently, duties to third parties in the codes tend to follow the common law and are not very extensive. The general duty 'not to take unfair advantage' is not very precise.

8

Social Responsibility

Duties owed to clients limit obligations that lawyers owe to the individual third parties they deal with. Therefore, as described in the previous chapter, duties that lawyers might owe to individual third parties are fairly restricted. The imposition of 'whistle-blowing' obligations on lawyers may be advocated on the ground that lawyers are uniquely placed to prevent certain kinds of social harm. Do the same limitations that apply to duties to individual third parties apply when the clients of lawyers are doing something harmful to society generally? Are lawyers more likely to be held responsible to collective entities, or the public interest, for client harms they could have prevented?

The imposition of professional responsibilities to society is controversial because it cuts across confidentiality. This diminishes clients' rights and clients' autonomy. Therefore, a duty on a lawyer to report suspicions that a client is engaged in money-laundering potentially undermines the obligation of loyalty lawyers owe clients. A duty not to let the client know that a report has been made contradicts the duty of disclosure to the client of all information known to the lawyer.

Because of their primary orientation to clients, there are practical difficulties in making lawyers responsible for preventing social harms. The problem is finding the right balance between client-facing and public-facing duties. The task is to preserve both the legitimate right of clients to confidentiality and privacy and the public interest in detecting and punishing crimes or preventing social catastrophes.

This chapter considers the balance between lawyers' traditional role of counselling and defending individual clients and fulfilling a policing role in relation to clients. It looks, in particular, at legislative obligations imposed on lawyers and exceptions to legal professional privilege. It concludes by considering whether there should be general or specific duties to prevent widespread public harms imposed on lawyers.

Lawyers' Duty to the Public Interest

It is generally assumed that professions serve the public interest. It is only over the last thirty years or so that these claims have been called into question. The next chapter examines the benefits of organising lawyers into professions. This chapter examines the ways in which lawyers balance their service to clients with obligations to the state and public at large.

An obvious manifestation of the way a balance is struck between client interests and the public interest is the duty to the court. This requires that a lawyer does not mislead any court when presenting a client's case. This duty is well represented in the codes of conduct and is dealt with in chapter ten: Litigation and Advocacy. This chapter explores other ways in which lawyers must compromise their duties to clients and prioritise public-facing duties.

The expectation that lawyers will weigh other considerations than their clients' interests is clearly expressed in the Legal Services Act 2007 section 1. The first regulatory objective set out in the Act is 'protecting and promoting the public interest'. Other regulatory objectives, such as 'improving access to justice' and 'protecting and promoting the interests of consumers', are manifestations of the first objective, but it is assumed that they are separate and distinct objectives.

The last regulatory objective is 'promoting and maintaining adherence to the professional principles' and the first of these, set out in section 1(3)(a), is that 'authorised persons should act with independence and integrity'. These words are also longstanding features of codes of conduct. The message that they are intended to convey is that lawyers are not merely agents for whatever purposes their clients have. They are expected to weigh other criteria before doing whatever their clients want. They must also manifest their independence in ways that are consistent with their primary duty to clients.

The classic example of lawyer independence, explored further in chapter ten is that, when a client insists on presenting evidence that will mislead the court, the lawyer must withdraw from the representation but preserve the client's confidentiality. It is not clear, however, whether independence goes much further than not becoming involved in clients' criminal designs and not misleading the court.

The test of lawyers' independence is not whether they can resist the demands of clients in general, but whether they can resist control by powerful third parties. These might include corporations which expect total obedience from their lawyers. It might also include third party funders such as insurance companies providing before or after the event legal expenses insurances. It might even include agencies that pay for the legal work done for clients, such as legal aid authorities. The obligation of lawyers to retain their independence includes maintaining loyalty to clients when they are not the ones paying directly for the legal services they receive.

Respecting the duty to the court exemplifies a situation where lawyers must put a public interest first; other situations are less clear. Do lawyers, for example, have any responsibility to the shareholders of companies ruined by their director clients or to communities harmed by environmental damage caused by their manufacturing clients? This chapter begins by looking at the clearest examples of situations where lawyers must put public obligations before those owed to clients. It then works towards those that are more debatable.

Engaging in Criminal Purposes

Context

Lawyers, accountants and other professions involved in business activities are vulnerable to being targeted, as willing or unwilling participants, for involvement in criminal activities by clients. The main offences are not confined to lawyers, but lawyers are an obvious target because of their duty of confidentiality, the protection of legal professional privilege and their contacts with business.

In addition to the general prohibition on ordinary criminal activity, there is range of legislation that is specifically targeted at or relevant to business professionals. This is because in the Proceeds of Crime Act 2002 (POCA) the government attempted to clamp down on organised crime by recovering or 'taxing' the proceeds of crime. Modern criminals have therefore had to become increasingly sophisticated in covering their tracks.

The POCA covered primary offences which business professionals might be implicated in. They also impose obligations to report suspicions that clients may be involved in certain kinds of activity, such as money-laundering and terrorism. If lawyers assist their criminal clients in committing an offence they are likely to be prosecuted as participants, conspirators or accessories in whatever offence has been committed. It is not unusual for lawyers who have been engaged in criminal activity to also be called before a professional disciplinary tribunal and struck off or disbarred.

Primary Offences

The POCA creates a number of offences which solicitors, in particular, have to be wary of committing while undertaking work for clients. For example, an offence is committed under section 329 if a person acquires criminal property, uses criminal property or has possession of criminal property. Under section 327, a person commits an offence if he conceals, disguises, converts, transfers criminal property or removes it from England and Wales, Scotland or Northern Ireland. Solicitors can protect themselves by disclosing suspicions about particular transactions to the authorities under POCA section 338 and obtaining consent to complete the work the client wants them to do.

Under the POCA, section 328(1), it is an offence for a person to enter into or become concerned 'in an arrangement which he knows or suspects facilitates (by whatever means) the acquisition, retention, use or control of criminal property by or on behalf of another person'. Criminal property is defined as a benefit obtained from criminal conduct. Solicitors would again be protected by making authorised disclosures of the arrangement under section 338 and obtaining the appropriate consent.

The Terrorism Act 2000 (as amended) is the primary legislation creating terrorism offences. It covers participation in and providing material support for terrorist activity. The principal property offences are contained in sections 15–18 of the Act. They cover raising funds that a person knows or has reasonable cause to suspect may be used for terrorist purposes, using or possessing money or other property for terrorist purposes, and becoming involved in an arrangement which makes money or other property available for suspected terrorist purposes.

The Terrorism Act also covers money-laundering, meaning entering into or becoming concerned in an arrangement facilitating the retention or control of terrorist property by, or on behalf of, another person.[1] This includes concealing property, removing it from the jurisdiction or transferring it to nominees. Additionally, lawyers, by operating in the regulated sector, can commit further offences based on failing to report knowledge or suspicions that the primary offences have been committed.

Reporting Requirements

Even if they are not involved in relevant illegal activity, both the POCA and the anti-terrorism legislation contain provisions requiring that solicitors, and

---

[1] Terrorism Act 2000 s 18.

others, report suspicions of possible offences planned or carried out by clients. The relevant legislation typically prevents the person reporting the suspicious activity informing the client that they have done so. If the person reporting the activity lets the person they have reported know, he or she may be guilty of a 'tipping off' offence. Rules against tipping off cut across lawyers' responsibility to disclose to clients matters within their knowledge relevant to their matter.

There are three main activities which are considered so serious that they override the lawyer's duty of confidentiality in this way. The first legislative duty is to report suspected money-laundering, the recycling of money traceable to illicit activity.[2] Lawyers and others, such as bank officials and accountants, are obliged to inform the authorities if they suspect a client of laundering the proceeds of crime. The statute requires that reporting takes place without the client's knowledge.

The second significant incursion into the lawyer's duty to respect client confidentiality is the duty to report suspected terrorist activity. The anti-terrorism legislation requires a person who has information which he 'knows or believes might be of material assistance' in either preventing an act of terrorism or securing the apprehension of a person who has committed such an act, to reveal it.[3]

The advice of the Law Society is that the duty to report suspected terrorist activity only applies to solicitors where the information is *not* covered by legal professional privilege (LPP). Two sections of the relevant legislation are specifically stated not to require disclosure by a professional legal adviser of information which he obtains in privileged circumstances.[4]

If it is not protected by LPP, suspected terrorist activity may still be notionally protected by a duty of confidentiality. However, the solicitor may be guilty of an offence unless the information is also protected by legal professional privilege. Confidentiality alone is not a defence. The information must be disclosed to those with a legitimate interest in receiving the information, ie the police or other relevant enforcement authority. Informing a newspaper would not be a disclosure in the public interest.

The third area in which a reporting requirement may cut across a duty of confidentiality is in relation to tax avoidance schemes. These have to be reported to Her Majesty's Revenue and Customs so that they can investigated before they come into effect. In areas where breach of confidence is required by law, the position regarding LPP is the key to determining the obligation of the lawyer.

---

[2] Proceeds of Crime Act 2002, as amended by the Serious Organised Crime and Police Act 2005, the Serious Crime Act 2007 and Money Laundering Regulations 2007.

[3] Terrorism Act 2000 (as amended) s 38B.

[4] Ibid, ss 19(5)(a) and 21A(5)(b) and see Anti-Terrorism Practice Note issued by the Law Society, July 2007.

By imposing obvious restrictions on the duty of loyalty to clients and to the duty of confidentiality the state is demanding that lawyers put social responsibility first. The implication of this is that the circumstances in which they are expected to prioritise social over client responsibilities should be crystal clear. Usually, lawyers' social responsibilities are not so clearly drawn. The situation in relation to LLP illustrates this.

Legal Professional Privilege

Apart from the specific legislative requirements relating to money-laundering, terrorism and tax avoidance there is no requirement to break client confidentiality. Therefore, when lawyers know or suspect that clients are planning crimes there is no duty to report them. There is a question mark over whether they *can* report them, thereby breaking confidentiality and LPP. There is authority, set out below, saying that when clients use their lawyers for a criminal purpose they forfeit their right to confidentiality and the protection of LPP.

Context

As described in chapter six: Confidentiality and Privilege, the Police and Criminal Evidence Act (PACE) 1984 identifies two kinds of legal professional privilege. The first, legal advice privilege, is defined in section 10(1)(a). It covers communications between a 'professional legal adviser and his client' connected with 'the giving of legal advice to the client'. The second, litigation privilege, is defined in section 10(1)(b). It covers communications between lawyers, or their clients, 'and any other person' in connection with litigation or anticipated litigation.

LPP is a natural complement to the duty of confidentiality owed to clients. It protects confidentiality in the lawyer–client relationship by legally recognising that communications covered by privilege cannot be required to be produced for any purpose, including in court proceedings. There are, however, circumstances where LPP does not apply but confidentiality still does and circumstances where neither apply. These exceptions to LPP are restrictions imposed in the public interest.

A party may be aware that another party has documents for which LPP is claimed through the litigation process of disclosure. The process of standard disclosure is governed by the Civil Procedure Rules 1998 rule 31. A party is required to disclose a list of documents specifying which documents they hold or have held that are available for inspection. They must also specify documents for which privilege is claimed. The opposing party may apply to the court for a declaration that the document is not privileged.

A challenge to privilege can occur in ways outside the disclosure process. For example, a party may believe that an opposing party has documents that will help their case. It is, however, more difficult to make a case against privilege if they have no proof that such documents exist and their opponent denies that they do. The court may then decide that the applicant for disclosure is on a 'fishing expedition' and refuse to consider the matter. The position is further complicated where the applicant claims that privilege should be ignored because advice was taken for an illegal purpose.

The Illegality Exception to Legal Professional Privilege

By and large the courts protect lawyer and client confidentiality by recognising LPP. There are, however, two main situations where LPP may be held not to apply. These are (1) where the communication between the lawyer and client is aimed at furthering a criminal purpose; and (2) where items are held for a criminal purpose.

Communications Aimed at Furthering a Criminal Purpose

Communications aimed at furthering a criminal purpose are not mentioned in the PACE section 10, although the section does mention that items held for a criminal purpose are not protected by privilege. The common law has, however, always treated advice delivered for the purpose of furthering a fraudulent or criminal purpose as not covered by legal advice privilege.

There are therefore two vital requirements before legal advice privilege does not apply. First, the legal advice must be given with the intention of furthering a criminal purpose. The intention may be that of either of the lawyer, a client or a third party. In *Francis & Francis v Central Criminal Court*[5] the House of Lords decided that a lawyer need not intend to further a criminal purpose when holding items for privilege to be lost. In that case the lawyer and the client were both ignorant of the fact that the purchase money for a house provided by the client's relative was drug money.

Requirements for Overriding Legal Advice Privilege

It is important to distinguish advice taken with a view to committing a crime and advice taken for the purpose of defending oneself from actual or possible criminal charges. Advice about how to get away with a crime, or even to avoid

---

[5] *Francis & Francis v Central Criminal Court* [1989] AC 346.

legal responsibilities, may not be covered by LPP. Advice given to a client regarding an offence he has or may have committed is covered by privilege.

The courts sometimes have a difficult task balancing the idea that privilege is sacrosanct with the illegality exception. The cases raise a number of questions. One of the most important issues is how the court explores the possibility of illegality without breaching the privilege. In one of the founding cases, *R v Cox & Railton*, a review court was asked to consider circumstances where the advice given by a solicitor was related in court, by the solicitor. It appeared that the court of first instance had not considered whether the defendants' privilege should have prevented the solicitor giving his testimony.

R v Cox & Railton (1884) 14 QBD 153

The defendants were partners and owners of *The Brightonian*, a newspaper. M sued the newspaper for libel and the second defendant, R, entered appearance. R lost the case and was ordered to pay damages. In default of payment M sent a bailiff to seize the goods of the R. The bailiff was presented with a Bill of Sale transferring R's goods to the first defendant after the judgment.

C and R were prosecuted for conspiring to cheat M of his damages. It was alleged that the bill of sale and a deed dissolving their partnership were antedated. A solicitor, Goodman, was called to give evidence and confirmed that he had advised the defendants that a bill of sale to Cox would not defeat the judgment because they were partners. The judge's summary of the solicitor's evidence was as follows:

> On the 28th of June, or thereabouts, Railton and Cox came to me. Railton said, 'I suppose you have heard the result of the Munster case.' I said, 'Yes.' He said, 'Can anything be done to prevent the property being seized under an execution?' I said, 'Only a sale to a *bona fide* purchaser.' He said, 'Could the property be sold and I remain in possession as manager?' I said, 'No, you must go out of possession.' He said, 'That won't do. Can I give a bill of sale to Mr Cox?' I said, 'No, you cannot, because of the partnership.' Railton said, 'Does anyone know of the partnership except you and ourselves?' I said, 'No, not that I am aware of, only my clerks.' Cox said, 'Then you don't think a bill of sale will do?' I said, 'Certainly not.' They then asked my fee and paid it, and left the office. Nothing was said about a dissolution at that interview. The interview was with me as a solicitor, and I was paid my fee. It was expressly arranged that the partnership should be kept secret. Nothing either way was said about a dissolution.'

On this account, of course, the defendants were one-off clients of the solicitor and the solicitor was not a party to any fraud that took place. More importantly, it is not clear that he was certain, before giving his evidence, that he had unwittingly participated in a fraud. The defendants appealed against conviction on the grounds that the case against them depended on their solicitor's evidence and that his testimony should not have been admitted because it was privileged. On appeal the judge reserved the issue to be decided by the Court for Crown Cases Reserved. This was a review court later superseded by the Court of Criminal Appeal. This court plainly had difficulty with the case. It decided that the decision had to stand but reserved full reasons.

It seems that the court was particularly troubled by two points. First, what were the grounds for looking behind the advice given, particularly if the solicitor was innocent of any subterfuge? Second, should the court have admitted the evidence of the solicitor in the absence of any foundation laid at trial for the allegation that a crime had been committed? As Lopes J observed 'Here there were, so far as appears, no facts to destroy privilege given in evidence before Mr. Goodman was called. It is impossible to say you are to have the secret of the client disclosed in public, so as to see if it ought to be disclosed.'

Stephen J quoted with approval (at 175) Bovill CJ in *Tichborne v Lushington* who had said,

'I believe the law is, and properly is, that if a party consults an attorney, and obtains advice for what afterwards turns out to be the commission of a crime or a fraud, that party so consulting the attorney has no privilege whatever to close the lips of the attorney from stating the truth. Indeed, if any such privilege should be contended for, or existed, it would work most grievous hardship on an attorney, who, after he had been consulted upon what subsequently appeared to be a manifest crime and fraud, would have his lips closed, and might place him in a very serious position of being suspected to be a party to the fraud, and without his having an opportunity of exculpating himself. ... There is no privilege in the case which I have suggested of a party consulting another, a professional man, as to what may afterwards turn out to be a crime or fraud, and the best mode of accomplishing it.'

[However, although there is no privilege, there is a problem] ... The privilege must, it was argued, be violated in order to ascertain whether it exists. The secret must be told in order to see whether it ought to be kept. We were earnestly pressed to lay down some rule as to the manner in which this consequence should be avoided. The only thing which we feel authorized to say upon this matter is, that in each particular case the Court must determine upon the facts actually given in evidence or proposed to be given in evidence, whether it seems probable that the accused person may have consulted his legal adviser, not after the commission of the crime for the legitimate purpose of being defended, but before the commission of the crime for the purpose of being guided or helped in committing it. We are far from saying that the question whether the advice was taken before or after the offence will always be decisive as to the admissibility of such evidence.

Courts must in every instance judge for themselves on the special facts of each particular case, just as they must judge whether a witness deserves to

be examined on the supposition that he is hostile, or whether a dying declaration was made in the immediate prospect of death. In this particular case
the fact that there had been a partnership (which was proved on the trial of
the interpleader issue), the assertion that it had been dissolved, the fact that
directly after the verdict a solicitor was consulted, and that the execution
creditor was met by a bill of sale which purported to have been made by the
defendant to the man who had been and was said to have ceased to be his
partner, made it probable that the visit to the solicitor really was intended
for the purpose for which, after he had given his evidence, it turned out to
have been intended. If the interview had been for an innocent purpose, the
evidence given would have done the defendants good instead of harm. Of
course the power in question ought to be used with the greatest care not to
hamper prisoners in making their defence, and not to enable unscrupulous
persons to acquire knowledge to which they have no right, and every precaution should be taken against compelling unnecessary disclosures.

Q8.1   What was the issue for the review court?

Q8.2   If the solicitor had claimed that his conversation with the defendants
       was privileged do you think the court would have ordered him to
       disclose details of it?

Q8.3   Should the defendants' solicitor have given evidence for the Crown
       so readily?

Q8.4   In your opinion, should a lawyer breach a client's confidentiality
       without an order from the court that LPP is overridden?

Items Held with the Intent of Furthering a Criminal Purpose

Under the PACE section 10(2) items held with the intent of furthering a
criminal purpose are not protected by privilege. This creates some difficulty
for claimants alleging that a criminal purpose defeats privilege. How can they
show that a party was aware of a criminal purpose if they cannot see the
relevant documents?

One on the issues that the court in *R v Cox & Railton* struggled with was
when it could be satisfied that a fraud or crime might have been committed.
A certain threshold had to be crossed to justify examining privileged material.
The problem, however, is that it might take this examination to confirm that
privilege should be overridden. In effect, the privilege must be broken to see
if the material should be admitted in evidence. The court therefore needs to

be satisfied that the intrusion on confidentiality and the breach of privilege is justified. How much evidence of a criminal purpose is needed?

Bullivant and Others. Appellants; v The Attorney-General for Victoria (on behalf of Her Majesty) Respondent **[1901] AC 196**

A deceased testator was alleged to have executed voluntary conveyances of property 'with intent to evade the payment of duty', an offence under statute. The testator's solicitors objected to producing the notes and records of their instructions regarding the conveyances on the ground that they were privileged communications between solicitor and client for the purpose of obtaining advice. The Attorney-General for Victoria alleged that the privilege was lost because of the illegal intent to evade duty. The court found that evading duty was an ambiguous term that did not necessarily carry an imputation of fraud. Therefore, there was no proof of, or even any allegation of, any fraud or illegality to displace the privilege.

Earl of Halsbury LC (at 200–01)

> I think the broad propositions may be very simply stated: for the perfect administration of justice, and for the protection of the confidence which exists between a solicitor and his client, it has been established as a principle of public policy that those confidential communications shall not be subject to production. But to that, of course, this limitation has been put, and justly put, that no Court can be called upon to protect communications which are in themselves parts of a criminal or unlawful proceeding. Those are the two principles, and of course it would be possible to make both propositions absurd, as is very often the case with all propositions, by taking extreme cases on either side. If you are to say, 'I will not say what these communications are because until you have actually proved me guilty of a crime they may be privileged as confidential,' the result would be that they could never be produced at all, because until the whole thing is over you cannot have the proof of guilt. On the other hand, if it is sufficient for the party demanding the production to say, as a mere surmise or conjecture, that the thing which he is so endeavouring to inquire into may have been illegal or not, the privilege in all cases disappears at once.

> The line which the Courts have hitherto taken, and I hope will preserve, is this— that in order to displace the *primâ facie* right of silence by a witness who has been put in the relation of professional confidence with his client, before that confidence can be broken you must have some definite charge either by way of allegation or affidavit or what not. I do not at present go into the modes by which that can be made out, but there must be some definite charge of something which displaces the privilege.

Q8.5   Had the Attorney-General for Victoria succeeded, what would have
        been the consequence regarding the solicitor's duty of confidentiality?

Q8.6.   Had the equivalent PACE section 10(2) been enacted at the time, do
        you think that this case would have been decided the same way?

In *O'Rourke v Darbishire and Others*[6] the Court of Appeal confirmed that the
court had to take every precaution against compelling unnecessary disclosures.
The mere allegation of fraud was not enough. There had to be (1) a reasonably clear allegation of fraud in the pleadings connecting with the fraud the
document sought to be disclosed; and (2) the Court had to be satisfied that
there was a reasonable probability of fraud. If, as in *Bullivant*, the statements
of fact are perfectly consistent with the innocence of the respondents it will
not be enough. The judge said: 'Looking at all the circumstances of the case,
this is a fishing action of a most fantastical kind, and the pleader has cast
about to see how he could frame some sort of pleading.' The application to
lift privilege therefore failed. By this time the courts had adopted the term
'iniquity' rather than crime, fraud or illegality. This is an old-fashioned word
meaning something like a gross injustice.

Accidental Disclosure of Privileged Material

In a case where advice or documents have accidentally come into the hands
of opposing parties it is arguable that privilege should apply to exclude them
from proceedings. There is, however, a problem if the documents constitute
evidence of iniquity. Should the courts exclude them even though a party
would not otherwise have been ordered to produce them? The court may well
take the view that there is no point trying to put the cat back in the bag if
a criminal purpose is revealed by the confidential information. The case of
Butler v Board of Trade pre-dates the cases which raised the current importance attached to LPP to a fundamental principle. It is therefore interesting to
consider whether it would be decided the same way today.

Butler v Board of Trade [1971] Ch 680

A solicitor handed the papers of a company for which she had acted to the
Official Receiver who was winding-up the company. The papers included
a copy of a letter to the appellant, who was connected to the wound-up
companies, warning of possibly serious consequences if he did not take care.
The Board of Trade wished to use this letter as evidence of the claimant's

---

[6] *O'Rourke v Darbishire* [1920] AC 581.

wrongdoing and as evidence that he was on notice as to the consequences. The claimant asked the court for a declaration that the original of the letter was privileged and the copy was therefore confidential. The Board contended that the original letter was not privileged as it was relevant to criminal proceedings.

The court confirmed that LPP was destroyed when advice was given in preparation or furtherance of a crime or fraud. On the facts of this case the advice was not tendered on that basis. It confirmed also that, as the original letter was privileged, the copy was confidential, but that, in the circumstances, legal advice privilege did not apply.

The rationale offered for the decision was that 'although there had been a breach of confidence and, in such circumstances, an innocent recipient of information could be restrained, there were good reasons why it would not be proper for the court to interfere in cases where there was a conflict between the private right of the individual in equity and the duty of the state to prosecute offenders. Accordingly, the recipient here being the Board of Trade, and the intention being to use the letter in a public prosecution, the court's equitable jurisdiction in confidence would not be exercised and the action must be dismissed' (690D–H).

Q8.7　What was the outcome of this action?

Q8.8　Would the outcome have been different if the Board of Trade had known such a letter been written but it had not been inadvertently disclosed to them?

Q8.9　Would the outcome have been different if the defendant had been, for example, a shareholder of the company and not the Board of Trade?

Q8.10　Do you think that, if the case were heard today, either (a) *Three Rivers District Council & Others v Governor and Company of the Bank of England* or (b) PACE section 10 would make a difference to the outcome?

Overriding Litigation Privilege

The courts have been keen to maintain a distinction between legal advice privilege and litigation privilege. LPP is a fundamental guarantee of the rights of criminal defendants. Therefore, the courts are very reluctant to override LPP where lawyers are advising clients regarding their past actions, or defending them in criminal proceedings.

R v Ataou [1988] 1 QB 798

Three men were charged with conspiracy to supply heroin. The appellant, A, who had been in a car with the other two, claimed he was an innocent passenger who did not know their plans. A's solicitors, B & Co, also acted for H, a known drug-dealer arrested in the car with A.

H pleaded guilty and gave evidence for the prosecution. H gave evidence that he and A had conspired to supply heroin. During the course of H's evidence, a clerk from B & Co found a note of a meeting in which H had said that A was not involved. A's barrister was refused permission by the trial judge to refer to the note in the cross-examination of H. This was because H had made the statement in circumstances in which it was privileged. A was convicted and appealed. The Court of Appeal allowed the appeal because the trial judge failed to hear argument on whether H could claim privilege in the circumstances.

Q8.11 Was there a conflict of interest in *R v Ataou*? Could it have been avoided? How was it dealt with?

Q8.12 Which kind of privilege was H able to claim for the file note?

Q8.13 The Court of Appeal criticised the solicitors' clerk for passing on the note, but said that it was perfectly proper for the barrister to try to use it in cross-examination. Was this fair?

Q8.14 Is there an argument that the court should have admitted the note as prima facie evidence of a new crime, ie H's perjury?

As *R v Cox & Railton* showed, it might be difficult to separate legal advice and litigation privilege in some situations. The boundary risked becoming blurry in *Barclays Bank Plc and Others v Eustice and Others*.[7] The defendants were tenants of a farm. They borrowed money from the claimant bank to buy the freehold of neighbouring land. The bank took charges over the freehold. The defendants subsequently got into debt and, facing action by the Inland Revenue, assigned their tenancy of the farm and a tenancy of the freehold to one the defendants' sons for £1. The bank sought relief from the court, including a declaration that the transfers were void and unenforceable.

On appeal the Court of Appeal upheld the judge's decision that the purpose of the transfers was a prohibited purpose and contrary to the insolvency legislation. On the question of whether privilege applied, the Court concluded that the dominant purpose of the defendants in consulting lawyers was not prospective litigation. Rather they wanted to know the best way to protect

---

[7] *Barclays Bank Plc and Others v Eustice and Others* [1995] 1 WLR 1238.

their assets from legitimate claims. This purpose was sufficiently iniquitous for communications between the defendants and their legal advisers about setting up of the transactions should be discoverable.

One of the issues concerning the court in *Barclays Bank Plc and Others v Eustice and Others* was whether the privilege that was being overridden could be seen as litigation privilege. This was why the Court held that the client's 'dominant purpose' was seeking legal advice and not defending proceedings. In *Kuwait Airways Corporation v Iraqi Airways Company* it was held that strong prima facie evidence of fraud defeats a claim to litigation privilege.[8]

In principle, therefore, neither form of privilege protects communication aimed at furthering a criminal purpose. This position has to be clearly distinguished from a situation where a client asks a lawyer for representation against a criminal charge or civil claim. In that case, information passing between them relates to a past conduct and must be treated as confidential and privileged.

JSC BTA Bank v Mukhtar Ablyazov and others, Mukhtar Ablyazov, Syrym Shalabayev, Clyde & Co LLP, Stephenson Harwood LLP, Addleshaw Goddard LLP [2014] EWHC 2788 (Comm)

A had been Chairman of the claimant bank in Kazakhstan until it was nationalised in February 2009. A fled to London claiming that the takeover was because he was a political opponent of the government. The bank claimed that A had used the bank's resources for his personal purposes and began various proceedings to recover sums in excess of $6 billion. At different points in these proceedings A instructed different English law firms to resist the bank's claims. Four sets of proceeding ended with A ordered to repay $4.6 billion but A absconded and continued to fight the actions from undisclosed locations.

A engaged in transactions using proxies, including S, to transfer and dispose of resources that were subject to freezing orders by the English courts. At one point in the proceedings Rix LJ had said:

> Mr Ablyazov's contempts have been multiple, persistent and protracted, have embraced the offences of non-disclosure, lying in cross-examination and dealing with assets, and have been supported by the suborning of false testimony and the forging of documents. Mr Ablyazov, emboldened perhaps by the wealth at his disposal, which enables him to travel, hide and still instruct lawyers on a prodigious scale, he continues to obstruct justice with an attempt at impunity for the consequences of this litigation.

Eventually, A was debarred from defending the proceedings. The bank, attempting to track the various assets held by A, sought disclosure of docu-

---

[8] *Kuwait Airways Corporation v Iraqi Airways Company* [2005] EWCA Civ 286.

ments held by his law firms. Popplewell J had to consider whether the documents fell within the fraud exception even though they had been prepared in anticipation of, or for the purposes of, litigation. He adopted the reasoning in *R v Snaresbrook Crown Court Ex p DPP* [1988] QB 532 and *R v Central Criminal Court Ex p Francis & Francis* [1989] AC 346 and accepted that litigation privilege is not prevented from attaching merely because the solicitor is engaged to conduct litigation by putting forward an account of events which the client knows to be untrue and which therefore involves a deliberate strategy to mislead the other party and the court, and to commit perjury. In the *Snaresbrook* case Glidewell LJ said (537–538):

> Obviously, not infrequently persons allege that accidents have happened in ways other than the ways in which they in fact happened, or that they were on the correct side of the road when driving while actually they were on the wrong side of the road, and matters of that sort. Again, litigants in civil litigation may not be believed when their cases come to trial, but that is not to say that the statements they had made to their solicitors pending the trial, much less the applications which they made if they applied for legal aid, are not subject to legal privilege. The principle to be derived from R v Cox and Railton applies in my view to circumstances which do not cover *the ordinary run of cases such as this is.* (emphasis supplied)

Popplewell J also quoted Lord Goff of Chieveley who, in *Francis & Francis*, went out of his way to approve Glidewell LJ's reasoning (at 397) 'that the common law principle of legal professional privilege cannot be excluded, by the exception established in *R v Cox and Railton* ... where a communication is made by a client to his legal adviser regarding the conduct of his case in criminal or civil proceedings, *merely because* such communication is untrue and would, if acted upon, lead to the commission of the crime of perjury in such proceedings.'

Popplewell J continued (at para 93):

> I would conclude, therefore, that the touchstone is whether the communication is made for the purposes of giving or receiving legal advice, or for the purposes of the conduct of actual or contemplated litigation, which is advice or conduct in which the solicitor is acting in the ordinary course of the professional engagement of a solicitor. If the iniquity puts the advice or conduct outside the normal scope of such professional engagement, or renders it an abuse of the relationship which properly falls within the ordinary course of such an engagement, a communication for such purpose cannot attract legal professional privilege. In cases where a lawyer is engaged to put forward a false case supported by false evidence, it will be a question of fact and degree whether it involves an abuse of the ordinary professional engagement of a solicitor in the circumstances in question. In the 'ordinary run' of criminal cases the solicitor will be acting in the ordinary course of professional engagement, and the client doing no more than using him to provide the services inherent in the proper fulfilment of such engagement, even

where in denying the crime the defendant puts forward what the jury finds to be a bogus defence. But where in civil proceedings there is deception of the solicitors in order to use them as an instrument to perpetrate a substantial fraud on the other party and the court, that may well be indicative of a lack of confidentiality which is the essential prerequisite for the attachment of legal professional privilege. The deception of the solicitors, and therefore the abuse of the normal solicitor/client relationship, will often be the hallmark of iniquity which negates the privilege.

Q8.15 What is the dividing line between the 'ordinary run of cases', where LPP is preserved despite a client's lies and bad faith, and iniquity, which will cause litigation privilege to be lost?

Summary and Overview

The presence of an iniquitous purpose in seeking legal advice or in an aspect of the conduct of litigation is sufficient grounds for the courts to override LPP. If their clients lose this protection lawyers could be ordered by the court to give oral evidence. They are more likely to be asked to produce their files. Before ordering that privilege be ignored the court must have before it an allegation of fraud or other conduct and be satisfied that there was a reasonable probability of it amounting to iniquity.

The iniquity exception does not arise because a lawyer is engaged by a client to conduct litigation by putting forward an account of events which the client knows to be untrue. Although this may involve a deliberate strategy by the client to mislead the other party, and the court, and to commit perjury, this is deemed to be in the normal run of litigation; it is what the courts are for.

The removal of the protection of LPP does not necessarily remove a lawyer's obligation of confidentiality. The court order lifting privilege may apply to very specific materials. The client may retain privilege in relation to other matters. Also, because the privilege has been lifted in relation to the court and specific parties, it does not mean that lawyer need not keep the information confidential from all other parties and from the public.

The Public Service Dimension of the LPP Exception for Iniquity

As will be clear from most of the cases, lawyers are typically involved in defending their clients' claims to privilege when those rights are challenged. However, the case of *R v Cox & Railton* demonstrates that lawyers may not always regard their clients so benignly. The case raises the question of whether lawyers might have either a duty or a permission to report clients who have used their services for iniquitous purposes.

In the *Ablyazov* case Popplewell J said that the reason why LPP failed was because the prior duty of confidentiality had failed. This raises the question of what the lawyer is supposed to do when she believes that a client has used her for an iniquitous purpose, but no party or court is pressing her for breach of confidentiality. Does the lawyer have a duty to report the client? As we have seen, where there is a situation that calls for reporting, such as suspicions of money laundering, the legislature has created a clear duty. This leaves the issue of whether there is an implied permission to report a client who involves an unwitting lawyer in an iniquitous plan.

In *R v Cox & Railton* Stephen J's judgment implied that lawyers may have a right to report clients that have involved them in a criminal purpose. He suggested that it would be a 'grievous hardship' for a lawyer to sit by and have people think that he was party to the criminal act. In circumstances where there is no application to avoid LPP, people may continue to think that a lawyer is complicit in their client's scam. Nevertheless, it seems safer to conclude that, in the absence of a clear duty to report, there is no such duty.

What Are the Policy Arguments for LPP?

Many people may find the conclusion that there is no duty to report clients involved in some criminal scheme surprising. It is therefore instructive to return to the rationale for confidentiality and LPP and to consider the policy reasons for privilege and for ignoring it.

R v Derby Magistrates Court ex parte B [1996] 1 AC 487

Lord Taylor of Gosforth CJ at 507C–E:

> The principle which runs through all these cases and the many other cases which were cited, is that a man must be able to consult his lawyer in confidence, since otherwise he might hold back half the truth. The client must be sure that what he tells his lawyer in confidence will never be revealed without his consent. Legal professional privilege is thus much more than an ordinary rule of evidence, limited in its application to the facts of a particular case. It is a fundamental condition on which the administration of justice as a whole rests.

Three Rivers District Council and Others v Governor and Company of the Bank of England (No 6) (House of Lords)

Baroness Hale of Richmond (at para 61):

> It is in the interests of the whole community that lawyers give their clients sound advice, accurate as to the law and sensible as to their conduct. The client may not always act upon that advice (which will sometimes place the lawyer in professional difficulty, but that is a separate matter) but there is always a chance that he will. And there is little or no chance of the client taking the right or sensible course if the lawyer's advice is inaccurate or unsound because the lawyer has been given an incomplete or inaccurate picture of the client's position.

Barclays Bank Plc and Others v Eustice and Others

Schiemann LJ:

> I do not consider that the result of upholding the judge's order [overriding LPP] in the present case will be to discourage straightforward citizens from consulting their lawyers. Those lawyers should tell them that what is proposed is liable to be set aside and the straightforward citizen will then not do it and so the advice will never see the light of day. In so far as those wishing to engage in sharp practice are concerned, the effect of the present decision may well be to discourage them from going to their lawyers. This has the arguable public disadvantage that the lawyers might have dissuaded them from the sharp practice. However, it has the undoubted public advantage that the absence of lawyers will make it more difficult for them to carry out their sharp practice. In my judgment the balance of advantage is in permitting inspection of the material as ordered by the judge.

Q8.16 Is the difference in the policy considerations expressed explicable by the different issues the court in each case is considering?

Q8.17 If a lawyer was allowed to breach a client's legal advice privilege when that lawyer had been used for an iniquitous purpose would you expect that permission to be clear in the code of conduct?

Q8.18 In the light of the policy considerations expressed by the different judges do you think the balance the courts are striking between privilege and disclosure is (a) about right, (b) too much to the clients' benefit or (c) prejudicial to the right to a fair trial?

Q8.19 If there is no challenge to the privilege in the courts, should the lawyer be allowed to speak to protect his reputation?

Should Lawyers Be Under a Duty to Act in the Public Interest?

The Issues

Closer examination of the illegality exception to LPP underlines the fact that lawyers have no duty to protect third party interests from their clients. They have a duty not to participate, but that is potentially the limit of their responsibility. This relative absence of clear social responsibility is sometimes seen as a moral weakness at the core of lawyers' ethics. This weakness may become even more glaring if the stakes involved in legal representation are magnified. If, for example, a client's illegal actions could lead to catastrophic social consequences, should lawyers still be under no reporting duty?

Advanced industrialisation and the globalisation of trade and finance and the massive scale of global corporations have increased the risk of catastrophic events. This fact has been graphically illustrated by recent events in the world's financial industry. The collapse of global companies such as Enron, WorldCom, Allied Irish Bank and Tyco International often reveals wrongdoing by directors. Similar company collapses are partly blamed for precipitating the global financial crisis beginning in 2007/8. People lost savings and pensions, national economies were plunged into debt, millions of people lost jobs.

The catastrophic consequences of repeated corporate collapse caused loss of confidence in the regulation of the financial sector. This led to a search for measures that might prevent future crises, including examination of the role of professional advisers, such as accountants and lawyers. Lawyers may or may not be involved in corrupt activity, but they may be in a position to prevent it happening. In fact, the work that lawyers do for companies means that they are well positioned to detect certain kinds of malpractice.

Lawyers are central in the process whereby shares and securities are offered on financial markets, including verifying the initial public offering. They are often regarded as 'gatekeepers', who prepare, verify or assess the disclosures that are required by industry regulators. In fact, they are sometimes described as field marshals of the disclosure process.[9] Finally, because of these central and necessary tasks that they perform, lawyers also acquire the roles of trusted advisers.

Lawyers may be prevented from blowing the whistle by their duty of confi-

---

[9] SM Solaiman, 'The Enron Collapse and Criminal Liabilities of Auditors and Lawyers for Defective Prospectuses in the United States, Australia and Canada: A Review' (2006–07) 26(8) *Journal of Law and Commerce* 81.

dentiality or by LPP. Therefore, one way of policing and preventing corporate fraud would be to impose a duty on lawyers to warn public authorities when their corporate clients engage in misconduct.

A Duty to Act in the Public Interest?

Enron Corporation

A warning of the risks of corporate failure came in 2001 when US energy company Enron, one of the world's largest companies, went bankrupt. An investigation revealed significant financial wrongdoing. Enron used accounting loopholes and false financial reporting to hide losses of billions of dollars. The saga led to the dissolution of Arthur Anderson, at that time one of the five leading accountancy firms in the world.[10] They had ignored the financial wrongdoing or been deflected from taking action. They were also accused of destroying documents, e-mails and files relating to Enron auditing.

In the Enron debacle attorneys were heavily involved in many of the activities that led to fraud.[11] Senior in-house lawyers failed to investigate when given evidence of malpractice. Even the corporation's external lawyers were involved in some of this activity. Yet, despite the obvious conflict of interest, they agreed to undertake an 'external audit' of the company when allegations began to surface.

Despite the fact that some of the directors served prison terms, Enron shareholders recovered little of the $40 billion that was claimed through court action. The Enron affair called into question whether or not professionals involved in work for major corporations paid sufficient regard to the fact that the company, rather than a director, is the client. It also raised the issue of whether professionals should have a duty to report corporate clients involved in serious illegality.

The Sarbanes–Oxley Act (US)

As a result of major corporate scandals the US legislated so as to police the financial sector more effectively. The Sarbanes–Oxley Act 2002, named after its sponsors, created an infrastructure to curb financial irregularity in public companies. The Act aimed to ensure that company information filed with the US Securities and Exchange Commission (SEC) represented a full and reliable account of a company's position. The regime created by the Act required much more openness, particularly by directors.

---

[10] D Rhode and P Paton, 'Lawyers, Ethics and Enron' (2002-03) 8 *Stanford Journal of Law Business and Finance* 9; E Wald, 'Lawyers and Corporate Scandals' (2004) 7 *Legal Ethics* 54.
[11] Rhode and Paton, ibid, 15.

The Sarbanes–Oxley Act imposed obligations on company auditors and emphasised that the duty of auditors was to the various stakeholders, like shareholders, rather than to directors or other officers of the company. During the drafting of the Act there was discussion of whether it should impose a duty on attorneys to disclose wrongdoing to regulatory authorities. Reconciling such an obligation with confidentiality and LPP was an obvious problem.

In order to preserve client confidentiality it was decided that lawyers could not be expected to report specific wrongdoing. They could, however, be expected to withdraw from representation and to inform the regulator that they were doing so. This process was labelled a 'noisy withdrawal', the idea being that it would signal fairly clearly that something was wrong. The issue was how noisy the process needed to be; how far the reasons for withdrawal had to be disclosed.

In the event, the Sarbanes–Oxley Act did not deal with the issue of attorney reporting. It delegated the task of drafting subordinate rules to the regulator, the SEC. The Sarbanes–Oxley Act section 307 provided that the SEC rules must prescribe minimum standards of professional conduct for attorneys appearing and practising before it in the representation of issuers.

The SEC rules had to include requirements for attorneys reporting evidence of material violations of securities laws or breaches of fiduciary duty by or on behalf of the issuer (the company). The lawyer's first port of call was appropriate officers within the organisation and then, if there was no appropriate response, the chief executive officer. The rules also provided for 'noisy withdrawal' by notification to the SEC in specified circumstances.

Securities and Exchange Commission
Implementation of Standards of Professional Conduct for Attorneys
(www.sec.gov/rules/final/33-8185.htm)

205.3(d)(2) provides:

(2) An attorney appearing and practicing before the Commission in the representation of an issuer may reveal to the Commission, without the issuer's consent, confidential information related to the representation to the extent the attorney reasonably believes necessary:

(i) To prevent the issuer from committing a material violation that is likely to cause substantial injury to the financial interest or property of the issuer or investors;

(ii) To prevent the issuer, in a Commission investigation or administrative proceeding from committing perjury … suborning perjury … or committing any act … that is likely to perpetrate a fraud upon the Commission; or

(iii) To rectify the consequences of a material violation by the issuer that caused, or may cause, substantial injury to the financial interest or property of the issuer or investors in the furtherance of which the attorney›s services were used.

Q8.20 Are US lawyers under a duty to make relevant disclosures?

Q8.21 What consequences do you think would be appropriate if lawyers fail to make a disclosure they 'reasonably believe to be necessary'?

Q8.22 What are the arguments against lawyers having to report any financial misconduct by a corporate client?

The SEC consulted on these regulations before finalising them. Several comments on the proposals argued that permitting attorneys to disclose illegal acts to the Commission would undermine the relationship of trust and confidence between lawyer and client. Attorneys would have a duty to explain to the client at the outset this limitation on the 'normal' duty of confidentiality. This would, it was said, impede lawyers' attempts to steer their clients away from unlawful acts.

Opponents of the SEC provisions pointed out that they conflicted with obligations in the rules of professional conduct of some State Bars. Jurisdictions such as the District of Columbia, for example, prohibit the disclosure of information where it reveals past client misconduct. Respondents to the consultation argued that 'it is not a lawyer's job' in representing an issuer before the Commission 'to correct or rectify the consequences of [the issuer's] illegal actions, or even to prevent wrong-doing'.

Some respondents to the SEC consultation agreed with the thrust of the proposals but argued for tighter limits. They thought that disclosure provisions should be limited to illegal acts likely to materially impact on the market for the issuer's securities. Others suggested that there should only be a duty to report where there was ongoing criminal or fraudulent conduct by the issuer.

Commentators who were generally supportive of the SEC proposals expressed reservations that they did not go far enough. They noted that at least four-fifths of State Bars already permitted or required disclosures of ongoing client financial misconduct. Several of these commentators noted that the Commission could have required that lawyers make disclosures of any continuing fraud or illegal conduct. They wanted the Commission to clarify that the obligations did not override state codes of conduct making higher standards of disclosure mandatory.

Case Study
Sarbanes–Oxley and Lawyers[12]

Tom Sjoblom, a former trial lawyer for the SEC's enforcement division, told a legal magazine that the 'noisy withdrawal' provisions being discussed as part of the Sarbanes–Oxley legislation would place an undue burden on transactional lawyers.

In 2009 a large US corporation, Stanford Financial Group, collapsed amid allegations of fraud and financial irregularity. The Group's chief financial officer entered a guilty plea and made a plea agreement. This implicated Sjoblom, at the time a partner of private law firm Proskauer Rose LLP, in concealing relevant information from the SEC. The plea agreement was reported to state that in late 2008 Sjoblom was informed of irregularities in the bank's investment portfolio that had not been disclosed to investors. He later learned that about $6 billion of alleged investment was largely fictitious.

Sjoblom met SEC lawyers investigating the investment portfolio in January 2009. According to the court documents he 'falsely maintained' that the company's chief executive and chief financial officer did not have details of the fictitious investments portfolio and suggested that another executive, Laura Holt, would be best placed to talk about it. In February Sjoblom and Holt were allegedly told by the Stanford executives that the bank was probably insolvent because of the fictitious investment portfolio. On 10 February Sjoblom is said to have advised Holt when she told SEC lawyers under oath that she was unaware of the assets and allocations of the $6 billion of fictitious assets.

News reports suggest that Sjoblom informed the SEC on 11 February that his firm was no longer advising Stanford. The next day he sent a fax to Kevin Edmundson, an assistant director of the SEC, and the following day left a voice message. Two days after that he sent a text note to Edmundson: 'Kevin, this will advise the SEC, and confirm my voice message last evening, that I disaffirm all prior oral and written representations made by me and my associates … to the SEC staff regarding Stanford Financial Group and its affiliates.'[13]

On 17 February 2009 the SEC filed a complaint against R Allen Stanford and three of his companies, alleging a fraudulent, multibillion-dollar invest-

---

[12] A Afrati, 'The Stanford Affair: Another Bad Day for Proskauer's Tom Sjoblom', *Wall Street Journal Law Blog*, 27 August 2009 (http://blogs.wsj.com/law/2009/08/27/the-stanford-affair-another-bad-day-for-proskauers-tom-sjoblom/); B Baxter, 'Stanford Trial Drags Former Proskauer, Chadbourne Partner Back into Spotlight', *American Law Daily* 8 February 2012 (http://amlawdaily.typepad.com/amlawdaily/2012/02/tom-sjoblom.html).

[13] MS Melbinger, 'A Prominent Example of Noisy Withdrawal under SOX 307', 26 February 2009 (www.winston.com/en/executive-compensation-blog/a-prominent-example-of-noisy-withdrawal-under-sox-307.html)

ment scheme. Sjoblom and other lawyers faced multiple law suits from investors claiming that their inaction allowed investors to be defrauded.

Q8.23 Why might a lawyer make a 'noisy withdrawal' even though not required to do so under the legislation or rules?

Q8.24 To what extent does this case study demonstrate the effectiveness of section 205.3(d)(2) of the SEC rules on the Standards of Professional Conduct for Attorneys?

Q8.25 Did this 'noisy withdrawal' meet the requirements of section 205.3(d) (2)?

An English equivalent of the Sarbanes–Oxley Act might already have existed in the form of the Companies Act 1985. Part XIV of the Act provided for the investigation of companies and their affairs by inspectors appointed by the Secretary of State. Under section 431 such investigations could take place on the application of companies, shareholders or members. The Companies (Audit, Investigations and Community Enterprise) Act 2004 made amendments to the 1985 Act to increase powers to require the production of documents

Under a revised section 447 of the Companies Act 1985 the Secretary of State may authorise an investigator to require the company or any other person to produce specified documents, meaning information recorded in any form.

Companies Act 1985 (as amended)

448A Protection in relation to certain disclosures: information provided to Secretary of State

(1) A person who makes a relevant disclosure is not liable by reason only of that disclosure in any proceedings relating to a breach of an obligation of confidence.

(2) A relevant disclosure is a disclosure which satisfies each of the following conditions—

(a) it is made to the Secretary of State otherwise than in compliance with a requirement under this Part;

(b) it is of a kind that the person making the disclosure could be required to make in pursuance of this Part;

(c) the person who makes the disclosure does so in good faith and in the reasonable belief that the disclosure is capable of assisting the Secretary of State for the purposes of the exercise of his functions under this Part;

(d) the information disclosed is not more than is reasonably necessary for the purpose of assisting the Secretary of State for the purposes of the exercise of those functions;

(e) the disclosure is not one falling within subsection (3) or (4).

(3) A disclosure falls within this subsection if the disclosure is prohibited by virtue of any enactment.

(4) A disclosure falls within this subsection if—

(a) it is made by a person carrying on the business of banking or by a lawyer, and

(b) it involves the disclosure of information in respect of which he owes an obligation of confidence in that capacity.

452 Privileged information.

(2) Nothing in sections 447 to 451—

(a) compels the production by any person of a document or the disclosure by any person of information in respect of which in an action in the High Court a claim to legal professional privilege, or in an action in the Court of Session a claim to confidentiality of communications, could be maintained;

(b) authorises the taking of possession of any such document which is in the person's possession.

Q8.26 Does section 448A(4) effectively prohibit a lawyer making a relevant disclosure, as defined by section 448A(2), to the Secretary of State?

Q8.27 Does section 452 effectively prevent lawyers producing documents that they might otherwise be required to produce under section 447 of the Companies Act 1985.

Lehman Brothers Holdings Inc

Lehman Brothers Holdings Inc (LBH) was another corporate collapse, but with an English connection; the law firm at the centre of the controversy was the City of London law firm Linklaters, one of the 'magic circle' of solicitors' firms. The consequences of the collapse of LBH were arguably even more far-reaching than those of other corporate collapses. When it went into liquidation in 2008 it was the fourth largest investment bank in the US. The demise of LBH is seen as one of the events precipitating the global financial crisis.[14]

---

[14] L Elliott and J Treanor, 'Five Years on from Lehman: 'We Had Almost No Control'' *The Guardian*, 13 September 2013.

The main reason for the collapse of LBH was that it held a large volume of property investments known as sub-prime mortgages. These represented money lent to borrowers against the security of properties which, in the event of default, might not cover the value of the money borrowed. LBH covered up the declining value of this investment portfolio using an accounting treatment called Repo 105. This had the effect of reducing financial liabilities on its balance sheet and hiding $50 billion of debt. Repo 105 would only pass regulatory scrutiny if transactions were shown as 'sales at law'. For this purpose LBH needed a 'true sale' opinion letter from a law firm. Under US law, repos were not legally sales, so LBH obtained a true sale letter from Linklaters addressed to its European branch. This was a clear attempt by LBH to avoid US financial regulation.

Kershaw and Moorhead suggest that the SRA Code of Conduct should cover this situation. They argue that where there is a *real, substantial and foreseeable* risk of client action that is unlawful, or probably unlawful, a finding of misconduct would be justified.[15] Kershaw and Moorhead argue that the foundation for a rule requiring reporting of clients lies in 'the core tenets of what it means for law to be a profession', specifically the professional principles of upholding the rule of law not doing anything that undermines public trust.

The high-level principles of the SRA Code of Conduct are, it is suggested, an inadequate basis for imposing new duties on solicitors. The SRA Code of Conduct would need a specific outcome to deal with social responsibility for risk of catastrophic financial harm. This might look something like the ABA Model Rules of Professional Conduct, Rule 1.6.

American Bar Association Model Rules of Professional Conduct 1983 (as amended)

Client–Lawyer Relationship

Rule 1.6 Confidentiality of Information

(a) A lawyer shall not reveal information relating to the representation of a client unless the client gives informed consent, the disclosure is impliedly authorized in order to carry out the representation or the disclosure is permitted by paragraph (b).

(b) A lawyer may reveal information relating to the representation of a client to the extent the lawyer reasonably believes necessary:

(1) to prevent reasonably certain death or substantial bodily harm;
(2) to prevent the client from committing a crime or fraud that is reasonably certain to result in substantial injury to the financial interests or property

---

[15] D Kershaw and R Moorhead, 'Consequential Responsibility for Client Wrongs: Lehman Brothers and the Regulation of the Legal Profession' (2013) 76(1) *Modern Law Review* 26.

of another and in furtherance of which the client has used or is using the lawyer's services;

(3) to prevent, mitigate or rectify substantial injury to the financial interests or property of another that is reasonably certain to result or has resulted from the client's commission of a crime or fraud in furtherance of which the client has used the lawyer's services ...

Q8.28 If this model rule were applied would it place lawyers under a duty to avoid physical or financial injury to third parties?

Q8.29 Should the codes of conduct of English lawyers contain a provision similar to ABA Model Rule 1.6?

While the SRA Code of Conduct does not include a provision similar to ABA Model Rule 1.6 it does contain two intriguing outcomes discussed in Chapter 10: You and Your Regulator. These read:

O(10.3) you notify the SRA promptly of any material changes to relevant information about you including serious financial difficulty, action taken against you by another regulator and serious failure to comply with or achieve the Principles, rules, outcomes and other requirements of the Handbook;

O(10.4) you report to the SRA promptly, serious misconduct by any person or firm authorised by the SRA, or any employee, manager or owner of any such firm (taking into account, where necessary, your duty of confidentiality to your client);

Q8.30 Looking at the indicative behaviours in Chapter 10, what do these outcomes appear to relate to?

Q8.31 Could these outcomes provide a basis for reporting the risk of third party harm where a client co-opts solicitors' breaches of financial regulations?

It can be argued that extensive third party duties for reporting financial risks are not necessary or that they would be antithetical to the lawyer's role. The role of lawyers under the rule of law is to seek recognition of their clients' rights within rules defined by the courts. So, it might be argued, they cannot do this effectively if they need to focus on the implications for third parties' rights.

Conclusion

Lawyers' ethics are sometimes criticised for the absence of a clear duty to the public interest. Critics might argue that it suggests that legal professional ethics are something of a mirage. Without duties to third parties legal ethics amounts to little more than service to clients and courts. Client duties are, largely, self-interested rather than altruistic; it is, after all, clients who are paying the bill. This deficit is particularly noticeable regarding collective responsibilities, such as those that might be owed to shareholders or the public generally.

Where society has required that lawyers put the public interest before client interests, legislation has been enacted. The responsibilities of lawyers who suspect their clients of money-laundering or terrorist activity are spelt out in some detail. Obligations of confidentiality have been made subject to these provisions. The issue of whether lawyers should have a duty to protect the public interest has achieved greater salience because of high-profile company collapses. These are increasingly seen as potentially having national and global implications.

Where lawyers are made responsible for policing clients their responsibilities undermine the promise of confidentiality and LPP. This underlines the difficulty of the issues. Regulation needs to maintain a free market, control risk and not undermine lawyers' fundamental role in relation to clients. Reporting obligations potentially undermine these goals. Likewise, the circumstances in which noisy withdrawal, ie informing the relevant regulator that the lawyer is withdrawing from representation, is justified are unclear.

It is argued that professional ethics is the wrong place to look for the imposition on lawyers of broad duties to third parties. If lawyers are to perform gate-keeping functions in financial or other markets the circumstances need to be specified, probably in legislation. Despite the temptation to minimise social risk, imposing broad duties on lawyers to anticipate and avoid harm arising from apparently innocuous activity is arguably too onerous a burden.

9

Professional Responsibility

When legal ethics became a compulsory subject for attorneys-to-be in the US it was usually presented under the title 'professional responsibility'. As a subject, professional responsibility included, but was broader than, professional ethics. It also embraced a number of contextual issues that affect professional life and which intending lawyers should arguably understand if they are to have a rounded appreciation of professional responsibility. In the US, these issues included admission to practice, judicial ethics and disciplinary matters.

The term 'professional responsibility' is a useful reminder that the social role of lawyers is not a narrow subject. Professions, and their members, arguably have ethical responsibilities that go beyond those set out in codes. These responsibilities might be based on a number of circumstances that are peculiar to professions and others that are peculiar to lawyers. These circumstances include their claim to special public recognition and prestige, their state-endowed monopoly of the provision of a social good and their ethical claims.

Membership of a profession might also be the basis for distinctive, ethically based relationships with other members. These obligations flow from the collegial ideal. They also follow from the fact that professions typically reserve the job of inducting entrants to the profession, through the equivalent of apprenticeship, to established practitioners. This confers special responsibilities for training and guidance, but also for ensuring that young professionals develop 'professional values'.

One of the underlying themes of this chapter is the way the profession has sought to regulate and mediate the relationship between employers and employees. It considers the professions' attempts to secure fairness of entry, fair treatment within organisations and continuing competence. It also considers the future of the tripartite relationship between professions, professionals and their employing organisations.

263

The Public Profession of Law

Lawyers often define themselves as members of 'public professions'. It is often not clear what this claim is based on and ambiguity is likely to be misinterpreted. Basset, for example, points out that the preamble to the ABA code uses the word 'public' ten times.[1] She argues, however, that the heavy focus on client loyalty in the code, and the relative absence of public-facing responsibilities, invalidates any claim to law being a public profession. This is a debateable conclusion, even based on analysis of the codes. It is particularly suspect, however, because a claim to being a public profession might refer to different kinds of public commitment.

The thrust of Basset's criticism is that the ethical rules that protect lawyers' relationships with clients are largely self-interested. Clearly, the commitments of a public profession should serve some higher goals. Commitments demonstrate a public orientation when they are not purely self-interested activity but support the public good. These activities may therefore be represented as a kind of public service. Cases could be made for various kinds of commitment demonstrating a public orientation, for example guaranteeing the competence of practitioners, supporting professional communities and engaging with public agendas, such as the provision of access to justice.

Professions support values that are not necessarily supported to the same extent, or in the same way, by other groups in society. The Chief Justice of Ontario's Advisory Committee on Professionalism identified ten elements of professionalism: scholarship, integrity, honour, leadership, independence, pride, spirit, collegiality, service and balanced commercialism.[2] While not every legal profession would prioritise the same values, it is arguably worth the effort. They provide standards by which professions can:

- educate and develop the next generation;
- monitor their own progress; and
- be judged and held accountable.

One of the ways in which it has been suggested lawyers might raise the importance of the values of legal practice would be to have them swear an oath equivalent to the Hippocratic oath sworn by doctors. The following has been suggested as an oath or declaration to be sworn by solicitors, perhaps on admission:

---

[1] DL Bassett, 'Defining the "Public" Profession' (2005) 36(3) *Rutgers Law Journal* 721.
[2] A Dodek, 'An Education and Apprenticeship in Civility: Correspondent's Report from Canada', www.lsuc.on.ca/media/definingprofessoct2001revjune2002.pdf.

Preparatory Ethics Training for Future Solicitors
(London, Law Society, 2009) 33

I promise to use my legal knowledge and skill to the best of my ability and, notwithstanding duties owed to clients and the Court, will at all times serve the interests of justice without fear or favour. As a lawyer, I shall work diligently, honestly, with integrity and independence to the highest standards and do my utmost to uphold the core duties of my profession whilst respecting the truth and avoiding unnecessary harm to public and third party interests. I shall uphold the rule of law, the democratic order, human rights, social justice, fair and expeditious process, and work toward the improvement and accessibility of the law, legal institutions and processes.

Q9.1 What are the pros and cons of lawyers being required to swear an oath before admission to their profession?

Q9.2 Does this oath or declaration capture the ethical commitments of solicitors?

Q9.3 What oath or declaration do you think might be suitable for lawyers generally?

Professional Commitments

The Social Importance of Professions

Early sociologists, such as Emile Durkheim, considered that professions' ethical commitments and internal discipline made them exemplary organisations. Their presence in society was therefore seen as a positive public benefit. Such assumptions have been challenged by economists and the consumer lobby. Nevertheless, professions often seem to assume that their very existence serves the public interest.

The main justification for the view that the very existence of professions is a public good lies in the fact that they are the organisations which hold knowledge about an intellectual discipline. Professions maintain and pass on this reservoir of know-how to future generations. However, professions may also play an important role in promoting public agendas. It is therefore important to consider the functions that professions perform beyond providing and enforcing a code of conduct.

Responsibility for the Intellectual Discipline

i. Sharing Knowledge and Skills

Roscoe Pound thought that one of the ways in which professions demonstrated a public interest orientation was by sharing knowledge rather than keeping it for professional advantage. Therefore, professionals give lectures on subjects where they have developed special expertise. They also sit on specialist committees where they share information with other practitioners outside their organisations.

ii. Contributions to Law Reform

The expertise of professions can play an important role in law creation. Lawyers are often involved in the work of the Law Commission. This is an independent body created by the Law Commissions Act 1965 and sponsored by the Ministry of Justice. Its role is to keep the law under review and to recommend necessary reforms. Lawyers are involved as contributors to committees considering law reform. They may also serve as legislative draughtsmen and engage in similar activities.

ABA Model Rules

Rule 6.4: Law Reform Activities Affecting Client Interests

Public Service
Rule 6.4: Law Reform Activities Affecting Client Interests

A lawyer may serve as a director, officer or member of an organization involved in reform of the law or its administration notwithstanding that the reform may affect the interests of a client of the lawyer. When the lawyer knows that the interests of a client may be materially benefitted by a decision in which the lawyer participates, the lawyer shall disclose that fact but need not identify the client.

Q9.4   Which Principle of the SRA Code of Conduct does Model Rule 6.4 illustrate?

Q9.5   Why do you think there is no equivalent outcome in the SRA Code of Conduct?

The contribution of legal professions to law reform is substantial. It would be difficult to replicate if the primary affiliation of lawyers was the (profit-making) organisation to which lawyers belonged. It would be more difficult to trust, for example, that contributions to particular reforms were made in the public interest or for the benefit of clients.

Responsibility for the Competence and Socialisation of Practitioners

Ensuring the competence and socialisation of students and trainees is one of the main functions of professions.[3] Socialisation is a term used in many social science disciplines to describe a process of assimilating the attitudes and traditions of a social group. Attitudes are an important part of professional character because they affect motivation.

Professionals are often identified with devotion to their work and career. This was regarded as important by one of the founding fathers of sociology, Max Weber. Therefore, it is possible to aver that professionals perform their work 'primarily for the psychic satisfactions and secondarily for the monetary compensation'.[4] If professionals are motivated purely by self-interest, they will be competitive. This is potentially damaging to collegiality.

As discussed in chapter one, doing professional work for its own sake can be described as intrinsic motivation. The importance of intrinsic motivation to professionals is captured in the philosopher Alasdair MacIntyre's analogy with the game of chess.[5] A player who cheats at chess may acquire the external goods of fame, fortune or prestige, but will not achieve the internal goods of the game. These come only to those who play honestly, according to the rules, *and* with knowledge and skill.

MacIntyre argues that the 'internal goods' of any practice, whether chess or professional work, is only achieved by 'subordinating ourselves within the practice in our relationship to other practitioners'.[6] This involves acquiring a set of attitudes including humility, curiosity, openness and a positive attitude to learning.

i. Inducting Entrants into the Profession

Professions perform an important function in passing on knowledge and values through education and training. Professional communities inculcate newcomers into practices performed well for their own sake. This is consistent

---

[3] LJ Tapp and FJ Levine, 'Legal Socialisation' in WM Evan (ed), *The Sociology of Law* (London and New York, The Free Press, 1980) 121.

[4] Bassett (n 1), quoting WE Snizek, 'Hall's Professionalism Scale: An Empirical Re-assessment' (1972) 37 *American Sociological Review* 79.

[5] AD MacIntyre, *After Virtue: A Study in Moral Theory* (London, Duckworth, 1985) 127.

[6] Ibid, 191.

with the role of professions in providing an alternative agenda to 'the tidal pull of the profit motive'.[7] This kind of commitment is central to ethically based conceptions of what it means to be a 'good lawyer'.[8]

Various mechanisms of induction are used by professions. They may be direct, for example apprenticeship-type arrangements; or indirect, for example by designing, validating and recognising qualifications as key components of the training process. Ideally, considerable thought goes into this process, so education and training produces professionals possessing suitable knowledge, skills and attitudes for the roles they have to carry out.

ii. Legal Education

There is no single model of legal education and training. One of the more unusual models is the US system, where law is studied as a second degree. Following this, students must pass whatever examinations are required by a local state bar. The New York State Bar Examination is a famous example of flexibility.[9] It accepts students with a variety of qualifications and experience in addition to a university law degree. Many students enrol to sit the examination following a period of self-study and pay a $750 entrance fee. This compares with course fees nearing £20,000 for some vocational law courses in the UK.

In the UK, and most other common law jurisdictions, the process comprises three distinct stages. These are, first, the undergraduate stage provided by university law schools to first-degree level. Second, a vocational stage is supplied by a range of private and university providers. Third, the training stage is provided by employers and, in the case of the Bar, individual practitioners within a chambers structure. There is surprisingly little required overlap between these stages.

The professional bodies require that law degrees cover a number of subjects as a prerequisite for graduate entry to vocational courses. These fill just over half of most law degrees. Undergraduate legal education has the task of providing mass education for legal careers. However, the required subjects only obliquely cover lawyers, legal work or legal ethics. The explanation for this is that the universities have fought hard to preserve the historic distinctiveness of law as a 'liberal' and an 'intellectual' discipline, in the process resisting any move that could be seen as 'vocationalism'.

There are several inherent ethical challenges that have not been fully embraced. The huge popularity of law courses may be partly explained by 'the promise of professionalism'—occupational prestige, satisfying work, adequate pay. Some argue that this promise of professionalism is outmoded in a com-

---

[7] WM Sullivan, 'Calling a Career: The Tensions of Modern Professional Life' in A Flores (ed), *Professional Ideals*, (Belmont, CA, Wadsworth Publishing, 1988) 41.

[8] AT Kronman, *The Lost Lawyer: Failing Ideals of the Legal Profession* (Harvard, MA, Belknap Press, 1993) 367.

[9] www.nybarexam.org/TheBar/TheBar.htm.

petitive capitalist economy. Others argue that it is unlikely to be fulfilled for some groups, such as part-time students, who may lose out in competition for the best-paid or most prestigious jobs.[10]

iii. Training

The rationale of work-based education and training is familiarisation with work, acquisition of skills and socialisation into the norms of practice. Ethics should underpin each of these areas and sometimes arises as an explicit issue. The intention is that the workplace provides assistance and guidance in translating the principles of conduct, learned about in the vocational stage, into practice.

In England and Wales employment training was introduced for different types of intending lawyers, including attorneys, notaries and solicitors, from the eighteenth century onwards. Articles of clerkship with an established practitioner, the principal, lasted for periods of between five and seven years and clerks paid a premium for their training. Standards of education were, however, variable until the Solicitors Act 1922 introduced mandatory attendance at law school for one year.[11]

By the late 1960s conditions for articled clerks began to change. Most entrants to the profession were not doing five years of articles. They were university graduates who only had to serve two years. Five-year articles were phased out after 1971 following the Ormrod Report.[12] From this time most solicitors' firms paid their articled clerks an 'allowance'.[13]

Burrage argues that the 'semi-servitude' of five-year articles encouraged a sense of service in solicitors.[14] In contrast, the university law schools, by focusing on legal study, undermined respect for traditions, including ethics, and the collective honour of the profession.

A two-year training contract replaced articles of clerkship when the Legal Practice Course (LPC) and the Professional Skills Course (PSC) were introduced in 1993. The LPC changed the focus of the vocational course, introducing students to practice contexts, legal skills and professional ethics. The PSC provided a 12-hour top-up before the end of the training contract.

Firms were vetted and monitored to ensure that they could provide a suitable training experience. A code of conduct was introduced requiring monitoring

---

[10] AM Francis and IW McDonald, 'All Dressed Up and Nowhere to Go? Part Time Law Students and the Legal Profession' in P Thomas (ed), *Discriminating Lawyers* (London and Sydney: Cavendish Publishing, 2000) 41.

[11] E Cruikshank, 'Building a Profession' (2003) 100(25) *Law Society Gazette* 32.

[12] The Hon Mr Justice Ormrod (Chairman), Report of the Committee on Legal Education (1971) Cmnd 4595.

[13] E Cruikshank, 'Surviving Hard Times' (2003) 100(32) *Law Society Gazette* 22.

[14] M Burrage, 'From a Gentleman's to a Public Profession' (1996) *International Journal of the Legal Profession* 45, 68.

and appraisal of trainees.[15] Trainees had to work in different departments, or 'seats', during training and a minimum salary was introduced. The current SRA regulations require supervision by partners, or other senior solicitors, regular feedback and at least three appraisals during training.[16]

Despite the introduction of professional ethics to the vocational stage, research conducted for the Law Society in the 1990s found that not much attention was paid to ethics in the training contract.[17] Principals regarded the ethics code as a reference work and even the Law Society's guidance to trainees barely mentioned the issue.[18] Trainees were told to record any professional conduct issues arising in their training contract record.

iv. Continuing Competence

Lawyers are expected to display competence, diligence, honesty and loyalty in relationships with clients. Fostering these virtues is a direct concern of both employers and of the wider profession. Both employers and professions promote virtues through employment practices, disciplinary processes and educational processes. Competence may be supported by post-qualification requirements as a condition of practice. Traditionally, practitioners were assumed to become more competent with experience. In the 1970s and 1980s many professions implemented continuing professional development (CPD) schemes. These were intended to help practitioners keep up to date with increases in professional knowledge. They were also intended to address concerns about low levels of professional competence in what was assumed to be a minority of members. Most CPD schemes sought to achieve both these objectives.

Houle observed that professions shared similar practical agendas when designing their early CPD schemes. They realised that self-motivated learning is the most effective, but that any population confronted with new challenges is likely to include innovators, pacesetters, a middle majority and laggards. The common agenda was 'how to speed up the learning of majority adopters and how to reach the laggards'.[19]

Early CPD schemes were typically established as a direct relationship between professional bodies and their members. Satisfying CPD requirements was an individual responsibility of professionals. This direct relationship between profession and professional was a useful monitoring mechanism. It is not uncommon that CPD 'laggards' also manifest other professional failings.

The original requirement for solicitors undertaking CPD was attendance

---

[15] Ibid.

[16] SRA Training Regulations 2011 Part 2—Training Provider Regulations Reg 6(1).

[17] T Goriely and T Williams, *The Impact of the New Training Scheme: Report on a Qualitative Study* (London, Law Society, 1996).

[18] Law Society, *A Trainee Solicitor's Guide to Authorisation* (Redditch, Law Society Monitoring and Training Department, 2000).

[19] CO Houle, *Continuing Learning in the Professions* (San Francisco and London, Jossey-Bass, 1980) 164.

at 12 hours of approved courses. Since 2001, all solicitors working at least 32 hours a week must complete a minimum of 16 hours of CPD annually.[20] In 1991 the Law Society introduced a compulsory 'Best Practice Course' for solicitors' to be completed by the third year following admission. The course provided 'a reference manual of basic management techniques suitable for application to private practice'.[21] The current course is called Management Course Stage 1, which contributes seven CPD hours to the annual requirement and costs up to £354.

Continuing professional development for solicitors is currently defined as 'a course, lecture, seminar or other programme or method of study (whether requiring attendance or not) that is relevant to the needs and professional standards of solicitors and complies with guidance issued from time to time by the SRA'.[22] In 1985, the Law Society introduced a requirement that solicitors in the first three years of practice complete compulsory CPD. This was extended incrementally to all solicitors from 1 November 1998.

When applying for an annual practise certificate, solicitors must certify that they have complied with CPD requirements in the last complete CPD year or agree to make up any shortfall by an agreed date. The training regulations require production of the CPD record to the regulator on demand. Training records may also be subject to random sampling.

Solicitors and barristers are in the process of liberalising and relaxing CPD requirements generally, particularly reporting requirements. This is to be welcomed on one hand because meeting the requirement, rather than meaningful learning, can easily become the point of the activity. There is a concern, however, that such moves will make it easier for laggards to avoid or pay lip service to CPD.

Legal Education and Professional Development—An Educational Continuum: Report of the Task Force on Law Schools and the Profession: Narrowing the Gap American Bar Association Section of Legal Education and Admissions to the Bar

(July 1992) 119–120

E. The Survival of a Single Public Profession

The Preamble to the ABA Model Rules expressly affirms the lawyer's several responsibilities as a representative of clients, an officer of the legal system and a public citizen having special responsibility for the quality of justice. To the extent lawyers have met these responsibilities of their professional calling, government

---

[20] www.sra.org.uk/solicitors/cpd/solicitors.page#cpd-scheme. For solicitors and RELs who work fewer than 32 hours per week, the requirements are reduced.
[21] R Steele, 'The Best Practice of Management' (1991) 20 *Law Society Gazette*, 29 May, 21.
[22] SRA, *Solicitors Training Regulations* (2009) Regulation 2(3) (Interpretation and Definitions) of Part 1.

regulation has been obviated and the profession has been permitted to remain largely self-governing under the ultimate authority of the courts.

The Preamble further notes that self-regulation helps maintain the legal profession's independence from government domination, permitting the profession to be an important force in preserving government under law, standing ready to challenge the abuse of authority. However, as the Preamble concludes, the legal profession's relative autonomy carries with it special responsibilities of self-government. Thus every lawyer is responsible for observance of the rules of professional conduct. Neglect of professional responsibilities compromises the independence of the profession and the public interest which it is to serve.

Together, the law schools and the organized bar can have no more important function than to pass to each succeeding generation of lawyers an understanding of the profession's relationship to the American legal system. If a single public profession of shared learning, skills and professional values is to survive into the 21st century, the law schools together with the bar and the judiciary must all work for the perpetuation of core legal knowledge together with the fundamental lawyering skills and professional values that identify a distinct profession of law throughout the United States.

Q9.6 Is it meaningful to talk of a public profession of law?

Q9.7 What do you think are the indicators of a 'public profession'?

Responsibility for Maintaining an Ethical Professional Community

Primary responsibility for maintaining a professional community rests on three groups: profession, employer and employee. Their responsibilities are partly defined by the general law, for example anti-discrimination legislation. Aspects of the relationship between employers and employees are also defined by the profession, particularly through prescribed education requirements. They are sometimes covered by regulation and sometimes by 'soft regulation' such as policies and 'best practice' guidance.

Because they are not directly involved in the workplace, management of the relationship between employers and employees is arguably one of the most testing tasks for regulators. Traditionally, both employer and employee were members of the same regulated profession. The regulator must hold their potentially competing interests in balance. It must ensure that practitioners are competent and that incompetent or dishonest members and failing organisations are managed effectively. It must ensure renewal of the profession through a steady flow of recruits.

Professional work is often seen as a career, rather than just a job. The word career has connotations of a personal quest, where education and work are intrinsically linked and involve other aspects of a person's journey through life. This affects why people choose 'professional life' above other occupations. A recent report from Birmingham University highlighted four main motivations for entering legal practice which lawyers at all stages, from initial stage to practice, agreed.[23] These were:

- Service—helping people, society, the administration of justice and the rule of law.
- Interest—interesting or enjoyable work or subject.
- Material benefits—including career, status, and money.
- Skills—including debating and arguing, public speaking, analysis and problem solving.

A reason why people choose professional careers, not mentioned in this list, is stability and security. Sennett suggests that the traditional, 'well-made road' of a career saved people from lives of aimlessness and personal failure.[24] They stayed with the same employer, possibly progressing through different levels of an organisation. This built mutual dependence and loyalty. The promise of a rewarding career is an enduring appeal of the legal profession.

The traditional returns of professional jobs include security of employment, job satisfaction, social prestige and high financial returns. Rewards may also be found through working in a collegial work environment. Collegiality connotes mutual respect for persons sharing a commitment to working for a common goal or purpose.

In a collegial environment it is assumed that individuals will be treated as equals and enjoy autonomy. It is usually assumed that colleagues accept responsibility for passing on the knowledge, skills and attitudes that characterise the community. It follows that they accept responsibility for the welfare of members. Since professionals operate in different workplaces this collegial responsibility is often monitored and enforced by the profession.

It is surprising that obligations to employees and potential employees only rarely feature in the legal ethics literature. Lawyers are often in as close a legal relationship with employees as they are with clients. Their legal obligations to their employers are defined, their moral obligations less so. Over the years there has been evidence that some legal employers occasionally treat those that work for them badly. This is a situation that the wider legal community might be concerned about.

---

[23] J Arthur, K Kristjansson, H Thomas, M Holdsworth, LB Confalonieri and T Qiu, *Virtuous Character for the Practice of Law* (Birmingham, Jubilee Centre for Character and Virtues, University of Birmingham, 2014).

[24] R Sennett, *The Corrosion of Character: The Personal Consequences of Work in the New Capitalism* (New York, WW Norton, 2000) 120.

i. Training Experience

Research in the 1980s[25] and 1990s found that trainees and recently qualified lawyers were often unhappy with their early experience of the legal profession.[26] The first problem was that experience of traineeship was sometimes extreme and far from uniform. Small firms often expected trainees to work well above their level of experience. Some demanded that they operate as fee earners almost straight away.[27] Large firms, however, often delayed trainees' exposure to clients until well into the post-qualification period. Large-firm trainees denied experience sometimes became bored and disaffected.

A second major problem reported by both trainee solicitors and pupil barristers was a disturbingly high incidence of harassment and bullying. Helplines operated by the professional bodies reported being besieged by calls from trainees. The matters they were reporting included sexual harassment, pressure to act unethically and improper use of prospective trainees as para-legals.

ii. Employment Experience

People have high expectations of professional life. Lawyers, however, are a market-based profession competing to sell their services. They therefore suffer from changes in the market both generally (they suffer similar pressures to other businesses) and locally (they suffer pressures peculiar to legal businesses). Therefore, many legal businesses suffered, just like other businesses, during the economic recession beginning in 2008. For specific reasons many marginal legal firms also suffered loss of profitability in specific areas of work.

At the top end of the market recession usually reduces the level of commercial transactions, with a knock-on effect on legal work. In the middle and lower end of the legal services market intense competition for conveyancing work, once the bedrock of most small and medium practices, has driven down prices. At the lower end of the market the decline in legal aid as a major source of income for the same firms has undermined profitability. This sometimes impacts on trainees' experience.

The declining profitability of legal services has many ethical implications for law firms. There is a temptation when times are hard for organisations to exploit employees. Staff may experience pressure to work long hours. Firms might use unpaid interns or low-paid para-legals rather than trainees. There may be pressure to cut corners, pad bills or break conduct rules to win a case.

---

[25] P McDonald, 'The Class of '81—A Glance at the Social Class Composition of Recruits to the Legal Profession' (1982) 9 *Journal of Law and Society* 267.

[26] R Moorhead and F Boyle, 'Quality of Life and Trainee Solicitors: A Survey' (1995) 2 *International Journal of the Legal Profession* 217, 218.

[27] Goriely and Williams (n 17).

While the recent period has been difficult for some law firms, long-term trends may also test the aspiration of professions to operate ethically.

Sennett has argued that since the 1980s the economic forces unleashed by globalisation have exacerbated the unpredictability of capitalist economies. In the US employees were more likely to be offered unpaid and short-term work. They are more likely to move between organisations, weakening the bond of loyalty. These developments have made the promise of legal careers less secure and undermined bonds between employers and employees. Similar phenomena have affected the UK and legal employment.

Entrants' to the legal professions tend to expect that they will be doing worthwhile work in a collegial environment while earning a good living. For a variety of reasons their experience does not always match these expectations. In the 1990s, the last survey in the Law Society's longitudinal study found high levels of satisfaction with professional life. A significant minority were unhappy. One reason was lack of mobility. Up to 20 per cent of intending solicitors took a training contract in an area of work they did not like and then found that they could not move.

Entrants to the legal profession report a range of problems across the employment spectrum. Those in small firms sometimes find that they were employed on low-value work and were under pressure to work hard and cut corners. Some solicitors in elite firms report boring work and a culture of long hours. Barristers report that some clerks discriminate when allocating briefs. The professions therefore have to work hard to ensure that organisations do not abuse their power. Firms and chambers are required to record the allocation of briefs, to have written anti-discrimination policies and complaints procedures.

Not all of the ethical issues arising in the employment relationship can be dealt with by simple adjustments to professional regulatory mechanisms. Some changes in the employment market are deeper and hidden in employment culture. One of Sennett's main points is that contemporary employment patterns reduce the significance of character in employment situations. As a result, personality, a much more superficial evaluation of a person's worth, has become more important.

Sennett defines character as 'the personal traits which we value in ourselves and which we seek to be valued by others'.[28] He argues that less secure and short-term employment arrangements shift the focus of parties from the long term to the short term. Because of this, employers may be more inclined to look for congenial, compliant personalities rather than solid individuals with integrity. If this assessment is correct, it presents problems for professions, which have traditionally prized exemplary character.

The current regulatory strategy of legal professions in England and Wales is to adopt broad conduct outcomes and to focus attention on the values of entrants to the professions. This follows the argument of adherents of the

[28] Sennett (n 24) 10.

virtue ethics tradition that people of good character make right decisions. It may seem implausible that just teaching law students about values will produce ethical lawyers. This is particularly so when most disciplinary infraction results from 'need or greed'.

J Arthur, K Kristjansson, H Thomas, M Holdsworth, LB Confalonieri, and T Qiu, *Virtuous Character for the Practice of Law* (Birmingham, Jubilee Centre for Character and Virtues, University of Birmingham, 2014)

4.5 OVERALL FINDINGS

To conclude this section, we provide a list of what we consider to be the most significant findings of our project:

In selecting six strengths expected in the 'ideal' lawyer, all four respondent groups chose judgement, perseverance, perspective and fairness. Judgement and honesty were selected by 84% of solicitors and 93% of barristers. Fairness and perseverance appeared in the top six choices for respondents selecting both ideal qualities and personal qualities.

Morality was viewed by the majority of respondents as being at the core of being a good lawyer. However, some respondents expressed concerns about moral standards with specific mention of tax law as an area where the nature of professional advice frequently required manipulation of the law and diverged from the expectations of ordinary morality. 60% of solicitors surveyed answered 'sometimes' to statements including 'my work requires that I hide my feelings', 'my work involves tasks that are in conflict with my personal values' and 'at work it is difficult to do the right thing'. Commercial factors were most frequently cited pressures but the positive influence of good role models was apparent. These findings indicate some constraints and anxieties about the maintenance of a virtuous character in the practice of law.

The majority of lawyers appeared to react appropriately and dutifully in their professional roles. Despite this, there are responses to ethical dilemmas which raise concerns. A dilemma on misuse of client accounts showed 5% of experienced solicitors would not have reported the action. A dilemma on 'rounding-up' 'billing' hours showed 16% of experienced solicitors prepared to accept guidance from a more senior colleague, even though it might be regarded as fraudulent.

Ethics education receives little attention in the curricula for undergraduate law students. At the vocational stage, ethics focuses narrowly on the application of professional codes of conduct. The data from the surveys and interviews confirm the research team's normative assumption that virtue ethics, with other ethical perspectives, provides a useful theoretical lens through which to explore the ethics of legal practice.

Q9.8   Is the notion of virtuous lawyers idealistic given their role in an adversarial system?

Q9.9   How far do you agree that focusing undergraduates' attention on virtues such as honesty or integrity will improve the conduct of lawyers?

Q9.10 What do you think is the best strategy for producing ethical lawyers?

Responsibility for Promoting Appropriate Professional Relationships between Practitioners

Because of the wider responsibilities of professions for their disciplines it is important that they maintain structures encouraging them to flourish. Internally, this may be achieved by supporting collegial relations between professionals. Externally, the aim may be furthered by maintaining the reputation of the profession.

Professions support collegial relations between members in a number of ways. They require communal training, they maintain committee structures served by members and they support events that members can attend. All of these activities serve to remind professionals that they are part of a larger collective. The structures may also support personal working relationships outside of the workplace.

As considered above, CPD is one of the areas in which professional bodies make a significant contribution to developing the levels of competence in a profession.[29] A common programme of CPD can also be used as a way of achieving other objectives. These may include introducing foundations for new expertise, or changing practice requirements, and helping to maintain a common professional identity.

Preserving Professional Reputation

Professions generally strive to preserve their reputation. This kind of commitment was found in the now defunct Solicitors Practice Rules 1990. These contained only six basic principles,[30] but one was that a solicitor should not do anything that impaired 'the good repute of the solicitor or of the solicitor's profession'. In *The Guide to the Professional Conduct of Solicitors* (1999),

---

[29] A Boon and T Fazaeli, 'Professional Bodies and Continuing Professional Development: A Case Study' in S Crowley (ed), *Challenging Professional Learning* (London and New York, Routledge, 2014) 31.

[30] N Taylor (ed), *The Guide to the Professional Conduct of Solicitors*, 8th edn (London, Law Society, 1999) Practice Rule 1.01.

guidance to Rule 1.08 stated that this covered solicitors' private lives and that '[d]isciplinary sanctions may be imposed if, for instance, a solicitor's behaviour tends to bring the profession into disrepute'.

The idea that lawyers owed a responsibility to the professional community to which they belonged is no longer as prevalent in the codes of conduct. The SRA Handbook, for example, contains no similar obligation. References to such responsibilities still occur, however, in disciplinary and judicially determined cases. Although previous 'golden ages' are often illusory, it may be that the idea that the professional community had mutual responsibility for professional reputation is declining.

Supporting and Defending the Rule of Law

Supporting and defending the rule of law is arguably a social responsibility and a professional responsibility of lawyers. It is highly debateable what falls within the scope of such an obligation. In a democratic society it may be no more than facilitating access to justice. This is likely to involve undertaking legal work pro bono, considered further in the next section. In some countries lawyers can be targeted for helping particular cases. There are, however, occasions when defence of the rule of law may go beyond representation to more radical action. Where the state takes action that threatens the rule of law, action may be taken through the courts, or possibly on the streets.

Suspension and Reinstatement of the Chief Justice of Pakistan: From Judicial Crisis to Restoring Judicial Independence?
Library of Congress, www.loc.gov/law/help/pakistan-justice.php
(edited, sections reordered, references removed)

Profile of Chief Justice; Cases Decided Under Him

Chief Justice Chaudhry was the Chief Justice of the provincial Balochistan Supreme Court when he became a judge of the Supreme Court of Pakistan in February 2000. He was appointed as the Chief Justice of Pakistan in June 2005. Holder of an LLB degree, he had practiced law since 1974, and served as the Advocate General of Balochistan in 1989–90. His early experience does not appear to display anything to foreshadow his activist role as Chief Justice. According to a former president of the Balochistan Bar Association, he acted autocratically when he was the Chief Justice of Balochistan. Baloch lawyers were generally skeptical of the Chief Justice. Upon his dismissal, his unpopularity in Balochistan is stated to be evidenced by the fact that out of 2,000 practicing lawyers, only twenty to twenty-five turned up in his support at a public rally.

In Pakistan's capital, Islamabad, however, it was speculated that the reasons behind the dismissal went beyond the stated allegations of the Chief Justice's misconduct in office. Pakistan is to have parliamentary elections later in 2007 and a possible presidential election to follow in 2008. Legislation enacted in 2004 has enabled President Musharraf, who assumed power following a military coup in 1999, to continue to rule until 2007 both as president and chief of the country's army. The question of his continuing as President, while still wearing a military uniform, has been a vexatious issue in Pakistan. President Musharraf's opponents claim that the real reason behind the dismissal is his fear that the Supreme Court, led by Chief Justice Chaudhry, would have prevented him from running for President in 2008 while retaining his position as Chief of the Army.

Chef Justice Chaudhry's independent streak had become evident soon after his appointment in Islamabad. Several populist rulings against the government displayed a type of judicial activism considered to be unsettling for a government used to a pliable court. Under him, the Supreme Court took action on its own initiative to question the government on the role of the military and apparent instances of injustices. According to a respected British weekly "[i]ndeed, wherever Mr Chaudhry heard so much as a rumour of injustice … he summoned officials and demanded investigations."

Suspension

On March 9, 2007, when the President of Pakistan, General Purvez Musharraf, met the Chief Justice of the Pakistan Supreme Court, Iftikhar Muhammad Chaudhry, and reportedly importuned him to resign, the Chief Justice's refusal unleashed an unprecedented revolt led by Pakistani lawyers in support of judicial independence and the rule of law in Pakistan. Labeled a 'Lawyers' Mutiny,' the movement also generated public protests that it is thought could even endanger President Musharraf's hold on office.

The Chief Justice's act of refusal against a generally powerful executive, and in the face of pressure, is unheard of in Pakistan, which has seen no less than four military regimes ruling the country for significant periods during its sixty-year history. In that time, executive-judicial relations have been strained and numerous judges have been removed, despite protective provisions provided in Pakistan's present Constitution, promulgated in 1973. A number of judges have resigned in the face of court-packing, reductions in retirement ages, requirements to take fresh oaths, and other tactics of the government of the day.

President Musharraf is stated to have asked the Chief Justice to resign, based on grounds of alleged misconduct, in the presence of Prime Minister Shaukat Aziz and six other uniformed generals. The Chief Justice's reported refusal resulted in his virtual suspension and becoming 'non-functional.' At the same time, President Musharraf also invoked his authority under Article 209 of the oft-patched 1973 Constitution of Pakistan to refer the alleged abuses of office by the Chief Justice to a Supreme Judicial Council (Council). This is the first time that a Chief Justice has been made 'non-functional.' Soon after, an Acting Chief Justice was sworn-in in a hastily arranged ceremony. As explained, the second senior-most judge was picked for the acting position because the senior-most judge was out of the country.

The reference to the Council, consisting of five Supreme Court Justices chaired by the Acting Chief Justice, went into session soon after the swearing-in ceremony. During the proceedings in camera, the Council ordered Chief Justice Chaudhry not to perform functions as the Chief Justice or as a judge of the Supreme Court until the reference was decided. The suspended Chief Justice was called upon to answer in a matter of days the allegations raised against him

...

Public Support

As the news of the Chief Justice's treatment by the executive reached Pakistan's legal community, political circles and the general public, a 'protest movement spontaneously initiated by the overwhelming majority of lawyers' gained momentum. The previously unsung Chief Justice was 're-born as a hero of Pakistan's long-dejected democracy.' After an initial period when he appears to have been held incommunicado, the Chief Justice went on speaking tours during which he avoided making comments on his own dismissal, but canvassed the concepts of the independence of the judiciary and the rule of law.

In contrast to the lack of support in Balochistan, when he began the series of cross-country public appearances, hundreds of supporters, including lawyers in their traditional black coats, cheered him at all places. In Karachi, Pakistan's large southern port city, clashes between factions supporting the Chief Justice and pro-government activists exacted a death toll of more than forty persons. Chief Justice Chaudhry was forced to cancel plans to attend the rally because of the streetfighting.

On July 17, at a gathering of lawyers near the Supreme Court in Islamabad, even a suicide bomber is reported to have aimed an attack at the Chief Justice's supporters, and killed at least twelve persons.

Q9.11 In what way was the rule of law threatened in this example?

Q9.12 Were the actions of the lawyers justified?

Q9.13 What other action might be taken by lawyers in defence of the rule of law?

Public Agendas

Professions may justifiably be called public professions if they voluntarily promote what could be seen as public agendas. There are two such agendas that are noticeable in this respect: access to justice and the diversity of professional membership. Both have been the subject of considerable debate, particularly over the past 20 years.

Supporting Access to Justice

The rule of law assumes equality before the law. This also assumes what is referred to as equality of arms. This means that both parties to a dispute have equal capacity to put their side of the argument. This is particularly true of criminal cases. Such a commitment is somewhat hollow unless the state also ensures that every criminal or civil litigant has legal representation. Arguably, it is no less true in civil cases, where a citizen's rights can also be defined and lost. The idea of equal arms was the idea behind the introduction of legal aid in 1948.

Legal Aid and Advice Bill
HC Deb 15 December 1948 vol 459 cc1221–327 1221

Order for Second Reading read.

The Attorney-General (Sir Hartley Shawcross)

I beg to move, 'That the Bill be now read a Second time.'

If I might translate a respected expression from the promissory and ephemeral field in which it has been misemployed of late into the sphere of intended enactment, I should be inclined to call this Bill a charter. It is the charter of the little man to the British courts of justice. It is a Bill which will open the doors of the courts freely to all persons who may wish to avail themselves of British justice without regard to the question of their wealth or ability to pay. Since the right hon. and learned Gentleman the Member for West Derby (Sir D Maxwell Fyfe), who is to speak for the Opposition on this Bill, and I have been at the Bar—indeed, going back further to the time when Magna Charta decreed that: To no one will we sell, deny, or delay right or justice. —it is an interesting historical reflection that our legal system, admirable though it is, has always been in many respects open to, and it has received, grave criticisms on account of the fact that its benefits were only fully available to those who had purses sufficiently long to pay for them.

There is the old taunt, the familiar taunt, about His Majesty's courts being open to all just as the grill room at the Ritz Hotel is open to all. Indeed, I suppose that taunt is even more applicable today when the charges at the Ritz Hotel, at any rate in the grill room, are largely controlled, but many of the costs of the litigant are not subject to any legal limit at all. …

The Government have received the fullest support from both branches of the profession. Neither the Bar Council nor the Law Society have spared themselves in helping to draw up a really workable scheme on the general lines laid down in the Rushcliffe Report. This Bill is the result of the work done between the two branches of the profession and the Government in order to implement the proposals of the Rushcliffe Committee. It is based upon those proposals, it follows them in most of its important details, and, indeed, I think it is right to say, although there may be a number of quite minor differences, that in only two significant respects does it depart at all from the general principles of the Rushcliffe proposals. In one case it extends the proposed facilities to a rather wider circle, and in the other it slightly restricts the classes of litigation in respect of which the facilities will be available. ...

For a similarity of reasons, not of principle or logic but of practicability and expediency, it has been felt necessary to exclude, at all events for the present, certain classes of litigation, and those classes are set out in the second part of the first Schedule. They include various classes of action in which experience has shown—and I think there will be general agreement on this broad statement of the position—that there is most room for bringing vexatious, frivolous, unmeritorious or unnecessary claims. The most important of these, I suppose, are libel and slander. I do not say an action for libel or slander is never properly brought. In some cases, quite obviously, it is properly brought and naturally I would readily agree that the character and reputation of a poor person is just as deserving of legal protection as that of the wealthy individual, but it is a form of action which is open to great abuse and, moreover, it is a most precarious and risky form of action.

Legal aid was launched by the Legal aid and Assistance Act 1948. At that time it covered 80 per cent of the population, subject to means testing.[31] By the 1970s it covered 40 per cent. Since the 1980s, governments of all political complexions further reduced the commitment to providing access to justice. Between 1998 and 2007 the estimated proportion of the population of England and Wales eligible for civil legal aid fell from 52% to 29%.[32] In 2013–14, acts of help and of civil representation fell by over half, from 1,000,000 in 2007 to 497,000.[33]

It has been argued that supporting access to justice is a particular responsibility of lawyers. Such a proposition can be based on several grounds. Since the state grants lawyers monopolies of litigation and advocacy, it could be argued that lawyers should share the burden of providing access to justice with the state. The decline of legal aid in providing access to justice has raised the issue of what responsibility, if any, lawyers have for filling 'the justice gap'.

One way for lawyers to discharge this burden is by reducing the duration

---

[31] S Hynes and J Robins, *The Justice Gap* (London, Legal Action Group, 2009).

[32] A Griffith, 'Dramatic Drop in Civil Legal Aid Eligibility', Legal Action (September 2008) citing *Hansard*, HC Written Answers cols 779W–780W, 20 February 2008.

[33] Legal Aid Agency, *Legal Aid Statistics in England and Wales* (London, Ministry of Justice, June 2014).

and cost of litigation. Lawyers are encouraged to be efficient and the courts encourage this, for example, by disallowing costs and by making wasted costs orders. The other way in which lawyers can contribute to an access to justice agenda is by providing free legal services, usually referred to as *pro bono publico* legal services, to those who cannot afford legal fees.

Pro Bono Publico

The argument that lawyers should provide free legal services to those in legal need is contentious. Some in the legal professions resent any attempt to single out lawyers in this way. They point out that lawyers are the only professional group asked to work for free. There is some truth in this, although the priority given to free health services reduces pressure on doctors to provide gratuitous medical treatment. Others might argue that this is not a recent phenomenon, but one of the oldest enduring traditions associated with legal professions.

While it is true that pro bono publico is an old tradition it is one that has changed dramatically since the 1990s. Whereas the delivery of free legal services was once voluntary and modest, it has moved centre stage in recent years. Under the direction of large firms in the City of London, free service is becoming an expectation of lawyers at a time when the idea of public service may be fading for lawyers and perhaps in society generally.

The rising profile of pro bono publico began in the 1990s, when declining eligibility for legal aid became particularly controversial. Lawyers were under some pressure from politicians to provide more free services. A report on the issue by a Law Society Working Party concluded that solicitors provided a large volume of free legal services, but that these should not increase to compensate for legal aid cuts. Some lawyers were unhappy with this conclusion and decided to take independent action.

A meeting at the Law Society in 1996 led to the formation of the Solicitors Pro Bono Group, now going under the title LawWorks. Together with a strong Bar Pro Bono Unit, these organisations engineered a significant increase in the volume of activity. In 2002, the founder of the Bar Pro Bono Unit, Peter Goldsmith, then in government, formed the Attorney General's Pro Bono Committee. This provided an umbrella for a national Pro Bono week involving the main legal professions.

The development of pro bono legal services gained an important fillip in 2008 when courts in England and Wales were empowered to make pro bono costs orders under section 194 of the Legal Services Act 2007. These orders apply where a case was won with pro bono help. Without such an order, the losing party would escape liability for costs because of the indemnity principle (a winning party can only reclaim the costs he would have been liable for).

The costs awarded under pro bono costs orders went to the Access to Justice Foundation. This is a national charity created under statutory instrument by the Advice Services Alliance, Bar Council, ILEX and Law Society to provide grant funding to support pro bono and advice agencies.[34] There was, however, an apparent lack of awareness of the availability of these costs orders among practitioners (a year after they were introduced 70–80 per cent had not heard of them). Anticipated difficulties in having them agreed or determined by the court may deter pro bono lawyers from seeking orders. This raises the question of whether such orders should be compulsory.

Since the 1990s there has also been a concerted effort to involve more law schools in delivering free legal advice. In 2011 a LawWorks Student Pro Bono Report revealed that more than 65 per cent of law schools in England and Wales were engaged in some form of pro bono activity.[35] This represented an increase of over 40 per cent since 2006.

Why Do We Engage in Pro Bono Work?
See more at: www.lawsociety.org.uk/communities/lawyers-with-disabilities/
features/a-case-for-pro-bono/#sthash.NbB3SNQv.dpuf

It seems curious that an entire profession has established an altruistic act like pro bono as a customary practice.

However, working at LawWorks has enhanced my confidence that, in the words of Margaret Mead, 'a small group of thoughtful, committed citizens can change the world'.

I receive emails every day from solicitors and law students seeking to volunteer their skills to help the community in whatever way they can. Witnessing the enthusiasm these professionals have for supporting the sector and advancing access to justice makes me believe that some real stars have emerged from the LASPO tunnel.

There is a popular mantra in the sector that enunciates: 'Pro bono: It's part of being a lawyer'. Another common refrain pronounces: 'Pro bono is adjunct to, but not a substitute for legal aid'.

Perhaps as much as anything, the pro-bono sector aims to spread the former message while empathising with the sentiment behind the latter.

LawWorks works to instil the ethos of pro bono in all lawyers from law school onwards, hoping that they will carry the enthusiasm with them through qualification and onwards to become the senior role models the profession badly needs.

Projects like Students Pro Bono and the Fellowship programme, while targeted at opposite ends of the profession, serve to fulfil the same objective: to ensure

---

[34] www.accesstojusticefoundation.org.uk/downloads/Access_to_Justice_Foundation_leaflet.pdf.
[35] http://lawworks.org.uk/tmp_downloads/d142c24h93g72e148u73b38k41b23t140u83y75p
9n10j121/lawworks-student-pro-bono-report-2011.pdf.

these pro bono stars shine on through the night. In this respect, the hashtag #probonostar for the LawWorks Pro Bono Awards 2014 seems even more apt.

Q9.14 Why should lawyers engage in pro bono publico legal services?

The Bar has always maintained a close relationship with barrister pro bono organisations. Indeed, barristers make a £30 contribution to the Bar Pro Bono Unit when paying their practising fee, unless they opt out. The Law Society generally maintained a more arm's length relationship with solicitor pro bono organisations. It has occasionally made grants and given expressions of support, but a stronger commitment was apparently withheld because of concern over 'replacing legal aid'.

In 2011 the Law Society announced that would establish a committee to make recommendations for a more 'developed policy' on pro bono. It acknowledged that its policy that pro bono is an adjunct to, rather than substitute for, legal aid was 'being challenged' by 'the increased demand for pro bono services in the face of severely diminished legal aid provision' and local authority cuts that will hit the third sector.

A paper released with the announcement linked pro bono publico with the government's 'Big Society' agenda. It stated that:

> In a world where the provision of legal services will be much more commoditised, there is strong support for a view that pro bono demonstrates the ethic of a true professional. Indeed the legal profession is considered a leader in this respect and something that other professions are keen to emulate.

The Law Society suggested that '[a] commitment to pro bono and an ability to articulate its impact help to counter the charges of self-interest that are levelled against the Law Society in relation to defending legal aid'. Issues falling for consideration by the committee were predicted to include:

1. Whether pro bono efforts should go into areas of law which are falling out of scope of legal aid.
2. Whether and to what extent pro bono is a professional obligation.
3. Whether pro bono will help distinguish solicitors from post-Legal Services Act competitors.

The Law Society currently contributes to the running of LawWorks.

From the Law Society website Junior Lawyers page
(http://juniorlawyers.lawsociety.org.uk/pro-bono-article)

Case study—Lovells

Pro bono projects at Lovells are managed by the pro bono team and the supervising partner or associate. Junior lawyers are given substantial responsibility to determine legal strategy, the approach to be taken and arguments to be advanced in conjunction with their supervisor and/or a member of the Pro Bono team.

The firm has five solicitor advocacy schemes: War Pensions Tribunal work with the Royal British Legion; Criminal Injuries Compensation case work for victims of crime, trafficking and forced labour; duty Solicitors schemes at Bow County Court to defend warrants of eviction, and representation for victims of domestic violence to allow them to seek injunctions to stop their abuse. Volunteers can also undertake legal research for international NGOs and non-contentious work for charities, not-for-profits and social enterprises.

The firm also works with the National Centre for Domestic Violence and the Women's Trust to provide pro bono assistance to domestic abuse victims ineligible for legal aid. Since 2006 the firm has advised and represented almost 100 clients with obtaining urgent injunctions.

A recent case involved Ms B, who had been attacked and injured by her abusive husband following the serving of divorce papers. On his release from prison, Ms B was afraid of further attacks against herself or her children after seeing him parking outside her house. In a team led by newly qualified litigation associate, Emma Higgs, Lovells represented Ms B to obtain an injunction against him, and supported Ms B throughout court proceedings which were complicated by the fact that the ex-husband's whereabouts were unknown. Based on a volunteer's submissions and advocacy before a district judge, a permanent Non-Molestation Order was obtained.

These results speak for themselves. The most satisfying thing about doing pro bono work, Kevin Poulter says, is 'a thank you, a smile, a relationship with the client'. He adds: 'You should also take pride in the work you are doing and in the knowledge that you are helping someone who otherwise would not have had access to your services.'

Q9.15 Why do lawyers engage in pro bono publico legal services?

Although there are reasons to treat claims for lawyers' pro bono contributions with caution there appears to have been a significant increase in the volume of pro bono work done annually over the past 20 years. According to Law Society data drawn from its Annual Omnibus Surveys, for example, solicitors provided £338 million worth of free legal services in 2006/7, £475 million in 2009/10 and £511 million in 2011/12.[36] These figures typically represent around 2–3 per cent of fees generated by all solicitors' firms.

In 2013/14, £0.9 billion was spent on criminal legal aid and around £0.8 billion was spent on civil legal aid.[37] Therefore, assuming the current contribution of pro bono legal services, estimated at £518 million, is accurate,[38] this represents about half of the investment in civil legal aid. Legal services donated pro bono are never likely to replace legal aid. Therefore, it could be argued that pro bono legal services should be used strategically. This may require that free work be reserved for cases that are likely to produce precedents affecting other cases.

The legal profession in England and Wales is proud of the development of pro bono publico in the jurisdiction. In fact, the Anglo-American legal professions are seen as world leaders. A Bar Committee has prepared a guide to overseas bar associations 'anxious to clarify the meaning and content of principles of lawyers' ethics and to find ways to enforce them in their home jurisdictions'.

A Guide to the Professional Conduct and Discipline of the Legal Profession
(London, The International Relations Committee of the Bar Council of England & Wales, January 2007)

2.02(3) MAKING LEGAL SERVICES AVAILABLE

Discussion

As previously mentioned lawyers have duties not only to their clients but also to the wider public interest. An important way of fulfilling their public interest duty is the provision of pro bono legal services, in particular to those unable to afford them. Those legal services may be given either free or at a reduced fee. They may be rendered to a group (a charity or faith group) or individually. By devoting time to pro bono work, lawyers ensure access to justice for those otherwise unable to assert their legal rights.

An issue is whether pro bono activities should be mandatory. While major jurisdictions treat the provision of pro bono legal services as highly desirable, they have rejected the notion of a mandatory duty. One reason for this is that it is difficult to impose a universal duty given that lawyers have such varied practices. For example, the lawyer concentrating on publicly funded work may already be receiving lower fees than those who practice for large commercial clients.

---

[36] eg www.lawsociety.org.uk/secure/file/190342/e:/teamsitedeployed/documents/templatedata/Publications/Research%20Publications/Documents/probonoreport2011.pdf.

[37] Legal Aid Agency, *Legal Aid Statistics in England and Wales* (London, Ministry of Justice, June 2014).

[38] www.theguardian.com/law/guardian-law-blog/2012/nov/06/national-pro-bono-week-2012-law-firms.

In some jurisdictions the issue of fixed (scale) fees arises. While these are generally abhorrent to competition authorities they are one way of securing access to justice. While this is a matter of public policy the professional code may need to contain an obligation on lawyers to comply with the scale fees and not to try to avoid them. A related aspect is whether lawyers have an obligation to undertake legal aid work at the rates payable by the legal aid authorities.

The third rule is drawn from of the Law Society of Upper Canada. Their commentary to this reads, in part: 'It is essential that a person requiring legal services be able to find, with a minimum of delay, a lawyer qualified to provide such services. The lawyer may assist in making legal services available by participating in the Legal Aid Plan and lawyer referral services, by engaging in programmes of public information, education or advice concerning legal matters, and by being considerate of those who seek advice but are inexperienced in legal matters or cannot readily explain their problems'.

Principle 2.02 (3)

(a) Lawyers must support pro bono work, which represents a commitment to good citizenship.

(b) Lawyers must comply with any fixed rates set for legal services.

(c) Lawyers shall make legal services available to the public in an efficient and convenient way that commands respect and confidence and is compatible with the integrity and independence of the profession.

Source: Law Society of Upper Canada

Q9.16 Should legal services delivered at a reduced fee be regarded as pro bono publico?

Q9.17 Why might differences in the profitability of legal practice justify lawyers not doing pro bono work?

Q9.18 In the context of the Law Society of Upper Canada rule, what might 'a commitment to good citizenship' mean?

Even apparently strong pro bono commitments can be weakened by lack of specificity. The Law Society of Upper Canada Principle 2.02(3)(a), for example, is mandatory: it states that lawyers 'must' support pro bono work, but it does not say how. Is it sufficient for a lawyer to support the idea of pro bono legal work? Is it enough to perform an hour of free services a year? Would a contribution to charity discharge the burden?

Neither of the main legal professions in England and Wales include a reference to pro bono obligations in their code of conduct. This may be, as the Bar committee notes, because of a reluctance to make pro bono obligations mandatory. However, pro bono obligations can be included in codes as aspirations. The ABA Model Rules are an example of this approach.

American Bar Association Model Rules
Model Rule 6.1

Every lawyer has a professional responsibility to provide legal services to those unable to pay. A lawyer should aspire to render at least (50) hours of pro bono publico legal services per year. In fulfilling this responsibility, the lawyer should:

(a) provide a substantial majority of the (50) hours of legal services without fee or expectation of fee to:

   (1) persons of limited means or

   (2) charitable, religious, civic, community, governmental and educational organizations in matters which are designed primarily to address the needs of persons of limited means; and

(b) provide any additional services through:

   (1) delivery of legal services at no fee or substantially reduced fee to individuals, groups or organizations seeking to secure or protect civil rights, civil liberties or public rights, or charitable, religious, civic, community, governmental and educational organizations in matters in furtherance of their organizational purposes, where the payment of standard legal fees would significantly deplete the organization's economic resources or would be otherwise inappropriate;

   (2) delivery of legal services at a substantially reduced fee to persons of limited means; or

   (3) participation in activities for improving the law, the legal system or the legal profession.

In addition, a lawyer should voluntarily contribute financial support to organizations that provide legal services to persons of limited means.

Q9.19 Should the state guarantee access to law for those who cannot afford to pay?

Q9.20 Why should lawyers provide free legal services?

Q9.21 Would it be reasonable to remove the words 'should aspire to' from the second sentence of the model rule and replace it with the word 'must'?

Promoting Diversity

A long line of UK equalities legislation, including the Equality Act 2010, requires organisations to eliminate discrimination and promote equality in relation to the 'protected characteristics' of age, disability, gender reassignment, marriage and civil partnership, pregnancy and maternity, race, religion and belief, sex and sexual orientation. There is no doubt that the legal professions have, for the past 25 years, also been under pressure to ensure that their membership is representative of wider society.[39] This is more difficult to achieve when it is not professions that directly employ lawyers.

Among the regulatory objectives imposed on approved regulators under the Legal Services Act 2007 are encouraging an independent, strong, diverse and effective legal profession and improving access to justice. It is therefore arguable that regulators are under a statutory duty, not only to eliminate discrimination, but to take positive steps to promote diversity.

Unless one regards legal professions as privileged 'public professions', it is not clear why they should carry a special responsibility to be diverse, any more than, say, plumbers should be representative of the general population. This is different from saying that organisations employing lawyers should not illegally discriminate. It is also different from acknowledging that there are reasons why professions, in their own interests, should reflect social demography.

There are reasons why a professional body of lawyers should be diverse. The argument that is most often heard in relation to the diversity of the legal profession is that it should be representative of wider society. In Western societies this tends to mean that professional groups proportionately represent the wider population in terms of ethnicity, gender and disability. On this basis it might also be argued that legal professions should try to achieve proportional representation in terms of class and sexuality.

There are also arguments that it is in a profession's self-interest to be diverse, particularly if they aspire to be public professions. First, for example, entry to a public profession should be based on merit rather than the vested interests of social elites. Second, lawyers can better serve all communities if they have roots in all communities. Third, delivering the promise of the rule of law in a diverse society requires lawyers able to understand the social, cultural and class backgrounds of the client body. Fourth, there are good reasons why the judiciary should be representative of society, and judges in common law countries tend to be drawn from the ranks of practitioners.

---

[39] W Twining, 'Access to Legal Education and the Legal Profession: A Commonwealth Perspective' in R Dhavan, N Kibble and W Twining (eds), *Access to Legal Education and the Legal Profession* (London, Butterworths, 1989).

Policies of Professional Bodies

Professional Policy

During the 1990s, society generally became more sensitive to the difficulties of securing equal opportunities. Relative lack of social mobility was increasingly seen as a serious problem. With social cohesion dependent on equal opportunity and fair distribution of privilege, access to opportunity came to be recognised as an ethical issue. The Law Society was a particularly keen promoter of a diverse profession.

The Law Society's model anti-discrimination policy, introduced in 1995, sought to have a direct impact on the recruitment practices of solicitors' firms. Solicitors without an anti-discrimination code were deemed to have adopted the model policy. This included 'good practice' in setting recruitment targets for members of ethnic minorities. For example, firms with between six and ten fee-earners were expected to have at least one fee-earner of ethnic minority origin, with proportionate increases for larger firms.

In 2000, the chief executive of the Law Society defended the profession's role in seeking the elimination of unlawful discrimination and promoting equality of opportunity and good relations between different racial groups.[40] There were, however, significant problems remaining at all stages of legal careers, from admission to employment, in terms of equal opportunity and equal treatment.

Admission

There are various barriers to becoming a lawyer, all of which may contribute in some way to denying access to legal careers. A student paying in full for fees and living expenses for both the undergraduate and vocational stages of legal education is likely to incur debts of at least £60,000. It is therefore necessary to ask whether these barriers are necessary or whether they constitute unfair impediments to access and, therefore, to achieving a diverse and representative legal profession. This raises the question of whether all the phases of legal education are necessary preparation for legal careers.

Availability of Training

The training process has often suffered from bottlenecks at the vocational and training stages. While vocational course places have now increased to exceed demand, there are usually fewer training contracts available than LPC graduates seeking training. This has exacerbated concerns about unfair recruitment

---

[40] 'Opinion—Janet Paraskeva' (2002) 16 *The Lawyer*, 11 March, 19.

practices, particularly to elite sections of the Bar and to the large commercial solicitors' firms.

Studies for the Bar and a longitudinal study for the Law Society pointed to potentially discriminatory recruitment practices.[41] Initial concerns were that the profession was being replicated by direct discrimination as a predominantly male, white and middle-class preserve. This was certainly true in some sectors of the profession, where recruitment was based on nepotism and the use of recruitment consultants rather than open interviews.[42] The various studies showed that more significant limits on equality of opportunity were embedded in the recruitment practices of elite organisations.

The Law Society longitudinal study showed that large solicitors' firms in particular recruited future trainees early, often before they had finished their degrees, in order to capture the 'high flyers' from elite universities. This meant that they were essentially relying on A levels as the measure of academic quality.[43] Some commercial barristers' chambers were following suit in order to compete for the most promising talent. This favoured students from privileged backgrounds at the expense of those from lower social classes and ethnic minorities.

The studies conducted for the professional bodies put pressure on elite legal organisations to try and accommodate the diversity agenda. Many have done so by broadening the recruitment net. They now use work placements to assess promising candidates from unconventional backgrounds. This, however, has only begun to address inherent problems in access to, and progress in, legal professional jobs.

In 2008 half of minority ethnic group solicitors worked in firms with four or fewer partners, compared with only 28 per cent of white Europeans.[44] This inevitably means that, as a group, they have lower salaries. Similar problems affect women solicitors. Although they are taken on as trainees in larger numbers than men, they are less likely to achieve partnership and more likely to leave the profession.

There are also problems with diversity at the other end of the spectrum. The declining impact of legal aid as a source of income for solicitors has put the

---

[41] D Halpern, *Entry Into the Legal Professions: The Law Student Cohort Study Years 1 and 2* (London, Law Society, 1994) (first survey); M Shiner and T Newburn, *Entry Into the Legal Professions: Law Student Cohort Study Year 3* (London, Law Society, 1995) (second survey); M Shiner, *Entry into the Legal Professions: The Law Student Cohort Study Year 4* (London, Law Society, 1997) (third survey); M Shiner, *Entry into the Legal Professions: The Law Student Cohort Study Year 5* (London, Law Society, 1999) (fourth survey); E Duff, M Shiner, A Boon and A Whyte, *Entry into the Legal Professions: The Law Student Cohort Study Year 6* (London, Law Society, 2000) (fifth survey).

[42] A Boon, L Duff and M Shiner, 'Career Paths and Choices in a Highly Differentiated Profession: The Position of Newly Qualified Solicitors' (2001) 64(4) *Modern Law Review* 563.

[43] H Rolfe and T Anderson, *The Recruitment of Trainee Solicitors* (London, Law Society, 2002).

[44] B Cole, N Fletcher, T Chittenden and J Cox, *Trends in the Solicitors' Profession Annual Statistical Report 2009* (London, Law Society, 2009) 20.

profitability of many areas of work at risk. This has affected recruitment of trainees in these areas. The Legal Services Commission regarded the problem as so serious that it set up a Training Contract Grant Scheme to help firms recruit trainees who were committed to legal aid work. The Ministry of Justice abandoned the scheme in 2010 as part of a cost-cutting exercise.[45]

Reform of Training

The continued efforts of the Law Society to combat direct and indirect discrimination have achieved results. Nevertheless, the policy of driving greater diversity provoked mixed reactions. A survey in 2007 showed that nearly 70 per cent of lawyers favoured hiring former comprehensive school students, but between 30 and 40 per cent were opposed to different forms of diversity monitoring.[46]

The cost barriers to qualification provoked continued discussion of training processes. A recurrent issue was fitness for purpose. Were the results achieved by the system of training achievable in different ways involving shorter and cheaper routes to qualification?[47] The training contract was an obvious target. It was a bottleneck in the qualification process, a cost to employers, in the form of training obligations, and a cost to new employees, in the form of reduced wages.

In 2005 the Law Society's Training Framework Review proposed Day One Outcomes that would need to be met by intending solicitors. The proposals did not specify any particular route for achieving the outcomes, except that a two-year period of work-based learning would be retained as a prerequisite for practice. It was suggested that this would not necessarily be based at a single firm, or at a firm at all, provided it was under the supervision of a solicitor. It proposed extending the range of training organisations and lifting the requirement of providing four seats (four areas of work experience).[48]

The Legal and Education and Training Review for England and Wales, which reported in 2013, provided further support for addressing problems in the education and training process.

---

[45] 'Djanogly Scraps Training Contract Grant Scheme' [2010] *Solicitors Journal*, 7 July.
[46] K Williams, 'Firms Rail against Diversity Monitoring' (2007) 21 *The Lawyer*, 10 September.
[47] C Thomson, 'Fairness for All' [1997] *The Lawyer*, 20 May (student supplement, vi).
[48] J Eldred, 'How to Put recruits through their Paces' (2002) 99(34) *Gazette*, 5 September, 21.

The Future of Legal Services Education and Training Regulation in England and Wales (June 2013)

Equality and diversity in entry

7.47 There is concern, and sometimes anger, among those who have invested much time and money in the initial stages of education and then been unable to find qualifying employment within the regulated sector. Respondents mentioned a lack of initial information about risks and career options; the potential for unfair treatment in recruitment; being left in a paralegal limbo; potential for exploitation, and a lack of recognition of prior experience.

7.48 Cost and bottlenecks obviously have implications for access, diversity and social mobility. Despite the good intentions of many employers, there are distinct barriers to entry. Three overlapping barriers to access in this respect were identified in Chapter 6: reliance on A-levels and tariff scores; access to work experience, and the focus on recruitment from elite universities. The current buyer's market may mean that employers are more averse to taking unnecessary recruitment 'risks', and prospective applicants who lack social and economic capital, may also be deterred by the risk of not succeeding.

7.49 A number of responses recognised the importance of diversity and demonstrated commitment to diversity initiatives. There has been limited evidence as to the amount of difference such initiatives actually make to the workplace (BSN data, for example, suggests improvements are apparent in diverse recruitment but not yet in progression). The commitment to proper evaluation of initiatives such as PRIME and the Pegasus Access Scheme is welcomed. Diversity and social mobility data on apprenticeships should be obtained and monitored.

7.50 A focus in existing schemes on attracting high achievers from non-traditional backgrounds into the elite universities may create a skewed approach to questions of social mobility, rather than necessarily putting resources into better enabling those non-traditional students who are already in the higher education system to break through into elite employment.

7.51 A number of ways of reducing regulatory burdens so as to open up opportunities are identified in Chapter 6: chiefly the use of contextual admission data; flexible education and training models, and access to good quality information. Commitments by the solicitors' profession to widen access to work experience are to be welcomed and encouraged, but problems continue to exist in terms of the accessibility of placements, particularly as access at secondary school level appears to be becoming increasingly important to future career opportunities as a solicitor. The growth in unpaid internships also raises a set of different concerns about employers taking advantage of the difficult market for trainee applicants.

Approved regulators should have formal guidance in place regarding the offering of internships.

Q9.22 Is it important that legal professions have diverse membership?

Q9.23 Is the legal professions' record on diversity good?

Q9.24 What measures might increase diversity in the legal profession?

Consideration of the ethical implications of diversity should not be limited to legal professions. If the promise of legal careers is ephemeral it is arguably unethical for higher-education institutions to recruit to law degrees in such large numbers. This raises the issue of whether the professions should require universities to provide more information about legal careers? Should universities provide more relevant pathways? In short, is there a moral duty to make students more aware of their opportunities, options and duties as future lawyers?[49]

The Weakening of Professional Responsibility?

The Decline of Professionalism

As we saw in chapter two, some academics have speculated that legal professionalism, in England and Wales at least, is in decline. Some have even declared it dead. It is interesting to speculate what would remain of professional responsibility, particularly for the kinds of public agendas that the legal professions have sometimes pursued, were this true.

Larson suggests that one of the reasons that the state creates professional monopolies is to protect the personal investments of prospective professionals in education and training. John Stuart Mill argued that legal work should provide lawyers with a good living so that they were not exposed to temptation while handling others' money.[50] These kinds of 'protectionist' arguments are less persuasive than they once were. Therefore, the state has seen no difficulty in weakening legal professionalism while expecting professional standards to be maintained.

The Legal Services Act 2007 undermined the notion of self-regulation by separating the representative and regulatory functions of professions. The decline of legal aid and the reduced profitability of legal practice at the lower

---

[49] A Boon, 'Ethics in Legal Education and Training: Four Reports, Three Jurisdictions and a Prospectus' (2002) 5(1) *Legal Ethics* 34.

[50] M Davies, 'The Regulation of Solicitors and the Role of the Solicitors Disciplinary Tribunal' (1998) 14(3) *Professional Negligence* 143.

end of the market has reduced the viability of small-scale legal practice. It is unknown what impact this will have on the ethical culture of the workplace or whether changes to education and regulation can offset deteriorating conditions. Such changes in the conditions of professions arguably call into question the extent of professional responsibility for public agendas.

Sample Problem Question

A solicitor (A) is asked by a client to instruct 'any barrister who is not female'. A consults the SRA Code of Conduct Principle 9 which provides that '[You must] ... run your business or carry out your role in the business in a way that encourages equality of opportunity and respect for diversity.' In Chapter 2 he finds the following Outcome:

> 'you do not discriminate unlawfully, or victimise or harass anyone, in the course of your professional dealings' (O(2.1))

A explains to the client that accepting an instruction only to instruct a male barrister is contrary to the code of conduct.

Q9.25 Is A correct and, if so, why?

Q9.26 If the client accepts A's advice and tells A to instruct Mark Smith, can A do so?

Conclusion

Professional responsibility is a term covering the conduct and wider ethical responsibilities of professions. What constitutes the wider ethical responsibilities is debatable. The term can be interpreted very narrowly so as to cover the ordinary, collegial activities that professions tend to maintain. It can also be interpreted broadly to bring in matters that tend not to be covered by codes of conduct. Such matters have recently included campaigns to increase the amount of pro bono legal services provided by lawyers and to make the legal profession more diverse.

It is not clear why lawyers are expected to have public interest burdens that other occupations do not share. One theory is that law is seen as a public profession and that this status, albeit ill-defined, carries special responsibilities. Another is that responsibility is the price of enjoying special privileges, such as self-regulation and monopoly markets. It remains to be seen whether levels of responsibility will remain high if the privileges of the legal professions decline.

Part IV

Practice Contexts

10

Litigation and Advocacy

Litigation is the process of investigating, initiating and bringing legal actions to court. Advocacy is the act of presenting and arguing cases in court. This chapter looks at the professional ethics of lawyers in the context of both criminal and civil litigation and advocacy. In criminal litigation there are differences in the duties owed by prosecutors and those owed by defence lawyers. Although there are clear distinctions in the ethos of different areas of work, the codes of conduct of the main professions are moving closer together.

In the civil areas of personal injury and family litigation, there are significant differences in how lawyers have been expected to work. These areas have been the subject of shifts in the underlying ethical basis of work. These shifts are manifest in distinct norms for specialist practice, reflected in codes and criteria for competence. The regulation of litigation illustrates the difference that context can make to the application of ethical principles.

In England and Wales, traditionally solicitors were identified with conducting litigation and barristers with advocacy, certainly in the higher courts. The Courts and Legal Services Act 1990 (CLSA) potentially opened up the fields of litigation and advocacy to competition between solicitors and barristers in both areas. Some solicitors qualified for higher court advocacy, but in relatively small numbers. It was not until 2014 that the Bar finally embraced the idea that barristers should be able to offer litigation services.

In the 1990s the initial signs were that private practitioners in both branches of the profession would stick to their traditional roles. Solicitors valued the opportunity to instruct eminent barristers in difficult cases and did not think that the time demands of high-level advocacy would fit in with their work patterns. This reluctance of solicitors to cross work boundaries has, however, increasingly broken down. It is expected that, as legally aided advocacy declines, more barristers will want to offer litigation services.

The Adversarial System

Ethos

Ways of resolving disputes are culturally and socially determined. The justice system in England and Wales evolved from adversarial origins and was developed by lawyers along adversarial lines. This gave rise to an 'ideology of advocacy', casting lawyers as 'champions' against state power and guarantors of citizens' rights. Despite its claims to provide a unique way to assess the truth of competing claims, the adversarial trial is an imperfect means of resolving all disputes. It is expensive, formal and potentially fallible. Its use is sometimes disproportionate to the issue.

Structures

The blueprint for the court system was created in the nineteenth century. County courts were created in 1846 to deal with low-value and routine civil matters. They were replaced by a single County Court under the Crime and Courts Act 2013.[1] The Supreme Court of Judicature, incorporating the High Court, was established by the Judicature Act 1870. The hierarchy included a built in route for appeals, via the Court of Appeal to the House of Lords. When the House of Lords became the Supreme Court under the Constitutional Reform Act 2005 the former Supreme Court of England and Wales became the Senior Courts of England and Wales.

The High Court is split into three divisions: Family, Queen's Bench and Chancery. The jurisdictions of Chancery and Queen's Bench overlap but, despite a growing Chancery interest in commercial litigation, its main work includes bankruptcy, estates and mortgages. The Queen's Bench Division deals with the bulk of tort and contract cases. The substantive civil jurisdictions of the County Court and High Court largely overlap.

The criminal court system comprises crown courts, which hear serious criminal cases and appeals. Magistrates' courts hear less serious cases, around 95 per cent of the million criminal cases tried annually. They also deal with applications for bail and for search warrants and some civil matters.[2] Most magistrates are part-time volunteers without legal qualification, being advised on the law by a justices' clerk, now often referred to as the court legal adviser.

---

[1] Crime and Courts Act 2013 s 17.
[2] See further the report of Auld LJ, *A Review of the Criminal Courts of England and Wales* (London, Stationery Office, 2001) particularly ch 3.

District judges and deputy district judges, who must have seven years' experience of advocacy before appointment, also sit in the magistrates' courts. There are 28,000 lay magistrates, serving 600 local justice areas, and around 105 district judges.

The Court of Appeal consists of the Civil Division and the Criminal Division. The Civil Division hears appeals from the High Court, county courts and from tribunals such as the Employment Appeal Tribunal, the Immigration Appeal Tribunal and the Lands Tribunal. The Criminal Division hears appeals from the Crown Court. The 12 Justices of the Supreme Court provide a final court of appeal for UK civil cases, and for criminal cases from England, Wales and Northern Ireland.

Since the Human Rights Act in 1998, the Supreme Court can declare a law incompatible with the European Convention on Human Rights. The expectation is that the government will then change such a law to make it compliant. When the UK became a member of the European Community in 1973, a further appeal to the European Court of Justice[3] was introduced for cases involving EU law.

Lawyers' Jurisdiction in Litigation and Advocacy

Context

In England and Wales, the right to conduct litigation in the place of clients was historically associated with attorneys and later solicitors. The process whereby barristers only took instructions from attorneys to appear in court began in the Elizabethan period but was entrenched by the nineteenth century. The role of advocacy has been associated with barristers since the Middle Ages, but access to higher courts became their exclusive preserve.

Before the CLSA 1990 solicitors appeared as advocates in the less senior courts and tribunals, notably the county courts and magistrates' courts. The exclusive access of the Bar to higher courts was the rationale for the split profession. Solicitors had day-to-day contact with clients but tended to instruct barristers for specialist drafting and advice.[4] 'Instructing solicitors' were expected to remain in court for the duration of the case to deal with witnesses and any issues that arose.

---

[3] Technically, this is now called the Court of Justice of the European Union (CJEU) but is invariably referred to as the ECJ.

[4] S Payne, 'Instructing Counsel' in S Payne (ed), *Instructing Counsel* (Croydon, Tolley Publishing, 1994) 3–4.

The Need for Specialist Advocates

The Case for Specialist Advocacy Services

There are several arguments for restricting advocacy rights to a specialist group. First, advocacy is a highly evolved skill. Developing adequate expertise requires constant practice. Both clients and the courts benefit from being served by experienced advocates. Second, specialist advocates are more effective because they do not have to run an office. They can focus on the presentation of the case as their priority.

The third argument for specialist advocates is that they are better able to observe the duty to the court because they have an indirect relationship with lay clients. Fourth, because the market demands excellence, specialist advocates can be taught a greater range of advocacy skills and given more experience in training. At the English Bar, they also have the considerable experience of specialist institutions to support them.

The fifth argument for specialist advocates is their relationship to the market for legal services. First, newly qualified barristers undergo a process of selection by the market. If they do not demonstrate sufficient competence they do not survive at the Bar. They have no firm and no other source of work to fall back on. Sixth, specialist advocates are selected by discerning professionals, whereas employed advocates are selected by their firms on behalf of clients.

Finally, the availability of a core of specialist advocates facilitates access to justice. The smallest firm can instruct the most eminent advocates without having to pay to keep them 'in-house'. This means that solicitors in geographically remote areas can, in theory, compete with metropolitan solicitors in providing a full litigation service.

The Case for Competition in the Provision of Advocacy Services

The case against maintaining a specialist cadre of advocates relates both to quality and to expense. As regards quality, having large numbers of specialist advocates does not necessarily improve the quality of advocacy across the board. The most inexperienced advocates tend to appear in large numbers of important cases, such as criminal defence, so as to increase their earnings. This is not advantageous to the administration of justice.

As regards expense, the specialist advocate will need someone else to prepare the case. Retaining a specialist advocate therefore involves paying for two lawyers rather than one. Appointing a QC generally involves appointing at least three lawyers: QC, junior counsel and solicitor. This arrangement was generally seen as inefficient and there were various proposals to abandon the higher court advocacy arrangements during the nineteenth century. The proposal to end the solicitors' monopoly of conveyancing caused the Law Society to campaign to end the Bar's monopoly of higher court advocacy.

The Marre Report, published in 1988, was seen as a last chance for the legal professions to agree a way forward on solicitor advocacy. The representatives of the professions reached stalemate. The majority made a plea to retain advocacy as an exclusive activity, pointing to the delicate balance that advocates needed to achieve in representation. It claimed that:

> [T]he client is frequently acting under physical, emotional or financial difficulties and may well wish to take every step he can, whether legal or extra-legal, to gain advantage over the other party. In this situation the lawyer has a special duty and responsibility to advise his client as to the legal and ethical standards which should be observed and not to participate in any deception or sharp practice.[5]

The Bar argued that it was important to separate advocacy from other legal roles, for example the decision to prosecute, or from the task of case preparation.[6] This was seen as fundamental to the Bar's unique modus operandi and ethos.

In 1989 the Lord Chancellor, Lord Mackay, published three green papers, the main one called *The Work and Organisation of the Legal Profession.*[7] The Green Papers were based on the idea that competition between the professions, even in advocacy, would 'give clients the widest possible choice of cost effective services'.[8] The Bar's response was that its strength lay 'in its independence, and in the "cab-rank" rule, made possible by the independence of barristers in private practice as sole practitioners'.[9] The Bar and members of the judiciary resisted the extension of rights of audience on the grounds that it was necessary to preserve the Bar's excellence, independence and special commitment to the administration of justice.

The government response to its consultation on the proposed reforms stated that 'independence is a matter of ethos, professional discipline and frame of mind, rather than a matter of how a lawyer is engaged or paid'.[10] Nevertheless, what was enacted was a revision of the proposals, which had envisaged that both solicitors and barristers would have access to lower courts on qualification and then acquire separate qualifications to access higher courts.

---

[5] Lady Marre CBE, *A Time for Change: Report of the Committee on the Future of the Legal Profession* (London, General Council of the Bar and Council of the Law Society, 1988) 6.1.

[6] A Thornton, 'The Professional Responsibility and Ethics of the English Bar' in R Cranston (ed), *Legal Ethics and Professional Responsibility* (Oxford, Clarendon Press, 1995) 53, 62.

[7] *The Work and Organisation of the Legal Profession* (Stationery Office Books, 1989) Cm 570.

[8] Ibid, para 1.1.

[9] General Council of the Bar, *The Quality of Justice: The Bar's Response* (London, Butterworth, 1989) paras 2.3–2.4.

[10] Ibid, para 2.9.

The Extension of Rights of Audience

Under the CLSA new bodies could be approved to grant their members rights of audience. Under section 17 professions seeking the power to award rights of audience were required to demonstrate that they had rules of conduct, 'appropriate in the interests of the proper and efficient administration of justice', effective mechanisms for enforcing them and the propensity to do so.

Under the CLSA the Law Society could grant rights of audience in higher courts to solicitors in private practice from 1993. Since then, legal executives, patent attorneys and costs lawyers have been allowed to regulate the exercise of rights of audience and can grant rights of audience in higher courts for some purposes. As an authorised body under CLSA section 27 and by virtue of the Solicitors' Act (1974) section 2, ILEX had existing rights to appear in chambers in county courts and the High Court.

ILEX became an authorised body for advocacy in civil and family proceedings in open court in county and magistrates' courts in 1998. It can grant rights to appear in magistrates' courts for some purposes and various other tribunals.[11] Patent agent litigators have rights of audience in the Patents County Court and limited rights in the High Court. Institute of Trade Mark attorneys have the right to conduct litigation in the High Court and county courts.

All of the professions, except the Bar, require members to take additional qualifications before they could take up higher rights of audience. Therefore, despite the broadening of powers to grant higher rights, the slow initial uptake by solicitors is attributed to the qualification procedures and also to economic, structural and cultural forces operating on solicitors. Most solicitors' firms were not geared up for advocacy in higher courts.[12] They either did not want it or did not think they could afford it in-house. Despite the opening up of the advocacy market, most solicitors outside of the commercial firms have stuck to their traditional roles.

So that barristers could be more competitive, the Bar Code was changed to allow barristers instructed by professional clients to appear, with the courts' permission, without those clients being present,[13] provided the interests of the lay client and the interests of justice are not prejudiced. They were also allowed to interview witnesses and take proof of evidence in such circumstances.[14]

As a result of the pressure to economise, it became rarer for solicitors to be in court when a barrister was instructed, particularly in legally aided

---

[11]   www.cilex.org.uk/careers/careers_home/graduates/law_graduates/the_legal_sector/rights_of_audience.aspx.

[12] A Boon and J Flood, 'Trials of Strength: The Reconfiguration of Litigation as a Contested Terrain' (1999) 33 *Law and Society Review* 595; M Zander, 'Rights of Audience in the Higher Courts in England and Wales Since the 1990 Act: What Happened?' (1997) 4 *International Journal of the Legal Profession* 167.

[13] Bar Standards Board, *Code of Conduct of the Bar of England and Wales*, 8th edn (London, Bar Standards Board, 2004) para 706.

[14] Ibid, para 707.

work. Later, barristers were allowed to act for members of the public directly in litigation, but only in an advisory capacity. Therefore, their clients had to take all the physical steps in preparing a case. Despite acquiring the right to take clients directly, through licensed and public access, barristers did not undertake litigation as such.[15]

Impact of the Changes

Competition with solicitors for elite advocacy has not ended the Bar as a profession of choice for many young lawyers. There are around 16,500 self-employed barristers available for court work and around 4,000 solicitors who also have higher rights. It is often suggested that solicitors and barristers are now competing for work that young barristers used to do.

The Bar's decision to regulate barrister entities conducting litigation from 2014 suggests a substantial demand among barristers to compete with solicitors by providing 'one-stop shops' for litigation and advocacy services. The traditional model, whereby a client instructs a solicitor, who in turn briefs a barrister as an advocate and consultant is becoming only one of a number of models for delivering advocacy services.

The Legal Services Act 2007

The right to carry out any reserved activity, including litigation and advocacy, is now covered by the Legal Services Act 2007. It depends whether an individual is an authorised person, or exempt, in relation to that activity.[16] Authorisation means being licensed by an approved regulator in relation to that activity.[17]

Legal Services Act 2007

Section 14 Offence to carry on a reserved legal activity if not entitled

(1) It is an offence for a person to carry on an activity ("the relevant activity") which is a reserved legal activity unless that person is entitled to carry on the relevant activity.

(2) In proceedings for an offence under subsection (1), it is a defence for the

---

[15] A Heppinstall, 'Public Access to the Bar Is Good for All'(2005) 155(7192) *New Law Journal* 1360; L Sinclair, 'Licensed Access: Opportunity or Blind Alley?' (2005) 155(7180) *New Law Journal* 895.
[16] Legal Services Act 2007 s 13(2).
[17] Ibid, s 20.

accused to show that the accused did not know, and could not reasonably have been expected to know, that the offence was being committed.

(3) A person who is guilty of an offence under subsection (1) is liable—

> (a) on summary conviction, to imprisonment for a term not exceeding 12 months or a fine not exceeding the statutory maximum (or both), and
> (b) on conviction on indictment, to imprisonment for a term not exceeding 2 years or a fine (or both).

(4) A person who is guilty of an offence under subsection (1) by reason of an act done in the purported exercise of a right of audience, or a right to conduct litigation, in relation to any proceedings or contemplated proceedings is also guilty of contempt of the court concerned and may be punished accordingly.

The Quality of Advocacy

The introduction of greater competition in the market for advocacy services did not end debates about the best way to secure the quality of provision. In 1993, the Royal Commission on Criminal Justice noted that the best barristers were outstanding, many very good but a small number 'incompetent, prolix and poorly prepared'.[18] The government continued its criticism of barristers in its 1998 consultation on rights of audience. It was said that barristers returned up to 75 per cent of CPS instructions at nine crown court centres and that standards of advocacy were poor at the junior bar.[19]

In 2008 the Legal Services Commission, which was responsible for criminal legal aid, initiated work on assuring the competence of advocates working on criminal legal aid. The Quality Assurance Scheme for Advocates (QASA) was taken over by the Law Society, Bar and ILEX in 2009 and resulted in *The QASA Handbook for Criminal Advocates*. This provides that criminal advocates must be accredited at one of four levels in order to conduct criminal advocacy. Level 1 covers magistrates' court and youth court work and the three higher levels cover crown court work. Level 4 covers the most serious offences.

Persons approved by the three regulators can work at Level 1 on qualification[20] but this right expires after five years. Re-accreditation depends on completing appropriate CPD to satisfy Level 1 requirements.[21] Advocates progress to higher levels by acquiring practical experience and undertaking

---

[18] *Royal Commission on Criminal Justice* Cm 2263 (London, TSO, 1993); A Owen, 'Not the Job of a Judge' *The Times*, 6 December 1994, 39.

[19] *Rights of Audience and Rights to Conduct Litigation in England and Wales: The Way Ahead* (Lord Chancellor's Consultation Paper, June 1998) para 2.11.

[20] Bar Standards Board, Solicitors Regulation Authority and ILEX Professional Services, *QASA Handbook for Criminal Advocates* (September 2013) para 2.14.

[21] Ibid, para 2.16.

courses, but must be assessed by a judge in a trial in order to retain their accreditation. Judges can report advocates they consider to be inadequate to their regulator. This may lead to observation and removal of the advocate's accreditation.

In 2013 barristers supported by the Criminal Bar Association sought judicial review of the Legal Services Board (LSB) decision to approve QASA.[22] They argued that the scheme threatened the independence of barristers and judges. The willingness of advocates to press their clients' cases would be undermined by fear of a negative assessment or referral to the regulator. Their claims were dismissed in the High Court, which held that the scheme was a proportionate exercise of regulatory power in order to achieve a legitimate goal: the competence of advocates.[23] The barristers appealed to the Court of Appeal (see chapter two for extracts from the case relating particularly to regulatory issues).

[2014] EWCA Civ 1276

THE QUEEN ON THE APPLICATION OF (1) KATHERINE LUMSDON (2) RUFUS TAYLOR (3) DAVID HOWKER QC (4) CHRISTOPHER HEWERTSON Appellants

- and -

LEGAL SERVICES BOARD Respondent

- and -

(1) GENERAL COUNCIL OF THE BAR (acting by the BAR STANDARDS BOARD) (2) SOLICITORS REGULATION AUTHORITY (3) ILEX PROFESSIONAL STANDARDS (4) LAW SOCIETY OF ENGLAND AND WALES Interested Parties

Lord Dyson, Master of the Rolls

...

The history of QASA

1. This is set out in some detail at paras 16 to 38 of the judgment of the Divisional Court to which reference should be made. What emerges from the history is that (i) there was strong evidence of poor quality advocacy in the criminal courts; and (ii) there was general (but by no means universal) acceptance of the need for some form of quality assurance scheme policed by the judges. From the LSB's perspective, the position is summarised in paras 2 to 33 of the first witness statement of Mr Kenny (its Chief Executive). He says that the key

---

[22] N Rose, 'BSB Presses Ahead with QASA Preparations Despite Judicial Review' [2013] *Legal Futures*, 17 September 2013, www.legalfutures.co.uk/latest-news/bsb-presses-ahead-qasa-preparations-despite-judicial-review.

[23] *Lumsdon, Taylor, Howker and Hewertson v LSB and others* [2013] EWHC 28 (Admin); D Bindman, 'QASA Given Green Light by High Court as JR Fails' [2014] *Legal Futures*, 20 January, www.legalfutures.co.uk/latest-news/qasa-given-green-light-high-court-jr-fails.

points were (i) the potential consequences of poor advocacy in the criminal justice system were extremely serious; (ii) there were significant concerns about poor quality advocacy; (iii) there were reasons to believe that, in the absence of appropriate action, such problems would increase over time; (iv) there was a lack of satisfactory evidence about standards, precisely because there was no scheme such as QASA in place (introducing QASA, with the commitment to a review of its operation after a relatively short period, will allow for any appropriate changes to be made in the light of better evidence); and (v) it was important for there to be a common approach to the regulation of standards in criminal advocacy (different standards for the three professions would undermine public confidence and would be inimical to competition and consumer choice).

...

14. The existence of the principle of the independence of advocates is not in doubt. It is a long-established common law principle and one of the cornerstones of a fair and effective system of justice and the rule of law. If clients are not represented by advocates who are independent of the state, the judge and their opponents, they cannot have a fair trial. The position was stated with great firmness and clarity by Lord Hobhouse in *Medcalf v Mardell* [2002] 3 All ER 721; [2002] UKHL 27, [2003] 1 AC 120 in these terms:

'51 ... It is fundamental to a just and fair judicial system that there be available to a litigant (criminal or civil), in substantial cases, competent and independent legal representation. The duty of the advocate is with proper competence to represent his lay client and promote and protect fearlessly and by all proper and lawful means his lay client's best interests. This is a duty which the advocate owes to his client but it is also in the public interest that the duty should be performed. The judicial system exists to administer justice and it is integral to such a system that it provide within a society a means by which rights, obligations and liabilities can be recognised and given effect to in accordance with the law and disputes be justly (and efficiently) resolved. The role of the independent professional advocate is central to achieving this outcome, particularly where the judicial system uses adversarial procedures.

52. It follows that the willingness of professional advocates to represent litigants should not be undermined either by creating conflicts of interest or by exposing the advocates to pressures which will tend to deter them from representing certain clients or from doing so effectively. In England the professional rule that a barrister must be prepared to represent any client within his field of practice and competence and the principles of professional independence underwrite in a manner too often taken for granted this constitutional safeguard. Unpopular and seemingly unmeritorious litigants must be capable of being represented without the advocate being penalised or harassed whether by the Executive, the Judiciary or by anyone else. Similarly, situations must be avoided where the advocate's conduct of a case is influenced not by his duty to his client but by concerns about his own self-interest.'

15. Ms Rose QC draws particular attention to the statement in para 52 that the willingness of advocates to represent litigants should not be undermined by 'exposing [them] to pressures which will tend to deter them from representing certain clients or from doing so effectively'. In a nutshell, her case is that QASA exposes criminal advocates who know that their performance is being assessed by a judge precisely to such a pressure.

...

30. Ultimately, it is a matter of judgment whether QASA will realistically tend to deter advocates from representing their clients effectively. There have already been formal constraints on the way in which advocates present their cases. 'Independence' does not mean that advocates should be at liberty to promote their clients' interests at all costs. Barristers have professional duties which may sometimes conflict with their clients' interests: see *Hall v Simons* [2000] 3 All ER 673 (HL); [2002] 1 AC 615, 686E per Lord Hoffmann. In our judgment, QASA does not pose a sufficient systemic threat to the independence of the advocate to be unlawful on that account. The fact that there may occasionally be an unfair judge who undermines the independence of a susceptible barrister is not a sufficient reason for holding that the scheme as a whole threatens the independence of the advocate. If it were necessary for us to decide whether QASA undermines the independence of the advocate, we would conclude that it does not do so.

...

112. For the reasons that we have given, we reject all the claimants' challenges to the lawfulness of QASA. It is clear that this is a controversial scheme on which opinions are sharply divided. It is no part of the court's function to express any view about the merits of the scheme. We can only interfere with the Decision if it is unlawful. Those who oppose the scheme can at least take some comfort from the fact that the approved regulators intend to review it after two years. That is an important safeguard. We cannot end this judgment without paying tribute to the quality of the submissions that we have received. We especially wish to express our deep gratitude to Baker & McKenzie and to Ms Rose, Mr de la Mare and their juniors for undertaking this appeal pro bono. This has been no ordinary piece of litigation.

Q10.1 What threat did the appellants claim QASA posed to the independence of advocates?

Q10.2 Did the court decide that QASA posed no threat to the independence of advocates?

Q10.3 Do you think that independence or competence is a more important principle to protect?

Q10.4 Do you think QASA was a proportionate response to a need to secure the competence of advocates?

Criminal Litigation

Lawyers conducting criminal litigation are subject to quite different expectations depending on whether they are prosecuting or defending. Prosecutors are responsible for deciding whether defendants are brought to court and on what charges. They must also decide whether a case continues, for example in light of evidence of the defendant's innocence.[24]

Prosecutors are expected to be even-handed in their presentation of the case and not to seek conviction at all costs. They should ensure that the defence is furnished with any relevant evidence, even if harmful to the prosecution case. The Code of Conduct for Crown Prosecutors provides detailed guidance on how the responsibilities are discharged.

Crown Prosecution Service, *The Code for Crown Prosecutors*
(January 2013)

General Principles

2.1 The decision to prosecute or to recommend an out-of-court disposal is a serious step that affects suspects, victims, witnesses and the public at large and must be undertaken with the utmost care.

2.2 It is the duty of prosecutors to make sure that the right person is prosecuted for the right offence and to bring offenders to justice wherever possible. Casework decisions taken fairly, impartially and with integrity help to secure justice for victims, witnesses, defendants and the public. Prosecutors must ensure that the law is properly applied; that relevant evidence is put before the court; and that obligations of disclosure are complied with.

2.3 Although each case must be considered on its own facts and on its own merits, there are general principles that apply in every case.

2.4 Prosecutors must be fair, independent and objective. They must not let any personal views about the ethnic or national origin, gender, disability, age, religion or belief, political views, sexual orientation, or gender identity of the suspect, victim or any witness influence their decisions. Neither must prosecutors be affected by improper or undue pressure from any source. Prosecutors must always act in the interests of justice and not solely for the purpose of obtaining a conviction.

2.5 The CPS is a public authority for the purposes of current, relevant equality legislation. Prosecutors are bound by the duties set out in this legislation.

---

[24] *Environment Agency v Stanford* [1998] COD 373, DC.

2.6 Prosecutors must apply the principles of the European Convention on Human Rights, in accordance with the Human Rights Act 1998, at each stage of a case. Prosecutors must also comply with any guidelines issued by the Attorney General; with the Criminal Procedure Rules currently in force; and have regard to the obligations arising from international conventions. They must follow the policies and guidance of the CPS issued on behalf of the DPP and available for the public to view on the CPS website at www.cps.gov.uk.

Q10.5 Why do you think prosecutors have been called 'ministers of justice'?

Q10.6 To what extent do you think prosecutors can play a partisan role?

The defence is arguably subject to less rigorous ethical requirements than the prosecution. Its main task is to counsel the defendant on plea and if, necessary, to provide the best available defence and/or mitigation. The defence is therefore allowed to be partisan in a way the prosecution is not. Lawyers for the defence are however required to observe rules governing the litigation and their duty to the court (see below).

Civil Litigation

Context

Civil litigation covers widely diverse fields. Approximately half of civil disputes involve damage to vehicles, divorce, accident or injury, and unpaid debts.[25] The majority involve minor issues and are settled. This section contains an outline of the general operation of the system. Then, rather than consider all of these fields in detail, it examines the evolution of practice in personal injury and family work and reflects on the changing ethos and professional ethics of litigation.

Litigation Framework

The ethics of litigators are shaped by the litigation framework. This is a system, comprising the court rules, the rules of litigation and the ethical rules

---

[25] National Consumer Council and the BBC Law in Action Programme, *Seeking Civil Justice: A Survey of People's Needs and Experiences* (London, National Consumer Council, 1995) 15.

of the professions. The structure is provided by voluminous rules currently called the Civil Procedure Rules 1998 (CPR). These cover everything from the form of documents to timescales for conducting different stages of cases. The rules are default rules; they apply unless the court states otherwise. Failure to follow the rules can result in an adverse decision, such as costs sanctions or the striking out of claims or defences.

The framework for litigation is also shaped by attitudes to litigation. Historically, attitudes in many jurisdictions have changed over time. Hazard notes that, in the United States in the 1930s, hostility to litigation was written into the conduct rules.[26] The ABA Canons of Professional Ethics provided that '[w]henever the controversy will admit of fair adjustment, the client should be advised to avoid or to end the litigation',[27] and that '[i]t is unprofessional for a lawyer to volunteer advice to bring a lawsuit, except in rare cases where ties of blood, relationship or trust make it his duty to do so'.[28] This was apparently an attempt to curtail actions between the wealthy and business classes. The prohibition was only finally abandoned in the 1983 Model Rules of Professional Conduct.

In England, supporting litigation, including financing or providing free legal assistance, was prohibited by a range of ancient criminal offences: maintenance, champerty and barratry. Modern attitudes tend to support access to justice and the right of citizens to litigate. They have also tended to be liberal regarding making the process of civil litigation available. This has resulted in novel funding arrangements, such as contingency fees, to replace legal aid (see chapter five: Conflicts of Interest).

Until the introduction of the CPR the litigation system imposed minimal constraints on handling litigation. The court fulfilled a largely neutral role, adjudicating where the parties could not resolve any issues between them. This left parties free to exploit the advantages that their situation bestowed on them. The strategy adopted tended to reflect the interplay of strategic options provided by the rules and the circumstances of the main players, ie lawyers and clients.

Strategic Constraints and Possibilities

Time and Cost

The key factors potentially determining the outcome of litigation are the merits of the case, time and cost. The interplay of these factors can affect whether or

---

[26] GC Hazard, 'The Future of Legal Ethics' (1991) 100 *Yale Law Journal* 1239 at 1256.

[27] American Bar Association, *Canons of Professional Ethics* (1936) Canon 8, and see Hazard, ibid, 1262.

[28] American Bar Association, *Canons of Professional Ethics* (1936) Canon 28.

not a claimant succeeds. In most cases, however, they help determine the level of damages recovered. Because of the impact of the other factors, the strength of the claimant's case, while important, is often not decisive.

A few simple examples illustrate the potentially limited impact of merit on outcome. First, the outcome of litigation is seldom guaranteed. There is often a risk attached. Second, litigation is expensive and beyond most people's personal finances. Therefore, if no finance is available, many people cannot pursue meritorious claims. Third, litigation can be a long process. If the sums involved are not significant, claimants may consider that claiming is not worth the time and effort involved.

The allocation of costs is an important consideration. In the English system, the loser usually pays the winner for work necessarily performed. Under the old system, the exception to this principle was when the defendant paid a sum into court in settlement of the claim.[29] The claimant could then accept that sum in full settlement, and recover the costs incurred up to that date. A claimant refusing a payment into court was at risk of not recovering costs. The claimant would normally recover their costs only if the damages awarded exceeded the sum paid in.

Parties

The profiles of parties to litigation can be broken down into typical types with different characteristics. Perhaps the most significant general distinction is between repeat players in litigation and those with no previous experience. As a group, repeat players are likely to include most corporations and public bodies, but can include wealthy individuals. 'One-shotters' are typically individuals with 'personal plight'-type claims, family or personal injury cases, who do not use lawyers on a regular basis.

Repeat players have advantages in the litigation process.[30] No one person in the organisation stands to gain or lose financially, so the personal risk to individuals is small. When litigants are individuals, particularly those funding litigation themselves, they are more likely to be risk averse and concerned about cost.[31] In most situations, organisations are content to let litigation run its course. Individuals want it to end. These attitudes to risk help to translate into a number of advantages for repeat players in the litigation process.

First, because of their past experience of litigation repeat players will know what is likely to happen. Indeed, they may have structured the relationship

[29] Civil Procedure Rules, Part 39.
[30] M Galanter 'Why the "Haves" Come Out Ahead: Speculations on the Limits of Legal Change' (1974) 9 *Law & Society Review* 95, 99; JP Heinz and EO Laumann. 'The Legal Profession: Client Interests, Professional Roles, and Social Hierarchies' (1978) 76 *Michigan Law Review* 1111.
[31] M Galanter, 'Law Abounding: Legalisation Around the North Atlantic' (1992) 55(1) *Modern Law Review* 1, 20.

with the other party from the beginning, for example by proposing the form of contract. Second, they are also geared up for the litigation process, with well-established procedures in place. Third, repeat players are more likely to have informal relationships that may be useful in litigation, such as tried and trusted experts they can resort to. Fourth, they will have advantages in negotiation (see chapter eleven: Settlement).

Repeat players can afford to take a long-term approach to litigation. Therefore, their fifth advantage is that they need not view each case as a one off. They can pick and choose which cases to settle or fight. Sixth, they can formulate a strategy for all potential cases. They can, for example, spend lavishly on a case that will set a helpful precedent, saving more money in the long term. Conversely, they can pay over the odds to settle a case that will create a damaging precedent. Repeat players are more likely to know which principles are worth defending. Finally, the individual concerned with litigation for a repeat player is unlikely to be personally concerned about the cost of legal proceedings.

'One-shotters' usually have none of the litigation advantages enjoyed by repeat players. The only ground on which there is an equal balance potentially relates to costs. If a one-shotter has legal aid, or a no-win, no-fee arrangement with their lawyers, they may be relatively immune to pressure caused by the financial risk of proceedings. The balance of advantage swings round when defendants are unlikely to recover costs against claimants.

Lawyers

The lawyers acting for repeat players may enjoy advantages in litigation. They tend to have ample human and other resources. In large commercial cases they can provide disclosure of a massive volume of documents, because they have staff who can read and list papers that may or may not be relevant. They can also cope if the other side give disclosure of a large volume of paperwork.

The lawyers of repeat players know their client and the client's business. They may have fought similar claims before. Corporations, for example, usually employ in-house lawyers who will manage a claim internally, gather evidence and choose external lawyers if necessary.

The lawyers available to one-shotters are also likely to be at a competitive disadvantage against the lawyers of repeat players. They are more likely to be handling a high volume of claims without high-quality support. They probably have to work harder to understand each client and their motivations and to build a trusting relationship with them.

Litigation Strategy

Before considering the operation of litigation in practice, it is necessary to consider two strategic and tactical options that litigation systems allow to some degree. The first option is to be aggressive, adopting a 'litigation-first' strategy. This involves pressing forward with each stage of litigation as quickly as possible, creating a momentum towards trial or favourable settlement.

The second option is to try and co-operate with defendants in what are judged to be appropriate cases. This strategy is based on past dealings with institutional or professional opponents. This approach can be described as conditional co-operation. Lawyers committed to a strategy of conditional co-operation only use a ligation-first strategy if the opposing lawyer has previously demonstrated bad faith.

The Civil Procedure Rules and the Overriding Objective

In the run up to establishing the CPR lawyers were criticised for running litigation in their own interests rather than in the interests of clients.[32] The litigation-first strategy was one example of how lawyer self-interest could be presented as highly competent and ethical practice. The CPR 1998 were based on different assumptions. The rules embodied the idea that litigation should be conducted in a co-operative spirit with the overriding objective of dealing with cases justly. What this involved was defined more closely in CPR Part 1.

Civil Procedure Rules 1998

Part 1—Overriding Objective

1.1 The Overriding Objective

(1) These Rules are a new procedural code with the overriding objective of enabling the court to deal with cases justly and at proportionate cost.

(2) Dealing with a case justly and at proportionate cost includes, so far as is practicable—

    (a) ensuring that the parties are on an equal footing;
    (b) saving expense;
    (c) dealing with the case in ways which are proportionate—
        (i)   to the amount of money involved;
        (ii) to the importance of the case;
        (iii) to the complexity of the issues; and

---

[32] See generally, AAS Zuckerman and R Cranston (eds), *Reform of Civil Procedure: Essays on Access to Justice* (Oxford, Clarendon Press, 1995) and particularly Zuckerman, 'Reform in the Shadow of Lawyers' Interests', 75.

(iv) to the financial position of each party;

(d) ensuring that it is dealt with expeditiously and fairly;

(e) allotting to it an appropriate share of the court's resources, while taking into account the need to allot resources to other cases; and

(f) enforcing compliance with rules, practice directions and orders.

...

1.3 Duty of the parties

The parties are required to help the court to further the overriding objective.

1.4 Court's duty to manage cases

(1) The court must further the overriding objective by actively managing cases.

(2) Active case management includes –

(a) encouraging the parties to co-operate with each other in the conduct of the proceedings;

(b) identifying the issues at an early stage;

(c) deciding promptly which issues need full investigation and trial and accordingly disposing summarily of the others;

(d) deciding the order in which issues are to be resolved;

(e) encouraging the parties to use an alternative dispute resolution(GL) procedure if the court considers that appropriate and facilitating the use of such procedure;

(f) helping the parties to settle the whole or part of the case;

(g) fixing timetables or otherwise controlling the progress of the case;

(h) considering whether the likely benefits of taking a particular step justify the cost of taking it;

(i) dealing with as many aspects of the case as it can on the same occasion;

(j) dealing with the case without the parties needing to attend at court;

(k) making use of technology; and

(l) giving directions to ensure that the trial of a case proceeds quickly and efficiently.

Q10.7 In what ways did the CPR seek to make civil litigation more fair?

Q10.8 In what ways did the CPR seek to make parties more co-operative?

Q10.9 How did the CPR seek to reduce lawyers' control of litigation?

While the CPR clearly signalled a desire for a new civil litigation ethos the rules also contained sanctions aimed at achieving this end. The CPR codified the inherent jurisdiction of the court to control litigation by making wasted costs orders. In the leading case, *Ridehalgh v Horsefield and another*, the Court of Appeal held that wasted costs could be awarded against both advocates and litigators. The court proposed a three-stage test and other practical guidance that subsequently became the basis of a Practice Direction in the CPR 46.8.[33] Although the wasted costs jurisdiction preceded the CPR, its inclusion probably signalled the intention that such orders become a more commonplace way of controlling the conduct of litigation.

Civil Procedure Rules—Part 46

PRACTICE DIRECTION 46—COSTS SPECIAL CASES

Personal liability of legal representative for costs—wasted costs orders: rule 46.8

5.1 A wasted costs order is an order—

(a) that the legal representative pay a sum (either specified or to be assessed) in respect of costs to a party; or
(b) for costs relating to a specified sum or items of work to be disallowed.

5.2 Rule 46.8 deals with wasted costs orders against legal representatives. Such orders can be made at any stage in the proceedings up to and including the detailed assessment proceedings. In general, applications for wasted costs are best left until after the end of the trial.

5.3 The court may make a wasted costs order against a legal representative on its own initiative.

5.4 A party may apply for a wasted costs order—

(a) by filing an application notice in accordance with Part 23; or
(b) by making an application orally in the course of any hearing.

5.5 It is appropriate for the court to make a wasted costs order against a legal representative, only if—

(a) the legal representative has acted improperly, unreasonably or negligently;
(b) the legal representative's conduct has caused a party to incur unnecessary costs, or has meant that costs incurred by a party prior to the improper, unreasonable or negligent act or omission have been wasted;
(c) it is just in all the circumstances to order the legal representative to compensate that party for the whole or part of those costs.

5.6 The court will give directions about the procedure to be followed in each case in order to ensure that the issues are dealt with in a way which is fair and as simple and summary as the circumstances permit.

5.7 As a general rule the court will consider whether to make a wasted costs order in two stages—

(a) at the first stage the court must be satisfied—

---

[33] CPR Practice Direction 46—Costs Special Cases: Personal liability of legal representative for costs—wasted costs orders: rule 46.8, Practice Direction 46: Costs Special Cases, para 5.5.

> (i) that it has before it evidence or other material which, if unanswered, would be likely to lead to a wasted costs order being made; and
> (ii) the wasted costs proceedings are justified notwithstanding the likely costs involved;
> (b) at the second stage, the court will consider, after giving the legal representative an opportunity to make representations in writing or at a hearing, whether it is appropriate to make a wasted costs order in accordance with paragraph 5.5 above.
>
> 5.8 The court may proceed to the second stage described in paragraph 5.7 without first adjourning the hearing if it is satisfied that the legal representative has already had a reasonable opportunity to make representations.
>
> 5.9 On an application for a wasted costs order under Part 23 the application notice and any evidence in support must identify—
>
> (a) what the legal representative is alleged to have done or failed to do; and
> (b) the costs that the legal representative may be ordered to pay or which are sought against the legal representative.

Q10.10 What is a wasted costs order?

Q10.11 When does an application for wasted costs take place?

Q10.12 On what grounds may a wasted costs order be made?

Q10.13 Could a lawyer against whom a wasted costs order has been made also be disciplined by his regulator?

Most lawyers welcomed the CPR.[34] This may be because it legitimised co-operation in an adversarial setting. Co-operation is arguably a more natural and honest foundation for behaviour, except when it comes to the presentation of the case.[35] In fact, the litigation strategy most consistent with the new CPR appears to be conditional co-operation. With the introduction of the CPR, lawyers could be more subtle in their choice of litigation strategy, choosing methods and strategies that best suit their client's situation and wishes.

While revision and harmonisation of the rules of civil litigation was welcome, the reforms did not avoid criticism. These included the fact that judges sometimes became too enthusiastically involved in cases. This controversially involved imposing costs penalties on those who did not respond to judicial suggestions that the parties mediate (see chapter eleven: Settlement). The introduction of the CPR also led to a marked fall in the volume of litigation.

[34] A MORI poll published in April 2000 showed that 80% of solicitors were happy with the CPR.

[35] M Ridley, *The Origins of Virtue* (Harmondsworth, Penguin, 1997) ch 3.

This was not necessarily a positive sign in a society committed to the personal autonomy of the individual and the vindication of rights.

Practice in Civil Litigation

Context

Different litigation fields may be characterised by expectations of different levels of co-operation. We can describe this as the 'ethos of the practice field'. In this context ethos refers to disposition, character or fundamental values peculiar to the culture of practitioners in that field.[36] The differences between fields of practice can be illustrated by looking at two areas, namely personal injury and family law. Prior to the Woolf reforms, personal injury lawyers were criticised for not being adversarial enough, while family lawyers where criticised for being too adversarial. It is arguable that these criticisms were addressed by lawyers working in these fields.

The impact of the introduction of the CPR on the ethos of civil litigation can be explored through closer examination of these two key practice environments. Both show a move towards more co-operative ethos in adversarial fields. This may be a reaction to the Woolf reforms, but in the case of family law, it is also due to lawyers seeking a less combative approach to problems through mechanisms such as mediation. The particular focus of this chapter is personal injury, while family law will feature more in the next.

Personal Injury

The Pre-CPR Ethos of Personal Injury Litigation

i. Litigation Strategy and Outcomes

Large numbers of personal injury victims, many involved in car accidents, support numerous specialist personal injury firms and provide work for general practices. Academic analysis of personal injury victims in both the US and UK recognised them as typical, infrequent users of lawyers, or 'one-shotters'. Rosenthal's study of personal injury victims in the US found that they generally had little control over their lawyers.[37] The lawyers therefore worked cases

---

[36] www.thefreedictionary.com/ethos.
[37] DE Rosenthal, *Lawyer and Client: Who's in Charge* (New York, Russell Sage, 1974).

as they pleased and probably under-settled claims. Similar claims were made about solicitors in England and Wales.[38]

Over the years, committees and royal commissions have expressed concerns about inexpert lawyers' incompetent handling of personal injury litigation.[39] The main issue was seen as delay and the possibility that claims were settled for less than they were worth. General practice solicitors were criticised for 'dabbling' in personal injury work, for being duped by defendant's delaying tactics, not preparing cases properly in expectation of settlement and settling for less than cases were worth. Delay sapped the morale of claimants, causing them to accept low sums.[40]

Genn's study of personal injury solicitors working in the pre-CPR litigation system supported the litigation-first lawyers.[41] In contrast to the failings of general practitioners, expert personal injury lawyers used aggressive litigation-first tactics. They tried to get cases to court to reduce the pressure of delay on the claimant and increase the pressure of costs on the defendant. This increased the defendant's incentive to negotiate and avoid escalation of costs. Therefore, lawyers who did not routinely issue proceedings and press on with the case undermined their ability to do the best for their clients.

The view that expert lawyers used 'litigation-first' strategies to combat defendants' delaying strategies became conventional.[42] As is often the case, later research called into question the conventional wisdom. It found that the institutional players in personal injury litigation, expert lawyers and insurance companies, did not fit the stereotype created for them by Rosenthal, Genn and others. Insurance companies did not necessarily delay settlement of claims[43] and even expert plaintiff lawyers offered 'reasonable opposition', rather than fierce competition.[44]

In practice expert litigators often varied their approach according to the

---

[38] TM Swanson, 'A Review of the Civil Justice Review: Economic Theories Behind the Delay in Tort Litigation' (1990) *Current Legal Problems* 185, 202–04; DR Harris, M Maclean, H Genn, S Lloyd-Bostock, P Fenn, P Corfield and Y Brittan, *Compensation and Support for Illness and Injury* (Oxford, Clarendon Press, 1984) 124.

[39] *The Report of the Committee on Personal Injuries Litigation* (Cmnd 3691, 1968); *Report of the Personal Injuries Litigation Procedure Working Party* (The Cantley Report, Cmnd 7476, 1979); *Report of the Royal Commission on Civil Liability and Compensation for Personal Injury* (The Pearson Report, Cmnd 7054, 1978); *Report of the Review Body on Civil Justice* (Cmnd 394, 1988).

[40] J Phillips and K Hawkins, 'Some Economic Aspects of the Bargaining Process: A Study of Personal Injury Claims' (1976) 39 *Modern Law Review* 497; M Joseph, *Lawyers Can Seriously Damage Your Health* (London, Michael Joseph, 1985).

[41] H Genn, *Hard Bargaining: Out of Court Settlement in Personal Injury Actions* (Oxford, Clarendon Press, 1987) 166.

[42] TM Swanson, 'A Review of the Civil Justice Review: Economic Theories Behind the Delay in Tort Litigation' (1990) *Current Legal Problems* 185, 198, 200; R James, 'Delay and Abuse of Process' (1997) 16 *Civil Justice Quarterly* 289.

[43] Lord Chancellor's Department, *Civil Justice Review: Personal Injury Litigation* (London, Lord Chancellor's Department, 1986) para 67.

[44] R Dingwall, T Durkin and WLF Felstiner, 'Delay in Tort Cases: Critical Reflections on the Civil Justice Review' (1990) 9 *Civil Justice Quarterly* 353, 363.

type of claim they were handling.[45] They usually aimed to settle small-value claims, often without even issuing proceedings. Because large claims were likely to settle later or go to trial, these cases were usually taken forward as far and as quickly as possible. Expert personal injury litigators therefore used strategies that depended on the value and difficulty of the claim.

Claimants' solicitors might also employ a 'tit-for-tat' strategy. Where a particular insurance company had been unreasonable in the past, for example, a claimant's solicitor might issue proceedings as early as possible and avoid negotiations. This both 'punished' insurers and provided extra leverage in negotiations. These experts were able to give and receive the benefits of 'professional courtesy' from those defendants' representatives they dealt with regularly.

ii. The Personal Injury Panel

The Law Society established a specialist Personal Injury Panel in the early 1990s. Delay, incompetent claims handling and the risk that inexperienced solicitors would be exploited by experienced opponents were all cited as reasons why it was needed. It was also noted that personal injury cases accounted for 10 per cent of the total paid out under the solicitors' indemnity fund in 1991.[46] Therefore, it is not surprising that the personal injury panel took solicitors using litigation-first strategies as models of how personal injury litigation should be conducted.

The Personal Injury Panel officially endorsed members' expertise and excluded non-members from access to clients referred by the Law Society's 'Accident Line' service. Applicants were required to be committed to 'the expeditious pursuit of proceedings and the readiness to go to trial if need be'.[47] Guidance notes asserted that it was 'essential that personal injury specialists approach the majority of their personal injury cases on the basis that the case will reach trial and not be settled'.[48]

Applicants to the Personal Injury Panel had to have 'actively supervised at least sixty personal injury instructions in the five years prior to the application or at least thirty six personal injury instructions in the three years prior to application'.[49] It is plausible that there was a measure of self-interest in this endorsement of litigation-first since it inevitably increased costs.[50]

---

[45] A Boon, 'Cooperation and Competition in Negotiation: The Handling of Civil Disputes and Transactions' (1994) 1(1) *International Journal of the Legal Profession* 109; A Boon, 'Ethics and Strategy in Personal Injury Litigation' (1995) 22(3) *Journal of Law and Society* 353.

[46] E Gilvarry, 'Council Backs PI Panel' (1992) 27 *Law Society Gazette*, 15 July, 4.

[47] D Skidmore, *Drawing the Line: A Report on the Law Society's Personal Injury Panel* (1993).

[48] The Law Society, *The Personal Injury Panel—Notes for Guidance* (London, Law Society, undated).

[49] *Rules and Procedures for the Law Society's Personal Injury Panel* (undated).

[50] See generally P Cane, *Atiyah's Accidents Compensation and the Law* (London, Butterworths, 1993); H Genn, *Paths to Justice: What People Do and Think About Going to Law* (Oxford, Hart Publishing, 1999) 83–96.

Personal Injury Litigation since the Introduction of the CPR

Personal injury work was affected by a number of specific changes introduced under the CPR and since. Perhaps the most significant change to practice came through the introduction of pre-action protocols. These required claimants to obtain and disclose a large part of the evidence in the case before issuing proceedings. This involved a massive front-loading of cost before an action could be begun. This arguably assisted insurance companies using a strategy of delay.

There were various adjustments to procedures to make settlement easier. In 2010 the government introduced an online portal for handling road traffic claims worth between £1,000 and £10,000. Claims submitted to the portal progressed to a settlement stage if an insurer admitted liability within 15 days and, should this fail, to a court hearing, and a paper-based assessment of damages. Claims dropped out of the process if the insurer did not respond in 15 days or denied liability.

The portal system was expected to handle 70 per cent of relevant claims. In the first six months of operation, a third of claims dropped out of the system at the first stage and, overall, a third failed to settle. For lawyers, however, there were two significant features of the scheme. First, personal injury victims could use the online application adequately without legal assistance. Second, only fixed costs were payable, whatever work was involved.

From the end of July 2013, the automated portal system for road traffic claims was extended. A Pre-Action Protocol for Low Value Personal Injury (Employers' Liability and Public Liability) Claims was introduced to deal with appropriate employers' and public liability claims worth between £1,000 and £25,000.[51] The threshold for claims to the existing motor claims portal was increased to £25,000. Despite the revolutionary nature of the portal, the most significant changes occurred in litigation funding. Before 2013, conditional or no win, no fee agreements imposed the risk of litigation failure on claimants' lawyers.[52] This discouraged lawyers from taking high-risk cases but provided an additional incentive to win at all costs. Deducting success fees from client damages was a disincentive to incur cost. Allowing recovery of success fees and insurance premiums from defendants restored some bargaining leverage to claimants' lawyers.

Many of the reforms of civil justice proposed by Lord Justice Jackson, introduced by the Legal Aid, Sentencing and Punishment of Offenders Act 2012 (LASPO), affected personal injury litigation. The ability to recover success fees and After the Event Insurance premiums from defendants in personal

---

[51] QBE, *Ministry of Justice Extension to the Claims Protocols—Maximising Opportunities* (London, QBE, 2013), www.qbeeurope.com/documents/casualty/risk/technical%20claims/QBE%20MOJ%20Claims%20Portal%20Extension%20June%202013.pdf

[52] Courts and Legal Services Act 1990 as amended by the Access to Justice Act 1999 s 27.

injury cases was removed. The Qualified One-way Costs Shifting (QOCS) regime introduced from 2013 mitigates the impact of this change.

Under QOCS, defendants will generally be ordered to pay the costs of successful claimants but, subject to certain exceptions, defendants cannot recover their own costs even if successful.[53] Claimants can only benefit from the protection of QOCS if they have behaved honestly.

Orders for costs against claimants can be fully enforced, without the permission of the court, where proceedings are struck out. This may be because they disclose no reasonable grounds, or are an abuse of the court's process, or because the conduct of the claimant, or someone acting on the claimant's behalf and with the claimant's knowledge, obstructs the just disposal of the proceedings.[54]

Costs orders can also be enforced against unsuccessful personal injury claimants in limited circumstances, with the permission of the court. These include where the claim is found on the balance of probabilities to be fundamentally dishonest or where the claim is wholly or in part for the benefit of a third party.[55] Since 2007 settlement was made easier by abolishing the requirement for payment into court. Claimants can now be penalised in costs simply for refusing a written offer to settle.[56]

Arguably, the QOCS regime again shifts the balance of power in personal injury litigation towards the claimant. This is because the defendant is generally at greater risk in terms of costs than the claimant and therefore has greater incentive to settle. Lawyers must, however, be aware of two major ethical issues. The first is advising their clients on which funding mechanism is most appropriate given the client's financial situation and the likely outcome of the claim. The second is being alive to the possibility that the protection of QOCS may be lost by improper conduct.

The Post-CPR Ethos of Personal Injury Practitioners

It is assumed that the changes to the procedures and rules of litigation affected the ethos of lawyers conducting the work. This may be reflected in the aspirations of the Law Society's panels. The Law Society's Personal Injury Accreditation Scheme[57] is open to solicitors and FILEX members able to demonstrate appropriate levels of experience and expertise. The experience is based on cases completed in the previous three years.

The expertise required of applicants to the Personal Injury Panel includes 'awareness of the ethical issues and problems arising in this area of work, for

---

[53] Civil Procedure Rules r 44.14(1).
[54] Ibid, r 44.15(1).
[55] Ibid, r 44.16(1).
[56] Ibid, Part 36.
[57] The Law Society, *Personal Injury Accreditation Scheme* (April 2013).

example in relation to the use of expert witnesses; signature of statements of truth; disclosure of medical records and reports and conflicts of interest'.[58]

Under the scheme criteria, only applicants dealing with defendant work are asked to demonstrate experience of 'pursuing cases expeditiously and demonstrating a readiness to take the case to a speedy trial'.[59] Therefore, it appears that the most serious historic criticisms of both claimant and defendant litigation lawyers have been quietly addressed. Defendant lawyers are encouraged not to use what was formerly their prime strategic option, delay. The requirement that claimant lawyers proceed expeditiously to trial has, however, been dropped.

Summary and Overview

The procedural changes introduced with the CPR 1998 made the use of aggressive litigation tactics in personal injury cases more difficult. The completion of pre-action protocols, judicial case management, mediation and cost sanctions were potential impediments to litigation-first strategies. The structure of the litigation system and the incentives it provides drive personal injury claimants, and their lawyers, towards co-operation in the conduct of proceedings.

Controlling Litigation Behaviour

Forum Controls

The courts control the behaviour in a number of ways including wasted cost orders. Ipp suggests that the English and Australian cases fall into four categories that tend to cause the court to act.[60] These are conducting cases expeditiously, duties of disclosure, avoiding abuse of process and avoiding corrupting the administration of justice. Duties of disclosure include the advocate's duty to the court.

Conducting Cases Expeditiously

As noted in chapter one, the efficient conduct of litigation, and particularly advocacy, has long been a goal of the legal system. It is an obligation occa-

---

[58] Ibid, 6.
[59] Ibid, 3.
[60] D Ipp, 'Lawyers' Duties to the Court' (1998) 114 *Law Quarterly Review* 63.

sionally enforced by the courts.[61] The description of the overriding objective in the CPR (see above, this chapter) makes that goal explicit. The case management power of judges can be used to achieve the efficient conduct of litigation. The possibility of incurring costs sanctions provides the incentive for lawyers to comply.

CPR Part 3—The Court's Case Management Powers

Relief from sanctions

3.9

(1) On an application for relief from any sanction imposed for a failure to comply with any rule, practice direction or court order, the court will consider all the circumstances of the case, so as to enable it to deal justly with the application, including the need –

    (a) for litigation to be conducted efficiently and at proportionate cost; and

    (b) to enforce compliance with rules, practice directions and orders.

(2) An application for relief must be supported by evidence.

Q10.14 What in this context does 'relief from any sanction' mean?

CPR r.3.13 requires parties to file budgets estimating the cost of litigation, and r.3.14 provides that lawyers failing to do so will be treated as having 'having filed a budget comprising only the applicable court fees'.

Avoiding Abuse of Process

i. Criminal Litigation

An abuse of process arises when something is so unfair and wrong with the prosecution that the court should not allow it to continue.[62] This means that it would (a) be impossible to give the accused a fair trial or (b) involve a misuse or manipulation of process offending justice and propriety to try the accused in the circumstances.[63]

An abuse of process must be plain before the principle that it is for the prosecutor, not the court, to decide whether to begin or continue a prosecution is ignored.[64] This is because a fair trial involves considerations of fairness to

---

[61] *Brennan v Brighton BC, The Times* 24 July 1996.
[62] *Hui Chi-Ming v R* [1992] 1 AC 34, PC.
[63] *Bennett v Horseferry Road Magistrates' Court and Another* [1993] 3 All ER 138, 151, HL.
[64] *Wandsworth London Borough Council v Rashid* [2009] EWHC1844 (Admin).

prosecution and public as well to defendants.[65] Courts must therefore consider whether measures such as excluding evidence or directions to the jury might allow prosecutions to continue.[66]

The inherent jurisdiction to stop a prosecution for abuse of process does not involve disciplining prosecutors. Indeed, courts should not stay proceedings as a means of showing disapproval of the prosecuting authorities.[67] The courts are encouraged not to rely excessively on precedent when considering whether there has been an abuse of process.[68] Material on the CPS website,[69] on which this section is based, suggests that there are broad categories into which most cases fall.

There are six categories of abuse of process for which a case might be halted. These are where a fair trial is impossible because of delay, where there has been non-disclosure of relevant material by the prosecutor, where the defence does not have an opportunity to examine the evidence, where vital evidence cannot be called, where the defence cannot cross-examine a prosecution witness and where there has been adverse media publicity.

DPP v Meakin **[2006] EWHC 1067**

The DPP appealed against a decision by magistrates to stay proceedings against the respondent upon a charge of drink driving on the ground of abuse of process (the prosecution had failed to disclose the name of an informer that they did not rely on as a witness). The Queen's Bench Division of the High Court held, allowing the appeal, that a stay should not be imposed unless a defendant showed that he would suffer such prejudice that a fair trial was not possible. In the instant case, at the very most the prosecution had erred in failing to disclose the name of the witness; but that was at least matched by the defence failure to ask for those particulars. The concept of a fair trial involved fairness to the prosecution and to the public, as well as fairness to the defendant. There was a clear public interest in bringing drunk drivers to justice. There would have been no unfairness whatsoever to the defence in allowing the trial to proceed, but there had been a considerable unfairness to the public and to the prosecution in staying the proceedings.

---

[65] *DPP v Meakin* [2006] EWHC 1067.

[66] *R (Ebrahim) v Feltham Magistrates' Court* [2001] EWHC Admin 103; [2001] 1 WLR 1293; *Mouat v DPP* [2001] 2 Cr App R 23; *DPP v Hussain* (1994) 158 JP 602.

[67] *R v Crown Court at Norwich ex parte Belsham* (1992) 94 Cr App R 382, QBD per Watkins LJ, 395.

[68] *R v Sheffield Stipendiary Magistrate ex parte Stephens* (1992) 156 JP 555; *R v Newham Justices ex parte C* [1993] Crim LR 130.

[69] CPS, *Abuse of Process*, www.cps.gov.uk/legal/a_to_c/abuse_of_process/#general.

Q10.15 Did the Queen's Bench Division decide the prosecution was right not to disclose the name of the infomer?

R v Rotherham Justices ex parte Brough [1991] COD 89

The CPS had deliberately taken steps to ensure that a defendant who was charged with an offence that would be triable only on indictment in the case of an adult did not appear before the court until he had reached the age where the justices ceased to have a discretion whether or not to deal with him themselves. Although the court viewed the procedure as incorrect, it was held not to amount to an abuse of process because, on the facts, the conduct of the prosecution showed, at most, a lack of judgment rather than misconduct or *mala fides*. Furthermore, there was no prejudice to the defendant because the delay involved had been minimal, the justices would probably have committed the case to the Crown Court anyway, and in the event of conviction the judge would undoubtedly take account of the defendant's age at the time of the offence and the circumstances of his committal.

Q10.16 Was the prosecutor right to delay the case until the defendant could be tried as an adult?

---

ii. Civil litigation

Abuse of process in civil litigation is likely to arise in different circumstances than in criminal litigation. The court's powers are contained in CPR 3.4(2).

Power to Strike Out a Statement of Case

3.4

(1) In this rule and rule 3.5, reference to a statement of case includes reference to part of a statement of case.

(2) The court may strike out a statement of case if it appears to the court –

    (a) that the statement of case discloses no reasonable grounds for bringing or defending the claim;

    (b) that the statement of case is an abuse of the court's process or is otherwise likely to obstruct the just disposal of the proceedings; or

(c) that there has been a failure to comply with a rule, practice direction or
court order.

(3) When the court strikes out a statement of case it may make any consequential
order it considers appropriate.

As in criminal matters there are no hard and fast categories of abuse of process
in civil proceedings. Each case must be argued on its own facts. One of the
examples of potential abuse is where proceedings are brought in relation to
matters that have already been litigated and settled or decided. In such cases
the court must balance the claimant's right to access to justice against the
defendant's legitimate right to achieve finality in proceedings.

A recent case in which these issues were explored was *Walbrook Trustees
(Jersey) Ltd & Others v Fattal & Others*.[70] In a dispute over the management
of a family trust there were various proceedings, following which there was
agreed discovery. As a result of information discovered through this process
new proceedings were issued. An application was made to strike out the subsequent proceedings on the grounds that the claim could have been made
previously.[71] The Court of Appeal reversed the decision of the High Court to
strike out the claim.

The Court of Appeal considered various factors in the appellants' favour.
These included the fact that the information on which the new claim was
based was not easily discoverable when the earlier claim was brought. Another
relevant consideration was the fact that the information disclosed could be
material to the outcome. Also in the appellants' favour was the fact that they
had brought their new claim immediately on discovering the information.
Finally, there was evidence that a witness for the respondents in the court
below had concealed the information when giving evidence. All of these considerations led the court to conclude that there would be no abuse of process
if the case proceeded.

Duties of Disclosure

i. Duty to the Court

The advocate's obligation to act in the best interests of clients is constrained
by a duty to the court. This is established in a number of cases, which duly
inform the legal professions' rules of conduct. From these rules it seems that

---

[70] *Walbrook Trustees (Jersey) Ltd & Others v Fattal & Others* [2009] EWCA Civ 297.

[71] For a fuller summary of the facts, see M Ahmed, 'Strike Out for Abuse of Process: Guidance
for Making and Resisting Applications' [2009] *Law Society Gazette*, 15 October.

the duty has two branches: avoiding misleading the court regarding procedural and legal errors, and avoiding misleading the court in presentation of evidence.

The first branch of the duty to the court is illustrated by the obligation to point out errors in law or procedure that may mean that the judge produces a decision that upholds the integrity of the legal decision. For example, if one side misses an authority in its favour, the opposing advocate has a duty to draw this to the attention of the judge. The same principle applies to a procedural error which neither the other side nor the judge is aware of.[72]

The second branch of the duty to the court is directed to ensuring that decisions are based on the correct facts. The specific obligation, though, is not to allow the court to be misled. This is therefore a more difficult area. It is problematic because the presentation of a legal case is based on a client's instructions. Those instructions may be based on an account of events that seems to be totally implausible to the advocate. However, so long as the advocate does not know the account to be false, they are probably obliged to present the case as instructed. Observing the duty to the court can be complicated by the obligation of confidentiality and the client's right to invoke privilege concerning communications.

In circumstances where a court discovers it has been misled after the decision has been handed down, there may have been a miscarriage of justice. A reason for setting aside the decision could lie in the proven perjury of a witness. The offence of perjury occurs when 'any person lawfully sworn as a witness or as an interpreter in a judicial proceeding wilfully makes a statement material in that proceeding, which he knows to be false or does not believe to be true'.[73] Sometimes, however, a witness may give misleading evidence that falls short of perjury. This may be achieved by the advocate's skilful arrangement of the presentation of evidence so that no lies are required.

What the advocate must not do is knowingly allow the presentation of misleading evidence. For the court to be misled the evidence must be material to the outcome of the case. In *Meek v Fleming*[74] a senior police officer defending a civil claim for assault was allowed to present his evidence in a way that hid his demotion for giving false police evidence in another case. This was deemed to be material to his credibility, meaning whether he is believed as a witness. The Court of Appeal overturned a decision in the police officer's favour on the ground that it was a miscarriage of justice.

A case with similar facts but with a different outcome was *Tombling v Universal Bulb Company Limited*.[75] The witness in that case was a former prison governor who, at the time of trial, was in prison for a driving offence. His barrister had conducted examination in chief so as to conceal this fact. No

---

[72] *Haiselden v P&O Properties* [1998] All ER (D) 180, [1998] EWCA Civ 773.
[73] Perjury Act 1911 s 1.
[74] *Meek v Fleming* [1961] 2 QB 366.
[75] *Tombling v Universal Bulb Company Limited* [1951] 2 The Times Law Reports 289.

new trial was ordered because the misleading testimony was not, in the judgment of the Court of Appeal, material. Therefore, it was not satisfied that, had the court been aware of the true position, it would have affected the outcome of the trial.

Basing these decisions on the advocate's duty not to mislead the court is a convenient way of obscuring the fact that courts are usually deciding between 'versions of the truth'. This protects the convention that advocates are bound to present their client's case, even if they suspect it is untrue. Advocates or litigators may be subject to discipline where they allow the court to be misled (see *Brett v SRA*, below, this chapter). The impact of these cases survived the introduction of the CPR, insofar as the application of the principles furthered the overriding objective of doing justice.[76]

ii. A Duty to the Administration of Justice

A duty to the court to act with independence in the interests of justice, and a duty to comply with rules of conduct of the body relating to the right, was first imposed by an amendment to the Courts and Legal Services Act 1990 in 1999. The section was replaced by the Legal Services Act 2007 (LSA) section 188, which specified that both advocates and litigators had 'a duty to the court in question to act with independence in the interests of justice' and to observe the conduct rules of their authorising body.

The LSA does not mention a duty to the administration of justice in the regulatory objectives or the professional principles. It is likely that any such duty is an overarching idea unifying the categories set out above. Alternatively it is a category intended to catch cases not falling within principles and rules underpinning other categories of forum control.

Conduct Controls

Although the overriding objectives of the LSA do not mention a duty to the administration of justice, section 1(3)(d) states a professional principle that authorised persons exercising a right of audience or conducting litigation should comply with their duty to the court to act with independence in the interests of justice. Section 188 also provides that advocates and litigators have 'a duty to the court in question to act with independence in the interests of justice' and to observe the conduct rules of their authorising body. This may be seen as similar to a duty to the administration of justice.

Although both professional bodies mention the administration of justice in their high-level duties, they appear to have interpreted it in different ways. The first principle of the SRA Handbook is to 'uphold the rule of law and

---

[76] *Hamilton v Al-Fayed (No 4)* [2001] EMLR 15.

the proper administration of justice'. The first core duty of the BSB Handbook is that 'You must observe your duty to the court in the administration of justice.' The BSB duty therefore seems to be more restrictive, limiting the duty to the administration of justice by aligning it with the duty to the court.

It is not clear whether any the duty to the administration of justice envisaged by the SRA is intended to exceed the obligations imposed in the CPR or the common law. There is an acknowledged overlap between the common law, the rules of court and the rules contained in codes of conduct. Indeed, the obligations of lawyers in litigation are often first defined by the courts or by legislation. An example is the principle that lawyers should not act in a case in which he or she might be called as a witness[77] which appears in the SRA Code as IB5.6.

Despite the SRA's apparently broader commitment to a wide conception of the administration of justice, the actual conduct rules contain very little specific to litigation. In a whole chapter devoted to solicitors and the court, none of the Outcomes go beyond what is required by the courts. The remainder are either patently obvious or describe illegal conduct, like bribing witnesses. Therefore, it seems likely that both professional bodies regard the commitment to independence and the administration of justice as co-extensive with existing forum controls, including the duty to the court.

SRA Code of Conduct

Chapter 5: Your client and the court

This chapter is about your duties to your *client* and to the *court* if you are exercising a right to conduct litigation or acting as an advocate. The outcomes apply to both litigation and advocacy but there are some indicative behaviours which may be relevant only when you are acting as an advocate.

The outcomes in this chapter show how the *Principles* apply in the context of your *client* and the *court*.

You must achieve these outcomes:

O(5.1) you do not attempt to deceive or knowingly or recklessly mislead the court;

O(5.2) you are not complicit in another person deceiving or misleading the court;

O(5.3) you comply with court orders which place obligations on you;

O(5.4) you do not place yourself in contempt of court;

---

[77] *Re Recover Ltd (in liquidation) Hornan v Latif Group SL and others* [2003] EWHC 536 (Ch).

O(5.5) where relevant, clients are informed of the circumstances in which your duties to the court outweigh your obligations to your client;

O(5.6) you comply with your duties to the court;

O(5.7) you ensure that evidence relating to sensitive issues is not misused;

O(5.8) you do not make or offer to make payments to witnesses dependent upon their evidence or the outcome of the case.

Q10.17 Can you allocate each outcome to one or more of the SRA Principles?

Q10.18 Consulting the SRA Handbook online, can you find an Indicative Behaviour relevant to O(5.4) or O(5.7)?

The BSB Code of Conduct is interesting in that the first two chapters are 'You and the Court' and 'Behaving Ethically'. 'You and Your Client' only appears as the third chapter. The first two outcomes of Chapter 1: You and the Court are:

oC1 The court is able to rely on information provided to it by those conducting litigation and by advocates who appear before it [and]

oC2 The proper administration of justice is served.

The relevant rules are set out in rC3-6.

Bar Code of Conduct 2014

rC3 You owe a duty to the court to act with independence in the interests of justice. This duty overrides any inconsistent obligations which you may have (other than obligations under the criminal law). It includes the following specific obligations which apply whether you are acting as an advocate or are otherwise involved in the conduct of litigation in whatever role (with the exception of Rule C3.1 below, which applies when acting as an advocate):

.1 you must not knowingly or recklessly mislead or attempt to mislead the court;

.2 you must not abuse your role as an advocate;

.3 you must take reasonable steps to avoid wasting the court's time;

.4 you must take reasonable steps to ensure that the court has before it all relevant decisions and legislative provisions;

.5 you must ensure that your ability to act independently is not compromised.

rC4 Your duty to act in the best interests of each *client* is subject to your duty to the court.

rC5 Your duty to the court does not require you to act in breach of your duty to keep the affairs of each client confidential.

Not misleading the court

rC6 Your duty not to mislead the court or to permit the court to be misled will include the following obligations:

.1   you must not:

   .a   make submissions, representations or any other statement; or
   .b   ask questions which suggest facts to witnesses which you know, or are instructed, are untrue or misleading.

.2   you must not call witnesses to give evidence or put affidavits or witness statements to the court which you know, or are instructed, are untrue or misleading, unless you make clear to the court the true position as known by or instructed to you.

Guidance

gC6 You are obliged by CD2 to promote and to protect your *client's* interests so far as that is consistent with the law and with your overriding duty to the *court* under CD1. Your duty to the *court* does not prevent you from putting forward your *client's* case simply because you do not believe that the facts are as your *client* states them to be (or as you, on your *client's* behalf, state them to be), as long as any positive case you put forward accords with your *instructions* and you do not mislead the *court*. Your

role when acting as an advocate or conducting litigation is to present your *client's* case, and it is not for you to decide whether your *client's* case is to be believed.

gC7 For example, you are entitled and it may often be appropriate to draw to the witness's attention other evidence which appears to conflict with what the witness is saying and you are entitled to indicate that a *court* may find a particular piece of evidence difficult to accept. But if the witness maintains that the evidence is true, it should be recorded in the witness statement and you will not be misleading the *court* if you call the witness to confirm their witness statement. Equally, there may be circumstances where you call a hostile witness whose evidence you are instructed is untrue. You will not be in breach of Rule C6 if you make the position clear to the *court*. See further the guidance at gC14.

gC9 Rule C3.5 makes it clear that your duty to act in the best interests of your *client* is subject to your duty to the *court*. For example, if your *client* were to tell you that he had committed the crime with which he was charged, in order to be able to ensure compliance with Rule C4 on the one hand and Rule C3 and Rule C6 on the other:

.1 you would not be entitled to disclose that information to the *court* without your *client's* consent; and

.2 you would not be misleading the *court* if, after your *client* had entered a plea of 'not guilty', you were to test in cross-examination the reliability of the evidence of the prosecution witnesses and then address the jury to the effect that the prosecution had not succeeded in making them sure of your *client's* guilt.

gC10 However, you would be misleading the *court* and would therefore be in breach of Rules C3 and C6 if you were to set up a positive case inconsistent with the confession, as for example by:

.1 suggesting to prosecution witnesses, calling your *client* or your witnesses to show; or submitting to the *jury*, that your *client* did not commit the crime; or

.2 suggesting that someone else had done so; or

.3 putting forward an alibi.

gC11 If there is a risk that the *court* will be misled unless you disclose confidential information which you have learned in the course of your *instructions*, you should ask the *client* for permission to disclose it to the *court*. If your *client* refuses to allow you to make the disclosure you must cease to act, and return your *instructions*: see Rules C25 to C27 below. In these circumstances you must not reveal the information to the *court*.

Q10.19 Can a barrister represent a client on a not-guilty plea (a) if the client has confessed or (b) if the lawyer suspects that the client is guilty?

Q10.20 Is there any difference in the defence that can be offered in the above circumstances?

Q10.21 How can lawyers reconcile their duty to the court to their duty to clients, particularly regarding their duty of confidentiality?

It is not known how frequent breaches of the rules for litigation are. Relatively few cases of misleading the court come before the disciplinary tribunals. This may be because breaches remain undiscovered. Sometimes such breaches come to light in unpredictable ways.

Brett v SRA [2014] EWHC 2974 (Admin) (edited)

Alistair Brett (B) was Legal Manager at Times Newspapers Ltd (TNL) for over 30 years. He was, in effect, their in-house solicitor. He was accused of breaching the code of conduct in connection with litigation in the High Court of Justice, Queen's Bench Division. A police officer sought an injunction against TNL preventing it from publishing a story revealing him as the author of a celebrated blog which he published under the name of 'Nightjack'. In a hearing in 2009 Mr Justice Eady dismissed the claim for an injunction.

B was charged with breaches of the Solicitors' Code of Conduct 2007. These were Rule 1, where a list of 'core duties' specifies that 'You must uphold the rule of law and the proper administration of justice' and 'You must act with integrity'. He was also accused of a breach of Rule 11 of the Code of Conduct 2007 which provides 'You must never deceive or knowingly or recklessly mislead the court'.

The guidance concerning Rule 11 provides:

> ... 12 Rule 11.01 makes a distinction between deceiving the court when knowledge is assumed and misleading the court which could happen inadvertently. You would not normally be guilty of misconduct if you inadvertently mislead the court. However if, during the course of proceedings, you become aware that you have inadvertently misled the court, you must, with your client's consent, immediately inform the court. If the client does not consent you must stop acting. Rule 11.01 includes attempting to deceive or mislead the court

> 13 You might deceive or mislead the court by for example:

> a.   submitting inaccurate information or allowing another person to do so;

> ...

> c.   calling a witness whose evidence you know is untrue...

There is no further guidance on the distinctions, within Rule 11.01, between deceiving the court and knowingly or recklessly misleading the court.

The Solicitors Disciplinary Tribunal found that B was in breach of his duty to the court in the proceedings. It suspended him for six months and ordered him to pay £33,000 costs. He appealed to the High Court.

Mr Justice Wilkie:

> Until early 2009 DC Horton (RH) a constable with the Lancashire Constabulary published an internet blog under the pseudonym 'Nightjack'. It was an anonymous chronicle of his life as a police officer. It acquired a high public profile. It attracted the Orwell Prize for Journalism in April 2009 when the author was still anonymous.

> In 2009 PF, a 24 year old junior reporter at *The Times*, told Mr Brett, in his role

as legal manager, that he had identified 'Nightjack'. PF claimed that RH was using confidential police information on his blog. This was a breach of police regulations giving a strong public interest in exposing RH. B asked how PF had identified RH and was told that he had gained unauthorised access to Nightjack's email account.

B told PF that the story could not be published, legally, unless it could be based on information in the public domain. Even if this could be done, the allegation would have to be put to RH before publication. Later, PF sent an email to B stating that he 'had cracked it and could do the whole lot from publicly accessible information'. B telephoned a junior barrister, AE, and was advised that although an offence under the Data Protection Act may have been committed there might be a Public Interest defence.

When PF contacted RH he instructed Olswang, solicitors to seek an injunction against TNL preventing publication. B instructed different junior counsel to represent TNL and he was not told about PF's email hacking of RH's account. Olswangs were suspicious about a statement by TNL's barrister that TNL had identified the author of the blog 'largely' by a process of deduction. This, they wrote to B, '… suggests that our client was so identified, in part, by a process other than deduction, most obviously we assume by a source'. The letter then set out a number of allegedly suspicious circumstances and asked detailed questions about how RH had been identified. One of these suggested that PF may have previously hacked an email account.

At this stage B became aware of the possibility that PF's access to the email account of RH could constitute a criminal offence in breach of Section 1 of the Computer Misuse Act 1990, to which there was no public interest defence. B sent Olswang a final draft of PF's witness statement. This provided details of how he had 'deduced' RH's identity but said nothing about accessing his email account. In B's written response to Olswang he said:

'the suggestion that [PF] might have accessed your client's email address because he has "a history of making unauthorised access to email accounts"'

He then said:

'I regard this as a baseless allegation for the sole purpose of prejudicing the Times Newspaper's defence of this action.'

Then there appeared a passage setting out an account of circumstances in which PF, when a student, was subject to a university disciplinary action concerning an allegation of unauthorised access to emails. Despite further probing from Olswang the case proceeded on the basis that RH had been identified by publicly accessible information. Proceeding on the basis that the claim for an injunction was based on an 'old fashioned breach of confidence', Mr Justice Eady held that the claimant failed to establish a right to privacy in relation to the particular information because '*blogging is essentially a public rather than a private activity*' (at paragraph 11). He indicated that it would probably also have failed at stage 2, the public interest test.

That would probably have been the end of the matter but for the *Leveson Inquiry*. TNL disclosed emails and other material relating to PF's hacking disclosure to B and the circumstances of non-disclosure to the court. B gave evidence before the Leveson Inquiry and was questioned extensively. Subsequently the SRA brought proceedings before the SDT against B.

In June 2013 the SRA decided that B was in breach of Rule 1.02, failing to act with integrity, and rule 11.01 '*knowingly allowed the Court to be misled...*'. At paragraph 2 it set out the particulars of the allegations in the following terms:

'2.1 On or about 2 June 2009, while conducting litigation in the High Court ... the respondent caused or allowed a witness statement to be served and relied on in support of TNL's defence, which knowingly, and/or recklessly, created a misleading impression as to the facts and matters deposed to in the statement.

2.2 On or about 4 June 2009 during a hearing before Mr Justice Eady the respondent knowingly allowed the Court to proceed on the basis of an incorrect assumption as to the facts and matters set out in the witness statement referred to at 2.1 above'.

...

B argued that there was a contradiction in the SDT's decision between finding that he did not act dishonestly and, on the other hand, finding him guilty of 'knowingly allowing the Court to be misled'. He contended that such a conclusion implicitly involves a finding of dishonesty. This is indistinguishable from an allegation of deceit which was specifically not charged, though it could have been, pursuant to Rule 11.01.

This Court has power under Section 49 to make such order on an appeal as it may think fit. A breach of Rule 11.01 can arise on the basis of deceit, or knowingly or recklessly misleading the Court. In this case at least one of the particulars is couched in the alternative as knowingly and/or recklessly misleading a Court. In my judgment, it is open to this Court, if it were to conclude that the finding of the SDT was wrong on the basis of Mr Brett having 'knowingly allowed the Court to be misled', nonetheless, to conclude that he was guilty of a breach of Rule 11.01 on the basis that he 'recklessly' allowed the Court to be misled if, on the facts properly found, that was the correct conclusion.

...

In my judgment that duty, not knowingly to mislead the court or not to take the risk that the court might be misled, is not incompatible with the duty of confidentiality owed to a person who has disclosed material on an occasion of legal professional privilege. Mr Brett was, like any other lawyer, always in a position to avoid misleading the court or to remove the risk of the court being misled without breaking that privilege.

There were a number of options available to him. One was to obtain the agreement of PF to waive privilege so that the true factual position could be presented to the court. A second was to correct the misleading impression given by the witness statement by making it clear that the witness statement only intended to convey that the identity of Nightjack as RH *could* have been revealed through publicly available sources, as evidenced by the fact that PF had undertaken such an exercise. In the absence of a waiver of privilege Mr Brett could have adopted the position that TNL was not prepared to say how it was that PF, in fact, discovered the identity of Nightjack. A third was for Mr Brett to disclose to his instructed counsel, Mr White QC and Barnes, the true position concerning the circumstances in which PF initially discovered the identity of Nightjack and to invite them to correct paragraphs 7 and 8 of the skeleton and in open court to make a statement, different from the one which Mr White QC made, which would similarly avoid giving a misleading impression to the court. A fourth was for Mr Brett, on behalf of his client TNL, to abandon defending the claim without revealing the information given to him by PF on an occasion of legal professional privilege.

None of these options would have involved breaking the confidence in which PF had made his disclosure to Mr Brett, but each of them would have avoided allowing the court to be misled.

In my judgment, therefore, the focus of Mr Brett on the significance of the issue of the legal professional privilege and/or the prohibition on self-incrimination is a red herring. The real focus of the SDT's considerations, and of this appeal, are the dual questions (a) was the court in fact allowed to be misled, and, (b) what was Mr Brett's state of mind when these circumstances arose in which the court was allowed to be misled?

(d) The misleading of the court

I am in no doubt that the court was misled. The passages in PF's statement to which I have referred can only sensibly be read as an account, by PF, of how he first identified Nightjack as RH using publicly available sources. That was, on any view, a misleading impression. What had happened was that PF had initially identified Nightjack as RH by using exclusively unlawful methods, his unlawful access to the email accounts. The exercise which he did undertake, to see whether he could identify RH as Nightjack using publicly available sources, was undertaken at the insistence of Mr Brett only after PF had disclosed to Mr Brett that he had identified RH by illegitimate means.

The use to which such exercise could legitimately be put was, as Mr Brett correctly advised, to demonstrate to a court that Nightjack could be identified as RH using only lawful means so as to provide a basis for seeking to resist the injunction.

O required PF to remove any uncertainty of what he meant in his witness statement by confirming, in a witness statement, that he did not, at any time, make any unauthorised access to any email account. Mr Brett's response, coming as it did from a hugely respected and highly experienced solicitor in the field, was understood by O to be a denial that PF had unlawfully accessed RH's email account.

Furthermore, TNL's counsel, in their skeleton argument, understood that to be the case. When O requested further clarification of the true position, either by a further witness statement from PF or a correction of the potentially misleading impression the skeleton argument gave, they received neither a witness statement from PF nor a correction.

In those circumstances, in my judgment, it is wholly understandable that Mr Tomlinson QC made, before Mr Justice Eady, the concession he made and invited the Judge to deal with the case on the basis that it was more likely than not that, based on PF's evidence, the identity of Nightjack as RH, was discovered by detective work, not by unlawful means.

...

In my judgment, the evidence, particularly that of the contemporaneous correspondence and the lack of any response by Mr Brett to the demands contained in it, pointed inevitably to the conclusion that Mr Brett acted recklessly, as described above, in allowing the court to be misled. On that basis it was inevitable that the SDT would, had it properly addressed the issues as it had defined them, have found him guilty of a breach of Rule 11.01 on the basis that he 'recklessly' allowed the court to be misled.

In my judgment it follows, similarly, that in so acting, he was guilty of a breach of Rule 1.02 of failing to act with integrity.

Accordingly, I would allow this appeal by Mr Brett, but only to the extent of quashing the decision of the SDT that he was guilty of a breach of Rule 11.01 by 'knowingly' misleading the court and substituting for it a finding that he was guilty of Rule 11.01 by "recklessly" misleading the court. I would reject his appeal against the finding of the SDT that he acted in breach of Rule 1.02 by failing to act with integrity on that occasion.

Lord Thomas of Cwmgiedd, CJ:

...

The reason why that is so important is that misleading the court is regarded by the court and must be regarded by any disciplinary tribunal as one of the most serious offences that an advocate or litigator can commit. It is not simply a breach of a rule of a game, but a fundamental affront to a rule designed to safeguard the fairness and justice of proceedings. Such conduct will normally attract an exemplary and deterrent sentence. That is in part because our system for the administration of justice relies so heavily upon the integrity of the profession and the full discharge of the profession's duties and in part because the privilege of conducting litigation or appearing in court is granted on terms that the rules are observed not merely in their letter but in their spirit. Indeed, the reputation of the system of the administration of justice in England and Wales and the standing of the profession depends particularly upon the discharge of the duties owed to the court.

Where an advocate or other representative or a litigator puts before the court matters which he knows not to be true or by omission leads the court to believe something he knows not to be true, then as an advocate knows of these duties, the inference will be inevitable that he has deceived the court, acted dishonestly and is not fit to be a member of any part of the legal profession.

As conduct that is dishonest, such as misleading the court with such knowledge will inevitably be, is so serious, it is of the utmost importance that in difficult circumstances which can confront any advocate or litigator, that advocate or litigator has at the forefront of his mind his duty to the court, the necessity to avoid breach of that duty and, if he has any doubt as to how to discharge that duty, by taking independent advice...."

Q10.22   The case against Brett was brought under the Solicitors' Code of Conduct 2007, which was in force when the breaches occurred. Do you think the case could have been presented and decided in the same way under the BSB Code of Conduct 2014 (see below)?

Bar Standards Board Code of Conduct 2014

gC4 Knowingly misleading the court includes inadvertently misleading the court if you later realise that you have misled the court, and you fail to correct the position. Recklessness means being indifferent to the truth, or not caring whether something is true or false. The duty continues to apply for the duration of the case.

Conclusion

Litigators and advocates owe duties to the court to act with independence in the interests of justice and to comply with rules of conduct of their regulating body. They can be sanctioned for breaches of this duty in a variety of ways, including by the imposition of a wasted costs order when their conduct comprises improper (a breach of ethics), unreasonable or negligent acts. However, perhaps because of the range of forum controls on litigators and advocates, conduct rules tend not to go beyond the standards set in the courts. In cases of serious misconduct lawyers may suffer forum sanctions and they may also be disciplined.

Despite the fact that the same kinds of rules apply to different areas of litigation work, different areas appear to have a different culture. Personal injury work is a good example of this. At one time lawyers were encouraged to be highly adversarial. Claimant lawyers were told to approach cases as if they expected trial. The CPR attempted to change the culture of litigation generally towards a more co-operative ethos. This trend, encouraging lawyers to be less adversarial and more co-operative in the way they conduct work, can also be seen in the culture of family law, explored in the next chapter.

Settlement

Settlement is the main way in which disputes are resolved. The principal methods of settlement are negotiation and alternative dispute resolution (ADR). These methods have much in common in terms of processes. Indeed, negotiation is sometimes seen as a form of ADR. For the purposes of this chapter the essential difference is that negotiation is a direct interaction between two parties, or their representatives, whereas ADR is a process involving a neutral third party.

Another difference between negotiation and ADR can arise because of context. Negotiation is a common feature of everyday legal work. It arises in both transactions and matters with a contentious element. ADR is usually only deployed at the instigation of the parties where there is some kind of dispute between them.

Negotiation is a process of trying to reach agreement by communication, which can be written or verbal. This chapter recognises the distinction that is sometimes made between the overall process of negotiation and face-to-face verbal exchange, which is known as bargaining. This chapter deals with negotiation in contentious matters, while the next covers the negotiation of deals, eg commercial contracts.

Government has a strong interest in the efficiency of the justice system because it funds most criminal litigation and some civil litigation. Failure to support the defence and pursuit of legal rights is a potent political issue. As the modern state grapples with the problem of demands on welfare, it has sought ways to meet legal needs more efficiently. The expense of adversarial justice has led to greater use of ADR to complement more formal processes.

Negotiation in Contentious Matters

Context

Negotiation with a view to settlement is such a natural part of litigation that the process has been referred to as 'litigotiation'.[1] While litigation and advocacy are ringed with procedural and ethical rules, negotiation is devoid of any specific regulation by codes of conduct. Courts sometimes intervene at the request of parties to review the process and outcomes of negotiation outcomes but, even here, the secrecy of negotiation is usually protected by what is known as 'negotiation privilege'.

The intention to claim negotiation privilege is usually shown by use of the words 'without prejudice' in discussions or correspondence. This means that, in ordinary circumstances, evidence of discussions conducted with a view to reaching settlement cannot be referred to subsequently in court proceedings. The effectiveness of this usage is, however, dependent on context (see chapter twelve).

Negotiation Theory

Problem Types

There are various possible approaches to negotiation. The literature often talks about distributive and integrative negotiation, but I think that it is more helpful to think of negotiation problems having distributive and integrative features and possibilities.

The approach taken may depend on the type of negotiation problem. Some problems offer only 'zero sum' options, meaning the gain of utility for one party involves corresponding loss for the other. The problem is essentially a *distributive* problem. Dividing a cake between children is a good example; more for one child means less for another. Most negotiation, certainly most legal negotiation, involves money. This is still essentially a distribution. Although the position may not be fixed, the principle, more for one means less for the other, still applies. The extent to which agreement is possible depends on the overlap of expectations. This can be graphically illustrated as a case of best-case and worst-case scenarios. Agreement is possible anywhere in the 'contract zone'.

---

[1] M Galanter, 'Worlds of Deals: Using Negotiation to Teach about Legal Process' (1984) 34 *Journal of Legal Education* 268.

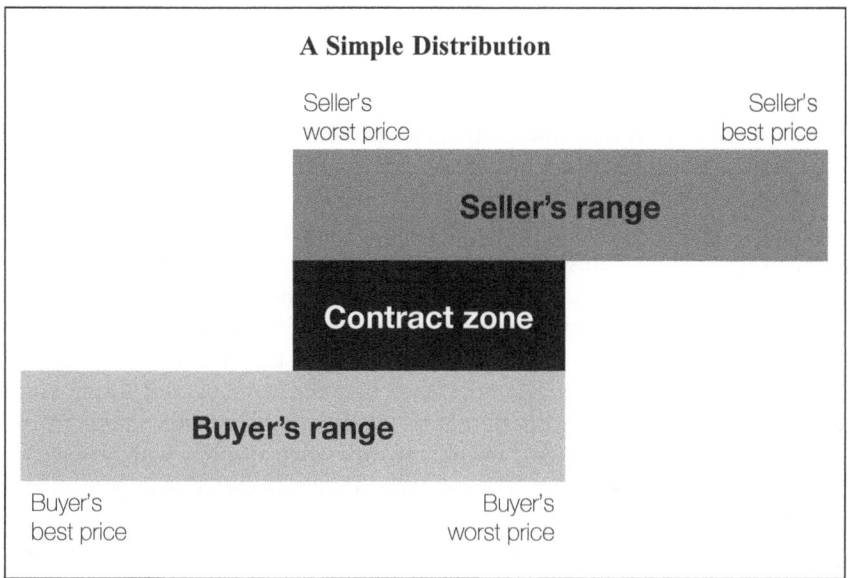

A Simple Distribution

Q11.1 Can you define the term 'the contract zone'?

Q11.2 Can you provide some figures to illustrate how a contract zone is defined in practice?

Not all negotiation problems are purely distributive. They may have non-distributive elements called *integrative* features. These may be matters that are peripheral to the main issue. Therefore, even a distributive problem may have integrative features. These integrative features may include issues such as the timing, location or form of payment. They can be used to make an agreement involving distribution more palatable.

Using the integrative elements of a negotiation problem involves offering the other side something they want which is peripheral to the main subject matter of the negotiation. These may be things that are of low cost to the party offering, such as early payment, but of high value to the recipient. Many situations in which negotiation occurs have the potential for parties to 'expand the cake'. There may be options for mutual gain, for example business opportunities created by the possibility of a continuing relationship between the parties. This is where the term integrative bargaining comes from.

Factors Affecting Settlement Outcomes

i. Valuation

While it is by no means always true, for present purposes it is assumed that litigation presents zero sum problems. Assuming that most litigation involves a simple claim, usually of money, the rationale for negotiation is that it eliminates the high risk of going to court. If attempted early enough it also reduces the cost and stress the parties suffer. The justification for negotiating a settlement is therefore that the parties achieve the likely outcome of the court proceedings while avoiding these disadvantages of the process.

The problem for parties and negotiators is that the outcome of court proceedings is unpredictable. The difference between winning and losing could depend on how one witness performs on the day, how the judge interprets one piece of evidence. Therefore, negotiators are often dealing with percentage chances of winning or losing. The estimate of risk associated with proceedings could produce widely different predicted outcomes to litigation.

In litigation over a breach of contract, for example, there could be different views on liability and the measure of damages. The claimants may think that they have a 65% chance of winning the case and that if wholly successful the damages would be £100,000. The defendants may think that the claimant's case has a 50% chance of success and value the claim at full liability at £60,000. Such divergent estimates would produce widely different settlement figures.

ii. Context

Outcomes in settled cases might be affected by a number of factors. Gross and Syverud found that the success of negotiators in California Superior Court cases varied greatly between and within 'fields' of work.[2] They concluded that these wide differences could only be explained by the differences in the fields that determined which cases were brought to trial. These include the parties' relationship, funding arrangements and the incidence of costs. The factors that might be relevant in any situation include the availability of insurance or other means of covering liabilities and the distribution of authority to settle as between claimants and others, eg insurers, and differences in success rates between fields.

iii. Approaches to Bargaining

Another explanation for variations in patterns of settlement could be the atti-

---

[2] SR Gross and KD Syverud, 'Getting to No: A Study of Settlement Negotiations and the Selection of Cases for Trial' (1991) 90 *Michigan Law Review* 319, 338.

tude to negotiation of the participants. The literature recognises two basic attitudes to bargaining: competitive and co-operative. These possibilities represent profoundly different aims in negotiators and different negotiating styles.

The competitive approach is geared towards one-sided gains. It is manipulative, coercive or both. The co-operative approach is more geared to achieving agreement. It is open, rational and conciliatory. The differences in the methods of competitive and co-operative bargainers are just as stark. Co-operators make concessions to show good faith and to encourage reciprocation. Competitive negotiators make few if any concessions.

An early study of US lawyers by Williams found that around 80 per cent had a co-operative approach to negotiation.[3] This could distort settlement data over a range of cases. It is logical to assume that, in zero sum negotiations, competitive negotiators are likely to do better. They will tend to exploit the propensity of co-operative negotiators to seek reasonable agreements and to make concessions.

Returning to the image of the contract zone, it is easy to see that that the competitive negotiator is more likely to come out with the best end of a deal. One of their main tactics is to offer an ultimatum. A colourful metaphor for this kind of tactic is two drivers, racing towards each other on a single-track road, playing chicken; the more likely winner is the one who throws his or her steering wheel out of the window. The problem is, if both drivers jettison their wheels, the outcome is disaster.

iv. Negotiating Strategies

The unpredictability of litigation, the high risks that parties run and the factors that might affect litigation outcomes makes settlement highly desirable. This raises the issue of what strategy lawyers should use when negotiating 'in the shadow' of litigation. Lawyers will be aware that the population of negotiators is likely to contain a relatively small proportion of competitive negotiators willing to use exploitative tactics in order to gain advantage for their client.

Some insight into how negotiators should approach the problem is offered by game theory. This models strategic behaviour by reducing strategic interactions to a score based on what they and others choose to do in a given situation.[4] The most familiar example is the 'prisoners' dilemma'. The prisoners' dilemma takes its name from a situation where two criminal accomplices must decide, in ignorance of what the other will do, whether or not to talk to the authorities and implicate each other, or remain silent and hope that their co-defendant does likewise.

In the prisoners' dilemma the two players must each decide whether to

---

[3] G Williams, *Legal Negotiation and Settlement* (St Paul, MN, West Publishing, 1983).

[4] DG Baird, RH Gertner and RC Picker, *Game Theory and the Law* (Cambridge, MA, Harvard University Press, 1994) 1.

'co-operate' with or 'defect' from the other. However, they have been kept apart and have no idea of what the other is going to do. Points are awarded depending on the outcome. The possibility for making strategic choices arises if the prisoners' dilemma is played between the same people a number of times. Then, of course, it is no longer useful to think of the game as being played between to prisoners but (say) two business people looking for the best deal in commercial transactions. It is interesting to compare the scores of different pairs of parties when this is done and to examine the reasoning behind their strategies.

The prisoners' dilemma pay-off structure

		Player B	
		Co-operate	Defect
Player A	Co-operate	A = 3 B =3 Mutual co-operation rewarded	A = 0 B = 5 One-sided defection rewarded
	Defect	A = 5 B = 0 One-sided defection rewarded	A = 1 B = 1 Neutral outcome from mutual defection

---

Q11.3 What is the most rational strategy in a one-off game of prisoners' dilemma?

Q11.4 What is a rational strategy for ten games of the prisoners' dilemma with the same person?

It can be argued that the prisoners' dilemma is useful in understanding negotiation strategy. This depends on the pay-offs mirroring the pay-offs of negotiation where co-operation equals co-operative bargaining and defection equals competitive bargaining. So, the total reward for a co-operative approach is six points, albeit shared equally, because co-operation leads to more satisfactory conclusions for both sides. The total reward for mutual defection is only two. However, there is a massive pay-off for defection against a co-operating opponent, where the defector grabs five points, the highest possible individual score.

In a one-off encounter in the prisoners' dilemma, when the other player's propensity for defection is known, the rational decision, given the reward structure, is to defect. This guarantees one point. There is no way of undoing the consequences of unreciprocated co-operation and, on an isolated occasion, there is no way of predicting how the other accused will react. As in real life, the selfish decision makes sense when there is no opportunity for payback. Therefore, in a one-off interaction the rational approach is to be competitive, at least until it can be established that the other party will reliably reciprocate co-operation.

v. Recurring Interactions

Lawyers often work in environments where they meet the same lawyers working in their field. Some of these will co-operatively try and seek a mutually acceptable solution while others will competitively seek one-sided advantage. How should negotiators respond? The first question is whether it is ethical in an adversarial culture to offer co-operation in negotiation.

At first sight it seems that co-operation is at odds with the adversarial ethic of litigation. This depends on whether the aim of negotiation is seen to be dispute settlement. If it is to achieve the same result as litigation, but at less cost, then a fair and reasonable settlement is an acceptable outcome. The co-operation that is likely to produce such an outcome is not, however, designed to take advantage of any weakness or mistakes of the other side.

In practice, co-operation is probably the best strategy for settling large numbers of cases cheaply,[5] where sensible discussion in an atmosphere of co-operation usually leads to amicable settlement. Lawyers employing conditional co-operation must ensure that their relationships with opponents do not become too 'cosy'. Combining co-operation with an appropriate degree of adversarial spirit is, however, what lawyers are trained to do.

The second question that arises where lawyers are involved in recurring interactions is: how should they deal with extreme competitors? A competitive negotiator will be extremely lucky to find an opponent who keeps on co-operating despite being taken advantage of. In repeated negotiations the rational strategy is mutual co-operation, because this will produce the best outcomes over time. The problem for negotiators, operating in a small pool of negotiators, where repeat interactions are inevitable, is to find a strategy that engenders co-operation in repeat interactions.

Among the attempts to discover the best strategy for playing the prisoners' dilemma Robert Axelrod's account is the most compelling. Axelrod organised a competition for computer programmers, mathematicians and gamers where each entrant played other programmes 100 times.[6] The most successful strategy was very simple. It was called 'tit for tat'. It simply co-operated on the first interaction and then repeated the opponent's previous move. In a competition

---

[5] RJ Condlin, 'Bargaining in the Dark: The Normative Incoherence of Lawyer Dispute Bargaining Role' (1992) 51(1) *Maryland Law Review* 1, 57.
[6] R Axelrod, *The Evolution of Co-operation* (London, Penguin, 1984).

against all other strategies tit for tat emerged as the winner in early rounds. In later rounds against better competitors it achieved even better scores.

Translation of tit for tat into human behaviour suggests four principles. First, be 'nice'; never defect first. Second, do not suffer provocation; punish betrayal of trust with reprisal. Third, forgive; return to co-operation when the other side indicates a willingness to do so. Finally, be transparent; do not conceal or be unpredictable.

This kind of conditional co-operation appears to be a good fit with principled negotiation. This is a method of negotiation developed by Roger Fisher and William Ury at the Harvard Negotiation Project.[7] It advocates four fundamental principles:

1. Separate the people from the problem.
2. Focus on interests not positions.
3. Invent options for mutual gain.
4. Insist on objective criteria (particularly on distributive issues).

These principles are said to protect negotiators from hyper-competitive tactics.

While the results of playing the prisoners' dilemma are thought provoking there are problems in applying it to real life and, specifically, to litigation. There are two obvious problems. The first is whether it is realistic that the same negotiators will meet so often as to make a tit-for-tat strategy effective. The second is whether the pay-off structure accurately reflects the realities of practice situations. For example, in negotiating the settlement of litigation, is the reward for co-operation as high as it is in the prisoners' dilemma?

vi. The Best Interests of Clients

The main consideration in deciding what negotiation strategy to use in any given situation is the best interests of clients. Applying the lessons of the prisoners' dilemma to litigation, it can be seen that working out the best interests of clients could be quite difficult. For example, using a 'litigation-first' strategy, a competitive rather than co-operative move, could be in the interest of a client. If using the strategy causes retaliation in future cases, its use could prejudice the interests of clients in future cases.

It seems plausible that a lawyer who consistently 'defects', by, for example, adopting 'litigation-first' tactics, must expect to develop a bad reputation. Other lawyers may 'punish' them by being unhelpful or awkward, to the disadvantage of their clients. It is debatable however, whether the competitive negotiator can be 'punished' sufficiently in repeat interactions so as to justify using a tit-for-tat strategy in repeat interactions.

---

[7] R Fisher and W Ury, *Getting to Yes: Negotiating Agreement without Giving In* (New York Penguin Books, 1981).

Civil Practice

Evaluating Negotiation Outcomes

The duties of the lawyer as advocate and of the lawyer as negotiator are different. The duty of the advocate is to advance the client's case within the limits of the law. For the negotiator, trial outcome is only one of a number of factors to be considered. The negotiator has the opportunity to achieve a settlement that reflects the client's preferences in terms of variables such as terms, cost and timing. The relevance of these factors depends on the client, the area of work and the circumstances of the particular case.

There are various criteria for evaluating negotiated outcomes. Lawyers undertaking negotiations in the shadow of litigation, as in divorce and personal injury actions, must anticipate what the outcome would be at trial. Since the rationale for this kind of negotiation is to reach a settlement that avoids trial but produces a similar outcome, it is natural that lawyers negotiating settlement of disputes explore the evidence, relevant arguments and applicable law.

One of the innovations of the CPR was to put judges under an obligation to promote mediation as a way of settling disputes. As we shall see, one of the perceived advantages of mediation is that it encourages consideration of 'extra-legal factors' in promoting compromise. Participants are encouraged to consider their interests rather than their rights. Under the CPR, parties could be punished by costs sanctions for not actively participating in mediation.

Variations in Practice According to Areas of Work

Personal Injury

i. Context

Most personal injury litigation cases are settled. The issues tend to be distributive, although the exact sum is arguable. Calculation of compensation can be complex, with factors such as liability, contributory negligence and the different elements of damages (eg physical injury, financial loss and future loss) each providing scope for argument. Winning the case may not be a foregone conclusion. A defendant may well argue that damages should be reduced to reflect litigation risk.

An insurance company tends to handle claims on behalf of defendants whom they have insured. Large sums are sometimes at issue, but early settlement can save large legal costs. Research suggests that personal injury bargaining can take the form of relatively crude 'horse trading'.[8] Delay may be used to put pressure on claimants and aggressive litigation tactics used to increase pressure on defendants. Claimants are usually 'one-shotters' with little understanding of the claim or process. A constant issue is whether claimants' lawyers are sufficiently adversarial in pursuing claims and settlements.

ii. Orientation to Settlement

During the 1990s approaches based on aggressive litigation strategies created a climate favourable to aggressive negotiation strategies on behalf of claimants. The climate changed with the introduction of the CPR. The new rules appeared to deliberately impede 'litigation first' by requiring the completion of pre-action protocols by the claimants. Later versions of the Law Society's Personal Injury Accreditation Scheme encouraged lawyers to keep client wishes in sight.[9]

Assessing a client's best interest could be problematic. An overly co-operative approach may result in low settlement figures but could be justified by avoiding the claimant's risk on costs. One such risk is that lawyers prioritise the rapid turnover of cases at the cost of doing the best that they reasonably can on each one. An insight into the consequences of routine claims handling and an inadequate adversarial orientation was gained from the so-called miner's costs scandal (see the case study in chapter five: Conflicts of Interest).

Analysis of the compensation for personal injury made to miners under the government-established compensation schemes suggested that some of the claims were 'under settled'.[10] One of the most common reasons was that diagnoses on which settlement rates were based were not challenged. Solicitors could maximise their incomes by processing large numbers of claims rather than fighting the arguable ones. Firms handling thousands of claims achieved widely different average levels of compensation.

One of the national, specialist personal injury firms settled at an average of over £9,000 per claim. Two of the three firms with the worst average recovery rates had partners struck off for other disciplinary offences.[11] The worst average recovery rate of the three firms was only £2,375 per claim. The next lowest recovered an average £2,559 and the median firm achieved £5,990. It

---

[8] H Genn, *Hard Bargaining: Out of Court Settlement in Personal Injury Actions* (Oxford, Clarendon Press, 1987) 134; HL Ross, *Settled Out of Court: The Social Process of Insurance Claims Adjustments* (Chicago, Aldine, 1970).

[9] Personal Injury Accreditation Scheme: Criteria and guidance Practice Management Standard F4.a(i) and (ii) (www.sra.org.uk/documents/solicitors/accreditation/personal-Injury-guidance.pdf (accessed 28 March 2008) 7.

[10] J Dean, 'Controversy Continues over Miners' Claims' [2009] *Law Society Gazette* 30 July, www.lawgazette.co.uk/news/news-focus-miners-compensation.

[11] See further A Boon and A Whyte, 'Icarus Falls: The Coal Health Scandal' (2012) 15(2) *Legal Ethics* 271 and chapter twelve: Commercial Practice.

was estimated that over 50,000 miners might have had 'under-settled claims'.[12] This example can be seen as a cautionary warning that there is a fine line between 'co-operation' and complacency.

Family

Family cases are a highly distinctive type of contentious work. They potentially involve disputes over marital status, children and property. Negotiators must deal with distributive issues, such as division of property and maintenance, while also considering the interests of children and the continuing relationships between parents. The parties often have complex emotions towards one another. Family litigation often provides an opportunity for spouses to avenge past wrongs.[13]

It is arguable that bad feeling often accompanying family breakdown can be exacerbated when lawyers take an aggressively adversarial approach. In the early 1990s one specialist family lawyer observed that opposing lawyers often acted 'as if war had broken out'.[14] The conduct of family litigation on a highly adversarial footing carried over into negotiation, with clients' bitterness and recrimination infecting correspondence and meetings between lawyers.

Other evidence suggested that family lawyers did not just pursue their clients' agendas. Research in the US found that, from the first meeting, divorce lawyers sought to manage their clients' perceptions and expectations.[15] They laid the foundation for the client accepting settlement terms less favourable than they had anticipated, a process known as 'cooling out'. In the early 1990s, research on English divorce solicitors found that they did not challenge their clients' preferences for settlement outcomes, but still sought negotiation when possible.[16] Very few financial settlements were decided by judges. This enabled solicitors to manage caseloads and maintain collegial relations with other solicitors.

Government policy on family law practice was based on a belief that lawyers increased tension and conflict between parties and attempted to disrupt the possibility of mediated settlements. During the 1990s, government policy favoured greater use of mediation to replace the conventional negotiation and

---

[12] J Dean, 'Coalminer Court Actions Set for "Special Hearing"' [2011] *Law Society Gazette*, 27 January, www.lawgazette.co.uk/news/coalminer-court-actions-set-039special-hearing; *VWF Professional Negligence Litigation (Various) v Raleys* (Claim No 00L00654), 3 May 2011, para 17 (approved judgment supplied to the author by Leeds County Court).

[13] RH Mnookin and L Kornhauser, 'Bargaining in the Shadow of the Law: The Case of Divorce' (1979) 88 *Yale Law Journal* 950.

[14] A Boon, 'Litigation Solicitors' in P Hassett and M Fitzgerald (eds), *Skills for Legal Functions II: Representation and Advice* (London, Institute of Advanced Legal Studies, 1992).

[15] A Sarat and WLF Felstiner, 'Law and Strategy in the Divorce Lawyer's Office' (1986) 20(1) *Law and Society Review* 93; J Griffiths, 'What Do Dutch Lawyers Actually Do in Divorce Cases?' (1986) 20 *Law and Society Review* 135.

[16] R Ingleby, *Solicitors and Divorce* (Oxford, Oxford University Press, 1992).

adjudication model. The Family Law Act 1996 was apparently prompted by a policy of reducing lawyers' involvement in family disputes.

The Act was intended to introduce a process of dissuading parties from divorce, requiring them to mediate before gaining access to legal aid. It was also proposed to reduce qualifying times for divorce by consent.[17] A decisive shift towards conciliation and mediation at the expense of negotiation and adjudication was averted by strong advice from the Law Commission.[18] This view was vindicated when mediation pilot projects had poor take-up.[19] A significant minority of those going through mediation evinced an even stronger inclination to see a solicitor.[20]

The government's determination to marginalise lawyers in family work was called into question by research. Research published in 1999 showed that most family cases were settled. Leaving aside consent orders, approved by judges to prevent the possibility of future applications for variation, possibly less than 5 per cent of divorce cases are adjudicated.[21] It is likely that the government's view of family lawyers ignored a transformation in lawyers' attitudes towards family work in the 1990s. This supports Lewis's conclusion that assumptions about lawyers he found in government policy documents contradicted the balance of evidence.[22]

In 2000 research by Eekelaar, Maclean and Beinart suggested that most divorce solicitors did a good job in difficult circumstances.[23] There was little evidence that solicitors were confrontational or exacerbated family conflict. The research noted that divorce lawyers, were often reluctant to pursue client wishes that they thought were dubious or excessive. Eekelaar et al concluded that lawyers should generally be entitled to act in this way, partly because they were sometimes successful against expectations, and partly because they should not have too much power to prejudge outcomes.

Eekelaar et al also considered that such clients' positions should be advanced moderately and that a retainer might be justifiably terminated, partly because the other party would be caused unnecessary expense by unjustified claims. Nevertheless, they concluded that, with regard to the sums in issue, the out-

[17] J Eekelaar, M Maclean and S Beinart, *Family Lawyers: The Divorce Work of Solicitors* (Oxford, Hart Publishing, 2000) 3.

[18] Law Commission, *The Ground for Divorce* (1990) Law Com No 192 and see Eekelaar, Maclean and Beinart, ibid, ch 1.

[19] A Ogus, M Jones-Lee, W Cole and P McCarthy, 'Evaluating Alternative Dispute Resolution: Measuring the Impact of Family Conciliation on Costs' (1990) 53 *Modern Law Review* 57, 59.

[20] Home Office, *Supporting Families: A Consultation Document* (1998) paras 4.31–33, Lord Chancellor's Department, Information Meetings and Associated Provisions within the Family Law Act 1996: Summary of Research in Progress (1999).

[21] G Davis, J Pearce, R Bird, H Woodward and C Wallace, *Ancillary Relief Outcomes: A Pilot Study for the Lord Chancellor's Department* (Bristol, University of Bristol, 1999).

[22] P Lewis, *Assumptions about Lawyers in Policy Statements: A Survey of Relevant Research* (Lord Chancellor's Department, 2000).

[23] Eekelaar et al (n 17).

comes and the costs, the way the legal process handled the cases was broadly satisfactory from the clients' point of view.

Many of the divorce lawyers interviewed for the research were members of Resolution, originally formed in 1982 as the Solicitors' Family Law Association. Resolution promoted a co-operative climate for the conduct of family disputes and constructive solutions to family breakdown. It consistently published a code of practice which discouraged members from taking an adversarial approach in family situations. Resolution advised members to 'encourage the attitude that a family dispute is not a contest in which there is a winner and a loser, but rather that it is a search for fair solutions … it is best for the whole family if the proceedings are conducted in a constructive and realistic way rather than in the midst of a war zone'.[24] Paragraph 2 of the code stated:

> You should encourage your client to see the advantages to the family of a constructive and non-confrontational approach as a way of resolving differences. You should advise, negotiate and conduct matters so as to help the family members settle their differences as quickly as possible and reach agreement.

Paragraph 4 further advised members to 'avoid using words or phrases that suggest or cause a dispute when there is no serious dispute.' Since 2008, Resolution has reduced its Code of Practice to a checklist of principles, and published a more detailed set of Guides to Good Practice dealing with specific areas.

Resolution Code of Practice
www.resolution.org.uk/editorial.asp?page_id=26 (6/1/2014)

Membership of Resolution commits family lawyers to resolving disputes in a non-confrontational way.

We believe that family law disputes should be dealt with in a constructive way designed to preserve people's dignity and to encourage agreements.

Members of Resolution are required to:

- Conduct matters in a constructive and non-confrontational way
- Avoid use of inflammatory language both written and spoken
- Retain professional objectivity and respect for everyone involved
- Take into account the long term consequences of actions and communications as well as the short term implications
- Encourage clients to put the best interests of the children first
- Emphasise to clients the importance of being open and honest in all dealings
- Make clients aware of the benefits of behaving in a civilised way
- Keep financial and children issues separate

---

[24] Resolution Code of Practice s 4 (www.divorceguideuk.co.uk/9-0.htm).

- Ensure that consideration is given to balancing the benefits of any steps against the likely costs—financial or emotional
- Inform clients of the options e.g. counselling, family therapy, round table negotiations, mediation, collaborative law and court proceedings.
- Abide by the Resolution Guides to Good Practice.

Q11.5 What are the advantages and disadvantages of groups of lawyers publishing their own codes of practice?

Q11.6 How consistent is the Resolution Code of Practice with the adversarial ethic?

Resolution also publishes Good Practice Guides on different aspects of resolving disputes, but none relate exclusively to conducting negotiations. It is implicit in this list of criteria, however, that Resolution members will encourage clients to take a very broad view of their interest in family disputes, for example by considering long-term family relationships. Eekelaar et al found that negotiation conducted by Resolution members used objective criteria to assess negotiation outcomes.[25]

Following the CPR, Resolution went from strength to strength. It is difficult to calculate accurately the number of family law practitioners, but Resolution claims to have 6,500 members. While Resolution is committed to dealing with family law disputes in a constructive way, there is no group promoting an adversarial ethos for family law.

Resolution also had an impact on Law Society policy relating to family law. The Law Society formerly operated two family law panels, both adopting Resolution's code of practice. These have been replaced by four accreditation schemes for solicitors and FILEX members: Family Law, Family Law Advanced, Family Mediation and Children Law. Eligibility for membership of these schemes is based on experience and expertise.

The influence of Resolution is reflected in the paperwork for the Law Society's Family Law panel, which identified the complex factors that needed to be kept in sight in negotiation. Element 2(i) of the panel's Advanced Knowledge and Skills criteria emphasised the need to consider 'the client's emotional state', 'underlying issues' and to keep 'the [case] strategy under review' Applicants seeking membership of the accreditation scheme may be refused membership if there is evidence that they are not a fit and proper person.' Such evidence may include 'delays in dealing with cases, failure to answer correspondence and failures or delays in responding to enquiries from regulatory and revenue authorities will raise doubts as to your competence to remain a scheme member'.

---

[25] Eekelaar et al (n 17) 123–25.

No particular orientation to litigation is specified as a requirement for entry to the Law Society's accreditation schemes. Former references to Resolution's Code of Conduct have been removed. The Family Mediation Accreditation Scheme refers to the Family Mediation Council and its Code of Practice.[26] This is a body representing six family mediation groups including Resolution.

Summary and Overview

The shift of ethos in family matters, away from adversarial assumptions, is arguably justified. It seems desirable that, whatever the feelings of separating couples, family lawyers should encourage the parties to focus on the future rather than the past, and explore their mutual interests in carrying on sustainable relationships. A contrary argument is that family lawyers are deserting their role in promoting individual autonomy in favour of a social agenda designed to promote settlement.

The movement of family law practitioners towards a more conciliatory ethos for practice was probably reinforced by the CPR 1998 and the Family Procedure Rules 2010 (FPR). The overriding objective of the rules set out in Rule 1.1 is enabling courts to deal with cases justly, having regard to any welfare issues involved. The removal of legal aid from most contested matters and promotion of mediation forces practitioners to think more actively about compromise.

Defining a Common Negotiation Culture

There are marked differences in the approaches to negotiation between solicitors specialising in family law and personal injury work. In both areas the current ethos of negotiation is markedly different from what was previously seen to be the norm. Personal injury lawyers were generally criticised for weak litigation and negotiation strategies. Expert litigators welcomed encouragement to legitimise hard bargaining tactics. In contrast, many family lawyers had already moved towards an ethos of conciliation. They were taking responsibility for persuading their clients to be co-operative and to take a broader view of their own interests.

Lord Woolf heralded the introduction of a more co-operative litigation environment with the introduction of the CPR. The heavy emphasis on ADR, particularly mediation, suggests a recognition that lawyers' negotiation would continue to be undertaken on an adversarial footing, hence the need for alternatives. It is arguable therefore, that the ethical picture for family lawyers

---

[26] www.lawsociety.org.uk/support-services/accreditation/family-mediation/.

is somewhat confused. Are they supposed to have the best interests of their clients or of their client's wider family as their ethical focus?[27]

There are very good reasons, particularly in terms of social policy, for promoting harmonious family relations. Yet, counselling clients to forego their day in court impinges on their personal autonomy and may not be in their personal best interests. It is particularly problematic in those extreme situations where compromise is not a fair and just solution to family conflict.

The inherent differences in areas of work, and the problems in defining an appropriate culture of negotiation, illustrate the difficulty of devising meaningful conduct rules except in the most general terms. Only the most general and high-level principles can cover the range of practices that are likely to be found 'on the ground'.

Regulating Negotiation Conduct

Acting in the Best Interests of Clients

The absence of specific rules on negotiation means that lawyers must look to core duties and principles and general outcomes for guidance on their duties in negotiation. The sections covering duties owed to clients and those owed to third parties are the most obviously relevant. These are, broadly, acting in the best interests of clients while not being unfair to third parties.

Acting in the best interests of clients was a core duty in the Solicitors Practice Rules 1990 and has featured in all subsequent versions of the conduct rules. In the 1999 edition of the Guide, Practice Rule 1 stated the duty as 'to act in the best interests of the client'.[28] In the light of Axelrod's conclusions, this raised the issue of whether litigation-first, adversarial or competitive approaches were in the interests of clients in general.[29]

The response to whose interests solicitors should focus on was apparent in the Solicitors' Code of Conduct 2007, where the core duty became acting 'in the best interests of each client'.[30] This formula was maintained in the SRA Code of Conduct 2011, both in the core principles and in the outcomes.[31] Outcome 1.2 is that 'you provide services to your clients in a manner which

---

[27] L Webley, 'Divorce Solicitors and Ethical Approaches—The Best Interests of the Client and/ or the Best Interests of the Family?' (2004) 7 *Legal Ethics* 230.

[28] N Taylor (ed), *Guide to the Professional Conduct of Solicitors*, 8th edn (1999).

[29] A Boon, 'Ethics and Strategy in Personal Injury Litigation' (1995) 22(3) *Journal of Law and Society* 353.

[30] Solicitors' Code of Conduct 2007, Rule 1, Core Duty 1.04.

[31] Solicitors Regulation Authority, *SRA Handbook*, SRA Principles 2011, Principle 4.

protects their interests in their matter, subject to the proper administration of justice'.

Acting in the best interests of 'each client' can be interpreted to mean being adversarial in each case, whatever the implications for future cases. The requirement may be fairly clear in personal injury matters where only distributive issues are at stake. Interpreting a client's best interests is more difficult in family matters where other issues are at stake.

Whatever lawyers perceive to be a client's best interests, they also have to be sensitive to a client's wishes. Therefore, on occasions, they may be required to follow a client's instructions, irrespective of what they think that client's interests are. On these occasions they must make sure, at a minimum, that the client understands the advice they have been given before they reject it.

Acting Fairly towards Third Parties

Whether lawyers have an obligation to treat others fairly is debatable. The provisions of Chapter 11 of the SRA Code, dealing with 'Relations with Third Parties', are based on 'ensuring you do not take unfair advantage of those you deal with and that you act in a manner which promotes the proper operation of the legal system'. Outcome 11.1 states that 'you do not take unfair advantage of third parties in either your professional or personal capacity'. Not taking unfair advantage is a lower standard than, for example, treating people fairly.

While the code is silent on the standard of behaviour required, the courts are occasionally required to review lawyers' negotiations. A good example is *Thames Trains Ltd v Adams*.[32] Lawyers for a personal injury claimant sent a fax accepting an offer of settlement, which was not received by the defendant's lawyers. They then accepted a later and higher offer made by the defendants.

The defendants argued that accepting the higher offer without mentioning the earlier purported acceptance was contrary to the Solicitors' Code of Conduct at the time. This imposed a duty of frankness and good faith in dealings between solicitors. The defendants argued that it would be unconscionable to uphold the deal. The court disagreed, on the facts of the case, but also indicated that, in slightly different circumstances, the decision could have gone the other way. This suggests that lawyers might be held to higher standards in negotiation than ordinary people.

The only other provision arguably relevant to negotiation in Chapter 11 is Indicative Behaviour 11.8. This covers

> demanding anything for yourself or on behalf of your client, that is not legally recoverable, such as when you are instructed to collect a simple debt, demanding

---

[32] *Thames Trains Ltd v Adams* [2006] EWHC 3291.

from the debtor the cost of the letter of claim since it cannot be said at that stage that such a cost is legally recoverable.

One reading of this would seem to make the consideration of integrative solutions to problems problematic, since they are, by definition, not legally recoverable. However, the example given suggests that this is not the intended interpretation.

The American Bar Association Model Rules may appear to retain a more onerous rule on 'statements of material fact' than do the SRA rules.

American Bar Association
Model Code of Professional Conduct **2004**

Rule 4.1.

[A] lawyer shall not knowingly a) make a false statement of material fact or law to a third person or b) subject to rules on client confidences, fail to disclose a material fact to a third person so as not to assist a criminal or fraudulent act.

Q11.7 Do you think Rule 4.1(a) would preclude bluffing in negotiation?

Q11.8 Should legal professions state how they expect members to conduct negotiation?

Q11.9 Should rules relating to negotiation be included in codes of conduct and, if so, why?

Alternative Dispute Resolution

Methods

Alternative dispute resolution is a term usually used to describe a range of dispute resolution methods including arbitration, mediation, conciliation, mini-trial and expert determination. There are different reasons why these methods can be described as 'alternative'. The main reason is that they usually sit outside state processes; they are alternatives to litigation. The second reason is that they involve different kinds of processes than are available in the litigation system. The processes of ADR may be less adversarial and therefore less confrontational and formal than litigation.

Some examples of ADR confound the explanation that ADR is an alternative to litigation. Arbitration and mini-trial, for example, can be very similar to state-sponsored litigation. They have a neutral third party who sits as a judge and use rules of evidence. The decision is usually binding on the parties. This emphasises the importance of the other factor that makes ADR alternative: at some stage the process is chosen and agreed to by the parties. Beyond this, the term ADR describes very different processes with very different aims.

The common factor in any ADR process is the agreement of the parties to use that method. The agreement may occur before a dispute occurs, as is often the case in commercial contract arbitrations, or after a dispute arises, as in mediation. The second feature is that, because the parties agree to use the method, they usually have some control over the process and can set the 'rules of engagement'.

The final distinctive feature of the different ADR processes is that the parties choose a third party to help to resolve the dispute. This person is generically referred to as a 'third party neutral'. Beyond these essential features, there are differences in the kinds of processes used and the kinds of outcomes reached.

Context

Alternatives to litigation have existed for well over 100 years, arbitration having been a popular way of resolving commercial disputes since at least the 1800s. During the 1990s there was growing interest in ADR to resolve an even wider range of disputes. Mediation is arguably the most important of these alternatives and is the focus of the remainder of the chapter. In 1999 the CPR sought to make greater use of mediation as an alternative to litigation and trials.

Many lawyers have sought expertise as mediators or in other new methods of ADR. They may act as third party neutrals or be asked to represent clients in ADR processes. It is therefore necessary to consider the implications of this shift in the methods of dispute resolution and of the different roles lawyers can fulfil.

The Meta-Ethics of ADR and Adversarial Processes

Chapter one compared the operation and values of the adversarial system with those of the inquisitorial system. This demonstrated that different methods of dispute resolution represent different values and make different claims to being ethical. Similarly, ADR claims distinctive values and makes a claim to ethicality that also sets it apart from adversarial justice. For example, ADR claims to be consensual, participative, and therefore empowering, and flexible, and therefore potentially creative.

A framework for considering these claims is provided by the principles of autonomy, beneficence, non-maleficence and justice (see chapter three: Regulation and Discipline).[33] Each of these principles can be applied to both the public and the private face of dispute resolution. This assists in identifying the benefits that individuals potentially derive from different forms of dispute resolution. It also enables consideration of the benefits that the forms of dispute resolution are capable of generating for the wider society. Finally, it encourages evaluation of what lawyers potentially bring to ADR and how it should interact with other dispute resolution processes.

Individual Ethics

i. Autonomy

The right of an individual to make his or her own choice is claimed as one of the main justifications of courts. ADR arguably achieves greater levels of autonomy in this respect. In the case of alternative modes of adjudication, individuals can choose their own rules and neutral third party. In the consensual examples of ADR, such as conciliation and mediation, participants also choose whether their matter is settled and the terms on which it is settled. In the case of transformative mediation (see below), the aim of the process is that people grow as individuals and are more able to help themselves in the future.

Critics of informal processes argue that they potentially exaggerate power imbalances between the parties. Judges can compensate for inequality,[34] but the absence of powers of compulsion means that mediators cannot. Poor parties cannot pay for expert preparation of the case, cannot predict the outcome of adjudication and are under financial pressure to settle.[35] Informality may also encourage unreasonable behaviour.[36] Mediation may therefore exacerbate unequal power relations between parties, whether financial or psychological.[37]

ii. Beneficence

Trials provide very little opportunity to act with the best interest of the other in mind. Generally, there is only one winner. The same may be true in adjudicative ADR. Mediation and conciliation, on the other hand, provide opportunities to consider the interests of the other and to satisfy these interests. In

---

[33] TL Beauchamp and JF Childress, *Principles of Biomedical Ethics*, 4th edn (New York and Oxford, Oxford University Press, 2001) 12.

[34] J Auerbach, *Justice Without Law? Resolving Disputes Without Lawyers* (Oxford, Oxford University Press, 1983).

[35] O Fiss, 'Against Settlement' (1983) 93 *Yale Law Journal* 1073, 1076.

[36] R Delgado, C Dunn, P Brown, H Lee and D Hubert, 'Fairness and Formality: Minimizing the Risk of Prejudice in Alternative Dispute Resolution' (1985) *Wisconsin Law Review* 1359.

[37] N Fricker and J Walker, 'Alternative Dispute Resolution: State Responsibility or Second Best?' (1994) 13 *Civil Justice Quarterly* 29.

transformative mediation (see below) acts of recognition provide benefits to other participants, irrespective of outcome.

iii. Non-maleficence

Any kind of adjudication inevitably involves collateral harms to one side and possibly to both sides. The loser is not only deprived of what they consider a right, they are also penalised in costs. The winner may not achieve all that hoped to from the process. There may be adverse psychological consequences of these various losses.

iv. Justice

Adjudication seeks a fair outcome according to rules set out in advance. This may be fair procedurally, but it does not necessarily achieve substantive justice, fairness and equality among individuals. It is arguable that consensual methods of ADR may be even more susceptible to failure in this respect.

Public and Private Provision of ADR

Both state-sponsored adjudication and ADR can claim to offer social benefits. ADR is seldom the only kind of dispute resolution available, whereas state adjudication may be. The issue is often whether ADR is provided alongside state adjudication and, if so, what model is adopted and what degree of compulsion exists to participate.

i. Social Benefits of ADR

Processes such as mediation offer social benefits as well as personal benefits to participants. Procedural flexibility increases the chance of accommodating the different interests and perceptions that individuals bring to disputes. Processes such as mediation potentially change how the parties regard their situation. They encourage understanding of the views of others, promoting greater understanding and social cohesion. These features are seen to be consistent with the aims of a plural, liberal society.

Mediation promotes agreements freely arrived at with full knowledge of legal and practical alternatives. The argument that this encourages compliance is supported by research showing greater compliance with mediation agreements than with court orders.[38]

The capacity to increase client participation stimulates client choice and

---

[38] CA McEwen and RJ Maiman, 'Small Claims Mediation in Maine: An Empirical Assessment' (1981) 33 *Maine Law Review* 237.

individual autonomy. This promotes individual agency and personhood, a key goal of the liberal state.[39]

The generation of solutions encourages exploration of mutual benefit, creating the possibility of satisfaction, and therefore 'justice', for both sides. These features make processes such as mediation attractive as inexpensive, accessible and community-orientated forms of dispute resolution, making justice achievable for all. [40]

ii. Social Benefits of State Adjudication

Society benefits when individuals assert their rights through the courts. Faith in the rule of law is vindicated and strengthened, publicity is given to the result and others are encouraged to assert their own rights. Society arguably becomes more cohesive, grows stronger and becomes more flexible as a result. In contrast, ADR is often a private process. Whatever the form of ADR, whether adjudicative or consensual, no publicity is given to the result. The outome does not reflect any universal standard and is therefore of minimal interest to anyone but the parties. This potentially inhibits the development of public standards[41] and slows the rate of social change.

The promotion of ADR processes at the expense of state adjudication may have negative consequences for parties. The availability of low-risk processes, and the uncertainty of outcome, can encourage petty disputes. Critics of informal processes argue that settlement, however achieved, is inherently 'second rate' or 'compromise' justice.[42] Worse, any compulsion to participate is a denial of choice and individual autonomy. Significant growth in ADR processes could therefore compromise the rights ethos of liberalism.

iii. State-Sponsored ADR

The individual attractions and social benefits of mediation sometimes encourage the state to introduce compulsory mediation to court processes. The introduction of mediation schemes in the North Americas during the 1980s had mixed results.[43] Court congestion was substantially reduced and the number of settlements increased.[44] Some argued that these gains, and the

---

[39] A Wellington, 'Taking Codes of Ethics Seriously: Alternative Dispute Resolution and Reconstitutive Liberalism' (1999) 12 *Canadian Journal of Law and Jurisprudence* 297.

[40] SE Merry, 'The Social Organisation of Mediation in Non-industrial Societies: Implications for Informal Community Justice in America' in RL Abel (ed), *The Politics of Informal Justice*, vol 2: *Comparative Studies* (New York and London, Academic Press, 1982) 17.

[41] MA Scodro, 'Arbitrating Novel Legal Questions: A Recommendation for Reform' (1996) 105 *Yale Law Journal* 1927.

[42] See particularly, Fiss (n 35).

[43] M Galanter, 'Law Abounding: Legalisation Around the North Atlantic' (1992) 55:1 *Modern Law Review* 1, 11.

[44] DR Hensler, 'What We Know and Don't Know About Court Administered Arbitration'

need to overcome widespread ignorance of alternatives, justified a degree of compulsion to participate in mediation.[45] Making mediation compulsory also vitiates some of the claimed advantages of the process.

Many critics strongly opposed state co-option of ADR to court processes. They argued that compulsory participation eroded the crucial, consensual nature of ADR. In some circumstances, compulsion could be unreasonable, as where parties are forced to mediate with abusive former spouses.[46] The increased formality of court-annexed schemes can lead to reduced client participation, stronger pressure to settle, less participant satisfaction and fewer durable agreements.[47]

Mediation

Like many other ADR methods, mediation involves a neutral third party, the mediator, to help the parties explore their differences. It has emerged as the main method of ADR used in conjunction with adjudication processes. The third party neutral could, in theory, be a judge sitting in the relevant tribunal or a lawyer, or non-qualified neutral providing an independent service.[48]

Processes

A typical role for mediators involves 'shuttle diplomacy', because they operate as a conduit for the ideas and proposals of the parties, who may or may not meet. It is difficult to definitively describe process however, because there are different types of mediation with different aims, outcomes and styles. Three examples are facilitative mediation, transformative mediation and evaluative

---

(1986) 69 *Judicature* 270; WK Edwards, 'No Frills Justice: North Carolina Experiments with Court Ordered Arbitration' (1988) 66 *North Carolina Law Review* 395.

[45] SB Goldberg, ED Green and FEA Sanders, *Dispute Resolution* (Boston, Little Brown, 1985) 490.

[46] FE Raitt, 'Informal Justice and the Ethics of Mediating in Abusive Relationships' (1997) *Juridical Review* 76; R Dingwall, 'Empowerment or Enforcement? Some Questions about Power and Control in Divorce Mediation' in R Dingwall and J Eekelaar (eds), *Divorce Mediation and the Legal Process* (Oxford, Clarendon Press, 1988).

[47] RL Abel, 'The Contradictions of Informal Justice' in RL Abel (ed), *The Politics of Informal Justice*, vol 1: *The American Experience* (New York, Academic Press, 1982) 267; Auerbach (n 34).

[48] A Boon, P Urwin and V Karuk, 'What Difference Does it Make? Facilitative Judicial Mediation of Discrimination Cases in Employment Tribunals' (2011) 40(1) *Industrial Law Review* 45.

mediation. The method that is used affects the approach of the neutral third party, including the process used and the skills that are brought to bear.

Facilitative mediation is the most popular form because it aims to help parties resolve disputes. It does so by encouraging them to take a broad approach to problems, to explore integrative features of a situation and to recognise the benefits of compromise. Transformative mediation is more concerned with the impact of the mediation experience on the parties involved. It is concerned with the personal growth of the participants. It uses the opportunities that disputes provide for the parties to receive recognition. Finally, in evaluative mediation the parties look to the mediator to value the claims of the parties as well as seek avenues for settlement.

Each of these approaches has advantages and disadvantages. The disadvantage of the transformative model is that it is not geared towards producing practical solutions to disputes. The evaluative model, on the other hand leans too far towards adjudication. The facilitative model is accused of reproducing power relations between the parties. This is because facilitative mediators are typically non-directive, meaning that the parties have a free choice whether or not to participate and whether or not to settle their dispute. Parties are not pressured to settle in a facilitative mediation although settlement agreements that are reached are in principle enforceable by the courts.

Application

Alternative dispute resolution, at least in the initial stages of development, is often undertaken on the initiative of parties in order to avoid state-run dispute resolution. In this phase of development the consensual, flexible and participative elements of the processes are emphasised. At some later stage the processes are formalised. The facilitative model of mediation has been promoted by government as part of a package of reforms introduced by the CPR.

After an initial heavy-handed approach, using costs awards to penalise parties who did not engage with mediation, the courts reasserted the consensual nature of participation. In *Halsey v Milton Keynes General NHS Trust*[49] the Court of Appeal refused to penalise a party with a good defence to a claim for refusing to mediate. In *PGF II SA v OMFS Company 1 Ltd*[50] the Court of Appeal found that a party must 'constructively engage' with any request for ADR even if they decide not to participate. Otherwise they may not be awarded their costs even if they win the case.

Costs are not the only way parties have been encouraged to mediate. Like the CPR, the FPR place a heavy emphasis on mediation.[51] Before making

---

[49] *Halsey v Milton Keynes General NHS Trust* [2004] EWCA Civ 576.

[50] *PGF II SA v OMFS Company 1 Ltd* [2013] EWCA Civ 1288.

[51] Family Procedure Rules 2010 (as amended by Family Procedure (Amendment) (No 5) Rules 2012).

an application, parties must follow the steps of a protocol requiring them to consider with a mediator whether the dispute is capable of being resolved through mediation.[52] Thereafter, the courts are required to consider mediation and opportunities for requiring the parties to participate in it.

An even more significant step towards encouraging mediation was taken by the Legal Aid, Sentencing and Punishment of Offenders Act 2012 (LASPO). This removed legal aid from most family cases except those involving domestic violence or child abuse. Legal aid was retained however, for family mediation.

The promotion of ADR reflects a conscious decision by the state that can be interpreted in different ways. The most benign interpretation is the desire to increase economical routes to achieve justice. A more neutral interpretation sees it as the expansion of civil society through the use of informal networks to replace formal institutions.[53] More cynical analysts see the expansion of state power using 'covert manipulation' through community justice schemes and the like and the weakening of the role of the courts.[54]

Lawyers and Mediation

Alternative dispute resolution is an area of activity that is relatively unregulated. Often, no special background or training is required to work as a third party neutral. They are often drawn from a variety of disciplinary backgrounds. Lawyers are prominent among ADR practitioners, either as mediators or participants representing the parties. Business lawyers are among the chief proponents of arbitration or other ADR methods.[55] This is probably because they are more familiar with alternative processes. Their clients prefer the informality and flexibility of 'customised dispute resolution' such as arbitration.

It is increasingly seen as natural for lawyers to develop skills in ADR as an adjunct to their more familiar skills in handling litigation and advocacy. They appreciate the scope for controlling a dispute resolution process more effectively than they can litigation. They can develop remunerative sidelines as representatives or mediators. There is often a different reaction from ordinary lawyers when ADR processes are engrafted onto litigation and under court control. Lawyers both in the US and the UK were initially suspicious of court-annexed mediation. It was suggested that they preferred court-based

---

[52] Family Procedure Rules 2010, Practice Direction 3a—pre-application protocol for mediation information and assessment, para 4.1.

[53] B de Sousa Santos, *Toward a New Legal Common Sense: Law, Globalization, and Emancipation* (London, Butterworths, 2002).

[54] Abel (n 47).

[55] Y Dezalay, 'The Forum Should Fit the Fuss: the Economics and Politics of Negotiated Justice' in M Cain and CB Harrington (eds), *Lawyers in a Postmodern World: Translation and Transgression* (Buckingham, Open University Press, 1994) 155.

solutions. One suspicion was that they did not like the increased involvement of clients which ADR allowed.[56]

Whether or not lawyers are enthusiasts for ADR, they occupy an ambiguous position in relation to consensual processes such as mediation. ADR processes could be seen to require skills and techniques that lawyers should possess. The attitudes that go with them can be seen as the very antithesis of the adversarial ethos in which lawyers are trained to operate. It is relevant to ask whether lawyers can, and if so whether they should, expand their expertise beyond litigation and advocacy. In short, should lawyers be involved in ADR processes in any capacity?

Advantages of Lawyers' Involvement

Lawyers bring to mediation the general advantages of legal knowledge, a facility with handling complex information and familiarity with negotiation. A further advantage of involving lawyers in mediation is that it provides basic protection against the exploitation of power and unfair outcomes. It has been argued that a legal perspective is helpful in neutralising the emotions and moral connotations that accompany blame. Some research suggests that this is a crucial barrier to settlement.[57] Non-lawyer mediators may have difficulty in attributing and encouraging acceptance of blame, but it is natural for lawyers to do so.

Legal expertise is also potentially useful in mediation. In complex legal situations, for example, having a lawyer involved could avoid the parties having to take independent legal advice. This potentially introduces delay and could be a barrier to settlement. Where a lawyer is present, they may be able to advise, for example, on the potential tax implications of a particular settlement.

Lawyers have particular advantages in evaluative mediation, where knowledge and experience enables them to balance the value of informal outcomes against the likely result of legal processes. Given the evaluative skills of lawyers, and the arguments for their involvement in mediation, it is surprising that legal professions are such enthusiastic advocates of the facilitative model.

Criticisms of Lawyers' Involvement in ADR

There are potential problems with lawyers participating in ADR. Lawyers may assume that their experience of legal negotiations equips them sufficiently for

---

[56] L Mulcahy, 'Can Leopards Change their Spots? An Evaluation of the Role of Lawyers in Medical Negligence Mediation' (2001) 8 *International Journal of the Legal Profession* 203.
[57] MJ Borg, 'Expressing Conflict, Neutralising Blame, and Making Concessions in Small-Claims Mediation' (2000) *Law and Policy* 115.

mediation. Often, this is not the case. At the beginning of the mediation boom, the National Consumer Council asserted that a 'mediator without legal knowledge is definitely preferable to a lawyer who is deficient in mediation skills'.[58]

Some critics suggest that the adversarial training that lawyers undergo produces deep-seated flaws in the legal psyche. Lawyers' litigious orientation is seen as an unsuitable basis for problem solving.[59] They are too used to working towards the narrow goals in the form of judicial remedies, damages and injunctive relief, and towards negotiation outcomes that mirror them. They are wedded to procedure rather than solutions, leading to overly legalistic processes and delay.[60]

A further difficulty of lawyers' involvement in ADR relates to clients. Many lay people may be confused when the person they look to for protection of legal rights adopts a different, more conciliatory role. A further concern is that lawyers' relationships with clients are often paternalistic. This encourages a dependent relationship, leading lawyers to make assumptions about their clients' best interests and obstructing client empowerment and informed decision-making.[61]

Critics of lawyers' involvement in ADR suggest that the combination of adversarial and paternalistic orientations make it difficult for lawyers to be constructive participants in a process such as mediation. They are neither good at considering interests, rather than rights, nor acting as 'healers of human conflict'.[62]

Reconciling Adversarial and Conciliatory Roles

Debates surrounding the involvement of lawyers in ADR date back to the early days of the introduction of mediation. These debates were manifestations of the tensions between practitioners of different types of mediations as well as concerns about lawyers joining a field dominated by non-lawyer mediation practitioners.[63] Underlying the debates, however, lay real concerns

---

[58] C Ervine, *Settling Consumer Disputes: A Review of Alternative Dispute Resolution* (London, National Consumer Council, 1993) 34.

[59] AJ Pirie, 'The Lawyer as Mediator: Professional Responsibility Problems or Profession Problems?' (1985) 63 *Canadian Bar Review* 378 and 'The Lawyer as a Third Party Neutral: Promise and Problems' in DP Edmonds (ed), *Commercial Dispute Resolution: Alternatives to Litigation* (Aurora, Canada Law Books Inc, 1989) 27, 35.

[60] J Flood and A Caiger, 'Lawyers and Arbitration: The Juridification of Commercial Disputes' (1993) 56 *Modern Law Review* 412; N Gould and M Cohen 'ADR: Appropriate Dispute Resolution in the UK Construction Industry' (1988) *Civil Justice Quarterly* 103.

[61] A Gutmann, 'Can Virtue Be Taught to Lawyers?' (1993) 45 *Stanford Law Review* 1759.

[62] W Burger, 'Isn't There a Better Way?' (1982) 68 *American Bar Association Journal* 274.

[63] S Roberts, 'Mediation in the Lawyers' Embrace' (1992) 55 *Modern Law Review* 258; R Dingwall and D Greatbatch, 'Who Is in Charge? Rhetoric and Evidence in the Study of Mediation' (1993) 15 *Journal of Social Welfare and Family Law* 367; M Roberts, 'Who Is in Charge? Effecting a Productive Exchange Between Researchers and Practitioners in the Field of Family Mediation' (1994) 16 *Journal of Social Welfare and Family Law* 439; and R Dingwall

about method. Mediators with a facilitative or transformative orientation to mediation were particularly anxious that more legalistic and evaluative forms did not take hold and dominate the field.

There was, however, some evidence that fears about the adversarial orientation of lawyers were exaggerated. US research suggested that lawyers are more likely to use integrated problem-solving in mediation than in negotiation.[64] This suggests that lawyers have the capacity to move between different kinds of dispute resolution methods and roles and choose between them as appropriate. This capacity might be attributed to the 'case method', which requires students constantly to shift perspective from that of judge to advocate. It also means that they can adjust their adversarial tendencies if circumstances require them to.

Lawyers also have some useful characteristic skills for ADR, such as conducting informal but orderly proceedings and skills in dealing with people.[65] It is arguable, however, that lawyers do need to be more aware of any paternalistic, competitive and aggressive traits that they might bring to the process. It may also be necessary for them to develop different attitudes and qualities and learn new skills, attitudes and techniques.

Mediation skills proceed from a different base than the skills lawyers use in client interviewing and litigation. Litigation skills tend to focus on the gathering and analysis of legally relevant information and are not geared to either client engagement or empowerment. Mediation requires a different toolkit, starting from a different base. Mediation requires a set of qualities and skills that constitute the core of counselling.[66] These are empathy, genuineness, listening and probing, together with creativity and foresight, analysis, advice, explanation and co-operation. These are also the foundation skills of problem-solving negotiation, but it is necessary to add strategy, persuasion and conciliation for mediation. In order to complete the skill-set for mediation, it is necessary to add respect for client autonomy, and the acceptance of individuals as rational, problem-solving entities.[67]

Lawyers and Mediation: An Overview

There are four different accounts or interpretations of the role of mediation.[68]

---

and D Greatbatch, 'Family Mediation Researchers and Practitioners in the Shadow of the Green Paper: A Rejoinder to Marion Roberts' (1995) 17 *Journal of Social Welfare and Family Law* 199.

[64] EE Gordon, 'Attorney's Negotiation Strategies in Mediation: Business as Usual? (2000) 17 *Mediation Quarterly* 377.

[65] RB McKay, 'Ethical Considerations in Alternative Dispute Resolution' (1990) 45 *Arbitration Journal* 15, 22.

[66] RM Bastress and JD Harbaugh, *Interviewing, Counseling and Negotiating: Skills for Effective Representation* (Boston, Toronto and London, Little Brown and Company, 1990) 5.

[67] SC Grebe, 'Ethics and the Professional Family Mediator' (1992) 10 *Mediation Quarterly* 155; DP Joyce, 'The Role of the Intervenor: A Client Centred Approach' (1995) 12 *Mediation Quarterly* 301.

[68] RAB Bush and JP Folger, *The Promise of Mediation: Responding to Conflict through*

Which account is accepted suggests what role lawyers should adopt in relation to ADR. The first account suggests that 'consumer satisfaction' with ADR processes indicates that they are better than adversarial dispute resolution. In this story, collaborative and integrative approaches reach win–win solutions that satisfy the needs of all parties, reducing economic and emotional cost.

The second account casts mediation as a method of organising people around a common interest. Individuals help themselves to solve problems, reducing the dependency of social groups lacking power and grassroots organisations. This empowers them to achieve social justice and limit exploitation.

The third perspective on the role of mediation emphasises its power to transform individuals and society by people defining their own problems and seeking their own outcomes. Parties are empowered by controlling their own dispute resolution processes and develop sympathy for the views and compassion for the other party in the process.

The fourth and final account is a story of oppression. This accuses mediation of allowing mediators too much control of parties and allowing stronger parties to manipulate the weak. In this account, mediation undermines the public interest by channelling and privatising class conflicts and public interest problems.

The role of lawyers in relation to ADR depends to some extent on which story of ADR is preferred. In the first story, lawyers must avoid subverting the potential of ADR. This requires that they develop the skills to conceive of and develop innovative solutions to problems and to disputes and avoid imposing their adversarial assumptions on the process. In the second and third stories, they must avoid colonising ADR so that the potential for community gains and individual empowerment are not lost. In the fourth story, they must be alert to the risk that ADR steals justice from the weak; they must demand formal justice for their clients when it is necessary.

Professional Regulation of ADR

Education and Training

The growing involvement of lawyers in ADR may have implications for legal education and training. Lawyers acting as third-party neutrals may need specified levels of experience or be required to undergo relevant training. At

Empowerment and Recognition (San Francisco, Jossey-Bass Publishers, 1994) ch 1; and for a more detailed summary H Burgess and M Yevsyukova, *The Promise of Mediation: Responding to Conflict Through Empowerment and Recognition* (Conflict Research Consortium, 1997) www. colorado.edu/conflict/transform/bushbook.htm.

the very least, lawyers must be able to distinguish the different processes if they are to offer competent advice. Ensuring lawyers have foundation skills for mediation could require that legal education and training take a different approach generally[69] and include training in ADR. When and how to teach lawyers about ADR is a subject not without difficulty.

Introducing students to ADR skills too late carries the risk that an adversarial mind-set is already entrenched in students, while introducing it early may encourage them to see legal practice as 'mastery of the arts of interpersonal manipulations'.[70] The balance of the arguments seems, however, to favour the early introduction of the full palette of dispute resolution techniques, allowing new lawyers to have a more sophisticated understanding of 'the morality of influence'.[71]

Conduct Rules

The growing involvement of lawyers in ADR raises issues about recognition of different processes and methods in conduct rules. On conflicts of interest, for example, there are likely to be restrictions on lawyers acting as mediators in matters involving present or former clients, as in the US and Canada.[72] The code of conduct might specify different obligations for lawyers acting as third party neutrals and providers of dispute resolution advice. It is also necessary to consider what responsibilities lawyers have in advising on dispute resolution.

Despite these considerations, the rapid growth of ADR has had relatively little impact on codes of conduct. Rather, the Law Society initially developed separate Codes of Practice for Commercial Mediation and for Family Mediation. While it still maintains the Commercial Code, solicitors accredited to the Law Society's Family Mediation Accreditation Scheme are bound by the Family Mediation Council's Code of Practice.[73]

The main section of the code is in Part 5, part of which is reproduced below.

---

[69] M Minnow, 'Some Thoughts on Dispute Resolution and Civil Procedure' (1984) 34 *Journal of Legal Education* 284.

[70] PD Carrington, 'Civil Procedure and Alternative Dispute Resolution' (1981) 34 *Journal of Legal Education* 298.

[71] P Brest, 'The Responsibility of Law Schools: Educating Lawyers as Counsellors and Problem Solvers' (1995) 58 *Law and Contemporary Problems* 6.

[72] Pirie (n 59) 45.

[73] www.lawsociety.org.uk/support-services/accreditation/family-mediation/.

Family Mediation Council Code of Practice
(www.familymediationcouncil.org.uk/us/code-practice/general-principles/)

5 GENERAL PRINCIPLES

5.1 Impartiality and Conflicts of Interest

5.1.1 It is the duty of the mediator at all times to ensure that he or she acts with impartiality and that that impartiality is not compromised at any time by any conflict of interest, actual or capable of being perceived as such.

5.1.2 Mediators must not have any personal interest in the outcome of the mediation.

5.1.3 Mediators must not mediate in any case in which they have acquired or may acquire relevant information in any private or other professional capacity.

5.1.4 Mediators must not act or continue to act if they or a member of their firm has acted for any of the parties in issues not relating to the mediation.

5.1.5 Mediators must not accept referrals from any professional practice with whom they are employed, in partnership or contracted, on a full or part-time basis and which is involved in advising one of the participants on matters which relate or are capable of relating to the mediation, even though the practices are separate legal entities.

5.1.6 Mediators must not refer a participant for advice or for any other professional service to a professional practice with whom they are employed, in partnership or contracted, on a full or part-time basis on matters which relate or are capable of relating to the mediation even though the practices are separate legal entities.

5.1.7 Mediation must be conducted as an independent professional activity and must be distinguished from any other professional role in which the mediator may practise,

5.2 Voluntary Participation

Participation in mediation is voluntary at all times and participants and the mediator are always free to withdraw. Where mediators consider that a participant is unable or unwilling to take part in the process freely and fully, they must raise the issue and possibly suspend or terminate the mediation.

5.3 Neutrality

Mediators must remain neutral as to the outcome of a mediation at all times. Mediators must not seek to impose their preferred outcome on the participants or to influence them to adopt it, whether by attempting to predict the outcome of court proceedings or otherwise. However, if the participants consent, they may inform them that they consider that the resolutions they are considering might fall outside the parameters which a court might approve or order. They may inform participants of possible courses of action, their legal or other implications, and assist them to explore these, but must make it clear that they are not giving advice.

5.4 Impartiality

5.4.1 Mediators must at all times remain impartial as between the participants and conduct the mediation process in a fair and even-handed way.

5.4.2 Mediators must seek to prevent manipulative, threatening or intimidating behaviour by any participant. They must conduct the process in such a way as to redress, as far as possible, any imbalance of power between the participants. If such behaviour or any other imbalance seems likely to render the mediation unfair or ineffective, mediators must take appropriate steps to seek to prevent this including terminating the mediation if necessary.

5.5 Confidentiality

5.5.1 Subject to paragraphs 5.5.3, 5.5.4 and 5.5.5 below mediators must not disclose any information about, or obtained in the course of, a mediation to anyone, including a court welfare officer or a court, without the express consent of each participant, an order of the court or where the law imposes an overriding obligation of disclosure on mediators.

5.5.2 Mediators must not discuss the mediation or correspond with any participant's legal advisor without the express consent of each participant. Nothing must be said or written to the legal advisor of one party regarding the content of the discussions in mediation which is not also said or written to the legal advisor(s) of the other.

5.5.3 Where it appears necessary so that a specific allegation that a child has suffered significant harm may be properly investigated or where mediators suspect that a child is suffering or is likely to suffer significant harm, mediators must ensure that the relevant Social Services department is notified.

5.5.4 Mediators may notify the appropriate agency if they consider that other public policy considerations prevail, such as an adult suffering or likely to suffer significant harm.

5.5.5 Where mediators suspect that they may be required to make disclosure to the appropriate government authority under the Proceeds of Crime Act 2002 and/or relevant money laundering regulations, they must stop the mediation immediately without informing the clients of the reason.

Q11.10   Which solicitors does this code of conduct apply to?

Q11.11   Is provision 5.3.3 consistent with the SRA Code of Conduct?

Q11.12   If a provision of this code conflicted with the SRA Code of Conduct, which do you think should prevail?

Conclusion

Negotiation is an important component in the settlement of disputes, including litigation. Despite this, regulations dealing with negotiation are not very well developed. In fact there is evidence that different areas of work will develop different cultures of negotiation, making the development of universal norms quite difficult.

Although negotiation takes place outside of the formal litigation process, it is often conducted along adversarial lines. It may be assumed that this serves clients' best interests, but it may not always be the case. This leaves some large questions unanswered. For example, do lawyers settling a claim that will otherwise be determined by trial have to be adversarial and, accordingly, competitive?

ADR escapes from the conflicts, of interests and ethics, attendant on adversarial justice. This is because it proceeds from different foundations. New dispute resolution mechanisms, such as mediation, aim to make access to justice more community based, less formal and less legalistic. It is arguable that the new spirit of co-operation provides a better ethos for dispute resolution.

The implicit tempering of the adversarial spirit must affect the way that lawyers interpret their role and the ethical obligations they are under. It may affect the way they approach the key litigation tasks of negotiation and advocacy. It also influences responses to the introduction of mediation as mainstream legal work. The tension in reconciling and managing adversarial and conciliatory roles is a new task for legal professional ethics.

In England and Wales the tone and content of legal professional ethics is informed, if not determined, by the model of the adversarial case and trial. At present, while there is some evidence that the practice of dispute resolution has become more collaborative, there is little evidence that the co-operative ethos has affected the codes of conduct.

Commercial Practice

Overview

The commercial practice of law receives relatively little regulatory attention. Large-firm lawyers infrequently appear before disciplinary tribunals. The codes of conduct rarely throw up competing duties for commercial lawyers, such as the duty of confidentiality to clients and the duty to the court. The first part of this chapter therefore highlights areas of special significance to lawyers conducting transaction work.

The second part of the chapter considers the international legal services market. This is a major focus of large law firms in England and Wales. Many of these firms are global players in intense competition to supply the international financial and commercial sectors. International legal work is being 'constructed' by international lawyers in much the same way as legal work was formerly constructed in domestic markets. Because English law firms are world leaders in this field they are major players in constructing a worldwide legal culture.

International law firms have relative freedom of operation because the international sphere is relatively unregulated. National governments and international agencies have no remit to control the international dimension of the conduct of lawyers. International lawyers are therefore seeking control of their work, just as they did nationally. In doing so they are using familiar ideological and rhetorical devices, including appeals for the rule of law.

Transactions

Context

Advising on and conducting clients' commercial transactions comprises a large part of legal work for many lawyers, particularly solicitors. The scope of this kind of work is vast. It covers a range of transactions from domestic conveyancing to the sale of massive public companies such as Royal Mail. In the mid-range transactions, lawyers are constantly working to complete large commercial contracts or to settle disputes arising from such transactions.

Application of General Principles

The SRA Principles apply to transactions so, for example, solicitors have to demonstrate integrity. In the same way, most conduct rules apply to both contentious and to 'non-contentious' work such as conducting transactions. Some, however, such as the duty to the court, can clearly apply only in litigation.

Legal Professional Privilege

It may be thought that principles such as LPP might apply differently in non-contentious contexts, where the liberty of the person claiming the privilege is unlikely to be at stake. The courts, however, are often involved in overseeing transactions and apply established principles just as zealously to transactions.

Banque Keyser Ullman v Skandia [1986] 1 Lloyds Rep 336

Four companies borrowed 80 million Swiss francs from banks under loan agreements. Under the terms of the agreements the borrowers lodged gemstones, accompanied by professional valuations, showing that the value of the stones lodged was more than twice the amount of the loan. Insurance policies were also taken out to cover the banks against failure of the borrowers to repay. Three of the borrowers assigned such policies to the banks. In the fourth case, the policy was issued directly to the bank.

    The loans were not repaid. In actions seeking to establish whether or not the insurers were liable under the policies the insurers contended that the policies were obtained by the fraud of the borrowers and therefore unenforceable. The insurers claimed the right to see documents, communications and notes passing between the banks and their solicitors at the time when the loans were made. These documents, the insurers claimed, were not privileged because of the fraud perpetrated by the borrowers.

On appeal to the Court of Appeal Lord Justice Parker:

> The learned judge accepted, as do I, that legal professional privilege does not exist in respect of documents which are in themselves part of a criminal or unlawful fraudulent proceeding or, if it be different, communications made in order to get advice for the purpose of carrying out a fraud, and that this is so whether the solicitor was or was not ignorant of the fact that he was being used for that purpose. I assume, as did the judge, that were the borrowers in this case the parties claiming privilege, either in litigation or in answer to a subpoena [seeking production of the documents], no claim to privilege in respect of documents or communications falling within the above descriptions could be maintained.

However, Mr Justice Staughton said at page 12 of the judgment:

> It is one thing to say that a party who has consulted his solicitor in the course of preparation or furtherance of crime or fraud ought not to be able to claim privilege for such communications. It is quite another to say that, because a party claims as assignee of a fraudsman, or because he has been the victim of fraud, he loses privilege, not for the fraudsman's communications with the fraudsman's solicitor, but for his own wholly innocent communications with his own solicitor.

It is clearly quite another thing, and the judge held that it was not the law.

Q12.1 What kind of privilege could the banks claim for the documents, communications and notes passing between them and their solicitors at the time when the loans were made? (See chapter six.)

Q12.2 On the basis of the reasoning of Parker LJ and Staughton J, should the insurance companies have been able to see the communications between the banks and their solicitors?

Negotiation

Methods

Those negotiating transactions are arguably in a very different position from those trying to settle litigation. The client of a transaction lawyer may have a long-term relationship with the other party or may wish to develop one. The clients may be open to creative ways of developing the relationship to the benefit of both sides. The transaction lawyer is therefore more likely to need to employ creative problem-solving in negotiation.

For commercial problems with integrative features a 'problem-solving' orientation is preferable. This involves identifying the parties' underlying needs and objectives and finding ways to meet those needs directly. Whenever possible, opportunities to expand the resources available and add value to solutions should be taken. Even where there is no perfect integration of the parties' interests, it may be possible to improve outcomes by understanding the different values that the parties place on the subject matter.[1] An identified problem of negotiation is that integrative potential can be obscured by distributive assumptions.

The implication of using an inappropriate method of bargaining is illustrated by the tale of two children arguing over the last orange in the fruit bowl. Neither is prepared to give it up. Their argument brings the intervention of a wise adult who establishes that one child wants the segments of the orange to eat while the other wants the skin as a cake ingredient. Both can have exactly what they want. A problem that the children interpreted as distributive was, in fact, integrative. Their competitiveness and lack of appreciation of negotiation methods obscured the solution.

In more realistic scenarios poor method choice is a potential barrier to effective negotiation. If the nature of a problem is unclear, there is a risk of using the wrong approach to resolve it. This is problematic when a situation has significant integrative potential, but the parties approach it as a purely distributive issue. In the real world, transaction may or may not have integrative features. Lawyers can only find out by being open about their clients' needs and preferences. This, however, can be dangerous. It can be difficult to predict whether divulging such information may disadvantage the client. The use of principled negotiation, as defined in the last chapter, may provide some protection against such risks.

Negotiation Privilege

Negotiations between lawyers can be protected by negotiation privilege. This is usually claimed when the parties agree that discussions are 'without prejudice'. Courts usually respect negotiation privilege where the negotiation takes place with a view to settling a dispute. The 'without-prejudice rule' is traditionally taken to reflect a public policy objective in promoting settlement. This would be less likely if any admissions made in the course of negotiation could later be held against a party.

Even where the 'without-prejudice' rule applies there are recognised exceptions. Therefore, for example, the court may examine whether without-prejudice communications resulted in a compromise agreement. It may also

---

[1] C Menkel-Meadow, 'Toward Another View of Legal Negotiation: The Structure of Problem Solving' (1984) 31 *UCLA Law Review* 754, 795.

do so to consider rectification of an agreement. Finally, when the court is construing an agreement, evidence of without-prejudice negotiation may be admitted to determine the parties' intentions at the time.

Provided negotiation was for the purpose of settlement, it does not matter whether or not the discussions were not stated to be 'without prejudice'. Similarly, if discussions did not take place with a view to settlement, claiming that they were 'without prejudice' will not prevent the courts examining the content of discussion for specific purposes. It is, however, not always clear how much of what passes in negotiation is covered or whether privilege only attaches to admissions.

Oceanbulk Shipping & Trading SA v TMT Asia Ltd
Also known as:
TMT Asia Ltd v Oceanbulk Shipping & Trading SA
Supreme Court [2010] UKSC 44; [2011] 1 AC 662

'Without-prejudice' negotiations took place between parties when the defendants failed to pay a sum due under commercial agreements. A settlement was agreed regarding the sum due. The claimant sued the defendants alleging breach of the settlement agreement. The defendants relied on communications in the 'without-prejudice' negotiations to support their interpretation of the clause. The claimant sought a declaration that evidence of the negotiations was inadmissible unless both parties agreed to waive privilege.

The Supreme Court reversed the Court of Appeal decision. It held that 'without-prejudice' communications were admissible for the purpose of determining how the terms of the agreement were to be construed. The language of the agreement should be construed in the same way and the relevant question should be the same, namely what a reasonable person having all the background knowledge which would have been available to the parties would have understood them to be using the language in the contract to mean.

Relevant background knowledge might well include objective facts communicated by one party to the other in the course of the negotiations. The process of interpretation should in principle be the same, whether the negotiations were without prejudice or not. In both cases, the evidence was admitted to enable the court to make an objective assessment of the parties' intentions.

Lord Clarke of Stone-cum-Ebony JSC quoted with approval dicta of Robert Walker LJ in *Unilever plc v The Procter & Gamble Co* [2000] 1 WLR 2436, suggesting that the without-prejudice rule is not limited to admissions but now extends much more widely to the content of discussions such as occurred in this case. According to Walker LJ:

Without in any way underestimating the need for proper analysis of the rule, I have no doubt that busy practitioners are acting prudently in making the general working assumption that the rule, if not 'sacred' (*Hoghton v Hoghton* (1852) 15 Beav 278, 321), has a wide and compelling effect. That is particularly true where the 'without prejudice' communications in question consist not of letters or other written documents but of wide-ranging unscripted discussions during a meeting which may have lasted several hours. At a meeting of that sort the discussions between the parties' representatives may contain a mixture of admissions and half-admissions against a party's interest, more or less confident assertions of a party's case, offers, counter-offers, and statements (which might be characterised as threats, or as thinking aloud) about future plans and possibilities. (2443H–2444C)

Q12.3 Can negotiation privilege be claimed for pre-contractual negotiation or only for negotiation attempting to settle disputes arising from transactions?

Q12.4 What material is potentially covered by negotiation privilege?

Undertakings

Promises given by lawyers to perform an action are usually referred to as undertakings. The glossary to the SRA Code of Conduct suggests that an undertaking:

> means a statement, given orally or in writing, whether or not it includes the word 'undertake' or 'undertaking', made by or on behalf of you or your *firm*, in the course of *practice*, or by you outside the course of *practice* but as a *solicitor* or *REL*, to someone who reasonably places reliance on it, that you or your *firm* will do something or cause something to be done, or refrain from doing something.

As this formula suggests, lawyers must be extremely cautious in what they promise to do, otherwise they may find that they have given an undertaking. Moreover, any ambiguous wording in the terms of the undertaking is usually construed in favour of the recipient.[2] Breaches of undertaking are often reported to the regulator by other solicitors. It is not uncommon for disciplinary action to be taken against solicitors for breach of undertaking. For an undertaking to be construed it is not necessary that the word 'undertaking' appears anywhere in relation to what is not promised.

---

[2] *Reddy v Lachlan* [2000] Lloyd's Rep PN858.

Solicitors Disciplinary Tribunal
Solicitors Regulation Authority Applicant
and
Asabe Georgina Adeyemo Respondent
Case No 10580-2010

Extract from the transcript

Allegation 1.1

8. In a letter dated 12 March 2009 GC & Co reported their difficulties in obtaining a file from the Respondent's firm on behalf of Mrs EG for whom the firm had previously acted in the purchase of a property. Mrs EG needed the file in connection with possession proceedings she wished to take against a tenant of the property. The firm responded to GC & Co on 23 October 2008 indicating that they were obtaining the file. They wrote again on 8 January 2009 in response to a further letter from GC & Co demanding a written undertaking. In the response the firm stated 'We confirm that we now have in our possession the file you request and you will be in receipt of a copy of the file no later than 12 January 2009.' Throughout the involvement of the SRA in this matter the file was not provided.

Allegation 1.2

9. On 17 April 2009 R Solicitors wrote to the SRA to complain of their inability to obtain the release of a sum of £2,000 retained by the Respondent on behalf of her purchaser clients as part of a transaction concerning a property in Croydon. The Respondent had written to R Solicitors on 7 March 2008:

'Further to our telephone conversation today and your subsequent faxed letter, we undertake to hold £2,000 to cover the arrears of ground rent and service charges for the period 24/03/07 until 06/03/08. If there are no arrears the full balance of £2,000 is to be returned to you to reimburse your client. If there are arrears, then any balance will be returned to you within one month of completion.'

Completion took place in March 2008. On 3 April 2008 R Solicitors wrote to the Respondent to indicate that the managing agents of the property had informed them that the Respondent had not served notice of Assignment of the Lease on them and requesting the return of the retention as a matter of urgency. Despite subsequent chasing as at 17 April 2009 the retention monies had not been returned.

10. In respect of allegations 1.1 and 1.2 the SRA wrote separate letters concerning each matter to the Respondent on 4 September 2009. The SRA also wrote to the Respondent's partner in the firm Ms A. On 8 September 2009 Ms A wrote two separate letters to the SRA in which she stated that she had been a partner in the firm but had ceased to be so in mid-September 2009. During her time there she asserted that the Respondent 'took all the major management decisions as she had worked as a property solicitor for a number of years.' Regarding the complaint the subject of allegation 1.1 Ms A said that she had contacted the Respondent on several occasions in order for her to resolve the matter and had managed to

do so in July 2009. The Respondent had apparently told her that she would deal with the matter. Ms A asserted the Respondent 'undertook full responsibility and possession of all the files.' While the undertaking regarding the file the subject of allegation 1.1 was not fulfilled, Ms A fulfilled the undertaking the subject of allegation 1.2 and paid to R Solicitors £2,000 in March 2010.

20. Allegation 1.1. Failed to comply with an undertaking given by her firm on 8 January 2009 to GC & Co in breach of Rule 10.05(1) of the Solicitors Code of Conduct 2007.

20.1 The Tribunal found that the Respondent's firm had given an undertaking on 8 January 2009 to GC & Co which had never been fulfilled and that this allegation was proved.

21. Allegation 1.2. Failed to comply with an undertaking given by her firm on 7 March 2008 to R Solicitors in breach of Rule 10.05(1) of the SCC.

21.1 The Tribunal found that the Respondent's firm had given an undertaking on 7 March 2008 to R Solicitors and that the Respondent had not fulfilled the undertaking in a reasonable time or at all. Monies had been paid instead by her former partner Ms A to discharge the undertaking in March 2010. The Tribunal found this allegation proved against the Respondent.

Sanction

32. Whilst the Tribunal had noted that no allegations of dishonesty had been made against the Respondent they considered that the allegations proved against her which were numerous were of a serious nature. Clients' monies had disappeared and no explanation had been offered. Lack of integrity had been proved against the Respondent. Her misconduct had affected several clients whom she abandoned along with her practice and her former partner. Her conduct was considered to have been likely to diminish public trust in the profession. It was also felt that having regard to the need to protect the public it was no longer appropriate for the Respondent to practise as a solicitor. The Tribunal had initially considered whether an indefinite suspension would suffice but the circumstances were such that it was not feasible in the circumstances to identify conditions which the Respondent might be required to fulfil in order for it to be appropriate for her to apply for such a suspension to be lifted. In all the circumstances the Tribunal felt that it had no choice but to strike the Respondent from the Roll.

Q12.5 Which Code of Conduct were the allegations against the respondent based on?

Q12.6 In relation to each charge, which words gave rise to an undertaking?

Q12.7 If the case were heard today, which of the current SRA Principles would the respondent be in breach of and which current SRA Outcomes would the respondent have failed to meet?

Despite the dangers in lawyers giving undertakings, they are necessary in many transactions. In conveyancing, for example, solicitors frequently give undertakings. They may promise to discharge mortgages, produce or return documents, hold monies to order or exchange contracts for the sale of land, or facilitate some other event. Much legal business could not be carried out speedily or efficiently without reliance on undertakings. The courts have enforced solicitors' undertakings in different ways, for example as a basis for creating trusts, ordering performance and awarding compensation.

Ordering Performance and Awarding Compensation

In relation to litigation, a court can exercise its inherent supervisory jurisdiction over solicitors and order the performance of an undertaking. The courts will order that lawyers discharge their undertaking if it is within their power to perform whatever acts are required. If discharge is no longer within the power of the lawyer, the court may order the lawyer to pay compensation and refer the matter to the relevant disciplinary body.[3]

International Legal Work

Domestic Regulation of Overseas Lawyers Coming to England and Wales

Lawyers qualified in overseas jurisdictions can practice in England and Wales in a number of ways. Most are registered and regulated by host professions.

Registered European Lawyers

In Europe, the potential for international legal practice was driven by the formation of the European Economic Community (EEC) and subsequently by the European Union (EU). In 1977, the European Commission passed Directive (EC) 77/249, giving EU lawyers limited rights to work in other Member States. Following Directive (EC) 98/5 in 1998, EU lawyers were permitted to practice in other Member States.[4]

European lawyers wishing to practice in another EU state under their home

---

[3] *Citadel Management Inc v Thompson* [1999] 1 FLR 21; *Udall v Capri Lighting Ltd* [1988] QB 907.

[4] Establishment of Lawyers Directive 98/5/EC.

title, without integrating into the local profession, must register with a professional body in the host country.[5] A Registered European Lawyer (REL) is an individual registered with the SRA under EC regulations.[6] They can practise from an office in England or Wales in their own right or with another domestically qualified or European lawyer, as permitted by the host professional body.[7] They can also practice as an employee[8] performing the same kind of work they would do in their home jurisdiction.

In order to decide the extent of the work they can do, the host profession is obliged to compare the qualifications and experience a European lawyer has gained in his or her other Member State. It must assess its relevance to the exercise of the work of the profession in question.[9] Depending on which European profession they belong to, RELs may be authorised by the SRA to undertake the same reserved work available to solicitors, subject to certain conditions.

The reserved work available to RELs includes work as an advocate using the rights of audience available to solicitors before the Courts and Legal Services Act 1990. This means, broadly, that they have access to county courts and magistrates' courts. They can also prepare documents in court and participate in immigration tribunal proceedings. In these two areas, however, they must act in conjunction with a solicitor or barrister authorised to do that work.[10]

Registered Foreign Lawyers

Overseas lawyers not subject to the Establishment Directive need not register with the SRA or be subject to solicitors' regulation provided they practice under their home title. A Registered Foreign Lawyer (RFL) means an individual who is not a European lawyer but is registered with the SRA. This follows from powers granted to the Law Society, under the Courts and Legal Services Act 1990 section 89, to apply key provisions of the Solicitors Act 1974 to RFLs. These include provisions relating to professional practice, conduct and discipline.

Under the SRA Practice Framework Rules Rule 3 practice as a RFL is confined to work as an employee of an SRA-authorised body or sole practitioner. RFLs must not be held out in any way which suggests that they are entitled to practise as a lawyer in England and Wales or undertake other reserved

---

[5] European Communities (Lawyer's Practice) Regulations 2000, Statutory Instrument 2000 No 1119. 'The Establishment Regulations' reg 1(3) and 16.
[6] European Communities (Lawyer's Practice) Regulations 2000 (SI 2000/ no 1119) regulation 17.
[7] Ibid, regulation 8.
[8] Solicitors Regulation Authority, *SRA Practice Framework Rules 2011*, Rule 2.1.
[9] Case C-313/01 *Christine Morgenbesser v Consiglio dell'Odine degli avvocati di Genoa* [2003] All ER (D) 190 (Nov).
[10] Solicitors Regulation Authority, *SRA Practice Framework Rules 2011*, Rule 8.1.

activities. They must not carry out any reserved work except advocacy before immigration tribunals, the preparation of documents in immigration tribunal proceedings and provision of immigration advice.[11]

Admission of Overseas Lawyers

Lawyers from overseas jurisdictions can also seek admission by virtue of European Directive 2005/36/EC and the Establishment Directive. To practice as a solicitor they must show that they are fully qualified lawyers entitled to practise in a recognised jurisdiction and can meet the SRAs English-language and character and suitability requirements.[12] Eligible candidates must then pass papers that the SRA specify from a number of English law subjects. These include substantive subjects, practice subjects, such as litigation and conveyancing, and professional conduct and accounts.

Lawyers from England and Wales Practising Overseas

A solicitor qualified in England and Wales is authorised to practice as a solicitor from an office outside England and Wales as a sole practitioner, employee or in a number of other ways.[13] English solicitors practising overseas are subject to the SRA Overseas Rules 2013. These are an adaptation of the general SRA Principles, but are intended to be applied so as to 'take account of the different legal, regulatory and cultural context of practice in other jurisdictions, which may require different standards of conduct to those required in England and Wales'.[14] This, it is said, does not imply a lower standard of general behaviour. Individuals practising overseas and responsible authorised bodies must comply with the rules and the SRA's character and suitability requirements.

Before lawyers from England and Wales can practice overseas, local regulators may require the SRA to issue certificates of good standing for individuals and authorised businesses. The SRA is usually expected to maintain regulatory control alongside the local regulatory regime. The SRA envisages that local regulation should prevail whenever there is a conflict.[15]

The only exception to local rules prevailing over the SRA's own rules is where this would cause conflict with Principle 6. Overseas Principle 6 prohibits doing anything bringing the overseas practice, the regulated individual, or the legal profession of England and Wales into disrepute. This is the only

---

[11] Ibid, Rule 8.4.
[12] SRA Qualified Lawyers Transfer Scheme Regulations 2011, regulation 2.
[13] SRA *Practice Framework Rules 2011*, Rule 1.2.
[14] SRA *Introduction to the SRA Overseas Rules 2013*, www.sra.org.uk/solicitors/handbook/introoverseasrules/content.page.
[15] Ibid.

Overseas Principle that must be observed at all times, even if to do so would result in a breach of local law or regulation.

The SRA Overseas Rules 2013 rules are brief. In addition to the principles of the SRA Handbook adapted to overseas practice, there is one substantive principle. Overseas Principle 3 states that: 'You must not allow your independence or the independence of your overseas practice to be compromised.'[16] There are also requirements for monitoring, reporting and notification of breaches. The rule repeats the statement that the SRA does not expect or require the same level as would be expected of a solicitor in England and Wales in relation to any of these requirements.[17]

The responsibility is to report 'any material or systemic breaches of the Overseas Principles that apply to you or to those for whom you are responsible' to the SRA when they occur, or as soon as reasonably practicable thereafter.[18] A material or systemic breach is defined as something relating to the character and suitability of an individual, the financial vulnerability of an overseas practice or a pattern of behaviour infringing Overseas Principle 6. This includes, for example, convictions by criminal courts or disciplinary action by another regulator.

SRA Overseas Practice Rules

2.1 With regard to the Overseas Principles set out in Rule 1:

(a) they apply to you if you are a regulated individual practising overseas, or a responsible authorised body in relation to each of its overseas practices;

(b) you will be committing a breach if you permit another person to do anything on your behalf which, if done by you, would constitute a breach of these rules;

(c) you should ensure that you and those for whom you are responsible under these rules comply with all legal and regulatory obligations applicable in the jurisdiction outside England and Wales in which you or they are practising. You, and those for whom you are responsible under these rules, should not cause, contribute to or facilitate a failure to comply with those legal or regulatory obligations by any other person or body subject to them;

(d) where there is a conflict between compliance with the Overseas Principles set out in Rule 1 and/or the Reporting Requirements set out in Rule 3 on the one hand, and any requirements placed upon you or those for whom you are responsible under these rules by local law or regulation on the other hand, the latter shall prevail, with the exception of Overseas Principle 6 [not bringing the overseas practice into disrepute], which must be observed at all times.

---

[16] *SRA Overseas Rules 2013*, Part 1: The Overseas Principles.
[17] *SRA Overseas Rules 2013*, Part 2: Application, Rule 3.1.
[18] *SRA Overseas Rules 2013*, Part 3: Reporting Requirements, Rule 3.2.

Q12.8 If a lawyer from England and Wales working overseas is asked to act for a client in a conflict of interest situation under the SRA code, can she act if local rules allow it?

England and Wales as Part of a Global Network

The International Legal Services Market

The international legal services market is a major focus of large law firms and for many barristers in England and Wales. Some London-based firms are among the elite law firms whose main business is international. These global players are in intense competition to serve the international financial and commercial sectors. Their firms often have a different character and different problems from those focused on the domestic market.

Many barristers also have practices that are primarily focused on international markets and institutions. They tend to specialise in advocacy in international courts. They are also found in judicial and quasi-judicial roles, such as arbitrators in international dispute resolution centres. Barristers are often instructed to appear in international courts, such as the International Criminal Court, or the courts of EU institutions.

Some barristers have rights of audience in foreign courts, notably within the Commonwealth and in the EU[19] Many also appear in international arbitrations. The 1,200 members of the Commercial Bar Association (COMBAR) specialise in international trade, shipping and aviation, banking and financial services, insurance, commodity transactions, international arbitration, insolvency, oil and gas/energy law and EU law.[20]

The international legal services market is relatively unregulated overall, although forum controls operate in the various international courts. National governments and international agencies have no direct remit to control the international dimension of the conduct of lawyers. The reach of domestic codes of conduct and the effectiveness of regulation is questionable. Often, international legal work has a different character to that performed in home jurisdictions.

---

[19] Bar Council, *Barristers in the International Market* 2102, www.barcouncil.org.uk/media/168701/barristers_in_the_international_legal_market_2012.pdf.

[20] See generally, www.combar.com/index.php and www.barcouncil.org.uk/about/specialistbar-associations/commercialbarassociation/.

Because of the lack of overarching regulation, international lawyers are constructing the field and seeking control of their work, just as they did nationally in previous ages. In doing so they are using tried and trusted methods. They are forming international associations of lawyers, devising international codes of conduct, and calling on familiar ideological and rhetorical devises, such as appeals to the rule of law.

For the first time we can see the potential for a new profession of international lawyer, with unique expertise and a distinctive legal role.[21] This possibility is driven by globalisation of the world economy, the process of European harmonisation, and regulation of international trade and investment. These processes have created an environment conducive to the international practice of law. Lawyers are moving increasingly easily between jurisdictions.

Globalisation and International Legal Institutions

Growth of the global economy and removal of trade barriers since the 1980s are part of a process that has been labelled 'globalisation'. This is usually taken to mean increasing levels of economic interdependence and cultural homogeneity. The process of globalisation has been furthered by international institutions for at least a century: the International Chamber of Commerce (ICC), was formed in 1919 in Paris by 'the merchants of peace' a coterie of elite businessmen wishing to promote trade and investment across frontiers and help business corporations meet the challenges and opportunities of globalisation.[22]

There are various centres for the international practice of law. The international centres of finance in London, New York and Tokyo are a strong focus of activity. Other centres include those specialising in dispute resolution, such as the centres of arbitration in London and Paris. Yet others are located around centres of multinational government, Brussels, Luxembourg and Strasbourg.[23] An obvious focus of activity is established and emerging centres of international commercial activity, such as India and China. The development of activity around these various centres is encouraged by international institutions.

The UN's key role in the field of international trade law is led by the United Nations Commission on International Trade Law (UNCITRAL), based in Vienna.[24] UNCITRAL is charged with removing legal obstacles to international trade by progressively modernising and harmonising trade law.

---

[21] R Badinter, 'Role of the International Lawyer' (1995) 23 *International Business Lawyer* 505.

[22] www.iccwbo.org/.

[23] RL Abel, 'Transnational Legal Practice' (1993–95) 44 *Case Western Reserve Law Review* 737, 743.

[24] www.uncitral.org.

Increasingly diverse systems of international dispute resolution lead to higher levels of legal activity.[25]

International commercial institutions, together with the United Nations (UN) and international financial institutions, promote the rule of law in order to create an environment of certainty in which international governments and corporations can operate.[26] The International Monetary Fund and European Bank of Reconstruction and Development only lend money to countries committed to promoting the rule of law.

London as a World Centre for Legal Services

In 2000, a geographic analysis of world cities mapped their 'network connectivity'.[27] This measures the interactions of firms servicing business. The analysis was based on 100 banking and professional service firms operating globally, in law, accountancy and advertising. Law firms engaged in international legal work were also analysed,[28] and it was found that, compared with general business services, some cities are relatively overprovided with global lawyers and others underprovided. London and New York are by far the largest centres of global network connectivity in law.

Whether or not global law firms choose to locate in a particular jurisdiction and city depends on two main factors: market demand and regulation. Market demand has to relate to the kinds of services the firm provides. Regulation relates to the kinds of restrictions that the host country and host profession impose on overseas lawyers and law firms. England (and Wales) is relatively open to overseas practices and overseas lawyers. It attracts international legal work because London, in particular, is a world centre for financial markets and for dispute resolution services.

A benchmark report prepared by the Legal Services Board noted significant growth in net exports of legal services, by over 30 per cent since 2005.[29] A large part of this was in provision of dispute resolution services. There were more international and commercial arbitrations held in London under English law than in any other city in the world. The largest percentage growth in net exports came was from Commercial Barristers Association members, with exports growing from £76 million in 2008 to £84 million in 2009.

---

[25] P Ruttley, 'The WTO's Dispute Settlement Mechanism' (1997) *Amicus Curiae* 4.

[26] *Jurisdictional Certainty is Essential in International Contracts* (2 April 2003) www.iccwbo.org/policy/law/iccef/index.html.

[27] P Taylor, G Catalano and D Walker, 'Measurement of the World City Network' (2002) 39 *Urban Studies* 2367.

[28] J Faulconbridge, J Beaverstock, D Muzio and PJ Taylor, 'Global Law Firms: Globalization and Organizational Spaces of Cross-Border Legal Work' (2008) 28 *Northwestern Journal of International Law and Business* 455, 474–77.

[29] Legal Services Board, *Market Impacts of the Legal Services Act: Interim Baseline Report* (April 2012).

Over 90 per cent of commercial cases handled by London law firms now involve an international party. The London Court of International Arbitration has seen an annual increase in references of around 10 per cent, with 310 references in 2013.[30] World Bank data, comparing the ease of enforcing contracts in different jurisdictions, put the United Kingdom 8th in terms of time taken and 13th in terms of cost compared with 15 other economies.[31] London was the favoured venue of nearly a third of respondents to a recent survey.[32]

Over half of the revenue of the largest 100 law firms in the UK is generated by international law firms based in London.[33] In 2015 the Law Society predicted growth in the UK legal services sector contributing growth in the net export of legal services to 7.9 per cent, from 3 per cent in 2014.[34]

The Practice of International Law

International Law Firms

The leading firms in the international legal market are English and American law firms, often multinational practices. The English firms are fewer in number but have performed strongly over time. In 2006, of the 100 leading world firms by turnover, 75 were from the US and 17 from the UK.[35] The average revenue of the UK firms was, however, 21 per cent higher than their US counterparts. In 2014, five of the top ten global firms by turnover had English origins.[36] These firms tend to have offices in several of the world centres of activity and in some emerging markets.

London and New York have large numbers of large and international firms. Because of their proximity to financial markets, the law firms in these centres have developed great expertise in dealing with large-scale financial and commercial matters. Of the top 50 firms, 12 are based in New York.

---

[30] London Court of International Arbitration, *Registrar's Report* (2013), www.lcia.org/LCIA/reports.aspx.

[31] Legal Services Board (n 29) para C.10.6.

[32] Queen Mary, University of London, *2012 International Arbitration Survey: Current and Preferred Practices in the Arbitral Process* (London, White & Case, 2012).

[33] The City UK Professional Services Series 'Legal Services' (2011), 1–12, 1, www.thecityuk.com/assets/Uploads/Legal-Services-2011.pdf.

[34] Law Society, 'Legal Services Boost Predicted for 2015', 28 August 2014, www.lawsociety.org.uk/news/press-releases/legal-services-boost-predicted-for-2015/.

[35] The Wall Street Journal Law Blog, 'Global Law Firms Chart Slow But Steady Growth', 29 September 2014, http://blogs.wsj.com/law/2014/09/29.

[36] Legal Week, 'Global 100 2012: Firm by Firm', 19 October 2012, www.legalweek.com/legal-week/news/2218379/global-100-2012-firm-by-firm.

Law firms are classified as international when 40 per cent or more of their lawyers are working outside their home country.[37] By this definition, in 2009/10 only 12 of the top 50 firms by gross fees were international firms. Most US firms were not international; their domestic market was sufficient to support their huge scale. The largest international law firm by gross fees is, however, the US-based firm Baker & McKenzie. Baker & Mackenzie has over 80 per cent of its lawyers based outside the US.[38] Today, most large firms chase growth by international expansion. More than 25,000 lawyers from the top 200 global firms work in more than 70 countries, with China, the UK and the rest of Europe the main centres of this activity, but with rapid growth in Australia, the United Arab Emirates and South Africa.[39]

Many of the leading English international firms have nearly 70 per cent of their lawyers overseas. In 2011 there were nearly 6,000 solicitors from England and Wales based overseas. The largest concentrations were in Hong Kong (15 per cent of the total), the United Arab Emirates (13 per cent) and Singapore (9 per cent).[40] In other countries, local conventions may limit the capacity of local legal professions to compete internationally. The Japanese profession has only recently begun to organise in large firms, a fact that has restricted their international reach.[41]

Firm Culture

International law firms are often concerned about maintaining their standards of service, about the integration of different parts of the business and maintaining firm identity between widely dispersed locations.[42] They consciously engineer relationships between lawyers in different offices world-wide through practice-group meetings, all-partner conferences and educational fora.

International lawyers can expect to move base several times, including on recall to their national firm in order to 'renew their corporate values'. Expatriated lawyers often have responsibility for the socialisation of lawyers in overseas offices. This includes convincing them of 'the importance and legitimacy of the American or English way of organising law firms and delivery legal services'.[43]

---

[37] 'Methodology' *The American Lawyer*, 20 September 2011, www.law.com/jsp/tal/PubArticleFriendlyTAL.jsp?id=1202516515870.

[38] IFSL Research, *Legal Services 2009 Legal Business/The American Lawyer.*

[39] Wall Street Journal Law Blog (n 35).

[40] The City UK, 'Legal Services February 2011',Table 5 Distribution of Solicitors Overseas, 4, www.thecityuk.com/assets/Uploads/Legal-Services-2011.pdf.

[41] KW Chan, 'The Emergence of Large Law Firms in Japan: Impact on Legal Professional Ethics' (2008) 11 *Legal Ethics* 154.

[42] Faulconbridge et al (n 28).

[43] Ibid.

International Legal Work

Transactions

Flood claims that international law firms are the only institution marching in step with the pace of change set by globalisation.[44] He suggests that '[n]o global transaction—contract, distribution agreement, securitization, franchise—can be engineered without them'.[45] Therefore, the main role of the international law firm is to bestow the legitimacy of expert knowledge on international transactions.[46] Developing commercial instruments is a matter of legal skill and improvisation. International lawyers adapt familiar commercial instruments, such as floating charges,[47] and recognised banking securities, such as the German Pfandbrief, for new purposes.[48]

Conducting work where there is no state control and no agreed procedures is sometimes called 'private ordering'.[49] This is self-regulation undertaken by private parties. Arbitration is a good example. International law work is said to rely heavily on this kind of innovation.[50] It is not possible without the ability to inspire trust in international markets. The necessarily high levels of trust are dependent on relationships, networks and social capital. This is not readily acquired. It has been built up by US and English firms through generations. It affects the way international lawyers are organised, the way they do their work, and how and what they are taught.

Disputes

International disputing is less likely to be dominated by large firms than transaction work. Two fields are considered here: arbitration and the work of the International Criminal Court.

i. Arbitration

There are various centres of international arbitration, of which the Interna-

---

[44] J Flood, 'Lawyers as Sanctifiers: The Role of Elite Law Firms in International Business Transactions' (2007) 14 *Indiana Journal of Global Legal Studies* 35.

[45] Ibid, 38.

[46] Ibid.

[47] See further A Dignam and J Lowry, *Company Law*, 6th edn (Oxford, Oxford University Press, 2010).

[48] P Quirk, 'Cover Me: The Economy Is on Fire (The German *Pfandbrief*)' (2010) *German Law Review* 1323.

[49] A Katz, 'Taking Private Ordering Seriously' [1996] *University of Pennsylvania Law Review* 1545.

[50] J Flood and E Skordaki, 'Normative Bricolage: Informal Rule-Making by Accountants and Lawyers in Mega-Insolvencies' in G Teubner (ed), *Global Law without a State* (Dartmouth, Aldershot 1997) 109–31.

tional Court of Arbitration (ICA) run by the ICC is one of the oldest and most venerable. The ICA was established in 1923 and is one of the biggest dispute resolution institutions in the world. It handles around 500 cases a year in centres in Paris, New York, Hong Kong, Singapore, Panama and Tunisia.[51] Its membership is drawn from almost 90 countries, calling on arbitrators with a wide range of nationalities and backgrounds.

The confidential procedures of the ICC are administered and monitored by the Court Secretariat in Paris. This fixes arbitrators' remuneration and scrutinises awards. Awards are enforceable in countries signing the 1958 United Nations Convention on the Recognition and Enforcement of Foreign Arbitral Awards. The rules of Arbitration of the ICC are widely used for institutional arbitration.

Dezalay and Garth use the example of the ICA to show how international arbitrators promote their natural characteristics and acquire the social capital that creates trust.[52] The old order of European arbitrators built social capital through publication and links to the institutions of conventional dispute resolution. They were often senior judges or academics, generalists, independent and often amateur. This model was challenged when US lawyers were brought to the European centres of arbitration in the 1970s. They were there because of the increasing importance of the market in eurodollars and petrodollars, fuelled by the oil crisis.

US lawyers demanded a more open ethical environment with declarations of conflicts of interest. They favoured a more litigious and combative style. The use of cross-examination increased and, and as a consequence, proceedings became more formal and expensive. The established European model gave way to a more rule-bound approach brought by the more combative US lawyers.[53] The models coexisted for a while but, from the 1970s, the common law model gained the ascendancy.

The triumph of the more litigious arbitral style was partly brought about by client demand. A wave of cases was brought by Western multinationals litigating over nationalisation of petroleum interests by third world countries. The governments of the third world countries preferred robust advocacy and partisanship to the studied detachment of the European jurists. Based on this example, Dezalay and Garth suggest that international arbitration reflects juris-

---

[51] International Chamber of Commerce, www.internationalarbitrationlaw.com/arbitral-institutions/icc/.

[52] Y Dezalay and B Garth, *Dealing with Virtue* (Chicago, University of Chicago Press, 1996).

[53] L Mistelis, 'International Arbitration—Corporate Attitudes and Practices—12 Perceptions Tested: Myths, Data and Analysis Research Report' (2004) 15 *American Review of International Arbitration* 525, http://qmul.academia.edu/LoukasMistelis/Papers/207153/International_Arbitration-Corporate_Attitudes_and_Practices-12_Perceptions_Tested_Myths_Data_and_Analysis_Research_Report; see also Price Waterhouse Cooper, International Arbitration: Corporate Attitudes and Practices 2008, www.pwc.co.uk/eng/publications/international_arbitration_2008.html.

dictional struggles between different groups of lawyers. Each tries to establish their preferred mode of practice and ethical regime.[54]

ii. The International Criminal Court

The international criminal jurisdiction grew out the trials to deal with the atrocities of the Axis powers in World War II, namely the International Military Tribunal in Nuremberg (the Nuremberg trials) and the International Military Tribunal for the Far East (the Tokyo Tribunals). The creation of a permanent international criminal court was agreed in principle in 1948, but the cold war rendered progress impossible.

In 1989 the idea of an international criminal jurisdiction was revived to curb growth in the trade in illegal drugs. Before the International Criminal Court (ICC) could be established, ad hoc tribunals were created to try war crimes in the former Yugoslavia and Rwanda. In 2002 the ICC was established as a permanent tribunal to prosecute individuals for genocide, crimes against humanity, war crimes and the crime of aggression.

The ICC is based in The Hague, but its proceedings may take place anywhere. Its jurisdiction is based on the premise that it is the primary responsibility of states to investigate and punish crime taking place in their national borders. The ICJ has jurisdiction when the accused is a national of a state party to the Rome Statute, when the alleged crime took place on the territory of a state party, or where a case is referred to the court by the UN Security Council. Further, the crime must have been committed after the inception of the court on 1 July 2002.

The ICC is served by lawyers drawn from all over the world. The majority working on particular cases at any one time tend to be from the area where the alleged crimes were committed. The next largest groups of lawyers are from the United States, Canada and the United Kingdom.[55] The current list of counsel authorised to appear runs to 15 pages and covers most countries in the world.[56]

The Office of the Prosecutor (OTP) of the ICC offers a range of legal and quasi-legal jobs for open recruitment, internships and visiting posts. It

> aims to foster an international cadre of active supporters and advocates who will be ideally placed within their respective professional and national communities, to raise awareness of the role of the Court; contribute to the strengthening of their national judicial systems; and promote cooperation with the Court, thus giving effect to the spirit of complementarity.[57]

---

[54] See above n 52.

[55] T Gut, *Counsel Misconduct Before the International Criminal Court* (Oxford, Hart Publishing, 2012) 9.

[56] International Criminal Court List of Counsel before the ICC, www.icc-cpi.int/iccdocs/PIDS/other/WebList_of_Counsel31.12.2014_EN.pdf.

[57] OTP website recruitment page: www.icc-cpi.int/Menus/ICC/Recruitment/.

The ICC has evolved its own rules of procedure and evidence. These draw very substantially on the adversarial tradition of criminal trial. Lawyers appearing in the court are subject to the Code of Professional Conduct for Counsel Appearing before the International Criminal Tribunal.

The ICC has also developed a range of sanctions, although most actions, including against lawyers, fall under the category of contempt of court. Penalties have gradually increased since they were introduced. The Disciplinary Board of the court can impose the following sanctions: admonishment, public reprimand, a fine of up to €30,000, suspension of the right to practice before the court for two years and a permanent ban on practice.[58]

Local Regulation

Because international legal work typically occurs outside of any specific host jurisdiction it is difficult for nationally based professions to regulate effectively. Courts and tribunals typically evolve their own rules to deal with this regulatory gap. For lawyers, accepting the tribunal rules is typically a condition of participation. This kind of control is absent in transaction work. In such areas, home professions must do their best to extend their regulatory reach to approved persons working overseas.

'Double Deontology'

The term 'double deontology' refers to the possibility of conflicts between the ethics of different legal professions. It therefore forms part of a discussion about whether or not international codes of ethics are necessary or desirable. One of the areas that is seen to be problematic is conflicts of interest. This issue is most salient in everyday commercial practice, particularly at the top end of the market.

With the increasing sensitivity of commercial information, corporations are alive to the possibility of the loss of market benefit or advantage to competitors. Lawyers are uniquely placed to gain such information and to exploit it for the benefit of other clients. Commercial clients are therefore the most likely litigators of conflict-of-interest issues.

The application of conflict-of-interest rules to commercial law firms is potentially fraught with difficulty. The more esoteric the expertise, the fewer firms can represent clients in that field. This problem is exacerbated by two factors. One is the increasing size of firms. This may decrease the number of organisations with appropriate expertise in the marketplace.

---

[58] ICC Code of Professional Conduct for Counsel (2005) Art 42, www.icc-cpi.int/NR/rdonlyres/BD397ECF-8CA8-44EF-92C6-AB4BEBD55BE2/140121/ICCASP432Res1_English.pdf.

The other factor complicating the application of conflict-of-interest rules are the relatively high levels of lawyer movement between organisations. This makes it difficult to track the flow of relevant information about clients or to locate it within firms. Hence, it may be difficult to identify potential conflicts of interest. Finally, the likelihood that the commercial transactions conducted by large firms will cross borders increases the importance of jurisdictional issues.

Chapter five explained that English law often approaches potential conflicts of interest between past and present clients as an issue of confidentiality. This is at variance with the situation in the US, where lawyers may be prevented from acting against former clients. The US approach therefore approaches the issue of acting against former clients as a loyalty issue and the English as an information issue.

Griffiths Baker and Moore point out that the difference in approaches to conflict of interest may create some difficulties in Anglo-American transactions and disputes. They also point out that the International Bar Association (IBA) approaches conflicts of interest from the US position.[59] This probably reflects the US origins of the IBA. Its Principles state that a conflict exists if 'there is a significant risk that the representation of one or more clients will be materially limited by the lawyer's responsibilities to another client, a former client, a third person or by a personal interest of the lawyer'.[60] This means that international law firms must have regard to 'double deontology': potential conflicts between ethics codes.

Griffiths Baker and Moore suggest that litigation arising from a past and present client conflict of interest involving an English international law firm is almost inevitable. They argue that it would be sensible to harmonise conflict-of-interest regimes or for lawyers to anticipate problems and to agree which conflict-of-interest rules will apply if problems arise in a transaction.

Some solicitors from England and Wales working overseas from England are still subject to the main provision of the SRA Code of Conduct. For example, those who are only temporarily overseas, or who are still providing reserved legal activities in England and Wales,[61] are still subject to the chapter on conflicts of interest. Those who are actually practising overseas on a more permanent basis are generally subject to the SRA Overseas Rules.

The SRA Overseas Rules largely comprise the SRA Principles, in some cases slightly varied. For example, Overseas Principle 6 provides that 'You must not do anything which will or will be likely to bring into disrepute the overseas practice, yourself as a regulated individual or responsible authorised

[59] J Griffiths Baker and NJ Moore, 'Regulating Conflicts of Interest in Global Law Firms: Peace in Our Time?'(2012) 80(6) *Fordham Law Review* 2541.

[60] International Bar Association International Principles for the Legal Profession, cmt 3.3 (May 28, 2011), available at www.ibanet.org/Document/Default.aspx?DocumentUid=1730FC33-6D70-4469-9B9D-8A12C319468C.

[61] SRA Code of Conduct 13A2.

body or, by association, the legal profession in and of England and Wales.' The overseas rules do not provide detailed outcomes relating to conduct. Rather, they provide that those practising overseas should follow local law and regulation.

The Global Legal Profession

Local Law

International law firms do not operate in a vacuum. Most established and leading English and US firms with offices overseas have practised the law local to the host jurisdiction as well as creating new legal approaches to international transactions.[62] This often involves employing locally qualified lawyers alongside staff qualified in England and Wales or the US.

Incoming lawyers to international law firms often bring culture, traditions and ethics with them. Some even take on a public service role in the host jurisdiction.[63] US law firms in London have, for example, been notable for their initiatives on pro bono and diversity issues.[64]

Local Regulation as a Barrier to Global Practice

The local Bars of many countries are resistant to international firms practising in their jurisdiction. They may prevent overseas lawyers practising and restrict their own lawyers joining incoming overseas firms. This presents difficulties for firms which normally try to employ most of their lawyers from overseas jurisdictions.

India is an example of a jurisdiction that gives indigenous lawyers a high degree of legislative protection.[65] Incursions are rigorously policed by practising lawyers, through litigation and political activism. Therefore, international law firms have a weak presence in, for example, Mumbai despite the importance of this world city.

---

[62] Faulconbridge et al (n 28).
[63] Abel (n 23) 743, 749.
[64] Legal Services Board, *Market Impacts of the Legal Services Act* (2012).
[65] J Krishnan, 'Globetrotting Law Firms' (2009) 23 *Georgetown Journal of Legal Ethics* 57.

The Professional Project of International Lawyers

The difficulty of operating globally across national borders has led many global law firms to advocate global liberalisation. Their aim is to create conditions that would allow international firms to operate freely. Some favour global regulation in order that common standards apply to all lawyers participating in international transactions. This is understandable if, for example, the lawyers on the other side are subject to lesser obligations of fairness.

International lawyers with a liberal reform agenda are supported by organisations such as the World Trade Organization (WTO), through a working party on professional services formed in the 1990s, and the International Competition Network and international professional groupings. These groups tend to be at the forefront of the spread of liberal democracy as the universal model of world government.

The rule of law is the totem of global legal institutions and international law firms alike. The process of regulating the international sphere has echoes of the process of professionalisation. This time, lawyers are attempting to convince international audience that professional self-regulation is needed in the international market for legal services.[66]

Harmonisation of Legal Professional Ethics

There are two international associations of lawyers with a particular interest in the harmonising the professional ethics of lawyers. One is the Council of Bars and Law Societies of Europe (CCBE) and the other is the IBA.

Council of the Bars and Law Societies of Europe

The CCBE was formed by the Bar associations of the six founding Member States of the European Economic Community. Thereafter, the CCBE was consulted on Directives concerning the cross-border activity of EU lawyers. In 1979, the CCBE intervened in *AM&S Europe Limited v Commission of the European Communities*.[67] The case concerned a claim of legal professional privilege for material disclosed to in-house counsel that was relevant to an EU competition investigation.

The European Court of Justice heard representations from a CCBE delegation led by a Scottish QC and subsequent president of the CCBE, David Edward. It also considered a report prepared for the CCBE by Edward on the

---

[66] TC Halliday and L Karpik (eds), *Lawyers and the Rise of Western Political Liberalism* (Oxford, Oxford University Press, 1997) 349.

[67] *Australian Mining & Smelting Europe Ltd v Commission of the European Communities (AM & S)* (155/79) [1982] ECR 1575.

differences in approach to privilege between Member States. Following the case, the CCBE maintained a permanent delegation to EU courts.

The CCBE is an international non-profit-making association to which European legal professions can be associated as full, associate or observer members. It represents all of the members on matters of mutual interest and in relation to its objects. There are three main objects, reflecting the CCBE's areas of interest and activity.[68] The first object, and main area of interest of the CCBE, is promoting the rule of law, the administration of justice, and substantive developments in the law at a European and international level.

The second object and activity of the CCBE is to act as an intermediary body in relation to its areas of interest. The role envisages operating between the European legal professions and the institutions of the EU and the European Economic Area.

The third object of the CCBE is to monitor defence of the rule of law and the protection of fundamental and human rights and freedoms. This focuses on access to justice and protection of the client, and the protection of the democratic values inextricably associated with such rights. The CCBE publishes two documents that are intended to affect the normative development of lawyers: a charter and a code of conduct.

i. Charter of Core Principles of the European Legal Profession

The Charter of Core Principles of the European Legal Profession ('the Charter') was adopted in November 2006. The core principles are said to be common to the national and international rules regulating the European legal professions. The Charter promulgates them for a variety of reasons.

The Charter aims, first, to provide a tool for bar associations struggling to establish their independence from the state. Second, it seeks to increase understanding among lawyers of the importance of their role in society. Third, it aspires to inform decision-makers, presumably in pan-European and state institutions and the public in general.

Charter of Core Principles of the European Legal Profession

Council of Bars and Law Societies of Europe, *Charter of Core Principles of the European Legal Profession Code of Conduct for European Lawyers* (November 2013). (http://www.ccbe.eu/fileadmin/user_upload/NTCdocument/EN_CCBE_CoCpdf1_1382973057.pdf)

---

[68] *Statutes of the Council of the Bars and Law Societies of Europe* (adopted November 2013), www.ccbe.eu/fileadmin/user_upload/document/statuts/statuts_en.pdf.

(a) the independence of the lawyer, and the freedom of the lawyer to pursue the client's case;

(b) the right and duty of the lawyer to keep clients' matters confidential and to respect professional secrecy;

(c) avoidance of conflicts of interest, whether between different clients or between the client and the lawyer;

(d) the dignity and honour of the legal profession, and the integrity and good repute of the individual lawyer;

(e) loyalty to the client;

(f) fair treatment of clients in relation to fees;

(g) the lawyer's professional competence;

(h) respect towards professional colleagues;

(i) respect for the rule of law and the fair administration of justice; and

(j) the self-regulation of the legal profession.

Q12.9   How far are these core principles consistent with those of the SRA or the core duties of the BSB?

Q12.10   Could these core principles provide the basis for regulation of a European legal profession?

The commentary on these sections is a revealing view of how the elite European legal professions view their role. In an account familiar to students of the English profession, it is asserted that the lawyer

> who faithfully serves his or her own client's interests and protects the client's rights, also fulfils the functions of the lawyer in society—which are to forestall and prevent conflicts, to ensure that conflicts are resolved in accordance with recognised principles of civil, public or criminal law and with due account of rights and interests, to further the development of the law, and to defend liberty, justice and the rule of law.[69]

The commentary goes on to suggest that the role fulfilled by lawyers demands independence from the state and from other powerful interests, including business associates and clients. It is claimed that the 'lawyer's membership of a liberal profession and the authority deriving from that membership helps to maintain independence, and bar associations must play an important role in

---

[69] Commentary on the Charter, Principle A, 9.

helping to guarantee lawyers' independence'. It is notable that the commentary to Principle J argues that self-regulation of the profession is vital in buttressing the independence of the individual lawyer. The commentary reflects concern at the danger of overt or covert state control.[70]

ii. The Code of Conduct for European Lawyers

The Code of Conduct for European Lawyers is the creation of the CCBE. It covers cross-border activities within the EU, the European Economic Area and the Swiss Confederation. To this extent, it claims to bind Member States and the Bars and law societies of these countries, whether they are full, associated or observer members of the CCBE.

The first Code of Conduct for Lawyers in the European Community was published in October 1988. The main English legal professions were early adopters. In September 1990, the CCBE code became binding on solicitors under rule 16 of the Solicitors' Practice Rules 1990 and rule 4 of the Solicitors' Overseas Practice Rules 1990.[71] The full code was reproduced in the Guide.[72] Some of the commentary in the code highlighted differences between national codes on particular issues.[73] The Bar incorporated it into the Code of Conduct and barristers were required to obey it unless would be inconsistent with the provisions of the Bar's Code.

The CCBE code has been amended three times, the last version dating from May 2006. The current version of the code comprises five sections. The first section is a preamble and the second deals with general principles. The preamble also features some familiar ideas. It states that:

> In a society founded on respect for the rule of law the lawyer fulfils a special role. The lawyer's duties do not begin and end with the faithful performance of what he or she is instructed to do so far as the law permits. A lawyer must serve the interests of justice as well as those whose rights and liberties he or she is trusted to assert and defend and it is the lawyer's duty not only to plead the client's cause but to be the client's adviser. Respect for the lawyer's professional function is an essential condition for the rule of law and democracy in society. A lawyer's function therefore lays on him or her a variety of legal and moral obligations (sometimes appearing to be in conflict with each other) towards:
>
> - the client;
> - the courts and other authorities before whom the lawyer pleads the client's
> - cause or acts on the client's behalf;
> - the legal profession in general and each fellow member of it in particular;

---

[70] Ibid, Principle J, 10.

[71] Adoption of the CCBE Code of Conduct 2006 (posted December 2013), www.ccbe.eu/fileadmin/user_upload/NTCdocument/Status_of_the_CCBE_C1_1386165089.pdf

[72] The Law Society, *The Guide to the Professional Conduct of Solicitors*, 8th edn (1999) 205–21.

[73] Commentary on rule 5.3: Correspondence between lawyers (ibid, 218).

- the public for whom the existence of a free and independent profession, bound together by respect for rules made by the profession itself, is an essential means of safeguarding human rights in face of the power of the state and other interests in society.[74]

This suggests, perhaps implausibly, that the ideology of legal professionalism is equally strong across European jurisdictions.

The CCBE code contains three substantive sections: 'Relations with Clients', 'Relations with Courts' and 'Relations Between Lawyers'. As might be expected in a document that claims to accommodate the norms of over thirty legal professions, the CCBE code expresses familiar principles at a high level of generality. For example, it states that: 'Subject to due observance of all rules of law and professional conduct, a lawyer must always act in the best interests of the client and must put those interests before the lawyer's own interests or those of fellow members of the legal profession.'[75]

The CCBE Code also reflects some ideas that are no longer general. For example, it provides that lawyers 'shall not be entitled to make a *pactum de quota litis*',[76] defined as an agreement that a client pays 'a share of the result'.[77] Such a description would fit a damages-based agreement, recently legalised in England and Wales. This raises the interesting question of whether such arrangements are forbidden to English lawyers operating in the EU.

The section on relations with other lawyers suggests that lawyers are under a positive obligation to raise breaches of rules with each other.[78] It goes on to suggest that disputes between lawyers from different Member States should be settled 'in a friendly way', if possible.[79] It then provides that lawyers

> shall not commence any form of proceedings against a colleague in another Member State ... without first informing the Bars or Law Societies to which they both belong for the purpose of allowing both Bars or Law Societies concerned an opportunity to assist in reaching a settlement.[80]

The current CCBE code shares many features of the previous versions. The original purpose of the code was expressed to be to 'mitigate the difficulties which result from the application of double deontology' arising from 'the continued integration of the European community and the increasing frequency of the cross-border activities of lawyers within the community'.[81] The code is

---

[74] CCBE, *Charter of Core Principles of the European Legal Profession Code of Conduct for European Lawyers* (November 2013), www.ccbe.eu/fileadmin/user_upload/NTCdocument/EN_CCBE_CoCpdf1_1382973057.pdf.
[75] Council of Bars and Law Societies of Europe, *Code of Conduct of the Bars of Europe*, para 2.7: The client's interests.
[76] Ibid, para 3.3.1.
[77] Ibid, para 3.3.2.
[78] Ibid, para 5.9.1.
[79] Ibid, para 5.9.2.
[80] Ibid, para 5.9.3.
[81] Ibid, para 1.3.1.

offered for adoption by local Bars and law societies. It urges members to take it into account in all revisions of national rules of professional practice with a view to their progressive harmonisation.

The CCBE code is curiously contradictory. For example, it still aspires to deal with the problem of 'double deontology'.[82] At the same time it notes that national rules arise in context and that it 'is neither possible nor desirable that they should be taken out of their context nor that an attempt should be made to give general application to rules which are inherently incapable of such application'.[83]

The CCBE code refers to the possibility of disciplinary proceedings, but the CCBE provides no mechanism for these. Its only real method for influencing lawyer conduct is through the mediation between lawyers disputing conduct issues offered by their home Bars or law societies.

The International Bar Association

The IBA was formed in 1947 by 34 national Bar associations.[84] It currently has a membership of over 200 Bar associations and law societies worldwide and is based in New York. Inspired by the formation of the UN, the aim of the IBA was to establish the rule of law and the administration of justice worldwide.

The IBA has three current objectives. The first is to promote an exchange of information between legal associations worldwide. The second is to support the independence of the judiciary and the right of lawyers to practise their profession without interference. The third is to support human rights for lawyers worldwide.

In 1970 individual lawyers were allowed to join the IBA. This led to growth in services for individual lawyer members and the growth of subject sections. Sections on Business Law, on Legal Practice and on Energy and Natural Resources Law were formed in 1970, 1974 and 1982, respectively. A Standing Committee on Human Rights and the Just Rule of Law was added in the 1980s. In 1992 the IBA launched a programme to investigate and observe trials where the independence of judges and lawyers was threatened. It also planned to support the independence of bar associations.

The IBA supports the development of associations for lawyers in countries where there is no tradition of an independent Bar. It runs a Human Rights Institute, which supports human rights for lawyers worldwide.

i. International Code of Ethics

The first version of the IBA International Code of Ethics was published in

---

[82] Ibid, para 1.3.1.
[83] Ibid, Preamble, para 1.2.2.
[84] www.ibanet.org/About_the_IBA/About_the_IBA.aspx.

1954 and the last version in 1988.[85] The original IBA code was fairly brief. It comprised only 21 rules, most of them only a couple of sentences long. The IBA code applied 'to any lawyer of one jurisdiction in relation to his contacts with a lawyer of another jurisdiction or to his activities in another jurisdiction'.[86] It was adopted by the Law Society, presumably intended to apply in situations or countries where neither its own code nor the CCBE code applied.

The IBA code was a recipe for what the CCBE called 'double deontology'. The first rule provided that:

> A lawyer who undertakes professional work in a jurisdiction where he is not a full member of the local profession shall adhere to the standards of professional ethics in the jurisdiction in which he has been admitted. He shall also observe all ethical standards which apply to lawyers of the country where he is working.[87]

The possibility of conflicting obligations was potentially strong.

ii. IBA International Principles on Conduct for the Legal Profession

The IBA also publishes General Principles of Ethics.[88] These comprise ten principles: independence; honesty, integrity and fairness; conflicts of interest; confidentiality/professional secrecy; clients' interest; lawyers' undertaking; clients' freedom; property of clients and third parties; competence; and fees. Each principle is quite brief, but supported by commentary.

The statement in the Principles relating to the lawyer's role and the independence of legal professions is exactly the same as that in the CCBE code statement of principles. It combines a vision of the lawyer as trusted advisor and ends with the assertion that the lawyer's functions are also to 'further the development of the law, and to defend liberty, justice and the rule of law'.[89]

Many provisions of the IBA Code were subject to national codes, for example in relation to advertising and soliciting and the delegation of work to non-qualified personnel.[90] The IBA described its code as a guide to what the IBA considers to be a desirable course of conduct by all lawyers engaged in the international practice of law. Although it reserved the right to 'bring incidents of alleged violations to the attention of relevant organisations'[91] it did not claim any regulatory status.

---

[85] International Bar Association, *International Code of Ethics* (1988).

[86] Ibid, Addendum.

[87] Ibid, rule 1.

[88] International Bar Association, *International Principles on Conduct for the Legal Profession* (adopted 28 May 2011), www.ibanet.org/Publications/publications_IBA_guides_and_free_materials.aspx#ethics

[89] International Bar Association, *Commentary on the International Principles on Conduct for the Legal Profession*.

[90] Ibid, paras 8 and 20.

[91] Ibid, preamble.

The IBA website suggests that the principles of conduct supersede the IBA Code of Conduct. This suggests that the IBA Code of Conduct has fallen into disuse, although it still appears on the website. The implication is that the IBA has recognised the implausibility of enforcing an international code of conduct. It may also reflect a shift in the aspirations of the IBA. It may now be more content to fulfil a lobbying and campaigning role rather than aspiring to be international regulator.

The Significance of the International Codes and Principles

The efforts of the CCBE and the IBA highlighted the commonalities, similarities and differences between lawyers' national codes of ethics. Harmonisation of the professional ethics of lawyers is likely to remain a long-term ideal, albeit one pursued with vigour by elite lawyers.[92] It is likely that some of the originators of the international codes considered the possibility that they could be used for regulation and for other purposes. These possibilities are now considered.

i. The Aspiration to Regulation

The desire of the international organisations to affect regulation has two dimensions. The first is to harmonise, as far as possible, the ethics codes of different legal professions. John Toulmin QC, a former President of the CCBE, foresaw the possibility of creating a worldwide code based on the US model rules and the Japanese and CCBE codes.[93]

Toulmin thought that the differences between the US and Western Europe were minimal. He considered areas of incompatibility, such as secrecy and confidentiality, advertising, conflicts of interest and contingency fees, to present greater problems in theory than practice. Since the formulation of the first CCBE code, differences have reduced further in some cases, such as contingency fees. Even in Japan, with a distinct legal culture, the legal profession is becoming similar to those in other countries.[94]

The idea of having a single worldwide code, acceptable to and enforced by all legal professions, is a long-term project fraught with problems. The national codes are often full of the kind of detail that upsets apparent consensus. The CCBE's ambivalence in relation to the differences between its members reflects inevitable cultural differences that brief codes of professional ethics struggle to resolve.

---

[92] See Halliday and Karpik (n 66).

[93] J Toulmin, A Worldwide Common Code of Professional Ethics?' (1991) 15 *Fordham International Law Journal* 673.

[94] K Economides, 'Anglo-American Conceptions of Professional Responsibility and the Reform of Japanese Legal Education: Creating A Virtuous Circle?' (2007) 41 *The Law Teacher* 155.

The second plausible regulatory function of the international codes could be regulation of international legal practice. Such an aim might suggest the development of a new legal profession, with an international regulatory body, for transnational legal work. Such a move is probably unnecessary at present.

If the main justification of professional ethics is protecting clients from the consequences of information asymmetries and power imbalances, international legal clients do not need them. The more plausible risk, that lawyers behave unethically towards fellow lawyers or are dishonest in international legal transactions, can be adequately covered by home-based disciplinary mechanisms. [95]

ii. Emulation of the International Business Elite

Efforts to internationalise legal professional ethics often meet with scepticism from academics. Picciotto suggests that an internationalist ruling class emerged between 1915 and 1975 based on the ideals of corporate liberalism and transatlantic unity.[96] He argues that the inadequacy of business regulation by the international state system led to the growth, since the 1960s, of 'international economic soft law' of which voluntary codes of conduct are an example.

Codes of conduct for international business were developed to convince interested parties that corporations could be trusted. Picciotto brands them 'a reaction to and an attempt to contain the growing criticisms of and actions against transnational corporations from the 1960s onwards'.[97] It would be possible to see the IBA Code as the emulation by commercial lawyers of their organisational counterparts in business rather than, for example, emulation of the UN.

iii. The Ideological Force of Professionalism and the Codes

The lack of serious regulatory intent behind the various international lawyer organisations, and the general tenor of the international codes, suggests that these have largely ideological or symbolic meaning. Halliday and Karpik suggest that legal professions may seek international solidarity as a means of encouraging lawyers' re-engagement with political liberalism.[98] Part of this role may involve determining the relationship of lawyers in different countries to the state. In England, for example, overseas observers saw professional

---

[95] Abel (n 23) 762, A Boon and J Flood, 'The Globalisation of Professional Ethics: The Significance of lawyers International Codes of Conduct' (1999) 2 *Legal Ethics* 29.

[96] S Picciotto, 'The Control of Transnational Capital and the Democratisation of the International State' (1998) 15 *Journal of Law and Society* 58 at 64.

[97] Ibid, 71.

[98] Halliday and Karpik (n 66) 8.

self-government as a pillar of civil society and a bulwark of liberal political society.

The position of English lawyers has changed to such an extent that they may no longer be seen as self-regulating. They are, possibly, among the European legal professions least formally independent of the state. There was little intellectual or political resistance and few attempts to mobilise public opinion against these changes. Worldwide alliances of professional associations might be more effective in checking the accumulation of state power, in the service of trade and corporations, by reasserting the pre-eminence of the rule of law.[99]

Some academics are sceptical of attempts to use the historic tradition of legal professions. McBarnett argues that the rhetoric of the rule of law is inconsistent with the role of business lawyers, whose advice to corporations, on tax avoidance for example, 'obviates rights and renders them ineffective'.[100] Whelan claims that rule-of-law rhetoric is used to bolster the advantage of international clients using lawyers.[101] Therefore, claims to confidentiality in the CCBE code are more extensive than they tend to be in members' national codes of conduct.

It is certainly the case that, in order to claim legitimacy for their international codes, elite groups must remain in professional unity with groups of lawyers often outside their sphere. These include those working in the fields of criminal defence, civil liberties or welfare law who are unlikely to be affected by the international codes. Indeed, these groups are more likely to face financial, language and geographical difficulties in engaging with international agendas.

Progressive Agendas for the Internationalisation Project

The scepticism surrounding the attempted internationalisation of professional ethics potentially obscures interesting possibilities. Large-firm transaction lawyers in New York have more in common with those in similar firms in London or Brussels than with sole-practitioner litigators in their own jurisdictions. Exploring these commonalities provides opportunities for both groups.

It arguably makes more sense for international transaction lawyers to be subject to their own international code than it does for them to be subject to a code designed predominantly for criminal defence lawyers. Such a reformulation would need to negotiate the deep-rooted and self-interested ideologies of national professions.

---

[99] T Johnson, *Professions and Power* (London and Basingstoke, Macmillan, 1972) 14, quoting KS Lynn, *The Professions in America* (Daedalus, 1967) 653.

[100] D MacBarnet, 'Law, Policy and Legal Avoidance: Can Law Effectively Implement Egalitarian Policies?' (1998) 15 *Journal of Law and Society* 113, 118–19.

[101] C Whelan, 'Ethics Beyond the Horizon: Why Regulate the Global Practice of Law' (2001) 34 *Vanderbilt Journal of Transnational Law* 931.

It is arguable that a reorganisation of the global legal profession is in the interests of global populations. Increasing globalisation brings less savvy citizens within the sphere of international markets. This arguably increases the argument for effective cross-border regulation of legal professions. On what basis this could be achieved is unclear. Legal professions often have different areas of reserved work and it is usually constructed in unique ways. It is fair to say, therefore, that the potential for the emergence of unified areas of global legal practice shows contradictory trends.

Q12.11   Are international codes of legal ethics binding on international lawyers?

Q12.12   What are the functions of international codes of legal ethics?

Q.12.13   What controls are there on the activities of international lawyers?

Conclusion

The English legal profession has a contradictory image, reflecting deep differences between different institutions and groups. In Europe, it is seen as conservative on the domestic front, resistant to European harmonisation, keen to preserve distinctive features, such as the split profession and distinct jurisdictions in England and Wales, Scotland and Northern Ireland.[102] In international practice, English lawyers are seen as highly specialised, competitive and particularly aggressive in international markets. The English are keen to deregulate and, certainly compared to most Europeans, open-minded on issues such as multidisciplinary practice.

While domestic law appears to contract, the international legal services market is large, profitable and dominated by Anglo-American law firms. It is also a relatively unregulated market, with lawyers operating under a combination of their domestic codes and local ethics regimes. In many cases, similar rules operate, but there are potentially significant cultural differences between international practitioners. This situation has led to collaboration across jurisdictions in designing international ethics codes.

Efforts to harmonise the various European professional regimes have been in progress for many years. This process seems to have in view the creation of

---

[102] K Gromek-Broc, 'The Legal Profession in the European Union—A Comparative Analysis of Four Member States' (2002) 24 *Liverpool Law Review* 109.

a common European code. This would seem to be a largely pointless exercise unless there are corresponding moves towards a European-wide regulatory regime for lawyers. There are also long-standing efforts by the IBA to build an international ethics regime. The focus of this seems to have shifted towards influencing national governments and professions.

In the longer term there are arguments for legal professions uniting across national boundaries. It would facilitate the globalisation of legal business. It could provide lawyers with greater ability to resist the demands of corporations. Finally, and perhaps more importantly, it could bolster the resolve of lawyers to resist encroachment on the rule of law by the state. Despite the internal fragmentation within domestic markets, movement towards international harmonisation might give global legal professions new energy and fresh legitimacy.

Index

Page numbers in **bold** indicate information displayed in tables.